SAMS PUBLISHING

KU-788-566

M T W T F S S **24**

Using the *Sams' Teach Yourself in 24 Hours* Series

Welcome to the *Sams' Teach Yourself in 24 Hours* series! You're probably thinking, "What, they want me to stay up all night and learn this stuff?" Well, no, not exactly. This series introduces a new way to teach you about exciting new products: 24 one-hour lessons, designed to keep your interest and keep you learning. Because the learning process is broken into small units, you will not be overwhelmed by the complexity of some of the new technologies that are emerging in today's market. Each hourly lesson has a number of special items, some old, some new, to help you along.

10 Minutes

The first 10 minutes of each hour lists the topics and skills that you will learn about by the time you finish the hour. You will know exactly what the hour will bring with no surprises.

20 Minutes

Twenty minutes into the lesson, you will have been introduced to many of the newest features of the software application. In the constantly evolving computer arena, knowing everything a program can do will aid you enormously now and in the future.

30 Minutes

Before 30 minutes have passed, you will have learned at least one useful task. Many of these tasks take advantage of the newest features of the application. These tasks use a hands-on approach, telling you exactly which menus and commands you need to use to accomplish the goal. This approach is found in each lesson of the *24 Hours* series.

40 Minutes

You will see after 40 minutes that many of the tools you have come to expect from the *Sams' Teach Yourself* series are found in the *24 Hours* series as well. Notes and Tips offer special tricks of the trade to make your work faster and more productive. Warnings help you avoid those nasty time-consuming errors.

50 Minutes

By the time you're 50 minutes in, you'll probably run across terms you haven't seen before. Never before has technology thrown so many new words and acronyms into the language, and the New Terms elements in this series will carefully explain each and every one of them.

60 Minutes

At the end of the hour, you may still have questions that need to be answered. You know the kind—questions on skills or tasks that come up every day for you, but that weren't directly addressed during the lesson. That's where the Q&A section can help. By answering the most frequently asked questions about the topics discussed in the hour, Q&A not only answers your specific question, it provides a succinct review of all that you have learned in the hour.

Sams'
Teach Yourself
LINUX
in 24 Hours

Sams'
Teach Yourself LINUX in 24 Hours

Bill Ball
Stephen Smoogen

SAMS
PUBLISHING

201 West 103rd Street
Indianapolis, Indiana 46290

To Cathy and Nat for their kindness, love, and warm fuzzies.—Bill Ball

FIRST EDITION

International Standard Book Number: 0-672-31162-3

Library of Congress Catalog Card Number: 97-68005

01 00 99 98 4 3 2

Interpretation of the printing code: the rightmost multi-digit number is the year of the book's printing; the rightmost single-digit, the number of the book's printing. For example, a printing code of 98-1 shows that the first printing of the book occurred in 1998.

Composed in AGaramond and MCPdigital by Macmillan Computer Publishing

Printed in the United States of America

Publisher Don Fowley
Executive Editor Jeff Koch
Managing Editor Sarah Kearns

Acquisitions Editor
Kim Spilker

Development Editor
Mark Cierzniak

Technical Editor
Steve Burnett

Project Editors
Andrew Cupp
Colleen Williams

Copy Editors
Margaret Berson
Howard Jones

Software Specialist
Jack Belbot

Team Coordinator
Tracy Williams

Cover Designer
Jay Corpus

Book Designer
Gary Adair

Production Team
Mike Henry
Linda Knose
Tim Osborn
Staci Somers
Mark Walchle

Indexer
Chris Wilcox

Overview

Contents

Acknowledgments

Thanks are due to the following people at Macmillan: Theresa Ball, Lynette Quinn, Mark Cierzniak, Jeff Koch, Kim Spilker, and the now departed but sorely missed Cari Skaggs and Colleen Williams (best of luck in your new jobs!). Thanks are also due to the great folks at Red Hat Software, Inc., including Michael Johnson, Terry Tomlinson, and Ed Bailey. Finally, thanks to Linus Torvalds for Linux, Richard Stallman for the GNU GPL, and Margaret Berson for her copy editing skills.

About the Authors

Bill Ball is a technical writer, editor, and magazine journalist and has been working with computers for the past 20 years. He first starting working with Linux, beginning with kernel version .99, after moving from BSD4.3 Machten for the Apple Macintosh. He has published more than a dozen articles in magazines such as *Computer Shopper* and *MacTech Magazine* and first started editing books for Que in 1986. An avid fly fisherman, he builds bamboo fly rods and fishes on the nearby Potomac River when he's not driving his vintage MG sports cars. He lives at Aquia Harbor in Stafford County, Virginia.

Stephen Smoogen lives in Chapel Hill, North Carolina where he currently is a technical support engineer at Red Hat Software, Inc. Stephen graduated from New Mexico Institute of Mining and Technology with a bachelor's in astrophysics and has been administrating networks with Linux since 1992. Stephen spends his spare time with his wife, Lisa, and their two cats, Pascal and Katrina, planning their future ranch in New Mexico.

Introduction

Welcome to Linux! You hold in your hands everything you need to install and use one of the most powerful computer operating systems in the world. This book is designed to help guide you through the process of learning about Linux.

Although the title of this book is *Sams' Teach Yourself Linux in 24 Hours*, you won't be alone while you learn. As you're taken from installation through system administration to playing games, you'll find advice, tips, and hints to help you along the way. Before you know it you'll be familiar with the terms, topics, and technical concepts dealing with the hottest and newest operating system in the world—Linux!

This book is designed to help you learn quickly. You'll find it an indispensable guide to installing Linux and getting right to work. This book helps you overcome technical obstacles, explains complex subjects in simple language, and shows you some neat tricks to make your computing experience easier.

Each section of this book gives you an hour's worth of knowledge and examples that you can run as you learn. By the way, you should know that this book was created, developed, and edited using the software included on the book's CD-ROM. We hope you enjoy teaching yourself Linux!

What is Linux?

Linux (pronounced Lih-nucks) is a UNIX-like operating system that runs on many different computers. Although many people might refer to Linux as the operating system and included software, strictly speaking, Linux is the operating system *kernel*, which comes with a *distribution* of software.

Linux was first released in 1991 by its author Linus Torvalds at the University of Helsinki. Since then it has grown tremendously in popularity as programmers around the world embraced his project of building a free operating system, adding features, and fixing problems.

Linux is popular with today's generation of computer users for the same reasons early versions of the UNIX operating system enticed fans more than 20 years ago. Linux is portable, which means you'll find versions running on name-brand or clone PCs, Apple Macintoshes, Sun workstations, or Digital Equipment Corporation Alpha-based computers. Linux also comes with source code, so you can change or customize the software to adapt to your needs. Finally, Linux is a great operating system, rich in features adopted from other versions of UNIX. We think you'll become a fan too!

Why Teach Yourself Linux?

You should teach yourself Linux for a number of good reasons. You'll expand your knowledge of your computer's hardware, which can be handy in troubleshooting problems. You'll also learn the basics of using a UNIX-like operating system loaded with state-of-the-art features. When you combine this knowledge of hardware and software, you'll be well on your way to becoming a power computer user.

You can use this book as a starting point in learning Linux basics. You'll learn all the skills needed to build and run a powerful and productive Linux workstation. While you won't learn how to program in Java, administer a network, or manage a Web server, you will learn that

- Using Linux is a great way to connect to the Internet for emailing, file downloading, or World Wide Web browsing.
- You can get to work right away, because this book's Linux distribution (on CD-ROM) comes with a rich assortment of popular productivity tools, such as word processors, calendars, emailers, and graphics programs.
- You can have fun with some wacky arcade games.
- In no time at all you can be on your way to joining the world-wide community of Linux users.

Who Should Use This Book?

This book is for someone who wants to quickly master the basics of how to install, run, and maintain Linux on an Intel-based personal computer. All of the tools you need are included.

Your computer should have a monitor, or display, keyboard, mouse, hard drive, floppy drive, and CD-ROM drive. Although you can jump right in and install Linux onto your hard drive, you should have some technical information about your computer and its hardware on hand before you start.

What's Included on the CD-ROM?

Everything you need! Included with this book is a CD-ROM, from Red Hat Software, Inc., which contains the latest and one of the most popular distributions of Linux, including the Linux kernel, utility programs, productivity programs, and even games. As you read through this book and install or configure software, you'll discover many of the reasons Red Hat's Linux was chosen to help you learn. Some of these are

- Red Hat Linux is easy to install.
- Red Hat Linux uses a convenient software-management system based on "packages."

- ☐ Red Hat Linux uses graphical tools to help you administer and maintain your system.
- ☐ Red Hat Linux software, and upgrades, are available on the Internet.

How to Use This Book

This book is designed to teach you topics in one-hour sessions. All the books in the Sams' Teach Yourself series enable you to start working and become productive with the product as quickly as possible. This book will do that for you!

Each hour, or session, starts with an overview of the topic to inform you what to expect in each lesson. The overview helps you determine the nature of the lesson and whether the lesson is relevant to your needs.

Each lesson has a main section that discusses the lesson topic in a clear, concise manner by breaking the topic down into logical component parts and explaining each component clearly.

Interspersed in each lesson are special elements, called Just a Minutes, Time Savers, and Cautions, that provide additional information.

JUST A MINUTE

A Just a Minute is designed to clarify the concept that is being discussed. It elaborates on the subject; if you are comfortable with your understanding of the subject, you can bypass it without danger.

TIME SAVER

Time Savers inform you of tricks or elements that are easily missed by most computer users. You can skip them, but often Time Savers show you an easier way to do a task.

CAUTION

A Caution deserves the most attention, because a Caution points out a problematic element of the topic being discussed. Ignoring the information contained in a Caution could have adverse effects on the task at hand. These are the most important special elements in the book.

Part I

Installation and Configuration

Hour

Part I

Hour 1

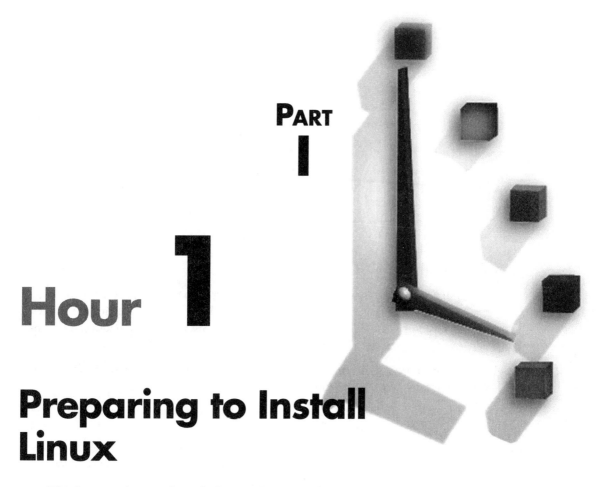

Preparing to Install Linux

This hour guides you through the initial process of installing Linux on your machine. Planning is one of the most important factors in a successful installation of any operating system. Your installation plan needs to cover how to install, where to install, and what the installation might affect. Planning isn't always a fun process, so it may help to keep in mind that working with the Linux operating system is a lot like being a hot rod mechanic back in 1955. All you've got is your parents' old car and a box of parts that were heading to the junk yard. The right tools and knowledge can turn that car into the fastest dragster on the strip.

With the hot rod mechanic in mind, look over the three steps that are covered in this hour:

1. Take inventory of your computer
2. Create the installation diskettes
3. Prepare your hard drive for installation

You should grab a pad of paper and a pen, because there are some numbers later in the chapter you may want to write down. You should also grab three formatted 1.44 MB floppy disks. Make sure one of the disks is bootable by using the `/s` switch with the `format` command from DOS.

JUST A MINUTE

> In order to install Linux from the CD included with this book, you need to have an operating system (such as DOS or Windows) already installed—or access to another computer.

Taking Inventory

First you need to take an inventory of your computer so that you can tell what you have to work with. Having an accurate inventory can come in handy if you have hardware problems. Taking inventory can be the most tedious part of the installation, but it also can eliminate a lot of larger headaches in the future.

It is easiest to begin by listing what external hardware you have. The following is a list of external items you should inventory:

Keyboard	Keyboards are a fairly standard item, but some are specialized for a language or other item.
Monitor	Make a note of the brand and size of your monitor. It's helpful if you have the monitor's manual, because it will have specifications like horizontal/vertical frequencies that you need later.
Mouse	The important information to know for your mouse is the brand, how many buttons it has, and what type of port (serial, PS/2, or bus mouse) it connects to.
Printer	You should write down the manufacturer, if the printer is capable of emulating another printer, and if your printer is a PostScript printer or not.

JUST A MINUTE

> Although not necessary for installation, it is a good idea to inventory anything else outside your computer: speakers, external disk drives, and so on.

Now comes the trickier hardware—the items that are inside your computer. There are many different kinds of hardware, and many different acronyms can be involved (such as SCSI, IDE, BIOS, and so on). However, it's not difficult to get through if you take things a step at a time.

Most of the information that you need can be obtained from your machine's BIOS. On many machines, as the system comes up you see instructions referring to a certain key (F1, Del, or some similar key) to enter the BIOS. Depending on the type, brand, and sophistication of the BIOS, you can find out all the information you need. If you're running Microsoft Windows 95 or NT 4.0, most of the information can be found in the Control Panel's system properties.

JUST A MINUTE

> If your BIOS doesn't give access to all the information asked for in this hour, don't worry. You can usually get this information from the computer's manufacturer; it will just take a little longer.

You'll need to know what kind of CPU you have. While Linux runs on many different platforms, the distribution included with this book only runs on Intel CPUs (or clones from AMD and Cyrix). So if your computer has a 386, 486, Pentium, Pentium Pro, Pentium II, or a clone of one of these chips, then you're set to go. Below is a list of internal items you should inventory:

CD-ROM	While Linux supports a large group of CD-ROM drives, those that are the easiest to install are those connected to the IDE bus or a SCSI card. If the CD-ROM is connected to the IDE bus, it needs to be an ATAPI-compliant CD-ROM.
Floppy Drive	The floppy drive you boot to has to be a 3.5" drive.
Hard Drive	Hard drives, like CD-ROMs, may be connected to either an IDE bus or a SCSI bus. It is a good idea to write down the number of cylinders shown in your computers BIOS. (Cylinders are discussed later in the hour.)
Internal Bus	This usually isn't an important issue except for people with IBM PS/2 machines. Linux doesn't currently support the Micro-Channel Architecture bus. Supported internal buses are PCI, ISA, EISA, and the VL Bus. Machines built from 1995 onward will probably have a PCI bus.
Memory	Linux requires at least 8 megabytes of RAM to run. The amount of RAM you have can usually be found at boot time or from the BIOS.
Sound Card	Not needed for installation, but if you have a Creative Labs Sound Blaster, or compatible sound card, you can get sound relatively easily.
Video Card	What's important here is the card's chipset and how much memory it contains. In the case of PCI video cards, this information can be probed during the installation. (This information is really only necessary if you plan to use the X Window environment.)

Hardware Considerations

Now that you've completed the inventory of your system, it's time to put the list to good use. The first thing you should do is compare the hardware in your inventory with a list of hardware that Linux supports. Table 1.1 contains a short list of supported items. A more comprehensive list is available on the Web at the following site:

```
http://www.redhat.com/support/docs/rhl/intel/rh50-hardware-intel.html
```

Table 1.1. A short list of Linux-compatible hardware.

Device	Compatibility
CD-ROM Drive	IDE ATAPI-compliant drives, and SCSI CD-ROMs on supported controllers.
Hard Drive	Virtually all IDE, EIDE, and SCSI hard drives are supported. Some newer Ultra DMA drives may not work because they aren't backwards compatible with the EIDE standard.
SCSI Controller	Most of the common controllers from manufacturers such as BusLogic and Adaptec are supported.
Video Card	Many cards from ATI, Cirrus, and Matrox are supported, as are most cards built around the S3 chipset.

If some of your hardware isn't supported, then you have the following alternatives:

- ☐ Change out the hardware with items that are supported.
- ☐ Check back later to see if support for the hardware is available.

It's a good idea to avoid any hardware that's labeled as Plug and Play ready. While Linux is starting to support plug-and-play hardware, it's currently not always a simple task to set up. It also would be prudent to avoid any hardware that's listed as a Win-item (like a Winmodem or a Winprinter). These items currently only work with a Microsoft Windows operating system.

Network Information

If your computer is connected to a LAN that's running TCP/IP, you will probably want to contact your network administrator to get the following information.

Hostname of Machine: ______________________
Domain Name: ______________________
IP Address: ______________________
Netmask: ______________________

1

Default Gateway: ____________________
Primary Nameserver: ____________________
2nd Nameserver: ____________________
NFS Server (optional): ____________________
FTP Server (optional): ____________________

Creating the Installation Floppies

The next step is to create the boot and supplemental floppies. You need the two blank, formatted floppies discussed earlier in the hour. Label the blank floppies "Boot Diskette" and "Supplemental Diskette." These diskettes are created by using the `rawrite` program located on the CD. The `rawrite` program works by writing a disk image to a blank floppy.

The following example assumes that your CD is drive E: on your system. Please substitute your drive letter if it's different. At the DOS prompt, change into the `\DOSUTILS` directory on the CD and run the `rawrite` program. You will be prompted by the following:

```
Enter disk image source file name: E:\images\boot.img
Enter target diskette drive: A:
Please insert a formatted diskette into drive A: and press --ENTER-- :
```

After the image is written, remove that floppy and insert the floppy you labeled "Supplemental Diskette," then rerun the `rawrite` program.

```
Enter disk image source file name: E:\images\supp.img
Enter target diskette drive: A:
Please insert a formatted diskette into drive A: and press --ENTER-- :
```

Your installation diskettes are now ready; the next step is to prepare your hard drive.

Preparing Your Hard Drive

Since you are installing Linux to a hard drive in your system, you need to make sure you have necessary room to perform the installation. If you already have a second hard drive or a partition set aside for Linux, you're pretty much ready to begin the installation. If you don't, you have to make space available on your existing hard drive by using a program that comes with the CD called `fips`. Before you do that, however, you need to have a basic understanding of partitions and file systems.

Partitions and File Systems

As discussed earlier, Linux should be installed into its own partition. All hard drives need to be partitioned before they can be used. When you partition a drive, you're designating a specific area of your hard drive for use. Partitions allow you to divide your hard drive so that not all information is stored in one area. Different operating systems write information to partitions in different ways, and these different ways are known as file systems.

Partitions

There are two types of partitions: primary and extended. Extended partitions can be subdivided into more parts through the use of logical drives; primary partitions cannot. A hard drive can contain both types of partitions at the same time, with some limitations. A drive can contain up to four primary partitions. To divide a hard drive up even further, one of these partitions may be designated as an extended partition. Each extended partition can be divided up using logical drives.

Figure 1.1 shows you an example of a drive that has been broken down into four distinct areas using one primary partition and one extended partition that has been further divided into three logical drives.

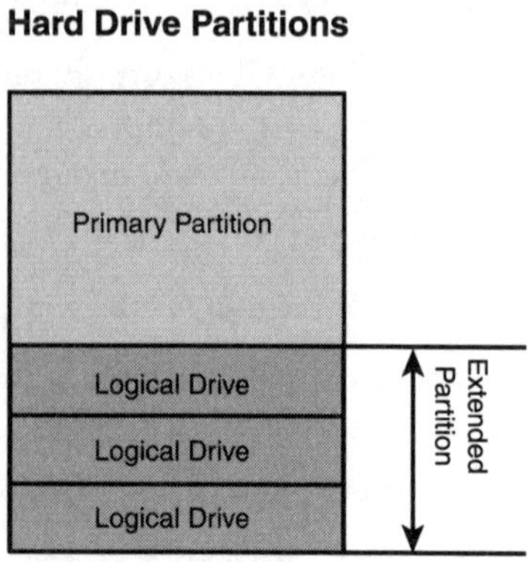

Figure 1.1.
Example of hard drive partition types.

File Systems

Whereas the partition tells the operating system "Write information in this area," a file system tells the operating system "Write the files in this format!" DOS versions 5.0–7.0 use a file system called FAT16 that allows for 512 megabyte partitions (and larger ones through some fancy footwork that are beyond the discussion of this book). Windows 95 OSR2 can use a FAT32 file system, which allows for much larger partitions. Linux primarily uses two file systems called EXT2 and SWAP.

CAUTION

If you're using Windows NT, OS/2, or have Windows 95 OSR2 with a FAT32 partition, you may have problems using the `fips` commands. You need to look to a commercial partition program (such as Partition Magic) to create the necessary space.

Creating Space

You need to have a minimum of 60 megabytes free on your hard drive for a bare-bones Linux installation. A more reasonable estimate is around 250 megabytes, and a complete installation takes up around 600 megabytes. This section takes you through the creation of space on your hard drive by showing you how it would be done on a fictional 1GB hard drive with 1024 cylinders. The drive has 600MB of space free.

Just a Minute

When looking at the data on the hard disk drive listed in the BIOS, you should have seen some items like Cylinders, Heads, and Sectors. The only important number here is Cylinders—they are the building blocks of partitions. If you partition half of the fictional hard drive mentioned in the preceding paragraph, you would be setting aside 512 cylinders for use.

To diagram how you want to layout the OS on the machine, the first step is to write down what's already on the hard drive(s), what cylinders those partitions cover, and what can be moved. Figure 1.2 shows the current configuration of the fictional drive as well as the planned configuration.

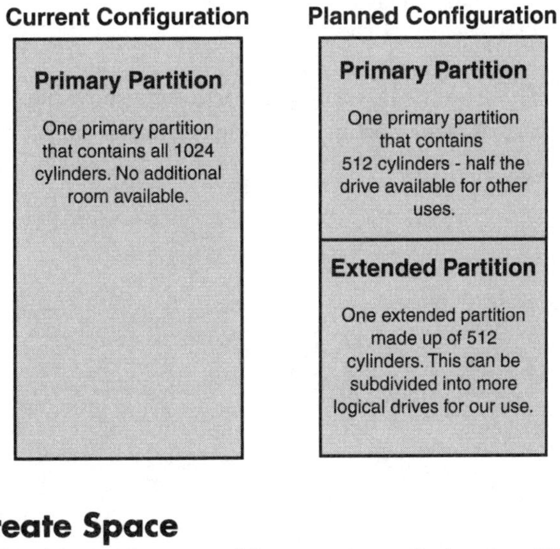
Current Configuration
Primary Partition
One primary partition that contains all 1024 cylinders. No additional room available.
Planned Configuration
Primary Partition
One primary partition that contains 512 cylinders - half the drive available for other uses.
Extended Partition
One extended partition made up of 512 cylinders. This can be subdivided into more logical drives for our use.

Figure 1.2.
Current and planned configuration of the fictional hard drive.

Using `fips` to Create Space

This example begins with a drive with one partition covering cylinders 1 to 1024. The goal is to shrink the first partition down to half its current size and create a new extended partition in the vacated space.

CAUTION

> It's always a good idea to backup your data before you change anything on your hard drive. Losing all of your data can be costly.

`fips` is located on the CD-ROM that comes with this book. First, read the documentation on the CD-ROM in the `\DOSUTILS` directory. It gives detailed instructions and may cover questions you have. Second, back up the data on the hard drive if at all possible (and verify the backup to make sure it worked). Third, copy the `fips.exe` program from the `\DOSUTILS` directory to the bootable floppy you created earlier in the hour.

`fips` works by reallocating the free space at the end of your drive. So the next step is to defragment your drive. Windows 95 comes with Disk Defragmenter in its System Tools. Users of DOS need to find another tool such as the Norton Utilities. In this example, defragmenting ensures all 600MB of free space on the fictional drive is at the end.

Once the defragmentation is done, you are ready to resize the partition. Restart the machine using the bootable floppy, and at the DOS prompt run the `fips` command.

CAUTION

> Be sure you have read the `fips` documentation located on the CD before you begin.

After you have finished resizing your partition, remove the floppy and reboot your machine. If all went well, your existing operating system should boot up and be ready to go.

PART I

Hour 2

Installing Linux

In Hour 1 you learned how to prepare your system for the installation of Linux. Before you actually begin installing, there are several items you should be familiar with.

The Installation Program's Interface

The installation interface is a character interface rather than a graphical interface. A mouse isn't used during the installation process; instead, various keystrokes are used to select items.

If you're in a text region that has multiple choices or selections, you can usually use the arrow keys to move around. To switch between regions, you can use the Tab and Alt-Tab keys.

To choose a button to select, you normally position the highlighted area using one of the movement keys. You can then press the Space or Enter key to press the button. To select check boxes, scroll through the entries, highlighting the desired option. Then use the Space key to select or toggle the option on or off.

The F12 key is special in that it takes the values as selected on the screen and proceeds to the next screen. If your keyboard doesn't have an F12 key, the combination Shift F2 should have the same results.

The installation program presents various diagnostic information for the user to determine what may be happening in various parts of the install. To not clutter the main screen with extra data, it uses a useful feature of Linux called the Virtual Console which can be seen via a single keystroke. Table 2.1 lists the keystrokes used to view each of the virtual consoles:

Table 2.1. Virtual console keystrokes.

Keystroke	Result
Alt-F1	This is the main installation dialogue.
Alt-F2	Once the CD-ROM has been found, you get a shell prompt that can be used to execute commands.
Alt-F3	The log from the installation program.
Alt-F4	The log from the kernel and other system level programs.
Alt-F5	Messages from disk formatting and some other programs.

For the most part, you won't need to ever leave the first virtual console, unless you are curious, or trying to diagnose a problem.

Beginning the Installation

To begin the installation, insert the boot diskette into the floppy drive and restart the computer. The machine should go through the normal process of booting from a floppy, then come to a screen with a `boot:` prompt.

JUST A MINUTE

> The installation process occurs in two stages. In the first stage you tell the installation program some basic information about your computer and where to find the installation files. The second stage performs the rest of the installation.

This initial screen contains helpful tips about starting the install, and allows access to some initial help screens before the boot process. To access these help screens, press one of the function keys, listed in Table 2.2, printed at the bottom of the screen. There is a short delay as the data is read from the floppy drive.

Table 2.2. Function keys and their results.

Function Key	Result
`F1 Main screen`	The one you initially saw at startup.
`F2 General`	Some general tips on what the boot process does.
`F3 Expert`	This screen explains the `expert` mode. This mode disables most of the autoprobing and autodetection.
`F4 Rescue`	This mode enables you to help repair a damaged system. You need both the boot and supplemental floppy for this mode.
`F5 Kickstart`	The `kickstart` is an advanced mode that uses a pre-configured text file. The use of `kickstart` mode is beyond the scope of this tutorial, but is documented on the CD-ROM.
`F6 Kernel`	A help screen on some options that you can pass to the kernel at boot time.

You can now type any options you require at the boot prompt, and press Enter to start the install. If you do not type anything or press any function key, the install automatically begins after one minute.

JUST A MINUTE

If you didn't get to this first screen, or received an error message, there may be something wrong with the floppy image. The most common causes are that the floppy disk had a bad sector, or that the floppy drive hardware has some sort of problems using the floppy. You need to recreate the boot floppy following the instructions in Hour 1, "Preparing to Install Linux."

After pressing Enter you should see the following output:

```
Loading initrd.img...................
Loading vmlinuz...........
Uncompressing Linux.......
```

If the diskette activity stops, and the initial screen doesn't appear, hardware problems or incompatibility are the likely culprit.

The First Stage

After a moment of floppy disk activity, you should see a black-and-white screen asking if you are using a color monitor, shown in Figure 2.1. This is the beginning of the first stage of the installation process. You next set up some basic hardware and the install attempts to find the installation media.

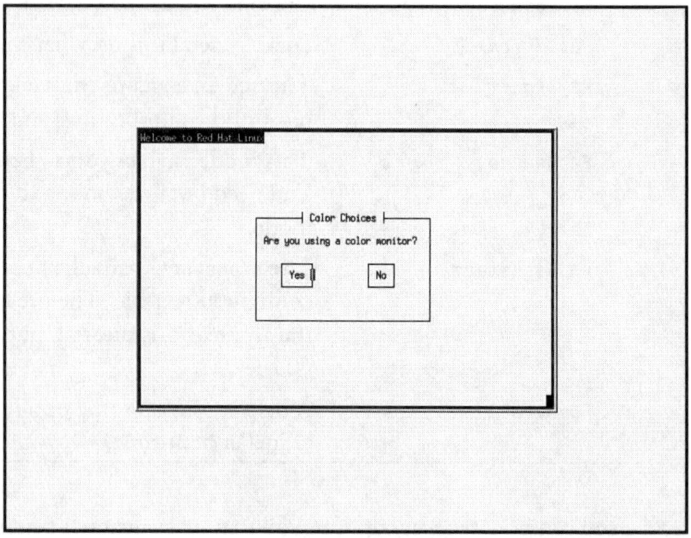

Figure 2.1.
Selecting the type of monitor you have.

The default choice on the first screen is `Yes`; you should see a blinking cursor or highlight near the `Yes`. If you see the cursor, or highlight option, press Enter and continue onto the next step. This walkthrough assumes that you have a color monitor.

TIME SAVER

> When selecting between options on the screen, you can use Tab to change the selection. If you have overshot your selection you can either press Alt-Tab to back up, or continue pressing Tab to wrap around to the other choices.

The next screen is a welcome screen, stating that the Red Hat installation guide also details the installation process. If you're ready to begin the install, press Enter.

Keyboard Selection

The next screen, shown in Figure 2.2, asks you to select the keyboard type you are using. If, after we have installed Linux, you want to change to a different keyboard type, the command `/usr/sbin/kbdconfig` can be used to change the keyboard type.

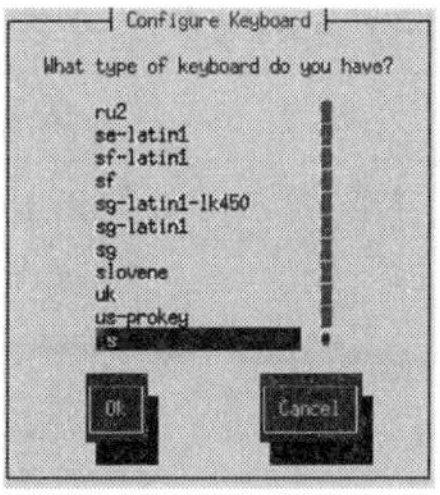

Figure 2.2.
Selecting the keyboard.

Most of the choices on this screen are for language-specific keyboards. The typical United States PC keyboard is the default choice. You can select a different choice by using the arrow up and arrow down keys. To the right of the screen you should notice a scroll bar with a # mark. This mark indicates that there are more types of keyboards than can be shown on the screen at present.

After selecting the keyboard for your machine, tab over to the Ok button and press Enter.

PCMCIA Support

Next, the program searches for a PCMCIA chipset in your computer. If a known PCMCIA chipset is found then you are asked to insert the supplemental floppy. When you have done this, you can select Ok and the program loads additional drivers from the floppy. If no known PCMCIA chipset is found, the program quietly goes on to the next step of the install.

Installation Method

The next screen, shown in Figure 2.3, asks you which kind of install that you want to attempt. There are four methods that can be used. This section only be details installation from a CD-ROM and a hard drive.

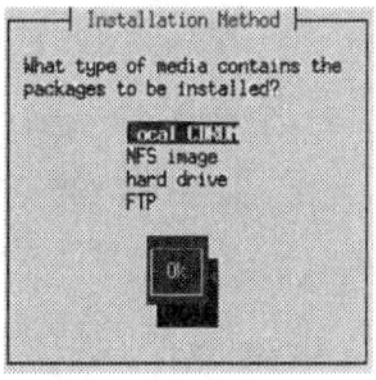

Figure 2.3.
Selecting where the installation files are located.

The four options are explained in Table 2.3.

Table 2.3. Explanation of the different installation methods.

Method	Explanation
Local CD-ROM	The default method of installing Linux to your hard drive. This method does not use the supplemental floppy.
Hard Drive	If you are unable to install from the CD-ROM, then you need to copy the `\RedHat\` directory tree over to a FAT16 (DOS) partition on your hard drive. This method then loads the supplemental floppy and continues with the install.
NFS	This method enables you to install from an NFS server (a type of network file system).
FTP	This method enables you to install from an FTP server.

This book will focus on the CD-ROM install.

Installing from CD-ROM

If you selected to install from a CD, the program asks you to insert the CD into the player. It then tries to auto-probe for an IDE CD on the system. If it doesn't find an IDE CD, it presents a screen asking what kind of CD-ROM you have. The choices on the screen are as follows:

SCSI — If your CD is on a SCSI adapter, it tries to find the SCSI adapter, and if it is unable to, it asks you for what kind of SCSI device it should try to load. You will be asked if you want to autoprobe for the device or if you want to give options to the device. In most cases, you shouldn't need to specify any options.

Other CD-ROM — If your CD isn't an IDE or a SCSI CD, it probably falls under this category. You are presented with a long list of drivers. Choose which driver matches your CD-ROM and if you need to, any special options.

Just a Minute

If you have an IDE CD and it wasn't detected, you'll need to restart the install and at the very first screen give the kernel a special option to point out where the drive is:

```
boot: linux hdX=cdrom
Where hdX =

Channel          Jumper          hdx
====================================
ide0             master          hda
ide0             slave           hdb
```

```
ide1            master          hdc
ide1            slave           hdd

ide0 = primary channel
ide1 = secondary channel
```

Once the CD has been detected, the program attempts to mount the Red Hat CD and go on to the next stage of the install.

The Second Stage

You are now ready to begin the second stage of the installation process. In this stage you create the necessary partitions and select which parts of the Linux distribution you want to install.

Selecting to Install Fresh or Upgrade

The next menu window, shown in Figure 2.4, asks whether you are installing or upgrading an existing system. This tutorial assumes that you are installing Linux for the first time.

CAUTION

> If you already have Linux on your system, an install using those partitions will overwrite all the data currently on there.

Figure 2.4.
Choosing to install fresh or upgrade an existing system.

SCSI Support

After choosing an installation option, the program tries to auto-probe for any SCSI adapters. If it is unable to locate any, it asks you if you have any SCSI adapters in your machine. If you do, select Yes and a dialog box asks which adapter you have. Choose the adapter you have in your machine, and another screen asking whether you wish to autoprobe or give options is displayed. Most SCSI drivers do not need options. If you don't have a SCSI adapter, choose No and press Enter.

Partitioning the Hard Drive

Before you begin partitioning the drive, it is important to understand how Linux references different partitions. In the DOS/Windows world, different partitions are given different drive letters. For example, if you had a drive with two partitions they would probably show up as drives C: and D:. Linux does away with drive letters, and partitions show up as what can best be described as different directories. So, to follow the example above, if you have two partitions under Linux, they might show up as `/` and `/data` in the user interface.

The next screen that appears begins the Disk Setup portion of the install, shown in Figure 2.5. You are given the choice of choosing between two partitioning tools that are shipped with Red Hat Linux. The first choice is the Disk Druid program, and the second is the `fdisk` command.

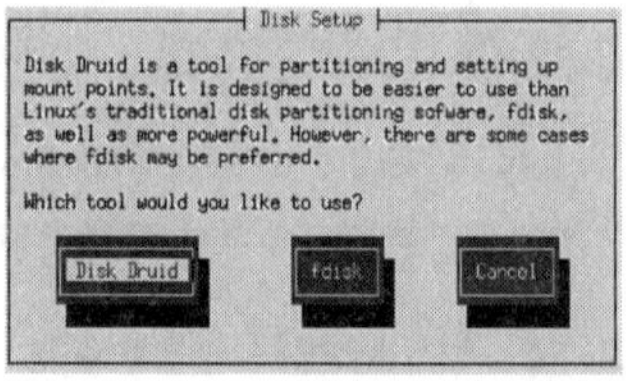

Figure 2.5.
Selecting the disk-partitioning program you want to use.

Disk Druid is a GUI-based disk management program. It is able to create and delete partitions, while also defining the mount points for those partitions. `fdisk` is a more esoteric partitioning tool. While it is more flexible than Disk Druid in certain situations (dealing with disk drives having odd geometries, for example), it also is less user-friendly.

You need to dedicate at least 2 partitions to Red Hat Linux. One needs to be the root mount point / and the other needs to be the Linux swap space. The recommended Linux swap space is usually equal to twice the amount of RAM you have. If you have 32MB or more of RAM you can set the swap space equal to the amount of RAM and feel safe.

The Disk Druid Interface

The Disk Druid screen, shown in Figure 2.6, contains a lot of information about your hard drives.

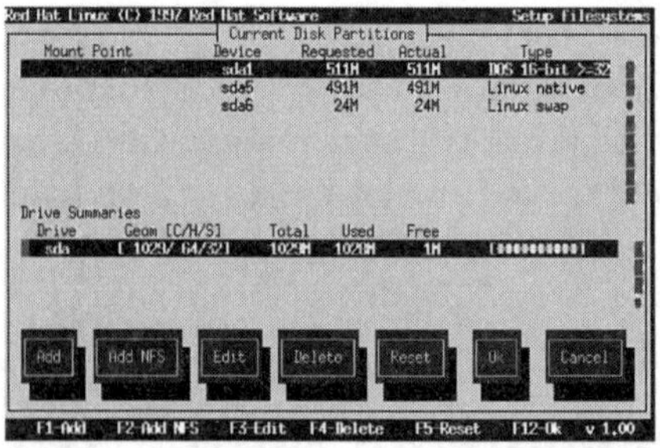

Figure 2.6.
The Disk Druid screen.

At the top of the screen, there's a section listing the Current Disk Partitions found on your hard drive. The middle of the screen is devoted to the Drive Summaries—the disk drives the installation program found. The bottom section lists the buttons and hot keys the program uses. All of the sections are described more fully in the following text.

Current Disk Partitions

This section details the partitions that already exist on your machine. Each listed partition has several fields that are (left to right):

`Mount Point` The name of the directory that you will mount the directory under in Linux. Not putting anything in this field means that the partition will not be mounted.

`Device` This field gives the device name of the partition.

`Requested` This field shows the minimum size that was requested when the partition was defined.

`Actual` This shows how much space is currently given to that partition.

`Type` This field shows the type of partition. Commonly seen types are DOS, NTFS, Linux native, or Linux swap. You might also see that the partition has not been allocated yet. This is usually due to the fact that there isn't enough disk space for the minimum amount originally requested.

Drive Summaries

The lines in this section represent the hard drives that are present in the machine. Each line has these fields:

`Drive` The hard drive's device name. IDE hard drives use the device names hdX, where X is a letter indicating which drive it is. SCSI hard drives are labeled by how they appear on the chain. The first drive found is sda, the second sdb, and so on.

`Geom [C/H/S]` The hard drive's geometry as detected by Disk Druid. The geometry is separated by the number of cylinders, heads, and sectors that were found. Compare these numbers to what you wrote down from the BIOS. If they do not match up, it usually indicates that you need to use fdisk.

`Total` This area reports the total amount of disk space the disk drive has. Compare this number with what you have already written in your inventory.

`Used` An area that indicates in Megabytes how much of the hard drive is currently allocated.

`Free`	This section shows how much of the hard drive is currently not allocated.
`#####`	The final area is a bar graph giving a rough visual guide to how much disk space is still available on the drive.

Disk Druid Commands

The bottom section contains the buttons that control Disk Druid. They can be used to Add, Delete, Change, Reset to the Beginning, or Finish the install.

The `F1-Add` option is used to add partitions. A pop-up menu, shown in Figure 2.7, appears when selected.

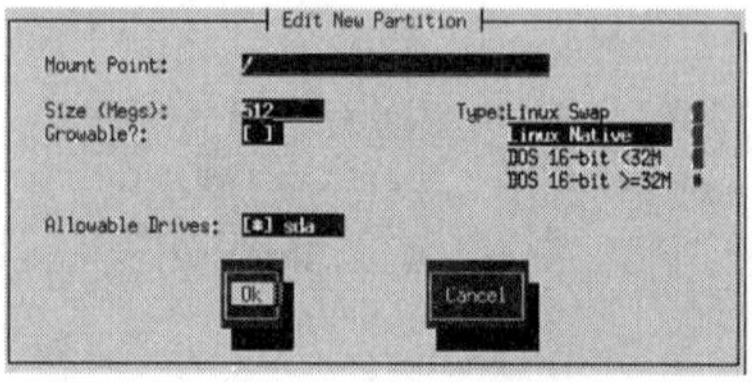

Figure 2.7.
This pop-up menu lets you specify the size and type of your partition.

The fields in this pop-up are explained in Table 2.4.

Table 2.4. Explanation of the `F1-Add` pop-up menu.

Menu Item	Explanation
Mount Point	Used to enter the partition's mount point. Remember that the entire space of the mounted hard drives are seen as subdirectories of the / partition. Therefore, you need to specify one Linux partition to be the root partition /.
Size (Megs)	Used to enter the minimal requested size of the partition. Unless changed, the minimum size is 1 meg.
Growable?	A check box to indicate that the size entered is a minimum or an exact size. If Growable is selected, the partition size tries to fit all available disk space on the drive.
Type	Used to choose the partition type to be used for the partition. This field is a highlighted scrollable section.
Allowable Drives	Another check box area that tells disk druid on which drives to try to create this partition.
Ok	Selecting this button tries to create the partition.
Cancel	Selecting this button aborts the addition of a partition.

The `F2-Add NFS` option is used to add NFS partitions. NFS partitions are network partitions and outside the scope of this section.

The `F3-Edit` option is used to change an already existing partition. The dialog box that appears enables you to edit various fields depending on whether the partition has been written to the disk already.

The `F4-Delete` option is used to remove the highlighted partition from the drive. A pop-up appears, asking to confirm this deletion.

The `F5-Reset` option is used to bring Disk Druid to the state it was before you made any changes. All changes that have been made are removed. Any data on the mount points also has to re-entered.

The Ok option is used to write changes to the disk drive. A confirmation pop-up appears, and if confirmed, the hard drives partition tables is written with the new data. The mount points that have been chosen are passed onto the installation program to define the filesystem layout.

The `Cancel` option bails you out of Disk Druid. Any changes made will be lost, and a pop-up dialog box is displayed, asking which step in the install should be to be done next.

Working with Disk Druid

Get out the pad of paper that contains your plan for your hard drive so you can be sure you know which partitions you want to delete, and which you want to keep. Select the deleteable partitions and press F4 to delete them.

CAUTION

> Remember that once you have removed these partitions and chosen the Ok option the information in these partitions is gone.

Press `F1` and you are presented with the Adding Menu. For the purposes of this walkthrough you will have two partitions: / and swap. The first partition will be /. In the mount point area type / and tab to the size field. For the purposes of this example, enter 250 megs (change this to fit with your earlier estimates). Select `Linux Native` as the partition, double-check all of your entries, and then select Ok. Create the swap partition in the same way, just be sure to select `Linux Swap` as the partition type and then choose Ok.

JUST A MINUTE

> If your attempt to create the partition fails for some reason, an error window pops up, explaining what the error is. More than likely the error is that Disk Druid could not allocate the disk space for the drive currently and you will need to edit the partition to be smaller or make other alterations to accommodate the partition.

Once you're done selecting the new partitions for your drive, select Ok or F12 and confirm that you want to make the changes. The install goes to the next stage.

Activating Swap Space

Once the partitions have been created, the install program searches for swap partitions. If it doesn't find any it will warn you, and you can go back to the previous step of partitioning the drives and set up a section to be swapped. If one or more swap spaces were detected, a screen, shown in Figure 2.8, asks which partitions you wish to use for swap. Select the check boxes of the partitions you want to use, and also select whether or not you want to check for bad blocks when it does the swap formatting. Once you are ready to continue, choose Ok.

Figure 2.8.
It's a good idea to have Linux check for bad blocks during formatting.

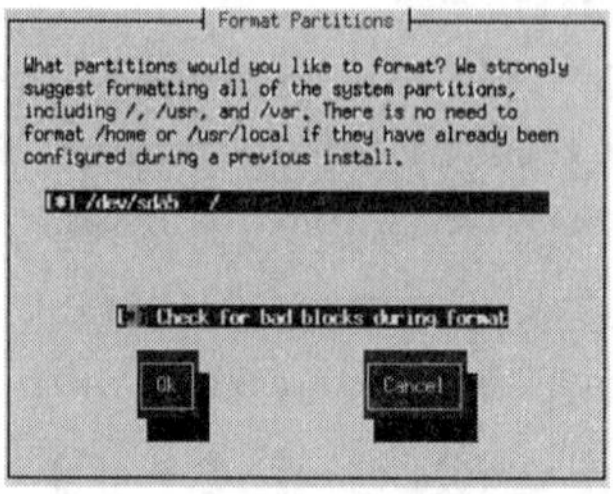

Formatting Partitions

Once the swap space has been selected, the next screen brings up a dialog box of the Linux Native partitions you need to format. You need to format any new partitions you created in the install process, and you should reformat any old partitions from previous Linux installs that do not contain data you want to keep.

Toggle the checkbox for each partition you want to format, and toggle whether you want to check for bad blocks during the format.

Selecting Which Components To Install

The next stage of the install is to select which packages you want on your Linux Box. A screen, shown in Figure 2.9, asks which components you would like to install on your machine. These components are sets of packages that work together or are similar in nature. The X Window System is all of the packages that give most of the X functionality (server, basic libraries, window manager, and some clients). Adding the X Games package installs various amusements.

If you want to install a minimal base 50 megabyte system, you need to unselect everything that has been auto-selected.

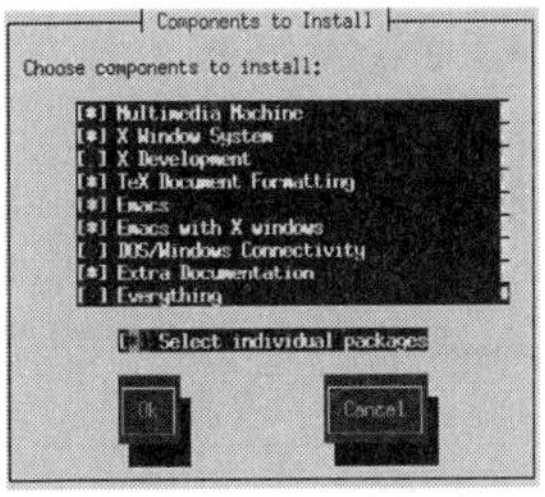

Figure 2.9.
This dialog box gives you a list of packages you can install.

For the person wanting to fine-tune the items in the component listings, you can select individual packages by toggling the so named switch. If chosen, another screen, shown in Figure 2.10, enables you to pick and choose which sub-packages you want to install. A scrolling menu of all the package groups available is displayed, and you can select or deselect any package inside of a grouping. In selecting or deselecting individual packages, the install program may ask you to either choose them again or will need to install other packages. This is due to the fact that other packages may depend on the un-selected package to properly work.

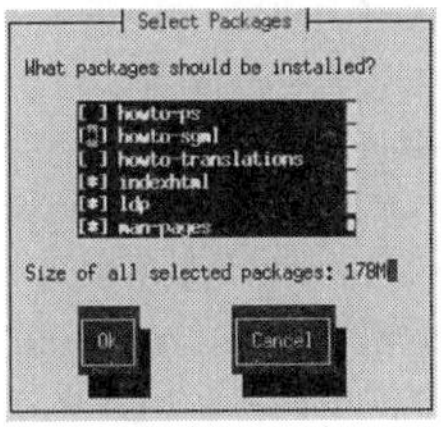

Figure 2.10.
Selecting individual packages for installation. Not recommended for beginners.

Finally, in this mode, you also can get more information on what each package contains or is supposed to do, by pressing the F1 key. To continue onto the next stage of the install, tab over to the Ok button and the installation begins.

Format and Install

Once any dependency issues have been resolved, the installation program lets you know that a complete listing of packages installed will be put in the `/tmp/install.log` file. Press Enter to continue on to the next stage. This stage is where each of the partitions that you chose previously to be formatted have new file systems placed upon them. Packages are now installed. You can follow the progress in the Install Status window.

Finishing the Installation

This final section of the chapter covers the items needed to finish the install and get your Linux system booted. You still need the pre-planning pad of paper.

Choosing a Mouse

The program probes your system for a mouse, and if it finds one, indicates the type and port that the mouse is connected to. Depending on the mouse, you may be asked for the number of buttons the mouse has, what protocol it uses, and if you need your 2-button mouse to emulate a 3-button model.

Just a Minute

> After the install has occurred, if you need to change the values for the mouse, you can use the program `/usr/sbin/mouseconfig`.

Configuring X Window

The next window that comes up asks you about the X Window server that you want to run. The configuration of X Window is detailed more in Hour 3, "Configuring the X Window System." However, this section walks you through a quick rundown so you can finish the initial installation.

Scroll down the list of video cards listed and try to find the card that is in your machine. One thing to note is that video cards, like cars, may have brand names very similar to one another, but the items under the hood (chipset in the case of the card) can be very different. If you can't find a card that matches what you have in your machine, choose the Generic VGA compatible card that every video card should be able to emulate. Once a card has been selected, the appropriate X server will be installed onto your machine.

The next screen tries to determine the model of monitor you have. It is very important that you select a monitor that matches your model exactly. If your model isn't listed, you need to choose custom and fill in the values that were researched earlier for your monitor.

Caution

> Entering incorrect values for your monitor can cause damage to the monitor. The author has smoked a monitor in the past by putting the wrong model's data into the settings.

If you have chosen the Generic VGA card, you are asked if you wish to probe for settings. Choose not to probe, and after a moment, you should move on to the next section of the install.

Network Configuration

If you will be installing this machine onto a Local Area Network (LAN), and you want to set up networking now, you should choose the Yes button. Otherwise choose No. If needed, you can configure networking after the install.

If you have chosen Yes, you are asked what network card driver the program should try. Scroll down the selection bar until you see one that matches your card. Tab to the Ok button and press Enter. You are then asked if you need to supply any options for the card. If you need to supply arguments for the card, they will be the IO address of the card (supplied in Hexadecimal), and the interrupt that the card is using (example: io=0x330 and irq=5). In most cases, the autoprobe will find the card.

If the card is found, the next screen presents you with choices to set up your network. If you have a bootp server running on your network that sets up the IP addresses and other data for your machines, toggle `[]Configure device with bootp` and select Ok. If not, input the information you received from your network administrator back in Hour 1.

Setting the Time Zone

You are next asked to set up your system's time zone and what your BIOS clock is set to. The first toggle area, shown in Figure 2.11, asks if your computer's BIOS clock is set to GMT. Using the BIOS clock at GMT enables Red Hat Linux to deal with daylight savings changes, but can have the effect of turning other OS's clocks off.

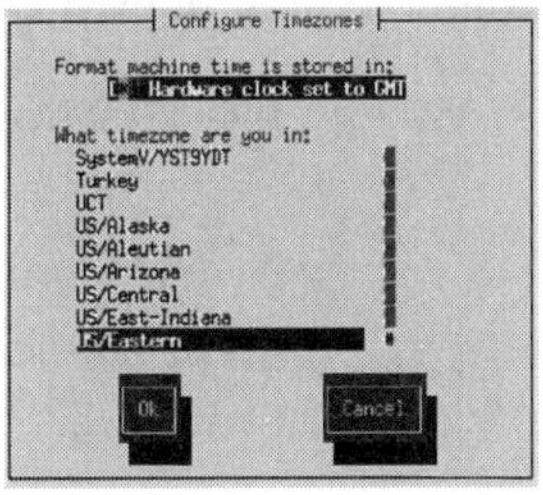

Figure 2.11.
If you're not sure what time zone you are in, you might check out your phone book.

The next selection area on the screen asks what time zone you are in. Scroll to the zone that best matches your time zone. Select Ok to continue with the install.

Selecting Which Services to Start

The next section of the install goes over the services or daemons to start when the system restarts. The dialog box shown in Figure 2.12, should contain a long scrollable list of check boxes linked to a service that starts when you boot the machine. You can choose to get more information on a service by scrolling to that service and pressing F1 to get a short description on the service.

Since you can get this screen after the installation by running the `ntsysv` command, you should look at each service and decide if you want to start the first time you run the box. For the most part, if a service was selected by default it should stay on, and if it wasn't turned on should only be enabled when you have configured it later.

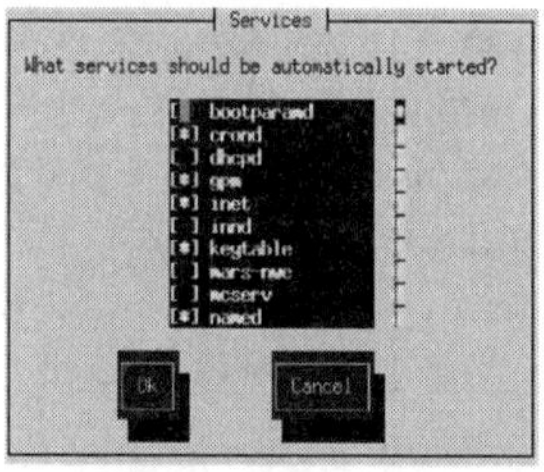

Figure 2.12.
Unless you're sure about what you are doing, leave the defaults as they are.

CAUTION

Certain services should only be turned off if you know what the consequences are. Otherwise you may run into a system that is not fully bootable. These services are as follows: `atd`, `crond`, `inet`, `kerneld`, `keytable`, `network`, and `syslog`.

Selecting a Printer

You are next asked to configure a printer. Select Yes if you want to do this now, or No if you don't have a printer or want to install it later.

Selecting Yes brings up a dialog box asking where the printer is. There are three selections available:

`Local`	Meaning a printer connected to the computer.
`Remote lpd`	This printer is one connected to your LAN that can communicate via lpd.
`LAN Manager`	If the network printer is printed to via a LAN Manager or SMB printer server.

Choosing Local Printer asks for you to name the printer queue (`lp` by default) and the spool directory that this printer will use. For the purposes of this install, you should probably choose the default values and select Next. The computer then tries to determine what printer ports are available, and asks you to match the printer to the ones found. Pressing `Next` sends you to the next section of the install.

JUST A MINUTE

If you're trying to connect to a network printer, it would be a good idea to skip this section until you can ask your system administrator for help. You can always come back and add the printer later through X Window.

Choosing `Remote lpd` printer brings up a dialog box asking you the name of the machine you will be printing to, and the name of the queue on that machine. For example, if the printer on the `lpd` print server is called laser, you would enter laser and in the next space the hostname of the print server. Pressing Next sends you to the next section of the install.

Choosing `LAN Manager` brings up a dialog box that will set up various `smbfs` items for you. The first selection is the LAN Manager Host name, the next is the IP address of that LAN Manager host, followed by the Share Name of the Printer and finally the Username and Password that are needed to access the printer. Pressing Next sends you to the next section of the install.

2

Finishing Printer Setup

The next screens complete the Printer setup. You are first asked what kind of printer you have. Choose a printer that is similar to your printer, and if not found, select a text-only printer. Select Next and press Enter to begin choosing paper sizes. If the printer has multiple resolutions available, choose the one that you want to use. Finally, select the `Stair Stepping` option, if your printer does not send a carriage return at the end of a line causing your printing to look tilted as everything becomes a run-on. When done with this screen, select Next and press Enter.

The next screen shows you all the values for the printer you have chosen. If you are happy with these items, select Done and press Enter. If not choose Edit you will go back through the printer selection. Once you're happy, press Done and you will go on to the next stage of the install.

JUST A MINUTE

> Other printers can be added, edited, or deleted after the install by using the X Window tool, `printtool`.

Entering Your Initial Password

The next screen, shown in Figure 2.13, asks you to type a root password for your computer. This password is used to log in the administrative account as root. Your first login is as root so that you can set up other accounts and finalize setting up any other system items before bringing the machine into "production."

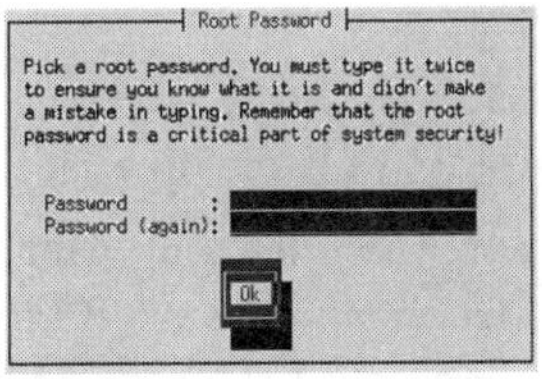

Figure 2.13.
Be sure to write this down—if you forget it you will have a lot of work to do to access your system.

In choosing a root password (or any password for that matter), you should choose one that is at least 6 characters, not a word found in a dictionary, a set of numbers, or some item that is easily guessable about you (your birthday date). Passwords that are considered to be good are a mix of numerals and case, and usually are acronyms of sentences or combined words. Examples of good passwords (at least until this is published) would be Fraz93Re, SH22puk, Iam99bal. Passwords are case-sensitive and commonly have a limit of only 8 characters (so Fraz93Rent and Fraz93Rex would both be considered the same password.)

Come up with a password for your machine, write it down on a separate piece of paper, and then enter it in the dialog areas. For security reasons, what you type does not show up on the screen. Because of this you need to enter the password twice to confirm that you are typing it the same way. When you have entered it twice, select Ok and press Enter. If the two passwords match each other, you will go onto the next screen. If they don't, you will need to re-enter them.

Remember, the root user has complete access and control over the system, having the ability to look into or change any file on the system, which is why this password should be kept secure.

Selecting Boot Options

You have reached the final stretch of the installation. This is the part where you decide how you will boot Linux after the installation.

The screen you are presented with, shown in Figure 2.14, gives you the choice of installing `LILO` (the bootloader) to two different parts of the system.

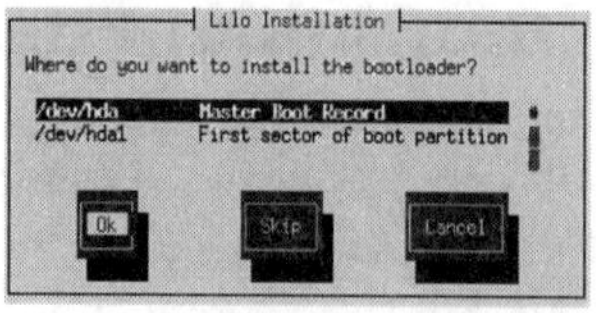

Figure 2.14.
Selecting where you want to install the bootloader. Most people should select the default `Master Boot Record` *option.*

- `Master Boot Record`. This replaces the master boot record of the system, causing a LILO prompt to come up each time you boot the machine. Useful in most cases.
- `First sector of the boot partition`. This option can be used if you have another boot loader on your system (OS/2, NT, Partition Magic, or System Commander are some examples). These boot loaders are already in the Master Boot Record of the primary drive and you don't want to replace them. With LILO installed to the root partition, you can then configure the other boot system to start that OS.

You also can choose to skip the installation of LILO to the hard drive. This is usually done when you want to use the LOADLIN program or if you installed Linux to an IDE system on the boot floppy. Choose the method you want and either select Ok or Skip.

If you selected either the First Sector of the root partition or the Master Boot Record, you are shown a screen asking for any boot options you need to pass to the machine or if you need to use the linear addressing mode to write to the system. For most systems, you don't have to choose anything going with the default.

Once LILO has been written to the boot record, you see a screen notifying you that the install is done, to remove the floppy disk from the drive, and to press Enter. If you do not get this screen, check the ALT-F3 and ALT-F4 screens to see if an error occurred during the LILO installation. In that case, you may need to skip the LILO installation and then use the alternative methods of booting.

Booting the System

Once LILO or LOADLIN have been installed, you can boot the Linux operating system. If LILO was chosen, you see what is called the LILO prompt:

```
LILO:
```

If you don't do anything at this point, the system automatically boots into Linux after a short timeout. If you have set up your system to boot to other operating systems, you can hit the Tab key to see what choices are available, and then just type in your option and press Enter.

```
linux dos
LILO:
```

After a few seconds, you see a set of text as the kernel boots up for the first time. After a short while, you should see the following prompt:

```
Red Hat Linux release 5.0 (Hurricane)
Kernel 2.0.32 on an i586

login:
```

You are now ready to login into the Red Hat Linux system. To do so, type **root** and you are prompted for a Password. Type the password you typed during the install, and you should get a # prompt indicating you have successfully logged in.

PART I

Hour 3

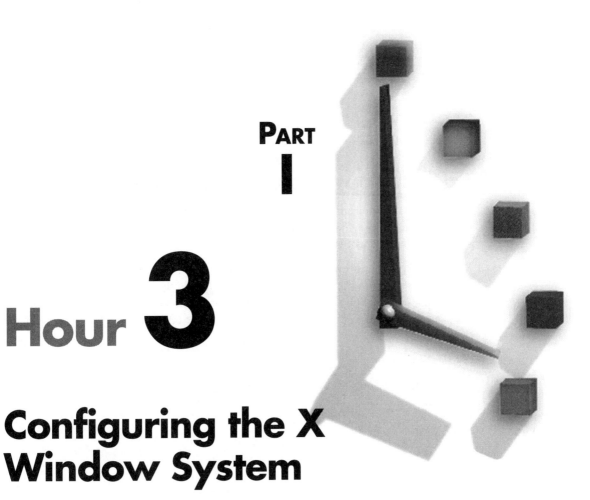

Configuring the X Window System

This hour looks at getting your X11 Window system up and running. X Window is the graphical windowing system that Linux and many other UNIX systems use. It is analogous to the windowing environment in Windows, OS/2, or Macintosh.

One of the differences between X11 Window and the other environments is that it was designed to be a machine/OS independent networked client/server program. As a result, the system is broken up into two major components: the X11 Window server that runs on the machine and interacts directly with the monitor and the video card, and the various clients that are displayed on the X11 server. These clients can range from terminal emulators (xterm) to eye candy (xpat2), or can manage the look and feel of the screen (the X11 Window Manager).

This hour begins by setting up the X Window system server that was skipped during the install, and finishes up by familiarizing you with the look and feel of the default windows that Red Hat offers. A later hour deals with customizing the system to different personal tastes. You need any documentation you have on your computer's video card and its monitor.

Checking Your Installation Files

The default X Window server that most Linux boxes come with (and the one on this book's CD) is supplied by the XFree86 Project. Other servers are provided from various commercial vendors and are discussed later in the hour.

First, check to make sure all of the files you need were installed during Hour 2, "Installing Linux." To see what X11 packages have been installed on the machine, you need to use the `rpm` command and pipe it through the `grep` command to find the lines that begin with X. The commands are covered in more detail throughout the rest of the book. If you enter the command

```
rpm -qa | grep ^X
```

you should receive output similar to the following:

```
X11R6-contrib-3.3.1-1
Xaw3d-1.3-13
Xconfigurator-3.25-1
XFree86-3.3.1-14
XFree86-75dpi-fonts-3.3.1-14
XFree86-libs-3.3.1-14
Xfree86-S3-3.3.1.14
```

JUST A MINUTE

> Pay special attention to the last line in the preceding listing. The `S3` portion of the line indicates the use of a video card with the S3 chipset. Knowing how the files are named makes it easier if you have to install a package for your video card later.

You're seeing what groups of packages were installed on the system. If you don't get any output but another hash prompt, there were no packages installed on the machine that begin with the letter X. If you don't get a list similar to the preceding one you need to install some extra packages to the system to get X11 up and running.

JUST A MINUTE

> If you followed the instructions carefully in Hour 2, you should have all the files you need to begin configuring your system.

Installing the X Files

In order to install the files you need, you must load the CD-ROM for Linux to see it, then get data off of it.

Insert the Red Hat CD-ROM and at the # prompt type the following:

```
mount /mnt/cdrom
```

After a few seconds you should see some activity on the CD-ROM and the # prompt, letting you know that you can continue. Change your current working directory to that of the CD-ROM's RPM area by typing the following command:

```
cd /mnt/cdrom/RedHat/RPMS
```

Further data, configuration options, and bug tips can be found at the following site:

```
http://www.xfree86.org
```


If no X items were installed, you need to install several RPM packages by using the `rpm` command. At the prompt, type the following commands one at a time, pressing Enter after each:

```
rpm -ivh X11R6-contrib*
rpm -ivh Xaw3d-1.3*
rpm -ivh Xconfig*
rpm -ivh XFree86-3*
rpm -ivh XFree86-75*
rpm -ivh XFree86-libs*
```

The preceding command lines will install everything you need except for the X server, which supports your specific video card. To install the correct server type in the following:

```
rpm -ivh Xfree86-YY*
```

Replace *YY* in your command line with the server name for your video card. Table 3.1 gives you a brief rundown of the servers and what chipsets they support.

Table 3.1. X servers shipped with Red Hat 5.0.

Server	What video chipsets this covers (short list)
Mono	2 color black-and-white.
VGA16	16 color VGA mode. Supports VGA with 256KB memory.
SVGA	Trident, Cirrus Logic, Chips and Technology, ET4000, S3V, and others.
Mach8	ATI boards with Mach8 chipset.
Mach32	ATI boards with Mach32 chipset.

continues

Table 3.1. continued

Server	What video chipsets this covers (short list)
Mach64	ATI boards with Mach64 chipset.
8514	IBM 8514/A boards and true clones.
S3	#9 boards, older Diamonds, others.
S3V	S3 Virge boards. Support is in SVGA.
AGX	All XGA graphic boards.
P9000	Diamond Viper (but not the 9100) and others.
W32	ET4000/W32 but not ET4000s.

Time Saver

If you're not sure which X server to install, run the `Xconfigurator` program (detailed in the following section) and it will detect most supported PCI video cards, letting you know which server to install.

Using `Xconfigurator` to Set Up X Window

At the `#` prompt, run the `Xconfigurator` command. You will get a welcome screen with an `Ok` button at the bottom, explaining the program.

Pressing Enter starts a PCI probe to see if `Xconfigurator` finds any video cards in your system. If it finds any, it shows which chipset and which X server need to be used. Pay special attention to this—if you installed the incorrect X server you are given the opportunity to correct your mistake. See Figure 3.1 for an example of the output when `Xconfigurator` successfully probes for a card. If the program can't find a card when probing, it brings up a list of cards and servers.

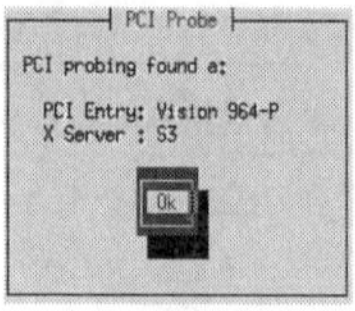

Figure 3.1.
Pay special attention to the information in this screen.

JUST A MINUTE

> If you manually installed the X server earlier and it doesn't match what the `Xconfigurator` finds, the configuration program aborts. Install the proper X server and then begin the configuration process again.

If you can't find your card on the list of servers, you should try to use the SuperProbe program. Running that probes the card directly and outputs what video chipset, amount of memory, and RAMDAC chipset it found.

CAUTION

> The `SuperProbe` command can lock up the machine and with a very few cards cause other problems. Read the man page on SuperProbe (`man SuperProbe`), and if you aren't comfortable with the possible risk, don't run it.

If you still haven't found a chipset that matches your system, you need to use the VGA16 or Mono server, as these are the lowest common denominators available. When choosing a video card, you also should be aware that video card manufacturers like to use name recognition but also use the best technology available for their card. Sometimes this results in two cards with similar names having very different chipsets—and it's the chipset Linux cares about. So, you may set up the servers thinking you have one chipset, and when finally starting the server get errors telling you that the card is not being detected.

Selecting Your Monitor

This section shows you how to configure the X server to choose your monitor type. You need to have the monitor specifications for your computer.

CAUTION

> Be very careful to select the settings that conservatively match your monitor. Choosing bad values can seriously damage your monitor.

After selecting a video card, you are asked to set up the monitor of the computer. You should then be presented with a screen, shown in Figure 3.2, that asks about the monitor on your system. Scroll down the list and choose a monitor name if it exactly matches your monitor's brand and model. If you know that your monitor is *very* similar to one in the list, you might be able to choose that one also. If you don't find your monitor listed, you need to select a generic monitor or the custom setting.

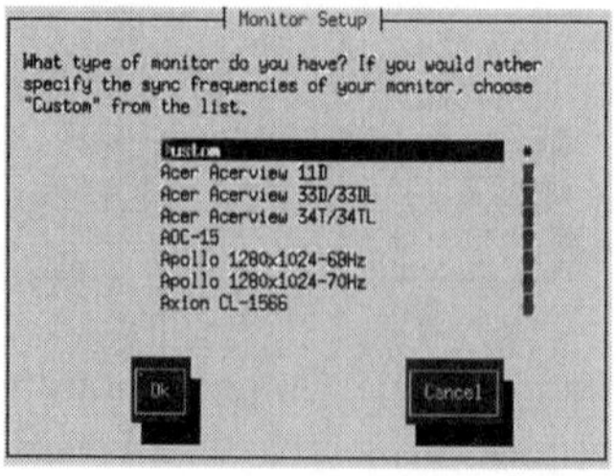

Figure 3.2.
The monitor selection screen.

Configuring a Custom Monitor

If you choose to use a custom monitor, you are presented with a screen explaining that you will be asked for the vertical and horizontal sync rates of your monitor. Your monitor's manual should give these listings, usually in the Specifications section. Select `Ok` to continue.

You are then asked for the horizontal sync range of the monitor. In choosing a rate, you should be very conservative about the type of settings if you don't see what your monitor is capable of. Most monitors should be able to display what is called Standard VGA. Next, you need to select the vertical range your monitor is capable of, and you again need to be conservative.

Final Server Configuration

The next screen depends on whether a PCI video card was detected or not. If one was detected, you are told that the installation will probe for correct video settings and ranges that are available. If no PCI card was detected, you are given a choice of probing or not. The reason for the choice is that some older ISA video cards do not accept probing and lock up the system if it is attempted.

Choosing to probe the system causes the screen to blink several times as `Xconfigurator` figures out what the card's available color depths are. You then see another screen that informs you what screens `Xconfigurator` recommends as a default setting, and gives you the choice to take those values or select others. In selecting others, you are given a selection of all video sizes and color depths that can be supported by the X server and monitor (see Figure 3.3).

Toggle through the check boxes you want (640×480 choices are always good selections). The 2/4/8/16/24 color depth is a listing of the number of colors that can be displayed at once. 4 bit is a 16-color choice of the original VGA selections. 8 bit allows for 256 colors, 16 bits allows for 65,000+ colors, and finally the 24-bit color allows the display of several million sets of colors. If your card is capable of higher sets of colors, then the more memory the card has, the higher the possible resolution of colors and screen size. When you have selected the screen sizes you want, select OK and the new `/etc/X11/XF86Config` file is written to your computer.

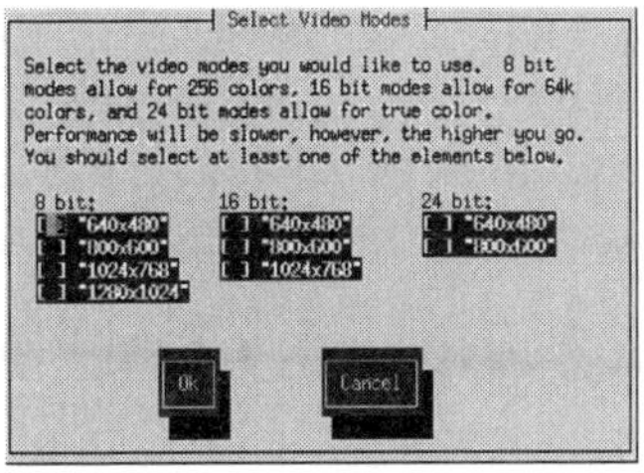

Figure 3.3.
Select the modes you want to use.

If you chose not to probe the monitor system, the next screen asks you how much video memory your card has. From either the documentation on the card or from the `SuperProbe` command, choose the amount of memory and select `Ok`. You are then asked to select a clock chip for the monitor. If your manual or the `SuperProbe` command didn't indicate a clock chip, you should choose the recommended no chip selection and continue on.

You are then presented with a screen that asks you to select the screen resolutions and color depths for your X environment. Choose a set of screen sizes and color depths that are suitable for you to work with. 640×480 resolution is always a good choice because most monitors can handle this setting. Upon selecting the screen sizes, a new `/etc/X11/XF86Config` file is written for your computer.

Testing the X Settings

Now that you have created X configuration settings that hopefully work for your computer, it's time to test them. To start the X server, run the `startx` command. This command sets up the internal environment, starts the server, and executes any client programs that need to be run.

CAUTION

> If the screen goes into what looks like a bad mode (flickering, garbage colors, and so on), press the following key sequence immediately: CTRL-ALT-BACKSPACE. This should exit you from the X server immediately. You should then check that your monitor is operating normally, and run the `Xconfigurator` command to make sure that the settings are all right. Choose a 640×480 setting to see if that works.

You should get a gray screen of little overlapping Xs (depending on the resolution you're running at, you may or may not be able to make out the Xs) This is the default X Window screen, and should be replaced after a short while by a blue-green screen and then a start bar at the bottom of the screen. If the color changes to a blue-green but no start bar appears, see if the bar is "off" the screen. X supports virtual desktops that are larger than what you can actually see on the screen. Moving the mouse to the bottom of the screen might show movement and a gray start bar at the bottom.

Common Problems and Their Solutions

This section covers most of the common problems you'll experience when starting X Window, and how to solve them.

Screen Remains Black

Wait for 30 seconds or so. On a 486/66 or slower machine X Window can take a while to start. For some video cards, the driver may be having problems using it properly. Type Control-Alt-Backspace and re-run `Xconfigurator`.

Screen Remains Black and Machine Does Not Respond

This is a worst-case scenario. You need to reboot the machine and let the machine check the disk drives for errors. The Linux filesystem keeps track of what parts are allocated and when a machine is shut down in a bad state, it needs to run the `fsck` command to fix these items. Most times the start-up scripts can handle this without user intervention.

Very Large Xs Appear on the Screen

In the case of very large overlapping Xs, the X server has probably gone into 320×200 mode versus 640×480. This problem occurs when the video card is not detected correctly by the server. Exit out of X either with the hot keys Ctrl-Alt-Backspace or cleanly via the Start button at the bottom of the screen. Check the file `startx.out` by using the command `less startx.out` and seeing if any errors that might help set up matters correctly were listed. Sometimes the problem is that you may need to select a different RAMDAC or some other option for that card.

Mouse Does Not Move or Acts Strangely

If the mouse doesn't respond correctly to user input, it can be due to several problems. The first is that the pointer section of the file was misconfigured by `mouseconfig` and `Xconfigurator`. `Xconfigurator` gets the values for the mouse from the settings that are set by the `mouseconfig` program. You should check the settings in the file `/etc/sysconfig/mouse` or via the `mouseconfig` program and then either rerun `Xconfigurator` or edit the `/etc/X11/XF86Config` file. The section of the file should look something like the following:

```
Section "Pointer"
    Protocol     "PS/2"
    Device       "/dev/mouse"
EndSection
```

The protocol says which type of mouse X should try to use and the device says which port it should look at. Further information on the types of mice supported can be found by running the command `man XF86Config`.

Another common reason for the mouse to fail is that the mouse is requiring special initializations or is conflicting with another program (usually `gpm`, which is a text mouse control program). In the case of possible conflicts, you should try stopping the `gpm` program (`/etc/rc.d/init.d/gpm stop`) and then try starting X again. If this solves the problem, you may find that you want to disable `gpm` altogether. To do this, run the `ntsysv` command and toggle `gpm` off.

For mice that need special configuration options the problem can sometimes be avoided by treating the mouse as a modem and using a serial program to turn it on. In these cases, changing mice can often be simpler.

TIME SAVER

> Many Linux commands have documentation in one of several places. Most commands are documented as a manual page that can be found with the `man` command. To quickly find all the items that are related to XFree86, try `man -k XF86`. This gives you a list of the documents to be called. A second place to look for documentation is in the directories `/usr/doc` and `/usr/doc/HOWTO`. The `/usr/doc` area contains documentation for packages that were installed onto your system. The `/usr/doc/HOWTO` contains a reference area of various HOWTOs and helpful tips on setting up items.

Having Your Machine Always Start in X Window

If you always want your machine to start the X Window manager so you don't have to type `startx` when you log in, you only have to edit one file.

Log in as root and edit the `/etc/inittab` file. This file is used by `init` to start various utilities. Changing the line beginning with `id` enables X to always start on boot.

```
# Default runlevel. The runlevels used by RHS are:
#   0 - halt (Do NOT set initdefault to this)
#   1 - Single user mode
#   2 - Multiuser, without NFS (The same as 3, if you do not have networking)
#   3 - Full multiuser mode
#   4 - unused
#   5 - X11
#   6 - reboot (Do NOT set initdefault to this)
#
id:5:initdefault:
```

The default run level of a Linux box is 3. Changing the number to 5, as it is in the preceding example, starts the X Window system, using the `xdm` program to manage logins.

Getting to a Virtual Terminal from X

While in X you can get back to a text virtual terminal by using the Control-Alt keystrokes versus the normal Alt keystrokes. To change from the X window (opened on terminal 7) to another console, press Ctrl-Alt-F2 to get to the second virtual terminal. To get back, press Alt-F7.

Part II

Learning Linux Basics

Hour

PART
II

Hour 4

Reading and Navigation Commands

This hour introduces you to the basic Linux commands you'll use for navigating, searching, and reading files and directories of your file system (the directories of your Linux partition). After working through the material, you should know how to get help on commands, find out where you are in Linux, and how to find files on your hard drive. The hour starts with navigating and searching your directory, and moves on to show you how to read directories and files. But first, you'll learn how to help yourself with the `man` command.

Getting Help with the `man` Command

One of the first things to know about Linux is that help is never far away. Like most implementations of UNIX, your Linux distribution comes with manual pages for nearly each utility, command, or programming system call. You can get information about nearly any command, including `man`, by typing

```
# man man
```

Manual pages started out in UNIX as one-page descriptions, available on-line, usually under the `/usr/man` directory. The file for each manual page is named with a single-digit extension, and placed in a subdirectory under `/usr/man`. For example, the manual page for `man` would be named and found as

```
/usr/man/man1/man.1
```

If you want to understand the format and placement of manual pages, you won't find this information in `man.1`, but in `man.7` under `/usr/man/man7`. If you look at Table 4.1, you'll see the locations and contents of each manual section.

Table 4.1. The Linux manual sections.

Directory	Contents
`/usr/man/man1`	Commands: commands you run from within a shell
`/usr/man/man2`	System calls: documentation for kernel functions
`/usr/man/man3`	Library calls: manual pages for `libc` functions
`/usr/man/man4`	Special files: information about files in the `/dev` directory
`/usr/man/man5`	File formats: details of formats for `/etc/passwd` and other files
`/usr/man/man6`	Games
`/usr/man/man7`	Macro packages: descriptions of the Linux file system, man pages, and others
`/usr/man/man8`	System management: manual pages for root operator utilities
`/usr/man/man9`	Kernel routines: documentation on Linux kernel source routines

Each manual page traditionally has a number of sections, with the documentation for the command broken down into sections. Look at Table 4.2 for the organization of a manual page.

Table 4.2. Organization of a manual page.

Section	Description
NAME	The name of the command and a brief description
SYNOPSIS	How to use the command and command-line options
DESCRIPTION	An explanation of the program and its options
FILES	A list of files used by command, and their location
SEE ALSO	A list of related man pages
DIAGNOSTICS	A description of unusual output
BUGS	Known problems
AUTHOR	The program's main author and other contributors

Online manual pages contain special typesetting codes for the `nroff` text formatting program (see Hour 15, "Preparing Documents"), using special macros (as documented in `man.7`). This format is critically important for other programs, such as `makewhatis`, `whatis`, and `apropos`, which you'll learn about later in this chapter.

You can also find more detailed documentation for Linux commands and other subjects under the `/usr/doc` directory, which contains files called Frequently Asked Questions, or FAQs, and HOWTOs, or How-To documents. Additionally, the Free Software Foundation, which releases the GNU software packages (many of the commands discussed in this book are GNU programs), puts much of its documentation in a special hypertext "info" format.

JUST A MINUTE

> Much of the software for Linux comes from the Free Software Foundation, or FSF, founded by Richard Stallman, author of the `emacs` editor (see Hour 14, "Text Processing"). The FSF distributes its software under the GNU General Public License, or GPL. Part of the success and popularity of Linux and GNU software is because of the terms of the GPL. If you want more information about the GNU software programs for Linux, the FSF, or the GNU GPL, you can try the `info` command, which is a reader for the GNU hypertext documentation, found under the `/usr/info` directory.

The `man` command normally searches for manual pages according to instructions detailed in the `man.config` file under the `/etc` directory. These instructions define the default directories in which to look for manual pages, and they match the directories to the `$MANPATH` environment variable, an abbreviated string of characters defined when you first start Linux and log in. Environment variables are discussed in Hour 6, "Using the Shell." The default places to look for these pages are

```
MANPATH /usr/man
MANPATH /usr/local/man
MANPATH /usr/X11R6/man
MANPATH /usr/lib/perl5/man
```

JUST A MINUTE

> A graphic version of the `man` command, called `xman`, is available for the X Window System. You can use `xman` not only to read manual pages, but to see directories of manual page entries. The `xman` program is handy and many users keep its small menu window active on their desktops.

Navigating and Searching the File System

This section introduces you to the basic navigation commands, and shows you how to move around your Linux file system, find files, and build file information databases, such as those for use with the `whatis` command. You'll also learn about alternative approaches and programs, and how to speed up searches to find files quickly.

Moving to Different Directories with the `cd` Command

The `cd` (change directory) command is the basic navigation tool for moving your current location to different parts of the Linux file system. You can move directly to a directory by typing the command, followed by a pathname or directory. For example, the following command will move you to the `/usr/bin` directory:

```
# cd /usr/bin
```

When you're in that directory, you can move up to the `/usr` directory with the following command:

```
# cd ..
```

You could also move to the root directory, or `/`, while in the `/usr/bin` directory by using the following command:

```
# cd ../..
```

Finally, you can always go back to your home directory (where your files are) by using either of the following commands:

```
# cd
```

or

```
# cd ~
```

Note that if you try to use the `man` command to read the `cd` man page, you won't find one. Why? Because `cd` is built into the shell. See `bash` in Hour 6, for more details.

Knowing Where You Are with the `pwd` Command

The `pwd` (print working directory) command tells you where you are, and prints the working (current) directory. For example, if you execute

```
# cd /usr/bin
```

and then type

```
# pwd
```

you'll see

```
/usr/bin
```

Although there's a man page for the pwd command, chances are that when you use pwd, you're using a pwd built into your shell. How do you tell? If you try calling pwd with the following command, you should see only the current working directory printed:

```
# pwd --help
```

Instead, try calling pwd with

```
# /bin/pwd --help
```

You'll see a short help file for the pwd command, and not the current directory.

Searching Directories for Matching Files with the `find` Command

The find command is a powerful searching utility you can use to find files on your hard drive. You can search your hard drive for files easily with a simple find command line. For example, to search for the spell command under the /usr directory, you would use


```
# find /usr -name spell -print
```

You can also use the find command to find files by date; you can also specify a range of times. For example, to find programs in the /usr/bin directory that you have not used in the last one hundred days, you can try:

```
# find /usr/bin -type f -atime +100 -print
```

To find any files, either new or modified, that are one or fewer days old in the /usr/bin directory, you can use

```
# find /usr/bin -type f -mtime -1 -print
```

The find command will also accept wildcards, which you'll learn about in Hour 5, "Manipulation and Searching Commands." As a simple example, you can use find to show you all the PostScript files (which you'll learn about in "Understanding Graphics Formats" in Hour 16, "Graphics Tools") in your /usr directory with

```
# find /usr -name '*.ps' -print
```

You should also know about one of the find command's handy options, -xdev. The examples so far show searches limited to the /usr directory. But what if you want to search starting at the root or / directory? Without using -xdev, which limits searches to the current filesystem (in this case, Linux), find will merrily continue its search through any mounted CD-ROMs, or your DOS or Windows partition, possibly finding files you're not interested in, slowing down the search, and cluttering up the search printout.

The `find` command has many different options and uses. For more details about `find`, see its manual page. Although `find` will rapidly search your hard drive (and any other filesystems), there are other ways of quickly finding files, especially programs. Read on to find out more!

Finding Files with the `whereis` Command

The `whereis` command can quickly find files, and it also shows you where the file's binary, source, and manual pages reside. For example, the following command shows that the `find` command is in the `/usr/bin` directory, and its man page is in the `/usr/man/man1` directory:

```
# whereis find
find: /usr/bin/find /usr/man/man1/find.1
```

You can also use `whereis` to find only the binary version of the program with

```
# whereis -b find
find: /usr/bin/find
```

If `whereis` cannot find your request, you'll get an empty return string, for example:

```
# whereis foo
foo:
```

Part of the problem could also be that the file is not in any of the directories the `whereis` command searches. The directories `whereis` looks in are hard-coded into the program. Although this may seem like a drawback, limiting searches to known directories such as `/usr/man`, `/usr/bin`, or `/usr/sbin` can speed up the task of finding files.

Although whereis is faster than using find to locate programs or manual pages, there's an even faster search utility you can use, called `locate`, discussed in the next section.

Locating Files with the `locate` Command

One way to speed up searches for files is not to search your file directories! You can do this by using a program like `locate`, which uses a single database of filenames and locations, and which saves time by looking in a single file instead of traversing your hard drive. Finding a file using `locate` is much faster than the `find` command because `locate` will go directly to the database file, find any matching filenames, and print its results.

`Locate` is easy to use. For example, to find all the PostScript files on your system, you can enter

```
# locate *.ps
```

Almost instantly, the files are printed to your screen. You may even find the `locate` command line a little easier to use than the `find` command. However, there is a catch: `find` will work "right out of the box," whereas with `locate`, you need to first build a database of all the files on your system. But don't worry, because the procedure is almost automatic.

After you install Linux, `locate` can't show any search results because it can't locate its database. To create this database, you'll need to use the `updatedb` command. Make sure you're logged in as the root operator (or use the `su` command; see Hour 20, "Basic System Administration"). At the prompt, enter

```
# updatedb
```

It may take a minute or so for the `updatedb` command to finish its work, but when it's done, `locate`'s database, `locatedb` (about 300,000 characters in size for 400MB worth of files), will reside in the `/var/lib` directory. The only downside to using the `locate` command is that after time, its database could become out of date as you add or delete files to your system. However, you can have its database updated automatically; see the command reference section at the end of this hour.

Getting Command Summaries with `whatis` and `apropos`

As you first explore your Linux system, you may come across programs whose function is not clear. Many Linux programs are designed to give at least a little help with a `?` or `-help` option on the command line, but you generally shouldn't run a program without knowing what it does.

The `whatis` command may be able to help you quickly find out what a program is with a summary line derived from the program's manual page. For example, to find out what is `whereis` (not `whereis whatis`!), you can enter

```
# whatis whereis
whereis (1)- locate the binary, source, and manual page files for a command
```

However, as with the `locate` command, you must first build a database of the command summaries with the `makewhatis` command, found under the `/usr/sbin` directory. To do this, make sure you're logged in as `root`, and enter

```
# makewhatis
```

The `makewhatis` command, like the `updatedb` command, will take a few minutes to build the `whatis` database, which, unlike `locate`'s, is called `whatis` and is found under the `/usr/man/man1` directory. The `makewhatis` command has several options, but it does not have a manual page. To see a quick summary, use

```
# makewhatis -?
```

Also, as with `locate`'s database, you'll need to periodically update the `whatis` database to keep track of any newly installed programs.

So far, you've seen how `whereis` and `whatis` can help you find programs or figure out what they do. But what if you want to do something and can't remember which program does what? In this case, you can turn to the `apropos` command.

For example, if you can't remember which command searches for files, you can enter

```
# apropos search
apropos (1)           - search the whatis database for strings
badblocks (8)         - search a device for bad blocks
bsearch (3)           - binary search of a sorted array.
conflict (8)          - search for alias/password conflicts
find (1)              - search for files in a directory hierarchy
hcreate, hdestroy, hsearch (3) - hash table management
lfind, lsearch (3)    - linear search of an array.
lkbib (1)             - search bibliographic databases
lookbib (1)           - search bibliographic databases
lsearch (n)           - See if a list contains a particular element
manpath (1)           - determine user's search path for man pages
strpbrk (3)           - search a string for any of a set of characters
strspn, strcspn (3)   - search a string for a set of characters
tsearch, tfind, tdelete, twalk (3) - manage a binary tree
whatis (1)            - search the whatis database for complete words.
zgrep (1)             - search possibly compressed files for a regular expression
zipgrep (1)           - search possibly zip files for a regular expression
```

You'll see a list of programs from the `whatis` database on your screen. The `apropos` command uses this database to search for the keyword you entered. If you keep your manual pages and `whatis` database up-to-date, you'll be able to use `apropos` to help you find the program you need.

Just a Minute

You can also use the `man` command's `-K` option to do the same thing as `apropos`, but the search will be slow, and you'll be presented each manual page in the search result. For example, to search for any programs dealing with PostScript, you can try

```
# man -K PostScript
```

This can result in the following output (before you quit with **q**):

```
/usr/dt/man/man5/DtStdAppFontNames.5? [ynq] n
/usr/dt/man/man4/dtdtsfile.4? [ynq] n
/usr/man/man7/unicode.7? [ynq] n
/usr/man/man7/suffixes.7? [ynq] n
/usr/man/man7/groff_char.7? [ynq] n
/usr/man/man1/convert.1x? [ynq] n
/usr/man/man1/xv.1? [ynq] n
/usr/man/man1/xdvi.1? [ynq] n
/usr/man/man1/dvips.1? [ynq] n
/usr/man/man1/afm2tfm.1? [ynq] n
/usr/man/man1/ps2pk.1? [ynq] n
/usr/man/man1/ps2frag.1? [ynq] q
```

4

Reading Directories and Files

Now that you know about directory navigation, searching for files, or how to find more information about programs, I'll introduce you to other basic Linux commands you can use. This section shows you how to list the contents of directories, make a catalog of your hard drive, and read the contents of files. You'll learn the basic forms of these commands to help get you started.

Listing Directories with the `ls` Command

The `ls` (list directory) command will quickly become one of your most often used programs. In its simplest form, `ls` lists nearly all of the files in the current directory. But this command, which has such a short name, probably has more command-line options (more than 75 at last count) than any other program!

In the simple form, `ls` lists your files:

```
# ls
News          axhome        nsmail        search
author.msg    documents     reading       vultures.msg
auto          mail          research
```

You can also list the files as a single line, with comma separations, with the `-m` option:

```
# ls -m
News, author.msg, auto, axhome, documents, mail, nsmail, reading,
➥ research, search, vultures.msg
```

If you don't like this type of listing, you can have your files sorted horizontally, instead of vertically (the default), with the `-x` option:

```
# ls -x
News          axhome        nsmail        search
author.msg    documents     reading       vultures.msg
auto          mail          research
```

But are all these just files, or are there several directories? One way to find out is to use the `-F` option:

```
# ls -F
News/         axhome/       nsmail/       search*
author.msg    documents/    reading/      vultures.msg
auto/         mail/         research/
```

As you can see, the `-F` option causes the `ls` command to show the directories, each with a `/` character appended to the filename. The asterisk (`*`) shows that the file search is an executable program. But are these all the files in this directory? If you want to see everything, you can use the `-a` option with `-F`, as follows:

```
# ls -aF
./                 .dt/               .neditdb           auto/
../                .dtprofile*        .netscape/         axhome/
```

```
.Xauthority         .festival_history  .newsrc           documents/
.Xdefaults          .forward           .oldnewsrc        mail/
.addressbook        .fvwm2rc95*        .pinerc           nsmail/
.addressbook.lu     .index/            .procmail/        reading/
.bash_history       .mailcap           .procmailrc       research/
.bash_logout        .mailrc            .tin/             search*
.bash_profile       .mime.types        .xinitrc*         vultures.msg
.bashrc             .ncftp/            News/
.desksetdefaults    .nedit             author.msg
```

Using the `-F` option is one way to see the files and directories in your listings, but if you have a color monitor, or use X11 in color, you can tell `ls` to show files, directories, or executable files in different colors. To do this, use the `--color` option. In X11, using the `rxvt` terminal, directories will be blue, programs will be green, and regular files will be black. You can also customize which colors are used for different types of files.

Look in the `/etc/` directory for the file named `DIR_COLORS`. Copy this file, renaming it to `.dir_colors`, and save it in your home directory. You can then edit this file to customize or add file types recognized for colorizing. See the `DIR_COLORS` file for details.

Long Directory Listing

Would you like even more information about your files? You can view the long format listing by using the `ls -l` option, for example:

```
# ls -l
drwxr-xr-x   2 bball    bball         1024 Nov 12 08:20 News
-rw-rw-r--   1 bball    bball         4766 Nov 12 07:41 author.msg
drwxrwxr-x   2 bball    bball         1024 Nov  5 10:04 auto
drwxrwxr-x   3 bball    bball         1024 Nov 12 13:54 axhome
drwxrwxr-x   2 bball    bball         1024 Nov 12 14:33 documents
drwx------   2 bball    bball         1024 Nov 12 14:02 mail
drwx------   2 bball    bball         1024 Sep 15 01:57 nsmail
drwxrwxr-x   2 bball    bball         1024 Oct 29 20:28 reading
drwxrwxr-x   5 bball    bball         1024 Nov  5 10:03 research
-rwxrwxr-x   1 bball    bball          200 Oct 24 13:24 search
-rw-rw-r--   1 bball    bball          801 Nov 11 22:46 vultures.msg
```

As you can see, there are eight different columns. The first column is the file's permissions flags, which are covered in Hour 21, "Handling Files." These flags generally show the file's type, and who can read, write (or modify or delete), or run the file. The next column shows the number of links, which are discussed in Hour 5, "Manipulation and Searching Commands." Next is the owner name, followed by group name. Owners and groups are discussed in Hour 21. The file size is listed next, followed by a timestamp of the file or directory was created or last modified. The last column, obviously, is each file's name.

Specifying Other Directories

You can also use the `ls` command to view the contents of other directories by specifying the directory, or pathname, on the command line. For example, if you want to see all the files in the `/usr/bin` directory, use

```
# ls /usr/bin
arch          dd             gzip       netstat        stty
ash           df             hostname   nisdomainname  su
awk           dmesg          kill       ping           sync
basename      dnsdomainname  ksh        ps             tar
bash          doexec         ln         pwd            tcsh
bsh           domainname     login      red            touch
cat           echo           ls         rm             true
chgrp         ed             mail       rmdir          umount
chmod         egrep          mkdir      rpm            uname
chown         false          mknod      sed            ypdomainname
cp            fgrep          more       setserial      zcat
cpio          gawk           mount      sh
csh           grep           mt         sleep
date          gunzip         mv         sort
```

The `ls` command also supports using wildcards, or regular expressions, which means you can use options similar to (and much more complex than) the examples you've seen with the `find` and `locate` commands. For example, if you only want to search for text files in the current directory, you can use

```
# ls *.txt
```

Finally, if you want to see all of the files on your system, you can use the `ls -R` option, which recursively descends directories to show you the contents. Although you can use this approach to search for files and build a catalog of the files on your system, you should be warned that it might take several minutes to list your files. The listing may also include files you don't want listed, or files on other operating system filesystems, such as DOS or Windows, especially if you use

```
# ls -R /
```

A better approach might be to use the `-d` option with `-R` to list only a certain number of directory levels. For example, the following command will search three directory levels along the root or `/` directory:

```
# ls -Rd /*/*/*
```

However, there's a much better utility for getting a picture of the directory structure of your system, the `tree` command, which is discussed later in this hour.

JUST A MINUTE

> Do you like how `ls -aF` shows your directories? Or would you prefer `ls` to use colors all the time? If you want the `ls` command to always show this sort of detail, see Hour 6.

Listing Directories with the `dir` and `vdir` Commands

If you just can't get the hang of using `ls` to list your directories, you can use the `dir` or `vdir` commands. These commands have only about 45 command-line options, compared to `ls`'s over 75, but they're just as capable. They work like `ls`, but with certain defaults.

The `dir` command works like the default `ls` command, listing the files in sorted columns, for example:

```
# dir
News          axhome        nsmail        search
author.msg    documents     reading       vultures.msg
auto          mail          research
```

The `vdir` command works like the `ls -l` option, and presents a long format listing by default, for example:

```
# vdir
total 15
drwxr-xr-x   2 bball    bball         1024 Nov 12 08:20 News
-rw-rw-r--   1 bball    bball         4766 Nov 12 07:41 author.msg
drwxrwxr-x   2 bball    bball         1024 Nov  5 10:04 auto
drwxrwxr-x   3 bball    bball         1024 Nov 12 13:54 axhome
drwxrwxr-x   2 bball    bball         1024 Nov 12 15:13 documents
drwx------   2 bball    bball         1024 Nov 12 14:02 mail
drwx------   2 bball    bball         1024 Sep 15 01:57 nsmail
drwxrwxr-x   2 bball    bball         1024 Oct 29 20:28 reading
drwxrwxr-x   5 bball    bball         1024 Nov  5 10:03 research
-rwxrwxr-x   1 bball    bball          200 Oct 24 13:24 search
-rw-rw-r--   1 bball    bball          801 Nov 11 22:46 vultures.msg
```

Although you won't find separate manual pages for `dir` or `vdir` (they're mentioned in the `ls` man page), you can get help with each command by using the `--help` option.

Graphic Directory Listings with the `tree` Command

You now know how to list the contents of your directories, but you may also be interested in the directory structure of your system, or the directory structure of a particular tree of your system (such as `/usr/X11R6`). For example, `ls -R` will recursively print out your directories, but how are these directories related to each other? If you would like a more direct, graphical view of your directories, a directory listing utility can help.

Steve Baker's `tree` utility will print a graphic view of any desired structure, and it has several handy features. First, `tree`'s syntax, or command-line, options are similar to several of those for the `ls` command. Wildcards or expressions are supported. The `tree` command also supports color in its listings, like `ls`. Finally, `tree` has a `-x` option similar to the `find` command's `-xdev` option, so you don't have to get a directory picture of operating systems if you choose to start your listing with the root or `/` directory.

The `tree` command is easy to use. For example, if you would like to see the contents of the `/var/lib` directory, along with all files, try the following:

```
# tree /var/lib
/var/lib
|-- alien
|   |-- applix-english_4.3-2.diff.gz
|   |-- applix_4.2-2.diff.gz
|   `-- applix_4.3-2.diff.gz
|-- games
|-- locatedb
|-- logrotate.status
|-- rpm
|   |-- conflictsindex.rpm
|   |-- fileindex.rpm
|   |-- groupindex.rpm
|   |-- nameindex.rpm
|   |-- packages.rpm
|   |-- providesindex.rpm
|   `-- requiredby.rpm
`-- texmf
    |-- fonts
    |   `-- pk
    |       `-- ljfour
    |           `-- public
    |               `-- cm
    |                   |-- cmbx10.600pk
    |                   |-- cmbx10.720pk
    |                   |-- cmbx10.840pk
    |                   |-- cmmi10.600pk
    |                   |-- cmmi10.720pk
    |                   |-- cmr10.420pk
    |                   |-- cmr10.480pk
    |                   |-- cmr10.600pk
    |                   |-- cmsy10.480pk
    |                   |-- cmsy10.600pk
    |                   |-- cmti10.600pk
    |                   `-- cmtt10.600pk
    `-- texfonts

10 directories, 24 files
```

The `tree` command also has a handy `-d` option to list only directories, and not files (unlike `ls`). This is one of the best ways to get an idea of what your Linux file system looks like from a directory standpoint. You can also use it to view the directory structure of installed software. For example, to see what is on your system after installing the Netscape Web browser, try

```
# tree -d /usr/local/netscape
/usr/local/netscape
|-- dynfonts
```

4

```
|-- java
|   `-- classes
|-- movemail-src
|-- nethelp
|   `-- netscape
|       |-- collabra
|       |-- composer
|       |-- confernc
|       |-- home
|       |-- messengr
|       |-- navigatr
|       |-- netcastr
|       |-- nscal
|       `-- shared
|-- plugins
`-- spell

17 directories
```

If you're interested in this utility (or other file utilities), you'll find a compressed archive containing its source, manual page, and ready-to-run binary at

```
http://sunsite.unc.edu/pub/Linux/utils/file
```

Listing and Combining Files with the cat Command

The cat (concatenate file) command is used to send the contents of files to your screen. This command may also be used to send files' contents into other files. Hour 6 covers terms such as standard input, standard output, and redirection, and this section shows you some basic uses for this command.

Although cat may be useful for reading short files, it is usually used to either combine, create, overwrite, or append files. To use cat to look at a short file, you can enter

```
# cat test.txt
This text file was created by the cat command.
Cat could be the world's simplest text editor.
If you read this book, you'll learn how to use cat.
This is the last line of text in this file.
```

The cat command also has a number of options. If you'd like to see your file with line numbers, perhaps to note a specific phrase, you can use the -n option:

```
# cat -n test.txt
     1  This text file was created by the cat command.
     2  Cat could be the world's simplest text editor.
     3  If you read this book, you'll learn how to use cat.
     4  This is the last line of text in this file.
```

You can also use cat to look at several files at once, because cat accepts wildcards, for example:

```
# cat -n test*
     1  This text file was created by the cat command.
     2  Cat could be the world's simplest text editor.
```

```
     3  If you read this book, you'll learn how to use cat.
     4  This is the last line of text in this file.
     5  This is the first line of test2.txt.
     6  This file was also created by cat.
     7  This is the last line of test2.txt.
```

As you can see, cat has also included a second file in its output, and has numbered each line of the output, not each file. Note that you could also see both files with

```
# cat test.txt test2.txt
```

The output will be exactly the same as if you'd used a wildcard. But looking at several files is only one way to use cat. You can also use the cat command with the redirection operator > to combine files. For example, if you would like to combine test.txt and test2.txt into a third file called test3.txt, you can use

```
# cat test* > test3.txt
```

You can check the result with

```
# ls -l test*
-rw-rw-r--   1 bball    bball         190 Nov 12 17:39 test.txt
-rw-rw-r--   1 bball    bball         108 Nov 12 17:45 test2.txt
-rw-rw-r--   1 bball    bball         298 Nov 12 18:00 test3.txt
```


But what if you want to combine test.txt and test2.txt without creating a larger, third file? In this case, you'd first decide whether you want the contents of test.txt to go into test2.txt, or the contents of test2.txt to go into test.txt. Then, using cat with the >> redirection operator, you might type

```
# cat test.txt >> test2.txt
```

This appends the contents of test.txt to the end of the test2.txt. To check the results, use cat again:

```
# cat test2.txt
This is the first line of test2.txt.
This file was also created by cat.
This is the last line of test2.txt.
This text file was created by the cat command.
Cat could be the world's simplest text editor.
If you read this book, you'll learn how to use cat.
This is the last line of text in this file.
```

Note that if you had entered the command

```
# cat -n test.txt >> test2.txt
```

The test2.txt file would look like

```
# cat test2.txt
This is the first line of test2.txt.
This file was also created by cat.
```

```
This is the last line of test2.txt.
     1  This text file was created by the cat command.
     2  Cat could be the world's simplest text editor.
     3  If you read this book, you'll learn how to use cat.
     4  This is the last line of text in this file.
```

Finally, here's a trick you can use if you want to create a short text file without running a word processor or text editor. Because the `cat` command can read the standard input (more about this in Hour 6), you can make the `cat` command create a file and fill it with your keystrokes. Here's how:

```
# cat > myfile.txt
```

Now, enter some text:

```
# cat > myfile.txt
This is the cat word processor.
This is the end of the file.
```

Then, when you're done typing, press Ctrl+D to close the file. To see if this works, try

```
# ls -l myfile.txt
-rw-rw-r--   1 bball    bball          61 Nov 12 18:26 myfile.txt

# cat myfile.txt
This is the cat word processor.
This is the end of the file.
```

You should also know that the `cat` command will print out the contents of any file, and not just text files. Although `cat` may be useful to look at one or several short files, what do you do when you want to read longer text files? Read on, and you'll learn about pager commands, which will make life easier when reading longer files.

Reading Files with the `more` Command

The `more` command is one of a family of Linux commands called *pagers*. Pager commands let you browse through files, reading a screen or line at a time. This can be extremely helpful, especially if you read a lot of manual pages, because the `man` command will use a pager to display each page.

The `more` command is a traditional pager in the sense that it provides the basic features of early pagers. You can use `more` on the command line with

```
# more longfile.txt
```

If you need help, you can tap the H key to see a help screen. You can also run other commands from inside `more` by using the exclamation character (`!`). Reading through a text file is easy because you can advance one screenful (the current screen size) by tapping the spacebar, and you can go backward one screenful by tapping the B key.

The more command also has a number of command-line options. You can customize the screen prompt (more displays the current percentage of the file you're reading), set the screen size (the number of lines shown when going forward or backward through your file), use multiple filenames or wildcards, and turn scrolling on or off, in addition to other options.

Although you may find the more command to be more than adequate in reading files, you might really like the less pager.

Browsing Files with the less Command

You'll find that less is more or less like more, but you'll also discover that less is much more than more. Confused? Don't be, because less, like more, is also a pager command. But its author, Mark Nudelman, has improved on a number of features in the more command, and added many others.

The less command offers a number of advantages over more:

- You can scroll backwards and forwards through text files using your cursor keys.
- You can navigate through files with bookmarks, by line numbers, or by percentage of file.
- Sophisticated searches, pattern options, and highlighting through multiple files.
- Compatible keystrokes with word processing programs, such as emacs.
- The less command won't quit on you when you reach the end of a file, or the end of the standard input.
- The information prompt at the bottom of the screen is more customizable and offers more information.
- Loads of options, including a separate key setup program, lesskey, so you can customize which keys control less.

You'll find that after you install Linux, the less pager is the default pager used by a number of programs, such as the man command. And if you need to read compressed files (those with a .gz extension, and about which you'll learn in Hour 5, "Manipulation and Searching Commands"), you can use the zless command, found under the /usr/bin directory.

Reading the Beginning or End of Files with the head and tail Commands

Although the head and tail commands are not pagers per se, they can make life a lot easier when all you want to do is read the beginning or end of a file. These programs, like most Linux commands, are designed to do one or two things, but they do these tasks well.

The head command has a number of options besides the traditional -n, which prints the first *n* lines of a file. You'll find that the head command in your Linux distribution, which is part of the GNU text utilities, will also print any number of 512-character, 1-kilobyte (1024 bytes), or megabyte-sized blocks from the beginning of a file. Like the cat command, head can also handle binary files.

If you use head in the traditional way, you strip off lines from the beginning of one or several files. For example, if you'd like to do a quick check of the formatting of all the manual pages for programs with names beginning with "xm" under the /usr/man/man1 directory, you can use the following command:

```
# head -5 /usr/man/man1/xm*.1
==> /usr/man/man1/xmpeg.1 <==
.TH XMPEG 1 "6 FEBRUARY 1993" "X Version 11"
.SH NAME
xmpeg - X11 MPEG-Player [Version 1.0]
.SH SYNOPSIS
.B xmpeg

==> /usr/man/man1/xmplay.1 <==
.TH XMPLAY 1 "6 FEBRUARY 1993" "X Version 11"
.SH NAME
xmplay - X11 directory browser for xmpeg [Version 1.0]
.SH SYNOPSIS
.B xmplay
```

Note that the default output from the head command is to include the filename. If you'd prefer just to have the information, use the -q option, for example:

```
# head -5 -q /usr/man/man1/xm*.1
.TH XMPEG 1 "6 FEBRUARY 1993" "X Version 11"
.SH NAME
xmpeg - X11 MPEG-Player [Version 1.0]
.SH SYNOPSIS
.B xmpeg
.TH XMPLAY 1 "6 FEBRUARY 1993" "X Version 11"
.SH NAME
xmplay - X11 directory browser for xmpeg [Version 1.0]
.SH SYNOPSIS
.B xmplay
```

The tail command is especially useful when you're faced with the task of reading through large files where the most useful information is at the end of the file. One example task is if you want to look at the system messages for errors. One message file, located in /var/log, contains details of system operations, but the log is updated at the end of the message file (in other words, text is appended, so the most recent messages are at the end of the file). To look at the last 12 lines in the message file using tail, make sure you're logged in as root, and type

```
# tail -12 /var/log/messages
Nov 12 21:02:02 localhost cardmgr[152]: initializing socket 0
Nov 12 21:02:02 localhost cardmgr[152]: socket 0: ATA/IDE Fixed Disk Card
Nov 12 21:02:02 localhost cardmgr[152]: executing: 'insmod /lib/modules/2.0.30/p
```

4

```
cmcia/fixed_cs.o'
Nov 12 21:02:03 localhost kernel: hdc: SunDisk SDCFB-4, 3MB w/1kB Cache, LBA, CH
S=123/2/32
Nov 12 21:02:03 localhost kernel: ide1 at 0x100-0x107,0x10e on irq 3
Nov 12 21:02:03 localhost kernel:  hdc: hdc1
Nov 12 21:02:03 localhost cardmgr[152]: executing: './fixed start hdc'
Nov 12 21:02:03 localhost cardmgr[152]: initializing socket 1
Nov 12 21:02:03 localhost cardmgr[152]: socket 1: Serial or Modem Card
Nov 12 21:02:03 localhost kernel: tty01 at 0x02f8 (irq = 5) is a 16550A
Nov 12 21:02:03 localhost cardmgr[152]: executing: 'insmod /lib/modules/2.0.30/p
cmcia/serial_cs.o'
Nov 12 21:30:17 localhost PAM_pwdb[556]: (su) session opened for user root by
bball(uid=0)
```

Being able to read large files in this way is convenient, considering that the system messages can grow to more than a million characters.

Part

II

Hour 5

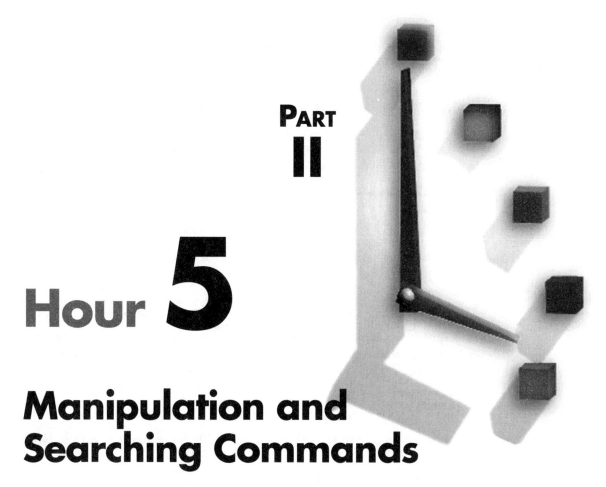

Manipulation and Searching Commands

In this hour, you'll learn about creating, copying, deleting, and moving files and directories. You'll also learn about searching through files and how to compress and uncompress files. This information will build on information you've learned in the last hour, and the commands you learn here will be used later on in this book.

Manipulating Files or Directories

Using Linux isn't different from any other computer operating system. You create, delete, and move files on your hard drive in order to organize your information and manage how your system works or looks. This section shows you how to do these tasks quickly and easily.

Although the graphical interface for Linux, the X Window System, may offer drag and drop or multiple selections in order to copy or delete files, many of the commands you'll learn here form the base of these operations. It is worth knowing how these programs work, even if you don't use Linux in the console mode.

Creating Files with the `touch` Command

The `touch` command is easy to use, and generally, there are two reasons to use it. The first reason is to create a file, and the second is to update a file's modification date. The `touch` command is part of the GNU file utilities package, and has several options.

To create a file with `touch`, use

```
# touch newfile
# ls -l newfile
-rw-rw-r--   1 bball    bball          0 Nov 13 08:50 newfile
```

As you can see, `touch` created a file with a length, or size, of zero. You can also use

```
# > newfile2
# ls -l new*
-rw-rw-r--   1 bball    bball          0 Nov 13 08:50 newfile
-rw-rw-r--   1 bball    bball          0 Nov 13 08:54 newfile2
```

Like `touch`, this creates a file with a length of zero. So why use `touch`, if you can do this at the command line? Because `touch` will update a file's date or time. You can even use `touch` to change a file's date or time to the past or the future, for example:

```
# touch newfile2
# ls -l newfile2
-rw-rw-r--   1 bball    bball          0 Nov 13 09:04 newfile2
```

As you can see, the file `newfile2` now has a timestamp 10 minutes younger. You can also set the time and date of a file to an arbitrary date, for example:

```
# touch -t 1225110099 newfile2
# ls -l —full-time new*
-rw-rw-r--   1 bball    bball          0 Thu Nov 13 08:50:00 1997 newfile
-rw-rw-r--   1 bball    bball          0 Sat Dec 25 11:00:00 1999 newfile2
```

Using the `--full-time` option and long format listing of the `ls` command shows that the file `newfile2` now has a timestamp of 11 a.m., Christmas Day, 1999 (which appears to be, and is indeed, a Saturday).

One use for `touch` is during backup operations. Either before or after backing up a series of files or directories, you can use `touch` to update the timestamps of your files so that the backup program has a reference time for the next backup session. Another use for `touch` is to control deletion or retention of log files during the next automated file cleanup by scheduled programs managed by `cron` (see "Using the `cron` Daemon" in Hour 24, "Scheduling"). If you make a log file old enough, it will be deleted. If you update it, the file will be retained.

Deleting Files with the `rm` Command

The `rm` command deletes files. This command has several simple options, but should be used cautiously. Why? Because when `rm` deletes a file, it is gone (you may be able to recover portions of text files, though; see the `mc` command or the Command Reference section for pointers).

Always running Linux while logged in as the root operator and using the `rm` command has caused many untold tales of woe and grief. Why? Because with one simple command you can wipe out not only your Linux system, but also any mounted filesystems, including DOS partitions, flash RAM cards, or removable hard drives, as follows:

```
# rm -fr /*
```

This command removes all files and directories recursively (with the `-r` option), starting at the root or `/` directory. If you must run Linux as root, make sure to back up your system, and read Hour 23, "Archiving."

The `rm` command will delete one or several files from the command line. You can use any of the following:

```
# rm file
# rm file1 file2 file2
# rm file*
```

One of the safer ways to use `rm` is through the `-i` or interactive option, where you'll be asked if you want to delete the file, for example:

```
# rm -i new*
rm: remove `newfile'? y
rm: remove `newfile2'? y
```

You can also force file deletion by using the `-f` option, as in

```
# rm -f new*
```

However, if `rm` finds a directory, even if it is empty, it will not delete the directory, and complains, even if you use `-f`, as in the following:

```
# rm -f temp*
rm: temp: is a directory
rm: temp2: is a directory
```

When you combine `-f` and `-r`, the recursive option, you can delete directories and all files or directories found within (if you own them; see Hour 21, "Handling Files"), as in the following example:

```
# rm -fr temp*
```

The `-fr` option also makes `rm` act like the `rmdir` command (discussed later in this chapter). Use this option with caution!

Some X Window managers, such as CDE, or utilities, such as TkDesk, offer "trash can" approaches to deleting files, but the files are not really deleted, just moved to a temporary directory. This is a safe, but not fail-safe, approach to deleting or recovering files. You may also be able to use the `mc` command, or Midnight Commander, discussed later in this chapter.

Creating Directories with the `mkdir` Command

The `mkdir` command can create one or several directories with a single command line. You may also be surprised to know that `mkdir` can also create a whole hierarchy of directories, which includes parent and children, with a single command line.

This command is one of the basic tools (along with `cp` and `mv`) you'll use to organize your information. Now, take a look at some examples. The following simple command line creates a single directory:

```
# mkdir temp
```

But you can also create multiple directories with

```
# mkdir temp2 temp3 temp4
```

You'd think that you could also type the following to make a directory named `child` under `temp`:

```
# mkdir temp/child
```

And you can, because the `temp` directory exists (you just created it). But, suppose you type

```
# mkdir temp5/child
mkdir: cannot make directory `temp5/child': No such file or directory
```

As you can see, `mkdir` complained because the `temp5` directory did not exist. To build a hierarchy of directories with `mkdir`, you must use the `-p`, or parent option, for example:

```
# mkdir -p temp5/parent/child
# tree temp5
temp5
`-- parent
    `-- child

2 directories, 0 files
```

As you can see, `mkdir` created not only the `temp5` directory, but also a subdirectory called `parent`, and a subdirectory under parent called `child`.

Now that you know how to create directories, take a look at how to remove them.

Removing Directories with the `rmdir` Command

The `rmdir` command is used to remove directories. To remove a directory, all you have to do is type

```
# rmdir tempdirectory
```

But there's a catch: the directory must be empty first! If you try to delete a directory with any files, you'll get an error message like this:

```
# rmdir temp5
rmdir: temp5: Directory not empty
```

In this example, `temp5` also contains other directories. The `rmdir` command would also complain if a directory contains only files and not directories. You can use the `rm` command to remove the files first (remember to be careful if you use the `-fr` option), or you can move the files somewhere else, or rename the directory, with the `mv` command, discussed next.

The `rmdir` command, like `mkdir`, also has a `-p`, or parent, option. You can use this option to remove directory hierarchies, for example:

```
# rmdir -p temp5
rmdir: temp5: Directory not empty
```

Hmm. That didn't work! How about

```
# rmdir -p temp5/parent
rmdir: temp5/parent: Directory not empty
```

Hey! That didn't work either. Now try

```
# rmdir -p temp5/*
rmdir: temp5/parent: Directory not empty
```

This is getting frustrating! Try it one more time:

```
# rmdir -p temp5/parent/child
```

Finally! As you can see, you must specify the complete directory tree to delete it. If you use the same command line, but without the `-p` option, only the child directory would be deleted. But what if there are two or more subdirectories, for example:

```
# mkdir -p temp5/parent/child
# mkdir temp5/parent/child2
# tree temp5
temp5
`-- parent
    |-- child
    `-- child2

3 directories, 0 files
```

In order to delete the entire directory system of `temp5`, you'd need to use

```
# rmdir temp5/parent/*
```

So far, you've seen how to create and remove directories. Next, you'll learn about the `mv` command, which you can use to move or rename files and directories.

5

Renaming Files with the `mv` Command

The `mv` command, called a rename command but known to many as a move command, will indeed rename files or directories, but it will also move them around your file system.

Actually, in the technical sense, the files or directories are not really moved. If you insist on knowing all the gory details, read the *Linux System Administrator's Guide*, available through

`http://sunsite.unc.edu/LDP/LDP/sag/index.html`

In its simplest form, `mv` can rename files, for example:

```
# touch file1
# mv file1 file2
```

This command renames `file1` to `file2`. However, besides renaming files, `mv` can rename directories, whether empty or not, for example:

```
# mkdir -p temp/temp2/temp3
# mv temp newtemp
```

Although `mv` has nine different options, this section concentrates on the two most commonly used. These options, `-b` and `-i`, allow you to use `mv` in a fairly safe way, because `mv` will not only rename, but overwrite silently and quickly! The first option, `-b`, creates a backup of any file or directory you rename to an existing name, for example:

```
# touch file1 file2 file3
# ls file*
file1  file2  file3
# mv file1 file2
# ls file*
file1 file2
```

As you can see, without using `-b`, `mv` not only renamed `file1` to `file2`, but deleted `file2` in the process. Is this dangerous? You bet! Now, try the `-b` option:

```
# touch file1
# ls file*
file1 file2 file3
# mv -b file1 file2
# ls file*
file2   file2~  file3
```

This example shows that although `file1` has been renamed, replacing `file2`, a backup of `file2` with a default extension of the tilde (~) has been created.

The `mv` command can work silently, or as with `rm`, you can use the `-i` (interactive) option, for example:

```
# mv -i file2 file3
# mv -i file2 file3
mv: replace `file3'? y
```

Here, the mv command asks if you want to overwrite the file (but will keep quiet if no overwriting takes place, even if you use -i). You can also combine the -b and -i options with

```
# mv -bi file2 file3
```

Now that you've seen how to delete, rename, or move your files, how do you copy files?

Copying with the cp Command

The cp, or copy, command is used to copy files or directories. This command has nearly 40 command-line options. They won't all be covered here, but you'll learn about some of the most commonly used options, which will save you time and trouble.

You'll most likely first use cp in its simplest form, for example:

```
# cp file1 file2
```

This creates file2, and unlike mv, leaves file1 in place. But you must be careful when using cp, because you can copy a file onto a second file, effectively replacing it! In this regard, cp can act just like mv. To show you how this can happen, try creating three files, each with a line of text, using the cat command:

```
# cat > file1
this is file1
# cat > file2
this is file 2
# cat > file3
this is the third file
# ls -l file*
-rw-rw-r--   1 bball    bball          14 Nov 13 16:12 file1
-rw-rw-r--   1 bball    bball          15 Nov 13 16:12 file2
-rw-rw-r--   1 bball    bball          23 Nov 13 16:12 file3
```

Now, copy a file onto another file, then check the file sizes and the contents of the new file:

```
# cp file1 file2
# ls -l file*
-rw-rw-r--   1 bball    bball          14 Nov 13 16:12 file1
-rw-rw-r--   1 bball    bball          14 Nov 13 16:14 file2
-rw-rw-r--   1 bball    bball          23 Nov 13 16:12 file3
# cat file2
this is file1
```

It should be obvious that file1 has replaced file2. To avoid this problem (unless you really want to overwrite the file), you can use the -b or -i options, which work just like mv. Here's an example:

```
# cp -i file1 file2
cp: overwrite `file2'? n
# cp -bi file1 file2
cp: overwrite `file2'? y
# ls file*
file1   file2   file2~  file3
```

Note that `file2`, which was overwritten, was backed up. The `cp` command may also be used to copy a number of files at one time. The following example shows how to copy all of the files in directory `tempdir1` to directory `tempdir2`:

```
# cp tempdir1/* tempdir2
# tree tempdir2
tempdir2
|-- temp1file1
|-- temp1file2
`-- temp1file3

0 directories, 3 files
```

Like the `rm` command, `cp` also has a `-r`, or recursive, option. You can use this option to copy one directory into another. For example, to copy the `tempdir1` directory and its files into `tempdir2`, use this syntax:

```
# cp -r tempdir1 tempdir2
# tree tempdir2
tempdir2
|-- temp1file1
|-- temp1file2
|-- temp1file3
`-- tempdir1
    |-- temp1file1
    |-- temp1file2
    `-- temp1file3

1 directory, 6 files
```

Finally, the `cp` command has the `-p` option, which is similar to `mkdir`'s `-p` option. Normally, when you copy a file inside several directories into another directory, only the file is copied. The following example will only copy `temp1file1` into `tempdir3`:

```
# tree tempdir2
tempdir2
|-- temp1file1
|-- temp1file2
|-- temp1file3
`-- tempdir1
    |-- temp1file1
    |-- temp1file2
    `-- temp1file3

1 directory, 6 files
# cp tempdir2/tempdir1/temp1file1 tempdir3
```

However, what if you'd like a file, along with its directory structure, copied? To do this, you can use the `-P` option:

```
# cp -P tempdir2/tempdir1/temp1file1 tempdir3
# tree tempdir3
```

```
tempdir3
`-- tempdir2
    `-- tempdir1
        `-- temp1file1

2 directories, 1 file
```

Not only has `cp` copied a single file, but it has also created the subdirectory structure.

Creating Hard and Symbolic Links with the `ln` Command

Linux supports both hard and symbolic links. Although it is not important that you understand how links work in Linux, you should understand the difference between these two types of links and how to use links while you use Linux. To create hard or symbolic links, you use the `ln`, or link, command.

The `ln` command creates both types of links. If you use the `ln` command to create a hard link, you specify a second file on the command line you can use to reference the original file, for example:

```
# cat > file1
This is file1
# ln file1 file2
# ls -l file*
-rw-rw-r--   2 bball    bball          14 Nov 13 18:54 file1
-rw-rw-r--   2 bball    bball          14 Nov 13 18:54 file2
# cat file2
This is file1
```

You can see that `file2` is exactly the same as `file1`. If you delete `file1`, `file2` will remain. If you make changes to `file1`, such as adding text, these changes will appear in `file2`, and if you make changes to `file2`, `file1` will also be updated. You should also know that although you can see two files, each 14 characters in size, only 14 characters of hard drive space are used (OK, technically more than that, but it depends on the block size of the partition or type of hard drive).

5

On the other hand, although a symbolic link can be useful, it also has a drawback. The next examples show you why. First, to create a symbolic link, use the `ln` command `-s` option:

```
# ln -s file1 file2
# ls -l file*
-rw-rw-r--   1 bball    bball          14 Nov 13 18:54 file1
lrwxrwxrwx   1 bball    bball           5 Nov 13 19:04 file2 -> file1
```

Note the arrow pointing from `file2` to `file2`. This tells you that `file2` is a symbolic link to `file1`. Also note that `file2` is shorter than `file1`. Symbolic links are different from hard links in that a symbolic link is merely a pathname, or alias, to the original file. Nothing happens to the original file if you delete the symbolic link. However, if you delete the original file, your symbolic link won't help you at all:

```
# rm -f file1
# cat file2
cat: file2: No such file or directory
```

Because the original file, `file1`, no longer exists, you can't access its contents through the symbolic link, `file2`. However, symbolic links do have an advantage over hard links. You can use a symbolic link to point to a directory on your file system. In the following example, if you try to create a hard link to the `/usr/local/games` directory, the `ln` command will complain and quit:

```
# ln /usr/local/games play
ln: /usr/local/games: hard link not allowed for directory
```

But you can use a symbolic link with

```
# ln -s /usr/local/games play
# ls -l play
lrwxrwxrwx   1 bball    bball          16 Nov 13 19:28 play -> /usr/local/games
```

Now, instead of typing a long command like

```
# cd /usr/local/games
```

you can use

```
# cd play
```

So far, you've learned about using the command line. If you're familiar with using more graphical interfaces to manipulate files, you'll like the next program, the `mc` command.

Handling Files with the Midnight Commander Program

The `mc` command, called Midnight Commander, is a graphical interface for handling files (see Figure 5.1). It is a visual shell (you'll learn more about shells in the next hour). To start `mc`, type the following at the command line:

```
# mc
```

This section does not cover all of the details of the `mc` command. But here are the highlights of its features:

- Provides visual interface to two directories at a time, and directory browsing with mouse clicks
- Allows menu-driven file operations with dialogs and mouse or keyboard (and function key) support
- Has an open command line to your shell

- Runs commands through mouse clicks
- Extensive, built-in hypertext help screens
- Emulates and supports the `ls`, `cp`, `ln`, `mv`, `mkdir`, `rmdir`, `rm`, `cd`, `pwd`, `find`, `chown`, `chgrp`, and `tree` commands
- Compares directory contents
- Uses customized menus so you can build your own commands
- Can use network links for telnet or FTP operations (see Hour 13, "Internet Downloading and Browsing")
- Offers mouse-click decompression of files (see `gzip`)
- Can undelete files (if your Linux filesystem is configured to support this)

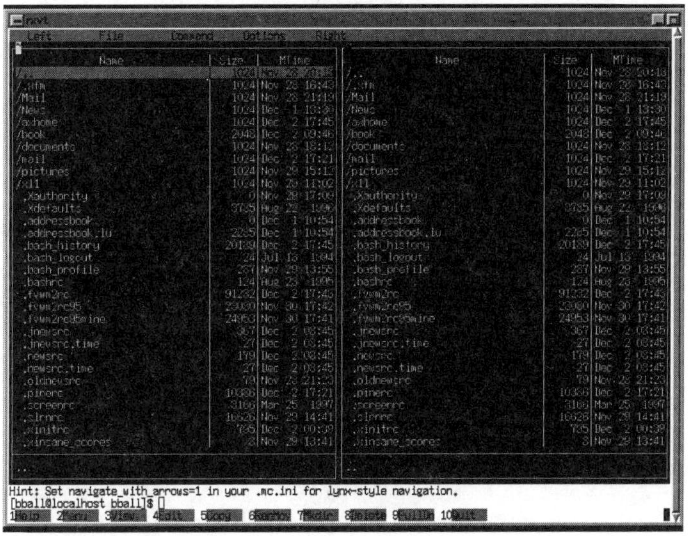

Figure 5.1.
The Midnight Commander visual shell displays a graphical interface to Linux file commands.

Midnight Commander is a handy and convenient tool to use for file handling and directory navigation. You will have to invest some time in learning how to use this program, but if you've used similar file-management interfaces, you'll feel right at home.

Searching Files

This section introduces you to the use of sophisticated wildcards, or regular expressions, along with short examples of file searches using the `grep` family of programs. If you understand and use these expressions, you'll be able to create refined search techniques you'll use again and again. You'll save time and effort during your work, and your learning investment will pay big dividends throughout your Linux experience.

What Are Regular Expressions?

Regular expressions are patterns, using special syntax, that match strings (usually in text in files, unless your search is for filenames). There are also extended regular expressions, but the difference, important for syntax, should not deter you from the valuable lesson of being able to construct patterns that will accurately match your desired search targets. This is important if you're looking for text in files, and critical if you're performing potentially dangerous tasks, such as multiple file deletions across your system.

You can build an infinite number of regular expressions using only a small subset of pattern characters. Here's a short list of some of these characters. You should be familiar with at least one (the asterisk) from the previous examples:

`*`	Matches any character
`?` or `.`	Matches a single character
`[xxx]` or `[x-x]`	Matches a character in a range of characters
`\x`	Matches a character such as `?` or `\`
`^pattern`	Matches pattern to the beginning of a line
`$pattern`	Matches pattern to the end of a line

This is not a comprehensive list of pattern characters. For more details, you can read the `ed` manual page (the `ed` command is discussed in Hour 14, "Text Processing"). For now, try several simple examples using different patterns.

You should know the asterisk, which is useful for finding matches to all characters. For example, if you want to find all the text files in your directory with an extension of `.txt`, you can use

```
# ls *.txt
14days.txt    96hours.txt   datalog.txt   datebook.txt  day67.txt
```

But suppose you wanted a list of all files in your directory with numbers in the filename? You can try to string multiple searches on the `ls` command line, like this:

```
# ls *0* *1* *2* *3* *4* *5* *6* *7* *8* *9*
08100097.db      14days.txt       backup001.file   phonelog.111597
08100097.db      32days.msg       day67.txt        phonelog.111597
08100097.db      32days.msg       day67.txt        phonelog.111597
08100097.db      96hours.txt      message.76
08100097.db      96hours.txt      message.76
14days.txt       backup001.file   phonelog.111597
```

Obviously, this is not the result you want, because the multiple searches have printed duplicate filenames. To find exactly what you want, use a regular expression that tells `ls` to list any file with a number appearing in the filename, for example:

```
# ls *[0123456789]*
0001file.0009    32days.msg       day67.txt
```

```
08100097.db       96hours.txt       message.76
14days.txt        backup001.file    phonelog.111597
```

This shows all files containing numbers in the filename, because you've specified a range of characters, or in this case, numbers in your search pattern. You can also use a regular expression shorthand to build a shorter expression to do the same thing, for example:

```
# ls *[0-9]*
0001file.0009     32days.msg        day67.txt
08100097.db       96hours.txt       message.76
14days.txt        backup001.file    phonelog.111597
```

How you specify your pattern characters in your expression is important. If you only want a list of files ending in a number, you can use

```
# ls *[0-9]
0001file.0009     message.76        phonelog.111597
```

If you only want a list of files beginning with a number, you can use

```
# ls [0-9]*
0001file.0009  08100097.db    14days.txt     32days.msg     96hours.txt
```

Here's a fun exercise: What if you want to list only those files with numbers inside or on both ends of a filename? Try these:

```
# ls *[-a-z][0-9]*
backup001.file  day67.txt

# ls [0-9]*[a-z]*[0-9]
0001file.0009
```

Finally, how do you match patterns when the pattern you're looking for contains a pattern-matching character? Easy! Use the backlash to "escape" the character, for example:

```
#  ls *\?*
cathy?.message
```

5

As you can see, using regular expressions can take some practice, but your efforts will be well rewarded. Try experimenting with different expressions to see if you can come up with results similar to the examples shown in this section.

Searching Inside Files with the `grep` Commands

This section introduces you to the family of `grep` commands. You'll learn about `grep`, `egrep`, and `fgrep`. In order to use these commands, you should know how to use some of the pattern-matching techniques already discussed. You'll use these commands to search through files and extract text. Each of these programs works by searching each line in a file. You can search single files or a range of files.

Each of the `grep` commands is basically the same and has nearly 20 different command-line options. The only real difference is that `egrep` uses a slightly different syntax for its pattern matching, whereas the `frep` command uses fixed strings. You'll see examples of each program, using some of the common options. For specific details about the pattern-matching capabilities of these programs, see the grep manual page.

To show you the difference in each program's search pattern syntax, I'll look for different patterns in Matt Welsh's *Linux Basic Installation Guide* (available at http://sunsite.unc.edu/LDP). For example, if you want to find all lines in the guide that begin with a number, use the following syntax:

```
# grep ^[0-9] guide.txt
1 Introduction to Linux                                                    1
2 Obtaining and Installing Linux                                          40
3 Linux Tutorial                                                          85
4 System Administration                                                  137
...
# egrep ^[0-9] guide.txt
1 Introduction to Linux                                                    1
2 Obtaining and Installing Linux                                          40
3 Linux Tutorial                                                          85
4 System Administration                                                  137
...
# fgrep ^[0-9] guide.txt
```

You can see that grep and egrep returned a search (I've deleted all the output except the first four lines). Notice, however, that fgrep cannot handle regular expressions. You must use fixed patterns, or strings with the fgrep command, for example:

```
# fgrep friend guide.txt
large extent  by the  window manager.    This friendly  program is  in
copy Linux from a friend who  may already have the software,  or share
(Unfortunately, the system was being unfriendly.)
```

Now use egrep to try searching for the pattern of the letter b in parentheses in the file:

```
# egrep "\([b]\)" guide.txt
(see Section 1.8 for a list of compatible boards), or (b)  there is an
connect to the  network, or  (b) you  have a  ``dynamic'' IP  address,
```

You see that there are exactly two lines in the file that match (b). See what happens when you search with grep:

```
# grep "\([b]\)" guide.txt
This is version 2.2.2 of the book, "Linux Installation and Getting
to PostScript printers. This document was generated by a set of tools
from LaTeX source, so there may be a number of formatting problems.
This is not the "official" version of the book! Please see
...
```

Whoa! Not exactly what you wanted, is it? As you can see, grep does not use the same syntax as the egrep command. But you can use a simpler approach:

```
# grep "(b)" guide.txt
(see Section 1.8 for a list of compatible boards), or (b)  there is an
connect to the  network, or  (b) you  have a  ``dynamic'' IP  address,
```

This pattern works with grep and fgrep. If you try this pattern with egrep, you'll get the same results as if you tried extended regular expressions with grep (each line with a b).

Each grep program accepts nearly the same set of command-line options. One popular option is -n, or line numbering. This is handy because you'll see which lines in the file contain matches. This example works for each grep program:

```
# egrep -n "friend" guide.txt
1242:large extent  by the  window manager.    This friendly  program is  in
1942:copy Linux from a friend who  may already have the software,  or share
5161:(Unfortunately, the system was being unfriendly.)
```

You can see that matches were made on lines 1242, 1942, and 5161. Another feature of these programs is that you don't have to retype your patterns each time you want to search. As a simple example, if you need to repeatedly search files for different words, you can put these into a file for grep to use. First, create a text file, then use the -f option to specify the file:

```
# cat > mywords
wonderful
Typewriter
War
# grep -nf mywords guide.txt
574:Typewriter Used to represent screen interaction, as in
617:software since the original Space War,  or, more recently, Emacs.   It
1998:Now you must be convinced  of how wonderful Linux  is, and all of  the
2549:inanimate object is a wonderful  way to relieve the occasional  stress
3790:    Warning:  Linux  cannot currently  use 33090  sectors of  this
7780:to wear the  magic hat when  it is not  needed, despite the  wonderful
10091:wonderful programs and configurations are available with a bit of work
```

Because you also used the line-numbering option, you should note that it had to come before the -f, or file option, or grep would report an error, complain it couldn't find file n, and quit.

You can make grep act like fgrep with the -F option, or like egrep with the -E option. You'll also find a unique version of grep on your system, called zgrep, which you can use to search compressed files, the topic of the next section.

Compressing and Uncompressing Files

This section introduces you to the basics of archiving and compressing files. However, for details concerning using these programs for the purpose of system management or backing up your system, see Hour 23, "Archiving." Read on, and you'll learn how to build your own archives and save disk space.

Creating Archives with the Tape Archive Command

The tar (tape archive) program has its roots in the early days of computing before floppy drives, hard disks, and CD-ROMs. Software was distributed and backed up on large reels of magnetic tape, so one of the first programs to run on computers was a tape reader. Over time, the tar program has proved its merit as a convenient way to transport files, and many programs you'll find for Linux come packaged in tar archives (your Red Hat CD-ROM uses the rpm program to package files; see Hour 22, "Red Hat Tools").

Using tar, you can create an archive file containing multiple directories and multiple files. The version of tar installed on your system also supports a -z option to use the gzip program to compress your archive (gzip is discussed later in this chapter).

The tar command has a bewildering array of options, but it's not hard to use. You can quickly and easily create an archive of any desired directory.

First, you'll create a directory with three files, and then create a subdirectory with another three files:

```
# mkdir mydir
# cd mydir
# touch file1 file2 file3
# mkdir mydir2
# cd mydir2
# touch file21 file22 file23
# cd ../..
# tree mydir
mydir
|-- file1
|-- file2
|-- file3
`-- mydir2
    |-- file21
    |-- file22
    `-- file23

1 directory, 6 files
```

Now that you have built a directory, create a tar archive with this command:

```
# tar -c mydir > mydir.tar
# ls -l
total 11
drwxrwxr-x   3 bball    bball        1024 Nov 14 16:48 mydir
-rw-rw-r--   1 bball    bball       10240 Nov 14 16:58 mydir.tar
```

Notice that your original directory is left untouched. By default, tar will not delete the original directories or files. You can use the --remove-files if you'd like to do this, but it's not recommended. If you'd like to see what's going on, you can use the -v option, like this:

```
# tar -cv mydir > mydir.tar
mydir/
mydir/file1
mydir/file2
mydir/file3
mydir/mydir2/
```

```
mydir/mydir2/file21
mydir/mydir2/file22
mydir/mydir2/file23
```

The `tar` command will show you what directories and files are being added. Does this mean you have to add all of the files in your directories? No! You can use the `-w`, or interactive option, and have `tar` ask you if you want each file added. This can be handy for selectively backing up small directories, for example:

```
# tar -cw mydir > mydir.tar
add mydir?y
add mydir/file1?n
add mydir/file2?y
add mydir/file3?n
add mydir/mydir2?y
add mydir/mydir2/file21?y
add mydir/mydir2/file22?n
add mydir/mydir2/file23?y
```

Here I've left out `file1`, `file3`, and `file22` from this archive. But how can you make sure? One way is to use two `tar` options, `-t` to list an archive's contents, and `-f`, to specify a `tar` archive to use, for example:

```
# tar tf mydir.tar
mydir/
mydir/file2
mydir/mydir2/
mydir/mydir2/file21
mydir/mydir2/file23
```

Note that the order of the options is important (like the `grep` example), or `tar` will complain and quit. Now that you know how to create and see the contents of an archive, you can learn how to extract the whole archive or a single file. To extract everything, you can use the `-x`, or extract option with `-f`. Just so you know what's going on, include the `-v` option, too:

```
# tar -xvf mydir.tar
mydir/
mydir/file2
mydir/mydir2/
mydir/mydir2/file21
mydir/mydir2/file23
```

If you want only a few files from your archive, you can again use the `-w` option:

```
# tar -xvwf mydir.tar
extract mydir/?y
mydir/
extract mydir/file2?y
mydir/file2
extract mydir/mydir2/?y
mydir/mydir2/
extract mydir/mydir2/file21?y
mydir/mydir2/file21
```

```
extract mydir/mydir2/file23?y
mydir/mydir2/file23
```

Here, I've gone through the archive, interactively extracting files. If you want just a single file from an archive, you can specify the file on the command line. For this example, the original `mydir` has been removed, and I'm using an empty directory:

```
# tar -xf mydir.tar mydir/mydir2/file23
# tree mydir
mydir
`-- mydir2
    `-- file23

1 directory, 1 file
```

As you can see, only one file was extracted. Be careful, though! The `tar` command won't overwrite whole directories, but it will overwrite files with the same name.

Try experimenting with `tar` before you start building archives. Some other features to try are selectively deleting files from an archive, or adding a file to an existing archive, which is something the next program, `cpio`, can do, too.

Creating `cpio` Archives

The `cpio` command copies files in and out of `tar` or `cpio` archives. Because it is compatible with `tar`, this section won't go into all the details of how it works, but it has some features that `tar` does not, such as

- Support for both `cpio` and `tar` archives
- Support for a number of older tape formats
- The ability to read filenames from a pipe (which you'll learn about in the next hour)

Very few, if any, software packages for Linux are distributed in `cpio` format. Chances are you won't run across any `cpio` archives in your search for new software across the Internet. But if you're interested in the details about `cpio`, see its man page.

Compressing Files with the `gzip` Command

The `gzip` command compresses files. This program is not only handy for saving disk space by compressing large, less often used files, but could be, in combination with `tar`, the most popular compressed file format for Linux. You'll often find files with the `.tgz` or `.tar.gz` format while searching for new Linux software across the Internet.

You'll also find that much of the documentation under your `/usr/doc` directory has been compressed with `gzip`. This can save a lot of space. According the Free Software Foundation folks in `gzip`'s manual page, `gzip` has a 60 to 70 percent compression rate for text files.

The gzip command is easy to use. To compress a file (or tape archive), enter

```
# gzip mydir.tar
```

By default, gzip will compress your file, append a .gz extension, and delete your original file. To uncompress your file, you can use gzip's companion program gunzip, or gzip's -d (decompress) option. You'll have to make sure the file has a .gz (or .Z, -gz, .z, -z, or _z) extension, or both gzip and gunzip will complain. If you want to specify your own extension, use the -S (suffix) option.

The gzip command also handles zip, compress, or pack compressed files. If you want more information during compression or decompression, you can use -l, or list option, to see the compressed or decompressed sizes of files.

Finally, gzip also has a helpful option, -t, to test the integrity of a compressed file. If the file is okay, gzip reports nothing. If you need to see OK, use -tv when you test a file.

Compressing Files with the compress Command

The compress command does just that—it compresses files. This is one of the earlier compression utilities for the UNIX world.

Files created with compress traditionally have a .Z extension. To compress a file, enter

```
# compress file
```

To uncompress a file, use

```
# uncompress file.Z
```

Like gzip, you must specify a filename with a .Z extension, or compress will complain.

JUST A MINUTE

> Interested in other compression utilities for Linux? Look on your system for zip, unzip, zipcloak, zipnote, zipsplit, zless, zcat, znew, zmore, zcmp, pack, compact, shar, unshar, or zforce. You might not find all of these installed.

PART

II

Hour 6

Using the Shell

In this hour you'll be introduced to the shell. Although the trend in personal computing in the last 10 years has been to move away from the command line to a point-and-click interface, the shell is still very much alive in Linux, and is used by many Linux programs.

This hour doesn't go into a detailed history of Linux or UNIX shells, or take sides in a debate over which computing interface is easier or better to use. Nor does this hour delve into shell programming—there's also not enough room in this hour (or even this book) to do so. This hour does, however, discuss the different shells you'll find on your CD-ROM, show you how to use the shell to make your Linux experience more enjoyable, and highlight some of the basics of using the shell and its command line.

What Is a Shell?

If you're not using the X Window System, the shell is one of the most important programs you'll use. The shell provides the interface to Linux so you can run programs. In fact, the shell is just another Linux program. While you can set up and run Linux without a shell (see Hour 20, "Basic System Administration," for details), you may find that you'll do a lot of typing at the shell's command line.

The shell is a command-line interpreter, and may be used to start, suspend, stop, or even write programs. The shell is an integral part of Linux, and is part of the design of Linux and UNIX. If you imagine the Linux kernel as the center of a sphere, the shell is the outer layer surrounding the kernel. When you pass commands from the shell, or other programs, to Linux, the kernel (usually) responds appropriately.

There are many types of shells, but at least five (not counting the visual shell Midnight Commander) are on your CD-ROM. You can determine which shell you'll use when you log in to Linux by either looking at the contents of the `/etc/passwd` file, or by searching the file for your username. Look at the following example:

```
# fgrep bball /etc/passwd
bball:OmB5tToB8fYLQ:500:500:William H. Ball,,,,:/home/bball:/bin/bash
```

Your shell will be listed at the end of your `passwd` file entry (`/bin/bash` in the fgrep search example).

What Shells Are Available?

This section lists the shells available for your system, along with some unique features of each to get you started. Each of these shells runs programs, and you may want to explore each to see how they work. This section highlights some of their differences and points out important files.

All of these shells support changing directories with a built-in cd, or the `change directory` command. Interestingly, the ash and tcsh shells do not have a built-in `pwd`, or print working directory commands, and must instead rely on the `pwd` command found under the `/bin` directory.

These shells have many, many features. You'll want to read the manual pages for each in detail. Some of the features to look for and explore include the following:

- What are the shell's built-in commands?
- How is job control (or background processes, discussed in a later section, "Running Programs in the Background") handled?
- Does the shell support command-line editing?
- Does the shell support command-line history?
- What are the important startup or configuration files?
- What environmental variables are important for each shell?
- What command-line prompts may I use?
- What programming constructs are supported?

JUST A MINUTE

> There are several other shells that also are included with Linux: tclsh, a simple shell and Tcl interpreter; wish, a windowing shell for X11; and rsh, a remote shell for running commands over a network. For details, see the tclsh, wish, and rsh manual pages.

Features of ash

The ash shell, by Kenneth Almquist, is one of the smallest shells available for Linux. This shell has 24 different built-in commands, and 10 different command-line options. The ash shell supports most of the common shell commands, such as `cd`, along with most of the normal command-line operators (discussed in the later section, "Understanding the Shell Command Line").

Features of the Default Linux Shell—bash

The bash, or Bourne Again SHell, by Brian Fox and Chet Ramey, is the default Red Hat Linux shell. It features 48 built-in commands and a dozen command-line options. The bash shell works just like the sh shell, and you'll find a symbolic link under the /bin directory, called sh, that points to the bash shell.

Not only does bash work like the sh shell, but it also has features of the csh and ksh shells. Because this is the default shell, bash is used for the examples in this hour. Later on you'll be shown how to customize your command-line prompt using the bash shell.

The bash shell has many features. You can scroll through your previous commands with the arrow keys, edit a command line, and if you forget the name of program, you can even ask the shell for help by using command-line completion. You do this by typing part of a command and then pressing the Tab key. For example, if you type l and press the Tab key, you'd see the following:

```
# l <TAB>
laser       less        listres     locale      look        lsac
last        lesskey     lkbib       localedef   lookbib     lsattr
lastb       let         lmorph      locate      lpq         lsc
latex       lex         ln          lockfile    lpr         lsl
lbxproxy    lha         lndir       logger      lprm        lynx
ld          lightning   loadkeys    login       lptest      lz
ld86        lisa        loadunimap  logname     ls
ldd         lispmtopgm  local       logout      lsa
```

The bash shell responds by listing all known commands beginning with the letter l. This can be very handy if you can't remember complex command names.

The bash shell also has built-in help, and lists all the built-in commands, as well as help on each command. For example,

```
# help
GNU bash, version 1.14.7(1)
Shell commands that are defined internally.  Type `help' to see this list.
Type `help name' to find out more about the function `name'.
Use `info bash' to find out more about the shell in general.

A star (*) next to a name means that the command is disabled.

 %[DIGITS ¦ WORD] [&]                 . filename
 :                                    [ arg... ]
 alias [ name[=value] ... ]           bg [job_spec]
 bind [-lvd] [-m keymap] [-f filena break [n]
 builtin [shell-builtin [arg ...]]    case WORD in [PATTERN [¦ PATTERN].
 cd [dir]                             command [-pVv] [command [arg ...]]
 continue [n]                         declare [-[frxi]] name[=value] ...
...
 while COMMANDS; do COMMANDS; done    { COMMANDS }
```

To get help with a particular command, type the command name after the help command. For example, to get help with help, type the following:

```
# help help
help: help [pattern ...]
    Display helpful information about builtin commands.  If PATTERN is
    specified, gives detailed help on all commands matching PATTERN,
    otherwise a list of the builtins is printed.
```

For more information about the bash shell, you'll find a manual page, info pages you can browse with the `info` command, and documentation under the `/usr/doc` directory.

The Public Domain Korn Shell—ksh

The pdksh, or public-domain Korn shell, originally by Eric Gisin, features 42 built-in commands, and 20 command-line options. This shell is found under the `/bin` directory, but a symbolic link also exists under the `/usr/bin` directory.

The pdksh shell is named ksh in your Linux system, and like the bash shell, reads the shell initialization script `/etc/profile` if a file called `.profile` does not exist in your home directory. Unfortunately, this shell does not support the same command-line prompts as the bash shell. However, this shell does support job control (discussed later this hour), so you can suspend, background, recall, or kill programs from the command line.

This shell is nearly compatible with commercial versions of the Korn shell included with commercial UNIX distributions. Documentation for this shell is in the ksh manual page, and in the pdksh directory under the `/usr/doc` directory.

Features of the csh-Compatible Shell—tcsh

The tcsh shell, by William Joy (and 47 other contributors), features 53 built-in commands, and 18 command-line options. This shell emulates the csh shell, but has many more features, including a command-line editor with spelling correction.

This shell is not only compatible with the bash shell prompts, it offers more prompt options than bash. Tcsh uses the file `csh.cshrc` under the `/etc/`directory if the `.tcshrc` or `.cshrc` file does not exist in your home directory. Like the bash shell, you can scroll through commands you've entered and edit the command line.

Get a list of the tcsh commands by using the `builtins` command (the tcsh does not have help like the bash shell).

```
# builtins
:          @          alias      alloc      bg         bindkey    break
breaksw    builtins   case       cd         chdir      complete   continue
default    dirs       echo       echotc     else       end        endif
endsw      eval       exec       exit       fg         filetest   foreach
glob       goto       hashstat   history    hup        if         jobs
kill       limit      log        login      logout     ls-F       nice
nohup      notify     onintr     popd       printenv   pushd      rehash
repeat     sched      set        setenv     settc      setty      shift
source     stop       suspend    switch     telltc     time       umask
unalias    uncomplete unhash     unlimit    unset      unsetenv   wait
where      which      while
```

For more information about this shell, read the tcsh manual page, or look in the tcsh directory under the `/usr/doc` directory. You'll find a Frequently Asked Questions file and other text files.

zsh

The zsh shell, originally by Paul Falstad, is one of the largest shells for Linux, and features 84 built-in commands. The zsh shell has more than 50 different command-line options, and also emulates the sh and ksh shell commands.

Like the bash and tcsh shells, the zsh shell enables you to scroll through previous commands and complete, edit, or spell check the command line. It also enables you to use job control to manage running programs. This shell features advanced command-line options for searching or matching file patterns.

Systemwide startup files for this shell are in the `/etc` directory:

```
/etc/zlogin
/etc/zlogout
/etc/zprofile
/etc/zshenv
/etc/zshrc
```

6

These files are parsed if the zsh shell cannot find equivalent files, but with a leading period, such as `.zlogin`, in your home directory. This shell also has more command-line prompt options than other shells, such as bash or tcsh. You'll find that this shell has features similar to all other shells, and can emulate the sh or ksh shells when called as a symbolic link (although your Red Hat Linux system has the sh shell linked to the bash shell).

There's a lot of information for this shell: 10 manual page files, along with a `/usr/doc` directory filled with help files, examples, and other up-to-date and useful information.

Understanding the Shell Command Line

When you use the shell to start a program at the command line, the shell interprets your command and the command echoes its output back to your screen. Using the shell, you can have the program's output sent elsewhere, such as to a file. The shell also can feed the program's input from another program or even another file. For example, you can redirect the standard output of the `ls` command to a file:

```
# touch /tmp/trash/file1 /tmp/trash/file2 /tmp/trash/file3 /tmp/trash/file4
# ls -w 1 /tmp/trash/* >trashfiles.txt
```

The first command line creates four files in the `/tmp/trash` directory. The second command line creates a text file, using the `ls` command's output, containing the names of the files under the `/tmp/trash` directory. The greater-than (>) character is called a standard output redirection operator, and is used to *redirect* the output of a command somewhere else. You also can use the less-than (<) character, or standard input redirection operator, to feed information to other programs. As a trivial example, you can use the file containing filenames created to build an archive using the `cpio` command. You can do this by using the standard input to feed the file names into the `cpio` command.

```
# cpio -o <trashfiles.txt >trash.cpio
1 block
```

This command line causes the `cpio` command to read a list of files from the standard input, the `trashfiles.txt` file, and then creates an archive by sending its output through the standard output to a file called `trash.cpio`.

Generally, most programs you run from the shell command line have the ability to read from the standard input and write to the standard output. Along with the standard input and standard output, there is also a standard error output (which almost always prints to your display). Using the previous example, if the list of files fed into the `cpio` command contains an error, the `cpio` command should complain, and send an error message to your screen:

```
# rm -fr /tmp/trash/file3
# cpio -o < trashfiles.txt >trash.cpio
cpio: /tmp/trash/file3: No such file or directory
1 block
```

One of the existing files has been deleted, but the input file, `trashfiles.txt`, which still contains the list of files has not been changed. When you try to use the list as a valid input to build an archive, the `cpio` command complains and sends an error message to your screen (but still builds the archive).

Each input and output also has an assigned file number in your shell. For the standard input, the number is zero (0). For the standard output, the number is one (1), and for the standard error, the number is two (2). Knowing this, you can run `cpio` silently, and can cause any errors to be sent to a file. Do this by combining the standard output redirection operator and the standard error's file number, as shown in the following example.

```
# cpio -o < trashfiles.txt >trash.cpio 2>cpio.errors
# cat cpio.errors
cpio: /tmp/trash/file3: No such file or directory
1 block
```

As you can see, the `cpio` command sent its errors, which normally would be sent to the standard error output (your display), to a file called `cpio.errors`.

Normally, each time you redirect output to a file, either the named file is created, or if it exists, the named file is overwritten and its previous contents are irrevocably lost.

CAUTION

> You should use file redirection carefully. If you redirect output to an existing file, you lose the original file, which may not be what you want.

If you'd like to retain the original contents of a file, you can append the output of a program to a file by using the concatenate (>>), or append redirection operator:

```
# cpio -o < trashfiles.txt >trash.cpio 2>>cpio.errors
```

This command line saves the previous contents of the `cpio.errors` file, and appends any new errors to the end of the file. This approach keeps a log of errors when you run the `cpio` command. This method is used if you've enabled system logging for Linux. Take a look at the contents of the file called `messages`, found under the `/var/log` directory.

If you recall the simple `cat` command text editor example from Hour 4, "Reading and Navigation Commands," you'll remember that the standard output redirection operator was used with the `cat` command to read input from the terminal to create a text file:

```
# cat >file.txt
this is a line
this is another line
EOF
# cat file.txt
this is a line
this is another line
```

The end-of-file, or EOF character, is used to close the file, and is entered by holding down the Ctrl key and pressing the d key. Add a new feature to this simple editor by using the << redirection operator, which tells the shell that the end of the input immediately follows the << operator:

```
# cat >file.txt <<.
This is a line of text
This is another line of text
.
# cat file.txt
This is a line of text.
This is another line of text.
```

You'll notice that the file is closed after typing a period (.) on a line by itself, which is handier than using a control key combination to close the file. Try this approach to build a simple, self-contained database file by combining the `grep` command (discussed in Hour 5, "Manipulation and Searching Commands") and input redirection. If you have a list of addresses, wrap the list by putting the `grep` commmand at the beginning, and the end of input character string at the end of the file. Call this database db. See the following example.

```
# cat >db <<.
egrep -i $1 <<zzzz
Debby, 275 Collins Ave., Vestal NY 13850
Cathy, 1001 N. Vermont St., Arlington, VA 22003
Scotty, 2064 N. 16th St., Arlington, VA 22001
Bill, 4000 N. Pennsylvania Ave., Washington, DC 10000
Fred, Slip 417, N. Woodward Ave., Boca Raton, FL 46002
zzzz
.
```

This text creates your short address database. The command line uses the `cat` command to redirect typing into the file called `db` until you type the end-of-input string, a period, on a line by itself. The database works by using the `egrep` command to read the file until the end-of-input string zzzz. The -i command line option tells the `egrep` command to ignore upper- and lowercase characters. The `$1` string is a shell variable (discussed in the next section, representing the command-line argument to be fed to the `egrep` command.

Input and output redirection with the shell may be used in many different ways. This discussion continues as you're introduced to shell variables and shown some handy tricks for customizing your shell.

Customizing Your Shell

When you use a shell, you're running the shell in an environment that contains environment variables. Environment variables are pre-defined in various resource text files, found under your home directory, and the `/etc` directory. For the bash shell, the default environment variables are defined in the `/etc/profile` file.

There are many different environment variables. Use the `printenv` command to see a list of the variables currently in use:

```
# printenv
...
PATH=/usr/local/bin:/bin:/usr/bin:.:/usr/X11R6/bin:/home/bball/bin
HOME=/home/bball
SHELL=/bin/bash
...
```

This hour doesn't list all of the environment variables, but you should know that one of the most important is the `$PATH` variable. This variable tells the shell where to find executable programs. Without this variable, you'd have to type the complete path, or directory hierarchy of a command, to run a program. For example, if you want to run the `ifconfig` command to check the status of your network connections, you might at first try to type its name on the command line:

```
# ifconfig
bash: ifconfig: command not found
# whereis ifconfig
ifconfig: /sbin/ifconfig
```

As you can see, this doesn't mean that the `ifconfig` command doesn't exist, or isn't installed on your system, it's just that your shell doesn't know where to find the program. To run the `ifconfig` command, you can type the full pathname before the command, but if you need to use this program repeatedly, include its directory in the list of known paths in your shell's `$PATH` environment variable.

Do this at the command line by adding the `/sbin` directory to your `$PATH` variable, using the bash shell's `export` command:

```
# ifconfig
bash: ifconfig: command not found
# PATH=$PATH:/sbin ; export PATH
# ifconfig
lo        Link encap:Local Loopback
          inet addr:127.0.0.1  Bcast:127.255.255.255  Mask:255.0.0.0
          UP BROADCAST LOOPBACK RUNNING  MTU:3584  Metric:1
          RX packets:436 errors:0 dropped:0 overruns:0
          TX packets:436 errors:0 dropped:0 overruns:0
```


As you can see, your shell now knows where to find the `ifconfig` command. But this is only temporary, and only lasts as long as you're logged in, or running a particular terminal. Make this change effective for each time you log in by adding the path to the file `.bash_profile` in your home directory, or if you're the root operator and want all users to benefit, to the file profile under the `/etc` directory.

Look for the line

```
PATH=$PATH:$HOME/bin
```

in the `.bash_profile` file, and add the `/sbin` directory.

```
PATH=$PATH:$HOME/bin:/sbin
```

If you're the root operator, look for the line

```
PATH="$PATH:/usr/X11R6/bin:/usr/games:/usr/lib/games"
```

in the profile file under the `/etc` directory. In this file, you'll also see a line like the following:

```
PS1="[\u@\h \W]\\$ "
```

Although this line may seem somewhat cryptic, this is the prompt string definition for the `$PS1` environment variable. You can change this string to define nearly any type of prompt string. The preceding definition is in the following form:

```
[username@host base_working_directory]$
```

The bash shell has 15 different prompts (18 for tcsh, and 35 for ksh) you can combine with character strings to customize your prompt. For example, you can have the current date and time in your prompt. If you use the bash shell export command, you can test different prompts from the command line:

```
# PS1='Date: \d Time: \t-> ';export PS1
Date: Sat Dec 27 Time: 20:09:53->
```

The time is updated each time you enter a command or press the Enter key. If you'd rather have the shell's name, along with the current directory in the command line, try the `\s` and `\w` prompt characters:

```
# PS1='\s:\w> '; export PS1
bash:/usr/bin>
```

You also can use different escape characters and terminal sequences to control the attributes of your prompt strings. You can use underlining, boldfacing, blinking, or other modes for your prompt strings:

```
# PS1='[\033[4m\u\033[0m@\033[4m\h\033[0m]:';export PS1
[bball@localhost]:
```

This example uses the proper escape sequences for the xterm X11 terminal (found with the `printenv` command, and by looking at the `$TERMCAP` variable) to change the prompt by underlining the username and hostname in the prompt. For more examples, and other prompt strings, consult your shell's manual page.

Changing the prompt is only one way to customize how you work in your shell. You also can define command shortcuts, or aliases, to tailor how your favorite commands work. You'll find at least one or two aliases defined for your system in the `bashrc` file under the `/etc/`directory.

System-wide alias definitions are entered by the root operator. You can put your own definition in the `.bashrc` file in your home directory, but if you're the root operator, you'll want to put in at least these three for all your users:

```
alias rm="rm -i"
alias cp="cp -i"
alias mv="mv -i"
```

These aliases provide at least some element of safety when deleting, copying, or moving (renaming) files. Without the `-i`, or interactive option, users may not think at least once before deleting or overwriting files.

You also can define aliases to build new commands, or provide variations of familiar commands to avoid typing long command-line options. For example, the `ls` command has many different options, but you can define several variations to make life easier. Some alias definitions you may want to try include the following:

```
# list the current directory using color filenames
alias lsc="ls --color"
# long format listing
alias lsl="ls -l"
# show all files except . and ..
alias lsa="ls -AF"
# show all file except . and .. in color
alias lsac="ls -AF --color"
```

After you've entered these changes into your `.bashrc` file in your home directory, you can use the aliases by using the bash shell's `source` command:

```
# source .bashrc
```

Now you can type `lsc`, `lsl`, `lsa`, or `lsac` without adding the command-line options. Just make sure that you don't redefine an existing command! If you come up with some really useful aliases, make sure they're defined for each of the shells active on your system.

Just because a shell is available on the system, it does not mean that a user may use a particular shell to log in. As the root operator, you can maintain a list of acceptable shells for your system by editing the file shells under the `/etc/`directory. As a default, the following shells are listed in this file:

6

```
/bin/bash
/bin/sh (a symbolic link to the bash shell)
/bin/ash
/bin/bsh (a symbolic link to the ash shell)
/bin/tcsh
/bin/csh (a symbolic link to the tcsh shell)
/bin/ksh
/bin/zsh
```

If you don't want your users to be able to use a particular shell, simply remove it from the list:

```
# chsh -s /bin/zsh
Changing shell for bball.
Password:
chsh: "/bin/zsh" is not listed in /etc/shells.
chsh: use -l option to see list
```

If you try to change your shell with the `chsh` command to use a particular shell for the next log in, the shell must be listed in the `/etc/shells` file. The `chsh` command complains and quits without making any changes. Note that this doesn't restrict a user from running a shell after logging in. The only way to effectively manage who may run a particular shell is to change a shell's ownership or file permissions (see Hour 21, "Handling Files," for details).

Running Programs in the Background

Most shells also offer a way to start and then run programs as a background process. This is a handy way to get work done, especially if you're working on a separate terminal, have limited screen space when working in X11, or have lots of memory. Although Linux offers virtual consoles when not working with X (accessed through the Alt and Function keys), and many X11 window managers offer separate desktops, you'll probably discover that you will run programs in the background many times while using Linux.

Programs are run in the background from the shell command line by using the &, or ampersand operator. For example, to start another terminal program under X11, you want the program to run in the background so that your current terminal is free for further input:

```
# rxvt &
```

This command starts the rxvt terminal, and your command-line prompt returns. The program is assigned a process number you can see using the `ps`, or process status command. For example,

```
# ps
...
  291   1 R    0:03 rxvt
...
```

In this example, to keep the list short, not all of the running processes have been listed. You can stop the program by using the shell's U command with the program's process number:

```
# kill 291
[1]+  Terminated              rxvt
```

Using the `kill` command is a crude way to control background programs. There is a more refined approach that uses other shell commands. Depending on your current shell, you can put running programs into the background, suspend the program, continue to run the program in the background, kill the program, or bring the program back to the terminal display. This is known as job control.

If you're running the bash shell, put a running program into the background and suspend its operation by holding down the Ctrl key and pressing the z key on your keyboard:

```
# pine
... program is running... (ctrl-z)...

Pine suspended. Give the "fg" command to come back.

[1]+  Stopped (signal)        pine
# fg
.... program returns
```

JUST A MINUTE

> In order to be able to suspend the pine mail program, you must enable suspension using pine's configuration menu. While running pine, press the s key, and then the c key. Then, scroll through pine's options until you highlight "enable-suspend," and press the x key and then the e key, followed by the y key, to save the changes. You'll now be able to suspend the pine mailer.

Sending a running program into the background and suspending its operation may be followed by the `fg` command to bring the running program back to your display, or by the `bg` command to continue to allow the program to run. This can be handy if you want to start a program, such as a newsreader (discussed in Hour 11, "Configuring Internet Email," and Hour 12, "Configuring Internet News"), then suspend and continue to run the program during lengthy operations (such as updating an internal list of newsgroups) while you run other programs in the foreground.

Using the bash shell, you can start, suspend, and run a number of programs, then selectively bring a background program back to your display by the program's job number:

```
# pine
... program is running (ctrl-z)...

Pine suspended. Give the "fg" command to come back.

[1]+  Stopped (signal)        pine
# sc
.... program is running (ctrl-z)...

[2]+  Stopped                 sc
# fg %1
... pine program returns...
```

In this example, the pine mail reader has been started, then suspended in the background to start the sc spreadsheet. Because pine is the first job suspended, the bash shell assigns a job number of 1 to the mail program. The sc spreadsheet was then suspended, assigned job number 2, and returned to the mail program by specifying its job number with the `fg %1` command.

If you run and suspend many jobs in the background, you may not remember a program by its job number, or remember which programs are suspended. You can get a list of the suspended programs by using the bash shell's jobs command:

```
# jobs
[1]   Stopped (signal)        pine
[2]-  Stopped                 sc
[3]+  Stopped                 emacs-nox
# fg %sc
... sc program is running ...
```

This shows that there are three jobs, the pine mailer, the sc spreadsheet, and the emacs editor, currently suspended in the shell. You should also note that instead of restarting the sc spreadsheet job by referring by its job number, the program was brought back to the foreground by using the `fg %` command with the name of the suspended job.

You also can stop programs using this same approach. Instead of using the `ps` command to find a program's process number, then issuing a `kill` command, you can use the kill with the % operator:

```
# kill %1

[1]-  Stopped (signal)        pine
# kill %emacs-nox

[3]+  Stopped                 emacs-nox
```

Here you see how to use the `kill` command to stop a program by its number or name. This is much easier than using the `ps` command, especially if there are a large number of programs or other processes running in the background.

Using your shell's job control facilities is a powerful way to work efficiently with multiple programs. All of the shells included on your CD-ROM include job control in one form or another. In the next section, you'll be shown another powerful way to use your shell to run multiple programs on a single command line.

How to Use Pipes

You've already seen how to redirect the output of a program into a file, and how to then redirect the contents of that file into another program. But you can do this all at once, without the use of a temporary file, by using the |, or vertical bar character, called a pipe. Using pipes to string commands together on the command line is a quick and powerful way to enhance the power of individual commands, and represents a unique strength of Linux and other versions of UNIX.

You'll definitely use piped commands as you begin to learn how to use Linux. Not only do pipes save you time, but you'll use different combinations of piped commands to tackle computing tasks particular to the way you work and the programs you run. At first your pipe commands may be simple, but as you gain confidence and understanding, you'll be able to construct fairly complex pipelines.

Pipes work well under Linux because many commands are also filters, which accept your shell's standard input and send output to the shell's standard output. Pipes may be used in nearly any computing task, and can be used to quickly find information, generate reports, transform data, or view results. First look at four simple examples.

```
# ls ¦ lpr
# printenv ¦ fgrep EDITOR
# nroff -man mymanpage.1 ¦ less
# cat document.txt ¦ wc ¦ mail -s "Document.txt Report" bball
```

The first command line pipes a listing of the current directory through the line printer command to print a report. The second example searches through a listing of your current shell environment and prints the value of the default text editor. The third example prints the formatted output of a manual page to your display so you can browse the document to check for errors. The last example pipes a text document through the word count command, wc, and then electronically mails a report on the number of characters, words, and lines in the document to the user bball.

You'll use pipes to confront and solve everyday problems not usually solved by individual programs. For example, if you have a lot of documents on your system, but can't remember which document contains a certain phrase, you can find this information quickly. Instead of running your word processor and opening each file, you could try typing the following:

```
# find /home -name *.doc ¦ xargs fgrep administration ¦ less
```

This command line uses the find command to search the `/home` directory for all files ending in .doc, then pipes the names into the `xargs` command. The `xargs` command then runs the `fgrep` command to search for the word administration in each file, with the results piped through the less pager. You also can use pipes to not only find information, but to process data, and create new files.

```
# find *.doc ¦ xargs cat ¦ tr ' ' '\n' ¦ sort ¦ uniq ¦ tee dict ¦ less
```

The preceding command line builds a file called `dict` that contains a sorted list of unique words contained in all your word processing files. What do you call this type of file? A dictionary! Although to be honest, not all the dictionary words may be spelled correctly. This command works by piping each found file through the `tr` command, which translates each character space into a carriage return to break the stream into one word per line. The stream of lines is then sorted, and the `uniq` command removes all occurrences of similar lines except for one. You'll notice that the `tee` command has also been used to save the output of the stream to a file.

Just a Minute

> The zsh shell contains some improvements on input and output redirection, so you may not need the tee command if you're using pipes on the zsh shell command line. See the zsh shell documentation for details.

The `tee` command is used to save the results of a pipe at a particular juncture. This is handy when you want to test your results when building pipes, or save results in a complex pipe. Look at the following example:

```
# xwd -out wd.xwd
# xwdtopnm < wd.xwd | ppmtogif | tee wd.gif | giftopnm | tee wd.pnm | pnmtotiff
➥>wd.tif
```

In this example, a window dump graphic has been created using the X11 `xwd` command, which captures and saves the contents of an X window or desktop. Then a single command line has been used to first convert this graphic into a portable bitmap graphic. The output of the `xwdtopnm` command is then fed into the `ppmtogif` command. The `tee` command is used to save the output, in GIF format, to a file, and then convert the file back into the portable bitmap format. This output is then saved as a portable bitmap graphic file, and also fed into the `pnmtotiff` command, which saves the file as a TIF graphic. One command line and four graphic conversions!

Using pipes with Linux is an easy way to get work done. As you continue to work with Linux, you'll soon develop your own set of favorite command lines. Once you've developed your favorites, you'll then want to build your own shell commands, which you'll read about in the next section.

Building Shell Commands

You don't have to be a programmer to write commands for Linux. After you become familiar with different programs and find yourself typing the same command lines over and over, save them into text files and turn them into commands. In the simplest form, a shell command may simply be one or several command lines you frequently use. Look at the following example

```
rxvt -geometry 80x11+803+375 -bg white -fg black -e pico &
rxvt -geometry 80x24+806+2 -bg white -fg black -e pine &
```

These two command lines start the pico editor and the pine mail program in two X11 rxvt terminal windows on the second desktop in an 800-by-600-pixel display. These certainly aren't command lines you'd want to type each time you want to run these programs. Although you can manually start the terminal windows after moving to the other desktop, it may take some time to correctly size the windows and then start the programs. Turn these command lines into an executable file by saving them into a file with your text editor, then use the `chmod` command to make the file executable:

```
# chmod +x d2
```

Now, when you want to run these programs, all you have to type is the following, which is certainly a heck of a lot easier!

```
# d2
```

You can make this new command even more flexible by using the shell variables `$1` and `$2`, which represent the first and second command-line arguments to a shell command. Edit the file you've created and change the program names to these variables:

```
rxvt -geometry 80x11+803+375 -bg white -fg black -e $2 &
rxvt -geometry 80x24+806+2 -bg white -fg black -e $1 &
```

Note that the order of the variables isn't important. Now when you run your command, you can supply the program names on the command line. For example,

```
# d2 pine pico
```

This has the same result, but from now on you'll be able to run nearly any program you want in the terminal windows.

This discussion of using the shell concludes with a simple shell script you can use to safely delete files. There's nothing special about this script in Listing 6.1 , rmv, but it demonstrates some of the power of shell scripts.

Listing 6.1. The rmv bash shell script.

```
#!/bin/bash
# rmv - a safe delete program
# uses a trash directory under your home directory
mkdir $HOME/.trash 2>/dev/null
cmdlnopts=false
delete=false
empty=false
list=false
while getopts "dehl" cmdlnopts; do
  case "$cmdlnopts" in
    d ) /bin/echo "deleting: \c" $2 $3 $4 $5 ; delete=true ;;
    e ) /bin/echo "emptying the trash..." ; empty=true ;;
    h ) /bin/echo "safe file delete v1.0"
        /bin/echo "rmv -d[elete] -e[mpty] -h[elp] -l[ist] file1-4" ;;
```

continues

6

Listing 6.1. continued

```
    l ) /bin/echo "your .trash directory contains:" ; list=true ;;
  esac
done

if [ $delete = true ]
then
  mv $2 $3 $4 $5 $HOME/.trash
  /bin/echo "rmv finished."
fi
if [ $empty = true ]
then
  /bin/echo "empty the trash? \c"
  read answer
  case "$answer" in
    y) rm -fr $HOME/.trash/* ;;
    n) /bin/echo "trashcan delete aborted." ;;
  esac
fi
if [ $list = true ]
then
  ls -l $HOME/.trash
fi
```

The first line of the script invokes the bash shell to run the script. After you've typed in this script using your favorite text editor, you should make the script executable by using the `chmod` command:

```
# chmod +x rmv
```

This script moves unwanted files to a directory called `.trash` in your home directory. When you're sure you want to delete the files, you can then verify the files and empty the trash. Because this script is supposed to act like a regular command, a short built-in help command has been included.

Caution

If you want to try the rmv script, make sure you type it in correctly, or change the line containing "rm -fr $HOME/.trash/* ;;" to "rm -i $HOME/.trash/* ;;" which is much safer than an unconditional delete. If you don't type this line correctly, you could delete your entire home directory!

The script works by first creating a .trash directory in your home directory (found with the `$HOME` environment variable). If the directory exists, any error messages generated by the `mkdir` command are discarded by sending the standard error output to the `/dev/null` device (a handy place to send all complaints!). Four internal script variables are then defined: cmdlnopts, delete, empty, and list.

The script uses the bash shell getopts command to look at your command line for any options. If a matching letter is found by the case statement, the script commands up until the two semicolons are executed. For example, if you want a reminder of how to use the script, you can use the -h, or help option:

```
# rmv -h
safe file delete v1.0
rmv -d[elete] -e[mpty] -h[elp] -l[ist] file1-4
```

This prints a short help message because the script found the letter h on the command line, then printed the message using the echo command. To delete files, you must use the -d, or delete command-line option:

```
# rmv -d graf.gif graf.pnm graf.tif
deleting:  graf.gif graf.pnm graf.tifrmv finished.
```

This deletes the four files by moving them to the .trash directory in your home directory. The d option was detected on the command line and the script then printed a message, echoed the file names back to your display, then set the delete variable to true. Because the delete variable was changed to true, the mv command found in the if ... then statement is executed.

You can verify that the files have been moved by using the -l, or list option, to see the contents of your trash:

```
# rmv -l
your .trash directory contains:
total 278
-rw-rw-r--   1 bball    bball         3299 Dec 28 22:38 graf.gif
-rw-rw-r--   1 bball    bball       272091 Dec 28 22:38 graf.pnm
-rw-rw-r--   1 bball    bball         6890 Dec 28 22:38 graf.tif
```

As before, because the letter l was detected on the command line, the script set the list variable to true, then executed the ls command to list the contents of your .trash directory. If you're sure you want to delete these files, you can then use the -e, or empty command-line option:

```
# rmv -e
emptying the trash...
empty the trash? n
trashcan delete aborted.
# rmv -e
emptying the trash...
empty the trash? y
# rmv -l
your .trash directory contains:
total 0
```

The rmv script asks if you're sure you want to empty the trash. If you type an n, the delete is aborted. If you type a y, the trash is deleted. Because the letter e was found on the command line, the empty variable was set to true and the statements following the if ... then test line were run. The script prints a message to your display, and then, using the read command, waits for you to enter an answer. The answer is then tested, and if yes, the files in the .trash directory are deleted.

Using the shell, you can quickly build simple programs to accomplish major tasks. Feel free to improve this program by adding features or improving on how file names are handled at the command line. One such improvement may be to add the ability to handle wildcards or whole directories. See the bash manual page for more information about other shell commands and operators you can use in your own shell scripts.

PART II

Hour 7

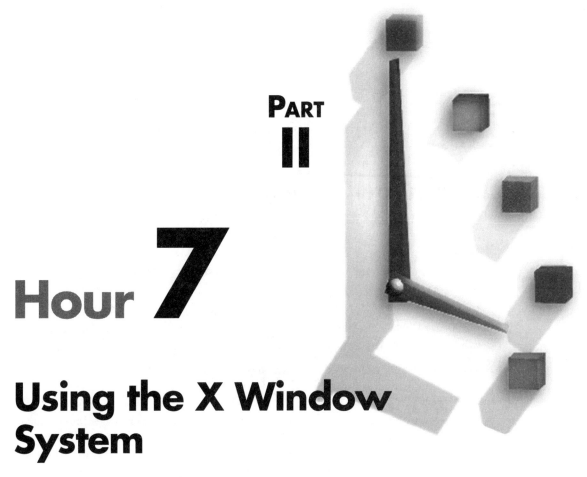

Using the X Window System

The X Window System installed on your computer, as you learned in Hour 3, "Configuring the X Window System," is a port of X11 from the XFree86 Project, Inc. This graphical interface includes about 3,500 files, with nearly 200 programs (clients), more than 500 fonts, and more than 500 graphic image files in nearly 50 megabytes of software. You'll find nearly everything (but not all files or programs) for X11 under the `/usr/X11R6` directory.

This book doesn't have enough space to discuss all aspects of using X11 with Linux. This hour shows you some of the different graphical interfaces, or window managers, you can use. It also discusses the different terminal programs (or shell consoles) you'll find on your system. You'll learn some of the basic operations you can perform while using X11, such as cutting and pasting text, adjusting your mouse speeds or cursor shape, or doing screen captures. The last section shows you a sampling of X11 clients you might want to try.

Just a Minute

> Note that many clients, such as text editors, graphics programs, and even other X11 Window managers, are discussed throughout this book.

X11 Window Managers

One of the great things about X11 is that you have freedom of choice in how you would like to manage your windows and programs on your screen. This screen management is through a window manager client. One of the bad things about X11 is that you have a confusing choice of window managers, and you might be initially overwhelmed with the array of configuration files, scripts, or resource settings.

This section covers the window managers included on your CD-ROM. In Hour 8, "Exploring Other X11 Window Managers," I'll introduce you to other new and exciting window managers you might want to try.

You can customize nearly every aspect of how your windows look.

Configuring the `fvwm2` Window Manager

The `fvwm2` window manager, by Robert Nation, builds on window manager improvements made by the `fvwm` window manager (discussed later). The window manager is set up to provide an appearance similar to that of other operating systems (see Figure 7.1) with a taskbar, hierarchical start menu, graphic icons, and three-dimensional window buttons and scrollbar. You can construct custom start menus, or menus for the root window, which are accessed by pressing the left mouse button on an empty space on the desktop. You can also build a custom icon taskbar to run programs at the click of a button, and add modules that add even more point-and-click functions (see the `fvwm2` manual page for a list of the modules and their manual pages).

You'll find the `fvwm2` window manager's configuration file, `system.fvwm2rc`, in the `/etc/X11/fvwm2` directory. You'll also find a symbolic link to the file, named `system.fvwm2rc`, in the `/usr/X11R6/lib/X11/fvwm2` directory. If you're the root operator, you can customize this file to support features and programs of your system for all users. If you'd like to make your own custom `fvwm2` features, copy the `system.fvwm2rc` file as `.fvwm2rc`, and save it in your home directory.

The main components of this file allow you to customize the following:

- ☐ Fonts for windows, icons, and menus
- ☐ Window colors (background and foreground)
- ☐ Operating modes (click in a window to activate it, or just move the cursor over it, and so on)

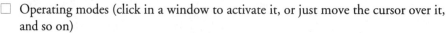

- Set how windows look
- Tasks to do when starting up, such as setting the background color of your desktop, and which modules to run
- Menu definitions, so you can customize the list of programs to match your system (a number of the programs defined in the default menus might not be installed on your system)
- Your mouse buttons' default operation or menus in the desktop, or you can define function-key utilities

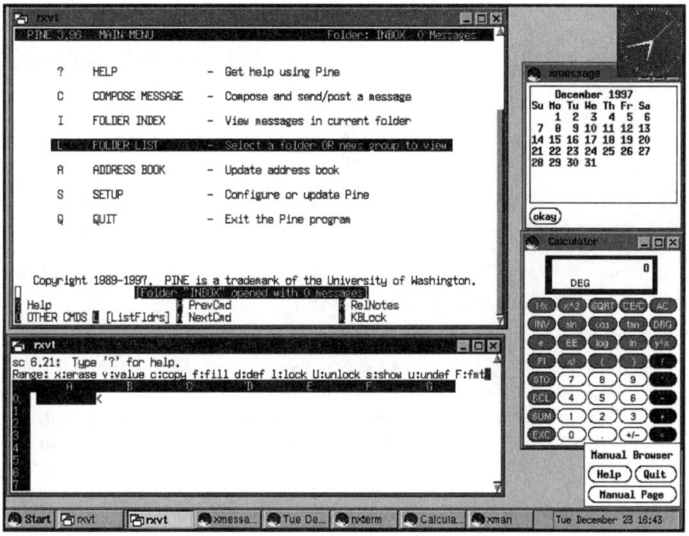

Figure 7.1.
The `fvwm2` *window manager for X11 under Linux offers decorative window borders and controls.*

If you find you like the `fvwm2` window manager, you might also want to try AnotherLevel, a sophisticated customization of `fvwm2`'s configuration files.

Configuring AnotherLevel

A more complex variant of the `fvwm2` window manager is AnotherLevel, based on Greg J. Badros' TheNextLevel, which uses the `fvwm2` window manager. The AnotherLevel `fvwm2` window manager configuration is the default X11 desktop for Red Hat Linux. You'll find an almost overwhelmingly complete menu system, and you can customize nearly any aspect of how your windows look, or how the window manager handles your keyboard or mouse.

Figure 7.2 shows the `fvwm2` AnotherLevel window manager.

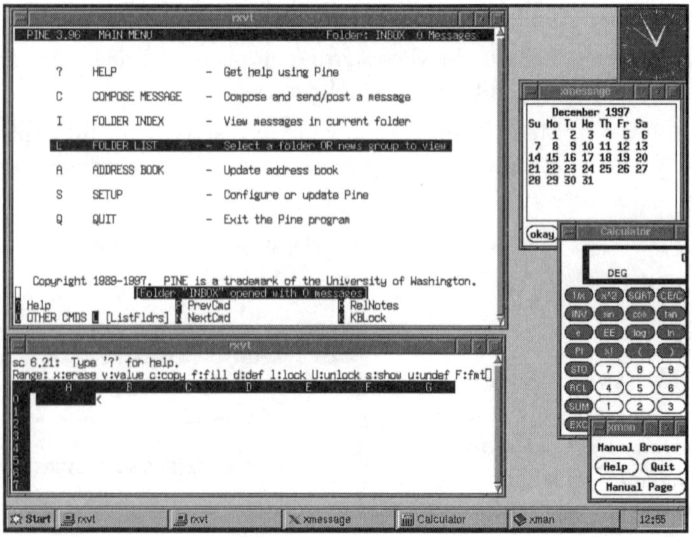

Figure 7.2.
The `fvwm2` *AnotherLevel window manager configuration comes with a set of files you can use to customize its windowing system.*

Unlike `fvwm`, `fvwm2`'s AnotherLevel has several configuration files, found under the `/etc/X11/AnotherLevel` directory. These files include

```
# ls -A /etc/X11/An*
decors              fvwm2rc.forms       fvwm2rc.m4          fvwm2rc.xlock
fvwm2rc.apps        fvwm2rc.functions   fvwm2rc.macros      scripts
fvwm2rc.decors      fvwm2rc.hostmenus   fvwm2rc.menus
fvwm2rc.defines     fvwm2rc.init        fvwm2rc.modules
fvwm2rc.defstyles   fvwm2rc.keys        fvwm2rc.mouse
```

If you're the root operator, you can make changes in these files to customize how this window manager will work for all your users. These files contain many different definitions you can change, including the following:

- Color options for menubars and menu items
- Options for enabling sounds
- Software toggles and switches for using icons, or color in menus
- Customized mouse and window operations, such as focus (whether a window is made active by mouse click or cursor location)
- Definitions for the number of virtual desktops
- Support for Windows 95 keyboards
- Options for tear-off menus

For customizing the applications supported in the window manager menus, you'll want to use the wmconfig program, found under the /usr/X11R6/bin directory. This program builds a window manager configuration file from definition files found under the /etc/X11/wmconfig directory. You can build configuration files for several window managers using this program.

First, create a directory called .wmconfig in your home directory. Then copy the files in the /etc/X11/wmconfig directory into your .wmconfig directory, for example:

```
# mkdir .wmconfig
# cp /etc/X11/wmconfig/* .wmconfig
```

You can then add, delete, or change the applications in the menus by creating, editing, or deleting the configuration files. For details concerning the format of these files, see the wmconfig manual page. When you've finished customizing the applications and menus, you can create a new configuration file using the wmconfig command, for example:

```
# wmconfig --output=fvwm2 --sysdir=/home/bball/.wmconfig >.fvwm2rc
```

This command line will cause the wmconfig program to parse the configuration files found under the .wmconfig directory and place the output in a new .fvwm2rc file.

If you like to use the taskbar at the bottom of the screen, but need the screen real estate, and don't want the taskbar to get in the way when you're working, you make it automatically hide by changing the settings in the fvwm2rc.modules file. Look for the section dealing with the taskbar, for example:

```
########################################################################
######## FvwmTaskBar
*FvwmTaskBarAutoHide
```

After you add the auto-hide setting, restart the window manager. The taskbar will disappear when you don't need it, but will appear when your mouse cursor is at the bottom of the screen.

You can also start programs from the fvwm2rc.init file. Although you can start programs by adding them to your .xinitrc file, it is important to add them to the fvwm2rc.init file if you want the programs' windows to have special features, such as visible minimize, maximize, or close buttons. Look for the SetupFunction section, then add the programs you'd like to run at startup, as follows:

```
# SetupFunction gets run at Init and Restart
AddToFunc "SetupFunction"
+ "I" Exec xsetroot -solid cyan4
+ "I" Exec rxvt -geometry 80x11+3+375 -bg white -fg black
+ "I" Exec rxvt -geometry 80x24+6+2 -bg white -fg black
```

These lines not only set the desktop color, but open two terminal windows in particular locations on the screen. The windows will feature any special buttons or window decorations you've enabled. You can also change how your windows react to your mouse cursor. Although you normally must click on a window or its title bar to make the window active, you can change this by removing a comment character in the `.fvwm2rc` file, for example:

```
# If defined, the focus follows the pointer. Otherwise focus is set by
# clicking on a window. Undefined this implements "ClickToFocus".
#define(`FOCUS_FOLLOWS_POINTER')
```

If you delete the octothorpe (or pound-sign character, #), a window will become active when your mouse moves over it. You can also set AnotherLevel to recognize the Windows key if you have a Windows 95 keyboard. To do this, search for the Win95 keyboard option in the `fvwm2rc.defines` file, and again, remove the comment character, for example:

```
# Uncomment below if you have a win95 keyboard (one w/ the extra keys)
#define(`Win95Keys')
```

After you remove the comment character and restart the window manager, you can use the Windows key to pop up the start menu on the taskbar. There are many other options and configurations for how you'd like AnotherLevel to manage your windows. You can read more about AnotherLevel by looking in the `/usr/doc` directory, or reading its manual page.

Configuring the `fvwm` Window Manager

The `fvwm`, or virtual window manager, found under the `/usr/X11R6/bin` directory, is a descendant of the `twm`, or Tab window manager (discussed next). The `fvwm` program, by Robert Nation, builds on the `twm` window manager, and offers several improvements:

- Supports virtual window to your desktop
- Consumes less memory
- Provides three-dimensional looks to window
- Introduces modules to support window operation sounds, pager utilities, icon docks, and many others

You'll find the configuration file for the `fvwm` window manager, `system.fvwmrc`, in the `/etc/X11/fvwm` directory. If you're the root operator, you can customize this file to support features and programs of your system for all users. If you'd like to make your own custom `fvwm` features, copy this file as `.fvwmrc`, and save it in your home directory.

Figure 7.3 shows the `fvwm` window manager.

If you'd like more information on how to set up and customize this window manager, see the `fvwm` manual page, along with the manual pages for each of its modules.

Figure 7.3.
The `fvwm` *window manager has virtual desktops, icon docking, and decorative window borders and controls.*

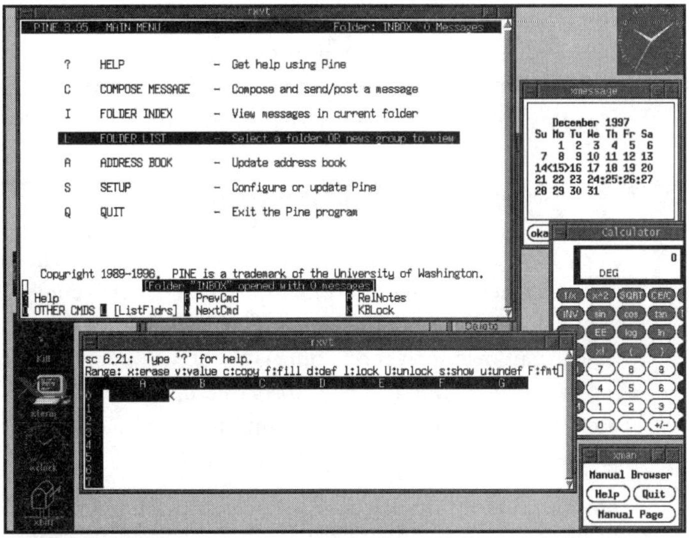

Configuring the `twm` Window Manager

The `twm`, or Tab window manager, found under the `/usr/X11R6/bin` directory, is one of the original window managers for the X Window System. The `twm` program, developed by Tom LaStrange and other authors, provides the most basic window operations, such as window titles, icons, root window menus, and other custom mouse or keyboard commands. Figure 7.4 shows the `twm` window manager.

Figure 7.4.
The `twm`*, or Tab window manager, provides basic X11 desktop displays with program lists, icons, and window controls.*

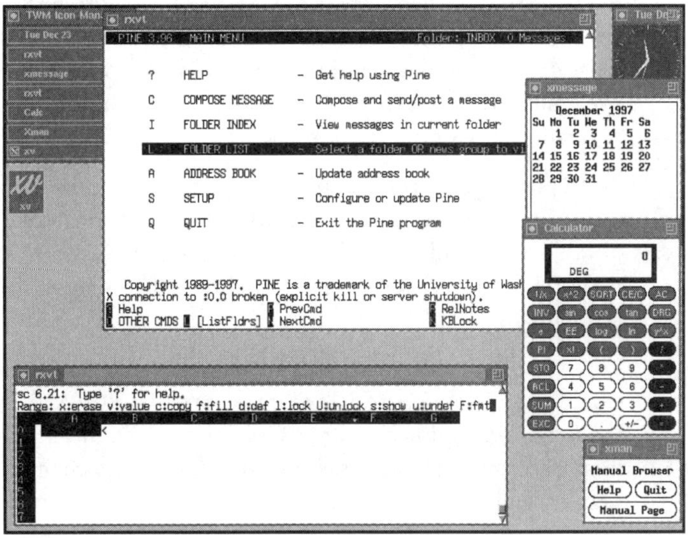

You'll find the configuration file for the twm window manager, system.twmrc, in the /etc/X11/twm directory. If you're the root operator, you can customize this file to support features and programs of your system for all users. If you'd like to make your own custom twm features, copy this file as .twmrc, and save it in your home directory.

X11 Terminal Programs

The X11 terminal clients give you a console with command-line access to the shell. Although you don't need to use a terminal program all the time, you'll probably have at least one terminal window open during your X11 sessions so you can start other programs. Having several windows open at one time is also a convenient way to learn new commands because you can have the manual page displayed in one window while you try out the program in another window. You can also use multiple terminal windows to copy and paste information between programs.

This section introduces you to two terminal programs you'll want to use with X11: xterm, or a color-capable version called nxterm, and the rxvt terminal. You'll learn how you can use these programs and some of their command-line options.

Changing the nxterm Terminal Settings

The nxterm client, or terminal emulator, is a color-capable version of the xterm client. Because these clients are basically the same with the exception of color, I'll discuss the features in the context of a terminal window.

The nxterm terminal emulator client displays an open window with a command line. You can run programs, do word processing, or perform nearly any function you'd normally do if you weren't running X11. Like most X11 terminal emulators, the nxterm client features a resizeable window that runs a shell. The upper left button on the window allows you to move, size, minimize, or maximize the window, and also close or kill the window and any running programs started from the window.

The upper right button also allows you to maximize or minimize the window. If you minimize a window, an icon can either appear on the desktop, or be placed in an icon dock or taskbar, depending on the window manager you're using at the time. By moving your mouse cursor to any corner of the window and holding the left mouse button down, you can resize the window.

You can tell nxterm how and where to initially display its window though the use of various command-line options. Some of these options, called X11 Toolkit options, are discussed in the section "Learning X11 Basic Operations" later in this hour. One feature you won't find in other terminal emulators is nxterm's capability to change features on-the-fly by using the Ctrl key and your mouse buttons.

For example, if you'd like your terminal to use a larger or smaller font, all you have to do is move the cursor inside the terminal window, hold down the Ctrl key, and press the right mouse button. A menu called VT Fonts with a list of sizes will pop up, from which you can select larger or smaller sizes.

TIME SAVER

> One really great feature of `nxterm`'s VT Fonts menu is the Selection option. Here's how it works. First, run the `nxterm` client, then start the `xfontsel` client from the command line. The `xfontsel` client displays different fonts in many different variations, and you can see the effects of different point sizes or orientation on a selected font. After you've found an extremely readable font for your display, click the Select button at the top of the `xfontsel` window. Then, move your mouse cursor to the `nxterm` window, hold down the Ctrl key, press the right mouse button, and select the VT Fonts menu item Selection. Voilà! Your `nxterm` window will now use the font you selected with the `xfontsel` client. This is handy for finding the best typeface to use for your terminal.

Many of the features of your terminal window can depend on the window manager you select. Although nearly all terminals support scrolling, not all terminal emulators have nicely drawn scrollbars. You can control whether or not scrolling is enabled and scrollbars are visible by holding down the Ctrl key and pressing the middle mouse button (for two-button mouse users, make sure you've enabled three-button emulation, and depress both mouse buttons). You'll find many other features you can change on-the-fly with this convenient menu facility.

The `nxterm` or `xterm` terminal emulators have many more features, including the ability to display Tektronix graphics. But if you don't need all these features, or need more memory to run programs, you might want to use the `rxvt` terminal emulator, discussed next.

Using the Memory-Efficient `rxvt` Terminal

The `rxvt` client, or terminal emulator, is a color-capable X11 console window with fewer, but possibly more useful, features, than the `nxterm` or `xterm` clients:

- Smaller, so this client uses less memory or swap space
- Color-capable terminal emulator
- Supports limited X Toolkit command-line options
- Does not have Tektronix 4014 emulation, which is not really needed for standalone Linux X11 workstations

You'll find that `rxvt` supports at least one of the same command-line options as `nxterm`—the `-e` option to run programs in a standalone X Window. The `-e` option is useful if you want to run programs under X that are normally run from a non-graphical environment (the console), for example:

```
# rxvt -e pico &
```

This command line will run the `pico` editor (part of the `pine` mail program) in a standalone window. You can create, open, edit, and save files, but when you quit the `pico` editor, the window will disappear. This is a great way to run interactive console programs under X.

The `rxvt` client also supports a number of X Toolkit options, as you'll see in the next section. By using these options, you can start your `rxvt` terminal at any location of your desktop, with any available font, and with a selection of foreground and background colors.

Learning X11 Basic Operations

A number of basic operations are important for you know about in using X11 and X11 clients. Many programs accept similar command-line options, so you can customize the size, color, and placement of client windows. This section introduces you to some of the more common command-line options and shows you how to use them.

TIME SAVER

> Not all X11 clients support the same X11 options, known as X Toolkit command-line options. For a full discussion of these options, see the X manual page, found under the `/usr/X11/man/man1` directory, or an individual client's manual page for details.

Using X11 Client Geometry Settings

You can use the geometry option, usually in the form of `-geometry widthxheight+xoffset+yoffset`, to manage how and where your client's window will be displayed.

For example, if you want to start an `rxvt` terminal in the upper left corner of your screen, you would use

```
# rxvt -geometry 80x25+0+0 &
```

This command starts an 80-character, 25-line `rxvt` terminal, and places its window at the upper left corner of your display. Here's a neat trick: If you are using a virtual-window-capable window manager, and have several desktops available, you can start terminal emulators not only in your current desktop, but also in other desktops.

For example, if your current desktop is 800×600, you can easily start other X11 clients in adjacent desktops by specifying the x and y offsets, as follows:

```
# rxvt -geometry 80x25+801+0
# rxvt -geometry 80x25+0+601
```

The first command line will start another terminal window, but at the upper left corner of the desktop immediately to the right. The second command line starts another terminal window, but at the upper left corner of the desktop immediately below. This is a handy feature to use if you want to set up not only your desktops, but others before you start X11. Using this approach, you can start word processing in one desktop, a Web browser in another, and a graphics program in a third (assuming you have enough memory).

The geometry specification is extremely useful for building organized, working screens. You can also use the very convenient "save desktop" features of the `fvwm` family of window managers to build your displays manually, and then save the window display settings to a file to be later edited into your `.xinitrc` window initializer file.

TIME SAVER

> The `.xinitrc` file usually resides in your home directory, and should be copied from the system `xinitrc` file, found in the `/etc/X11/xinit` directory.

Setting Background and Foreground Colors for X11 Clients

You can also usually set background and foreground colors for different parts of your X11 client's window with the `-bg` and `-fg` color command-line options. You'll find a list of colors supported by the XFree86 X11 servers in the file `rgb.txt` in the `/usr/X11R6/lib/X11` directory. For example, to start the `rxvt` terminal emulator with a red background with yellow text for the foreground, you would use

```
# rxvt -bg red -fg yellow
```

If you're not using X11 in the 8bpp (8 bits per pixel) mode (256 colors) with the XF86_SVGA server, you'll find a more limited selection of colors available. For example, you'll only have 16 colors available if you use the XF86_VGA16 server, or only black and white if you use the monochrome server, XF86_Mono. You might also try to see the available colors by using the `xcmap` client, which displays the colors in a grid, and gives the rgb (red, green, and blue) values of the color in base 16, or hexadecimal (see the X and `xcmap` manual pages for more information). Another program to try is the `showrgb` client, which will automatically list the contents of the rgb database, `rgb.txt`.

Other color options can include -bd for color choices of window borders, or the -rv and +rv reverse video modes, which are useful for monochrome displays.

Setting X11 Client Resources

The X Window System also supports further client configuration through the use of client resources. These are nothing more than text files that contain settings for different aspects of how a client looks or runs. You might also be able to set different resources of a client program when it first starts by using the -xrm command-line option to specify a resource string, but most programs will only use a resource file.

In order to change resource settings, you need to know what resources an X11 client uses. You can find this information by either reading the program's manual page, or looking for any installed settings in a file with (but not always) the client's name in the app-defaults directory under the /usr/X11R6/lib/X11 directory, as follows:

```
# ls -A /usr/X11R6/lib/X11/app-defaults
Beforelight     RXvt*         XGetfile      XPlaycd          Xgc
Bitmap          Seyon         XIdle         XScreenSaver     Xgopher
Bitmap-color    Seyon-color   XLoad         XSm              Xgopher-color
Chooser         Viewres       XLock         XSysinfo         Xloadimage
Editres         X3270         XLogo         XSysinfo-color   Xmag
Editres-color   XBanner       XLogo-color   XTerm            Xman
Fig             XCalc         XMailbox      XTerm-color      Xmessage
Fig-color       XCalc-color   XMdb          Xditview         Xmh
GV              XClipboard    XMem          Xditview-chrtr   Xvidtune
GXditview       XClock        XMixer        Xedit            xosview
Ghostview       XConsole      XPaint        Xfd
NXTerm          XFontSel      XPat          Xfm
```

You can see that there are quite a few files with application default settings, but that not all of the more than 200 programs for X11 have settings installed. Each file contains resource strings for a particular X11 client. The resource strings can provide not only information that determines how a program is displayed, but the contents and handling of menus, buttons, or other parts of a program.

The format of resource strings is defined in the X manual page, but many X11 client manual pages will list different resources, with examples, for a particular client. For example, if you look at the resource settings for the xpaint drawing program's main toolbox, you'll see the following values:

```
...
!
!  The top level operation/toolbox menu
!
XPaint.width:                 232
XPaint.height:                350
...
```

These values tell the `xpaint` client to draw a vertical toolbox. If you'd like a horizontal toolbox instead, you can resize the toolbox, note the dimensions shown by the window manager during the resize operation, and use the new settings to change the initial size of the toolbox in its default resource settings file, for example:

```
...
!  The top level operation/toolbox menu
!
XPaint.width:                     702
XPaint.height:                    122
...
```

For details about X resources, see the X man page. For details about different client resources, see the program's manual page or other documentation.

CAUTION

> Make sure your changes reflect your supported screen size, or programs might start off-screen, or with windows too large to be useful. Always use the exclamation character for comments, and if you edit the default, or original application resource file, copy the original settings first to a comment line.

Changing X11 Mouse and Cursor Modes

When you use X11, you might want to change the way your mouse works, or switch the order of the mouse buttons. This is especially handy if you're left-handed or if your mouse responds differently than the desired setup. You can also change the type of cursor used by your window manager.

In order to change your root window cursor, you need to know what cursors are available. You'll find a list of cursors in the `cursorfont.h` file under the `/usr/X11R6/include/X11` directory, for example:

```
...
#define XC_exchange 50
#define XC_fleur 52
#define XC_gobbler 54
#define XC_gumby 56
#define XC_hand1 58
#define XC_hand2 60
#define XC_heart 62
#define XC_icon 64
...
```


As you can see, many types of cursors are listed in this file. Knowing these different type of cursors, you can then use the `xsetroot` client, or root window utility program, to set your root cursor image, for example:

```
# xsetroot -cursor_name hand1
```

This will change the root cursor to look like a right-pointing hand. If you are left-handed, you might want to use the left-pointing `hand2` cursor!

Time Saver

> An easy way to see all the cursors is to use the `xfd`, or X11 font display, client found under the `/usr/X11R6/bin` directory. Used with the `-fn` command-line option, the `xfd` client will display the entire character set of the cursor font, `cursor`, located in the `/usr/X11R6/lib/X11/fonts/misc` directory.

If you find the left and right mouse buttons inconvenient, you can change how these buttons are ordered on your mouse by using the `xmodmap` client, found under the `/usr/X11R6/bin` directory. For example, to reverse the order of your mouse buttons, you can try

```
# xmodmap -e "pointer 3 2 1"
```

This example, from the `xmodmap` manual page, might help left-handed users.

Just a Minute

> The `xmodmap` client can also be used to change or alter the keys on your keyboard. See the `xmodmap` manual page for more information.

You can also customize other mouse settings using the `xset`, or user preference, client. For example, if you want to speed up your mouse acceleration, or how fast it travels across the screen, you can try these settings:

```
# xset m "40 4"
```

If this is too fast for you, try the following:

```
# xset m "4 8"
```

Experiment with different settings. You can really slow down your mouse with the `xset m "0 1000"` command line. See the `xset` client manual page for other X11 settings you can change, and see if some work with your system.

How to Copy and Paste in X11

Copying and pasting information in X11 involves transferring text between terminal windows, or graphics from one X11 client to another. For example, you can use the `xmag` program to select a portion of your desktop, then paste the copied graphic into an open `xpaint` drawing window (see Hour 16, "Graphics Tools"). To do this, first run the `xpaint` client, go to the File menu, and select New Canvas. Then start the `xmag` client. You'll see a tiny corner cursor. If you click over an area of the screen you'd like to magnify, the `xmag` client will then display the selection in a window. You would then move your cursor to the `xpaint` drawing window, go to the Edit menu, and select Paste. Your selected graphic will be pasted in the `xpaint` window.

If you're running a word processor or the command line in your terminal windows, you can also copy and paste text between windows. Both the `xterm` and `rxvt` terminals support copy and paste operations using your mouse cursor and mouse buttons. To copy text, you'll need to highlight the text first. If you just want a word, double-click on the word with your left mouse button. If you want a line of text, triple-click on the line. But if you want more than a word or a line, you'll need to highlight regions of text.

You can select text regions in terminal windows in two ways: You can move your cursor to the beginning or end of the text, and then drag with the left mouse button held down to highlight the selected text. You can also click at the beginning of the text with your left mouse button, then click at the end of the text to highlight your selection. There are also two ways to paste text into another window. One way to paste text is to use your keyboard by holding down the Shift key, and then pressing the Insert key. The other way is to press the middle mouse button (or the left and right mouse buttons simultaneously if you're using a two-button mouse to emulate three buttons).

You can also use the `xcutsel` client to copy from one window to another. When you run this client, you'll see two buttons called "copy PRIMARY to 0" and "copy 0 to PRIMARY." To copy text from one window to another, first highlight text in one window. Then click on the "copy PRIMARY to 0" button. You can then click on the "copy 0 to PRIMARY" button, then move to the window where you want to paste the text, and use either your keyboard or mouse to paste the text.

Another X11 client for copying and pasting text is the `xclipboard` client. This program is especially handy for copying sections of text from messages, FAQs, HOWTOs, or other files. Like the `xcutsel` client, `xclipboard` places the copied text into a buffer, but has the added benefit of displaying the text, which you can then save into a file, or copy into other windows or programs.

If you'd like to do more than just copy small bits of graphics or text, you can also capture pictures of whole windows or your desktop. The next section shows you how to capture, save, and display pictures from your X11 desktop.

Capturing and Dumping X11 Window

You can capture pictures of windows or your entire desktop using several X11 clients included on your CD-ROM. The first is the `xwd`, or X11 window dump, program. You can use this client to take snapshots of your screen, or any desired window.

The xwd program is easy to use. You'll want to specify a file on the command line, because if you don't, the file is sent to the standard output, and will scroll up your terminal window.

```
# xwd > mydump.xwd
```

After you type this command, your cursor will turn to a crosshair (+). If you click on the root desktop, the xwd client will dump, or capture, a picture of your entire screen. If you click in a window, the xwd client will capture the contents of the window, even if it is hidden or overlapped by another window.

This is handy if you want to capture a series of pictures of a running client, show off high scores of games, or create quick slideshows. The file is in an X11 windows dump format, but you'll find a number of clients you can use to view the image. One is the xwud (X11 window undump) client. To see your screenshot, you can use

```
# xwud -in mydump.xwd
```

You can also create a slideshow of your images with the xloadimage client, found under the /usr/X11R6/bin directory. For example, if you create a series of screen dumps, you can build a looping slideshow of the screenshots with

```
# xloadimage -fit 1.xwd 2.xwd 3.xwd -goto 1.xwd
```

Using this command line, you can repeatedly page through the dump files by pressing the N character on your keyboard, or press the Q character on your keyboard to quit. The xloadimage client has many features, and can also save your screen dump files into different graphics file formats. See the xloadimage manual page for more information.

JUST A MINUTE

Many other graphic utilities are included on your CD-ROM. See Hour 16 for an overview of paint and drawing programs, graphics conversion utilities, and other image viewers, such as the xv client, which not only captures screenshots, but edits, converts, saves, and prints graphics.

Customizing the X11 Root Window and Using Screensavers

If you have a color monitor, you might want to change the default color or pattern of the root, or desktop window. You can do this quickly and easily with several X11 clients. I'll also show you how to put pictures into your background, and how to set up and use screensavers in X11.

Setting the Background Color

You can change the background color of your display with the `xsetroot`, or root window utility, which is found under the `/usr/X11R6/bin` directory. Your choice of color, as I mentioned previously, depends on the number of color depth of your X11 server. If you're using the SVGA server, you'll have a choice of 256 colors. For example, you can change the color with

```
# xsetroot -solid red
```

Setting the Background Pattern

If a solid color is too hard on your eyes, or too plain for your tastes, you can also use one of nearly 90 different bitmap graphics files from the `/usr/include/X11/bitmaps` directory to set a desktop pattern. For example, to get a red basket-weave pattern for your desktop, use

```
# xsetroot -bitmap /usr/include/X11/bitmaps/wide_weave -bg red
```

This command line tells the `xsetroot` client to load the bitmap graphic file `wide_weave` from the X11 bitmap graphics directory, and display the pattern with a background color.

TIME SAVER

> Experiment with different colors and patterns. When you find one you like, place the `xsetroot` command line in your `.xinitrc` file so your background will be set the next time you run an X11 session.

If you're running a monochrome display, you're out of luck with colors. But you can change the pattern and apparent shade of your background display with different bitmap files. Try the `dimple1`, `dimple3`, or `flipped_gray` bitmap files.

Displaying Pictures on the Root Display

Many users like to display a favorite picture in the root window. If you have a favorite photograph you've scanned, or a graphic you like, you can display your image on the desktop with the `xsetroot` client, but the image must be in the X11 bitmap format.

You can use a client that's already been discussed—`xloadimage`. You can find out what graphics file format the `xloadimage` client recognizes with the `-supported` command-line option, for example:

```
# xloadimage -supported
Type Name  Can Dump Description
---------- -------- ----------
niff       Yes      Native Image File Format (NIFF)
sunraster  No       Sun Rasterfile
gif        No       GIF Image
```

```
jpeg        Yes     JFIF-style JPEG Image
fbm         No      FBM Image
cmuraster   No      CMU WM Raster
pbm         Yes     Portable Bit Map (PBM, PGM, PPM)
faces       No      Faces Project
rle         No      Utah RLE Image
xwd         No      X Window Dump
vff         No      Sun Visualization File Format
mcidas      No      McIDAS areafile
vicar       No      VICAR Image
pcx         No      PC Paintbrush Image
gem         No      GEM Bit Image
macpaint    No      MacPaint Image
xpm         No      X Pixmap
xbm         No      X Bitmap
```

The file formats `xloadimage` can use are listed in the left column. If you have a graphic you'd like to display, you can use

```
# xloadimage -onroot cathy.gif
```

This would load the graphic file, `cathy.gif`, and display it (depending on its size) in a tiled, or multiple-view, format. If you only want one large version of your graphic in the root display, use the `-fullscreen` command-line option, for example:

```
# xloadimage -onroot -fullscreen cathy.gif
```

This will cause the `xsetroot` command to load the graphic and zoom to fit the display. You'll have to experiment with different size graphics to get the best effect for your graphic.

Screensaver Settings and Programs

Although displaying a colored pattern or picture on your desktop can be fun, X11 screensavers also offer password control. Even though the utility of screensavers with late-model computer monitors might be questioned (most modern displays won't suffer from the "burn-in" effect of a continuous display), you'll find a variety of interesting screensavers included on your CD-ROM.

You can use the `xset` client, introduced earlier, to manage screensaving under X11. If you'd like to see the current settings, use the `q` command-line option (note that there is no hyphen used), for example:

```
# xset q
...
Screen Saver:
  prefer blanking:  yes    allow exposures:  yes
  timeout:  0    cycle:  600
...
```

You can turn on screensaving with the `xset` client by using the `s` command-line option, followed by the word `on`. To set the time in seconds, use the `s` option, followed by the number of seconds you want your X11 server to wait to blank the screen, for example:

```
# xset s 60
```

This will set the timeout interval to 60 seconds before the X11 screensaver is activated. To test the screensaver, which is built into your X11 server, you can then use the `s` option with the word activate, for example:

```
# xset s on
# xset s activate
```

This will display a blank screen. If you'd like to see a graphic and background pattern, you can use the `noblank` option for `xset`'s `s` command-line option, for example:

```
# xset s noblank
# xset s activate
```

As you can see, you'll find a large X displayed on the screen. To turn off screensaving, use the `s off` command-line option. If this isn't your idea of a screensaver, you can try the `xscreensaver` clients.

The `xscreensaver` and `xscreensaver-command` clients, by Jamie Zawinski, are found under the `/usr/X11R6/bin` directory. The `xscreensaver` client has 16 command-line options. Although this hour doesn't cover all of the options, the basic way to use this screensaver is to first run the `xscreensaver` client in the background as follows:

```
# xscreensaver -timeout 5 &
```

This command will set the screensaver to run after five minutes of no keyboard or mouse activity. You can control this client with the `xscreensaver-command` client, to turn the `xscreensaver` on or off, or to activate it immediately. Although the `xscreensaver` client has a `-lock` option to password-protect your display, you'll have to recompile the program to enable this feature.

The `xscreensaver` client comes with nearly two dozen different screensavers, which can also be run as standalone programs. For example, you can run the fractal drawing program, `hopalong`, in a window with

```
# hopalong
```

This will run the screensaver in a window so you can see what it looks like. For a list of the screensavers that will work with the `xscreensaver` client, read the file `XScreenSaver` in the `/usr/X11R6/lib/X11/app-defaults` directory. You'll find other settings in the file, which is the X11 resources file for this client.

You might also be interested in the `xlock` client. Although it is not a screensaver, `xlock` is a sophisticated terminal-locking program with nearly 50 command-line options and more than 50 different displays built in. The `xlock` client is helpful if you want to password-protect your display to prevent others from using your computer while you're away.

By default, after you start the `xlock` program, you must enter your password before you can use your display again. But you can use it as a simple screensaver without password protection to display a variety of animations, for example:

```
# xlock -duration 10 -nolock -mode random
```

This command line tells the `xlock` program to display a random selection of its animations, each of which will run for 10 seconds.

JUST A MINUTE

> The `xlock` client can also make your desktop an animated display if you use the `-inroot` command-line option. This won't protect your system, but you might find the visuals stimulating!

Exploring X11 Programs

There's not enough room in this hour to discuss all of the X11 clients on your CD-ROM. You will find discussions about different clients throughout the rest of this book, but this section shows you some helpful programs that will give you more information about your system, and some tips and tricks on how to use them.

Listing X11 Fonts with `xlsfonts`

If you'd like a list of all the fonts recognized by X11 on your system, you can use the `xlsfonts` client. You'll want to use a pager like `less` or `more` (discussed in Hour 4, "Reading and Navigation Commands") if you call the client without any options. You can also use wildcards or patterns to match font names. This can be handy to find a particular font on your system, for example:

```
# xlsfonts -fn *italic*
lucidasans-bolditalic-10
lucidasans-bolditalic-10
lucidasans-bolditalic-12
lucidasans-bolditalic-12
lucidasans-bolditalic-14
lucidasans-bolditalic-14
lucidasans-bolditalic-18
lucidasans-bolditalic-18
lucidasans-bolditalic-24
lucidasans-bolditalic-24
```

```
lucidasans-bolditalic-8
lucidasans-bolditalic-8
lucidasans-italic-10
lucidasans-italic-10
lucidasans-italic-12
lucidasans-italic-12
lucidasans-italic-14
lucidasans-italic-14
lucidasans-italic-18
lucidasans-italic-18
lucidasans-italic-24
lucidasans-italic-24
lucidasans-italic-8
lucidasans-italic-8
```

As you can see, this lists all the italic fonts installed or recognized by your X11 server. You can use the `xlsfonts` client to troubleshoot whether or not fonts are recognized or installed, or to find a font name to choose as a X Toolkit option when starting a client.

Getting Window Information with the `xwininfo` Client

You can use the `xwininfo` client, or window information utility, to get helpful information about a window. When you use this command, you can click on a another window to get a detailed information listing, for example:

```
# xwininfo
 xwininfo: Please select the window about which you
          would like information by clicking the
          mouse in that window.
```

After you click the desired window, you'll see a list of information, such as the following:

```
xwininfo: Window id: 0xc00002 "rxvt"

  Absolute upper-left X:  8
  Absolute upper-left Y:  397
  Relative upper-left X:  0
  Relative upper-left Y:  0
  Width: 574
  Height: 158
  Depth: 8
  Visual Class: PseudoColor
  Border width: 0
  Class: InputOutput
  Colormap: 0x21 (installed)
  Bit Gravity State: ForgetGravity
  Window Gravity State: NorthWestGravity
  Backing Store State: NotUseful
  Save Under State: no
  Map State: IsViewable
  Override Redirect State: no
  Corners:  +8+397  -218+397  -218-45  +8-45
  -geometry 80x11+3-40
```

This information can be helpful, for example, if you'd like to get the specifications about a window's geometry settings for the next time you run the program, or if you'd like to change the default behavior of a window by editing its resource file.

Making a Sticky Note Calendar with the `xmessage` Client

The `xmessage` client, by Chris Peterson and Stephen Gildea, is a handy way to create quick notes as reminders while you work. This deceptively simple client is easy to use. For example, if you want to make a quick note of a phone number, you can use

```
# xmessage "George called at 10:15; call him back at 555-1212" &
```

This command line will display the `xmessage` client window with the text of your message. Although this is a simple example, you can also use the `xmessage` client to display the output of program searches, or use it in your personal schedules to automatically send reminders while you work (see Hour 18, "Personal Productivity Tools," or Hour 24, "Scheduling," for details).

You can also use `xmessage` as a handy calendar display program if you need to keep a copy of the current calendar on the screen, or if you want a calendar on your desktop when you start your X session. You won't find a simple X11 version of the `cal` calendar program, but here's one you can use:

```
# cal | xmessage -file "-" &
```

This displays the output of the `cal` calendar program in a square `xmessage` client window.

JUST A MINUTE

> You will find the `ical` X11 client under the `/usr/X11R6/bin` directory, but this is a personal scheduling utility with a larger calendar display. See Hour 18 for details.

Keeping Time with X11 Clocks

If you're a habitual clock watcher, you're in luck using X11, as you'll find several clocks. You're sure to find one you like.

The `rclock` client is more than just a clock; it's an appointment calendar and mail notification program. You can run this client with a few simple options, for example:

```
# rclock -bg red -fg yellow -update 1 -geometry 80x80+718+0 &
```

This command line puts a square red clock with yellow hands (a second hand is created with the `-update 1` option) in the upper right corner of an 800×600 desktop. If you create a file called `.rclock` in your home directory, you can create automatic reminders, as the `rclock` client will not only pop up a reminder message at the appointed time, but can also be used to run programs at certain times (it checks the file every 10 minutes; when you have mail arrive, `rclock` reverses its display). Read the `rclock` manual page for more details on how to use its appointment and mail notification functions.

The `xclock` client displays time, by default, in a standard clock face, but you can make `xclock` look like a digital clock with the `-digital` option. You can also control the color of the standard clock hands or add a chime for the hour and half hour, for example:

```
# xclock -chime -hd red -hl red -update 2 -geometry 80x80 -bg yellow
```

This command displays an 80×80 pixel chiming `xclock` with a yellow face, red hands, and a sweeping second hand. If you want a digital version, you can use

```
# xclock -chime -update 1 -digital -bg yellow
```

This command displays a digital chiming clock with a yellow background. If you like digital clocks, you might also like the `xdaliclock` client, which uses animation for its digits, and has many options to control the digits, coloring, shape, or fonts used in the display, for example:

```
# xdaliclock -24 -cycle -shape -font 9x15 -geometry +697+3
```

This command display a floating, transparent digital clock with melting digits, which constantly change color. If you click the digital display, the current day, month, and year are displayed momentarily.

PART II

Hour 8

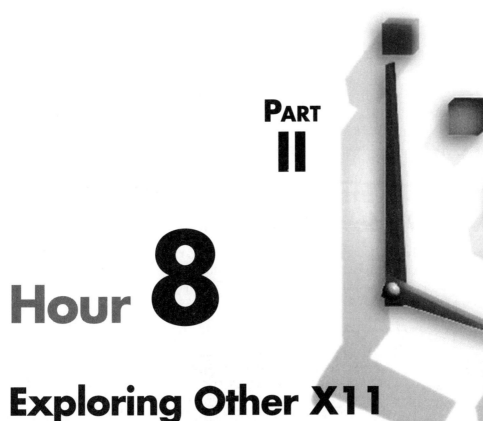

Exploring Other X11 Window Managers

In this hour you'll learn about several alternative window managers for the X Window System. There are more than 50 different window managers for X11, each with different themes, desktop colors, and decorations (for example, window controls). You're sure to find one you like. These window managers range from simple to complex, and some can be a challenge to install and configure.

Choosing a window manager is a matter of personal preference. Each window manager discussed in this hour handles terminal windows, but is different in ease-of-use, convenience, size, and style. These windows managers visibly demonstrate the graphic flexibility of the X Window System. You'll soon learn that there are no "standards" for the standard X11 graphical user interface.

TIME SAVER

> You can have all of these window managers installed on your system and use a different one whenever you want.

Obtaining, Installing, and Configuring Other Window Managers

Installing other window managers can be a daunting task. You won't find any of the following window managers installed on your book's CD-ROM. You'll have to find the software yourself, and either install pre-compiled versions, or build and install the software on your own.

JUST A MINUTE

> Don't be intimidated if you have to compile and install Linux programs from scratch. Many programmers make the job easier by providing shell scripts or other programs that automate the process. When you download a software package be sure to read the `INSTALL` or `README` file before you begin. If you're curious about Linux programming, see the Linux Programmer's Guide under the `/usr/doc/LDP` directory, and read the man pages for the make and xmkmf commands.

Fortunately, you can easily find these window managers by either using your favorite Web search engine, or browsing to Matt Chapman's site, which has a number of links to the sources:

`http://www.plig.org`

At this site the source code for many window managers is just a mouse-click away, along with beginner-UNIX tutorials and loads of details about X11 window managers.

The Motif Window Manager

The mwm, or Motif window manager, is part of the Motif software library distribution from The Open Group. Unlike the X11 XFree86 software installed on your system, Motif is distributed under a license, and you must pay for your copy. There are several Motif distributions for Linux, and many Linux users buy Motif to create Motif clients (which support drag-and-drop, along with other advanced features), or to run programs that require the Motif software libraries.

Unfortunately, you need to buy Motif to get the mwm window manager (see Figure 8.1). But you'll also receive a toolkit of programming header files, libraries, demonstration programs, and more than 600 manual pages. If you're interested in using mwm and Motif, you can find one version from Red Hat Software, Inc. at the following site:

```
http://www.redhat.com
```

Other companies also sell Motif for Linux besides Red Hat, and you can check their Web sites as well:

```
Caldera, http://www.caldera.com
InfoMagic, http://www.infomagic.com
Linux Systems Labs, http://www.lsl.com
Metro Link Incorporated, http://www.metrolink.com
Xi Graphics, Inc., http://www.xig.com
```

If you do a full installation of Red Hat's Motif, make sure there's at least 20 megabytes of free hard drive space on your Linux partition. You can get by with five megabytes of space if you install just mwm and the other Motif clients and libraries. Follow the instructions included with your distribution for proper installation.

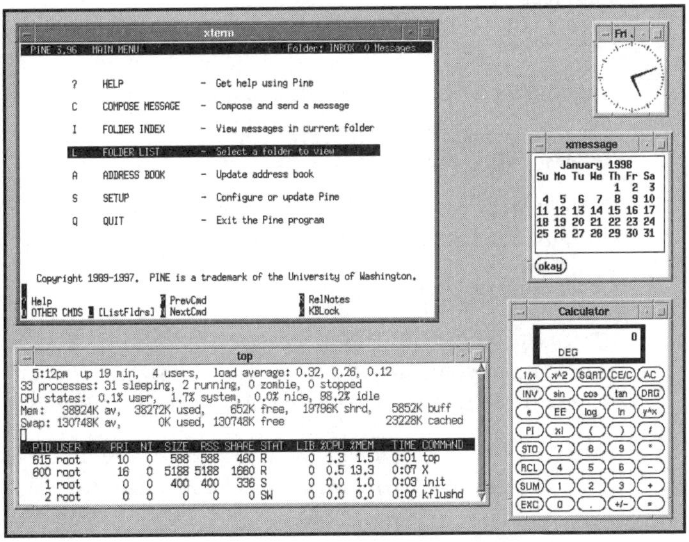

Figure 8.1.

The Motif window manager, mwm, is part of a commercially licensed Motif software distribution, and provides decorative borders and controls for windows, as well as virtual consoles.

After installing, customize mwm by editing a file called `.mwmrc` in your home directory. You'll find a copy, named `system.mwmrc`, under the `/usr/lib/X11` directory. This file contains numerous settings you can change to customize how mwm handles your mouse, windows, and desktop menus.

Installing and Using the LessTif mwm Window Manager

Don't want to spend money for a commercial distribution of Motif? You can try LessTif, an alternative software library, designed to be compatible with Motif version 1.2 and distributed under terms of the GNU General Public License. This software library comes with a window manager called mwm, along with the software libraries required to run many Motif programs.

You can download the source for LessTif and build it on your own, or your can get a binary distribution if you'd just like to try mwm. The latest copies of LessTif usually reside at the following Web site:

```
http://www.lesstif.org
```

This site also features' programming hints and a list of Motif clients that work with LessTif. To install the binary version of the LessTif distribution, move all of the unpacked directories to a single directory. Make sure you're logged in as the root operator, then type the following:

```
# gunzip lesstif-0.81-linux.tar.gz
# tar xf  lesstif-0.81-linux.tar
# cd less*
# mkdir /usr/local/lesstif
# mv * /usr/local/lesstif
```

Edit your `/etc/` profile, and add the following lines:

```
PATH=/usr/local/lesstif/bin:$PATH
LIBRARY_PATH=/usr/local/lesstif/lib
```

Save the file. To enter the new environment variables (see Hour 6, "Using the Shell") right away, use the bash shell's source command:

```
# source /etc/profile
```

Once you've used this command, either create a `.xinitrc` file in your home directory or comment out your current entries and use mwm as the last entry in the file. The next time you use the `startx` command, you'll be using the mwm window manager.

The LessTif version of mwm also uses a `.mwmrc` resource file in your home directory, so you can define your own Root menu (displayed when you hold down your right mouse button when your cursor is on the desktop).

You also can change how LessTif's mwm works by editing the file `Mwm`, located under the app-defaults directory (which you'll find under the LessTif directory).

Starting the Common Desktop Environment

The Common Desktop Environment, or CDE, is a graphical interface with many features common to other commercial operating systems. But it's much more than that: it is without a doubt one of the most sophisticated, complex, and complete GUIs for the X Window System. It has many features that other window managers lack:

- drag-and-drop actions (such as copy, move, or delete) for files and devices
- point-and-click dialog configuration of the desktop display colors, window borders, and themes
- programs and other data represented as icons on the desktop, or in windows with folder icons
- graphic configuration of your system's keyboard, mouse, and sound
- double-click convenience to edit files or graphics
- a desktop trash can for safer file deletions
- pop-up menus and built-in help for nearly any desktop action
- a suite of personal productivity tools, crafted to take advantage of the desktop interface and features, each with context-sensitive help and the ability to import and export data to other tools

CDE is a licensed product, based on Motif, that must be purchased from a vendor (see Figure 8.2). You can find CDE distributions for Linux from Red Hat Software, Inc., and Xi Graphics, Inc. You'll need nearly 50 megabytes of free disk space to run CDE comfortably, as well as at least 32 megabytes of RAM (without using swap space).

Figure 8.2.
The Common Desktop Environment is a commercially licensed X11 desktop environment with a suite of integrated personal productivity tools, including a calendar, mail, and an appointment reminder system.

Unlike other window managers that you run by entering the window manager name in the `.xinitrc` file in your home directory, CDE generally requires you to use the *xdm* client, or X Display Manager. This means that you must run X11 right after you start Linux, and have to log into your system through the xdm host chooser.

TIME SAVER

> When you use xdm to log in to Linux and run X11, you may find that you're unable to run programs as the root operator from a terminal window. This is because you must use the `xhost` command to temporarily add the hostname of your computer to the access list of your X server. To do this, you can use this formula: `xhost + localhost; su -c "rootcommand"`, where `rootcommand` is the name of command you want to run as the root operator (such as the control panel, or `printtool`).

Fortunately, you also can start the Red Hat distribution of CDE, from Triteal, Corp., from a console, or non-X11 display. To do this, create a text file containing the following line:

```
xinit /usr/dt/bin/Xsession
```

Save this with a filename like `startcde`, then make it executable by using the `chmod` command:

```
# chmod +x startcde
```

When you want to run CDE, use `startcde` on the command line. For more information about CDE, which was developed by Hewlett-Packard, IBM, Novell, and Sun Microsystems, browse to the following sites:

```
http://www.opengroup.org
http://www.triteal.com
```

For objective opinions about CDE, browse the `comp.unix.cde` Usenet newsgroup.

Obtaining, Building, and Installing KDE

One of the newest and most popular of the free software window managers for Linux and X11 is the K Desktop Environment. Like CDE, this window manager is more than just a window manager: it's a complete graphical environment for X11. KDE supports many of the same features as CDE, including the following:

- Network Transparent Access, or NTA, so you can click on a graphic document in an FTP listing and have a program on your computer automatically download and display the graphic.
- Mouse-click mounting of other file systems, such as CD-ROMs

8

- Menu control of terminal window scrollbars, fonts, color, and size
- "Sticky Buttons" to put an application or window on every desktop
- Pop-up mini-command-line windows for one-time single commands, in lieu of a terminal window
- JPEG graphic formats for background wallpaper graphics for the root display
- More than 100 integrated programs and games
- Session management, so open applications and window positions are remembered between sessions (like CDE)

In order to use KDE, you must install the free QT graphic software libraries from Troll Tech. You can download a copy from the following site:

```
http://www.troll.no/dl
```

After you install this package of libraries, you must then download the KDE distribution, found in eight different compressed archives. You can find copies at the following site:

```
http://www.kde.org
```

Download the KDE packages, then decompress and unarchive the file packages. If you download the files in RPM package format, make sure you're logged in as the root operator, and use the `rpm` command (discussed in Hour 22, "Red Hat Tools") to install the software:

```
# rpm -i kde*.rpm
```

For KDE you need about 13 megabytes of free hard drive space (less than one-third of CDE's requirement). You also need to make sure that your system's `/etc/profile` file contains the PATH environment variable pointing to the path for the KDE binary files, and the directory under `/opt/kde`:

```
PATH=/opt/kde/bin:$PATH
KDEDIR=/opt/kde
```

Insert the command `startkde` in your `.xinitrc` file and use the `startx` command to start X11 and run KDE (see Figure 8.3).

You'll be pleasantly surprised by how polished and feature-laden this desktop environment is, but you should know that KDE is a work in progress. Some documentation may be missing, and not all programs may work to your satisfaction. Even so, this is a usable X11 environment, and you'll definitely look forward to future versions.

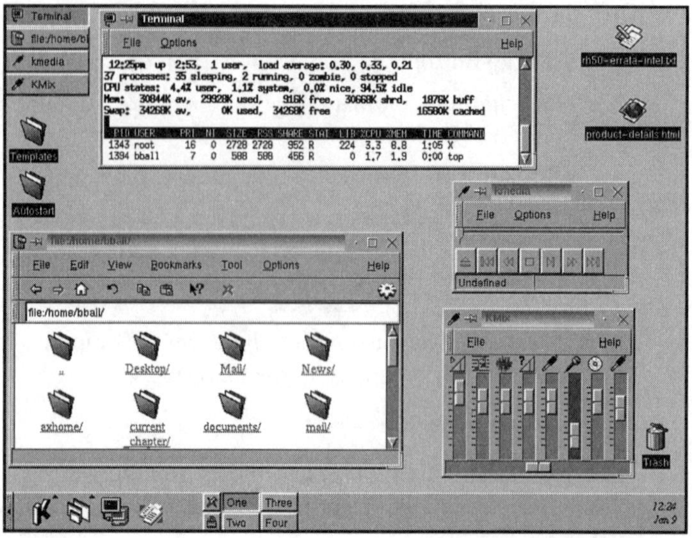

Figure 8.3.
The K Desktop Environment sports many advanced features, including Network Transparent Access, desktop icons and folders, and drag-and-drop actions.

While you're waiting for the next version, you also can play some of the games that come with KDE:

- asteroids—the classic space shoot-em-up
- mahjongg—provocative tile solitaire
- minesweeper—guess where the mines aren't
- patience—solitaire card game
- reversi—tile flip game
- samegame—unique scoring puzzle game
- shisen-sho—solitaire tile game
- snake race—evade the winding snake
- tetris—falling puzzle game

Documentation for KDE and its programs is under the `/opt/kde/share/doc/HTML/en` directory, and you can get help in each application and the desktop. Find out more about KDE by browsing to the following site:

`http://www.kde.org`

This site has the latest releases, along with documentation and bug fixes.

Installing the Enlightenment Window Manager

One of the most garish and outlandish X11 window managers is Enlightenment, by Carsten Haitzler and Geoff Harrison. Want to feel like you're hurtling through space, flying an alien spacecraft at the helm of an organic console? If your answer is "yes," then this window manager is for you.

Like other window managers, Enlightenment provides window controls, virtual consoles, scrollbars, and desktop menus (see Figure 8.4). But that's where the similarity ends. This window manager works by loading configuration files for various themes, and two themes, DEFAULT, and DEFAULT_small (for 800-by-600-pixel displays), are included.

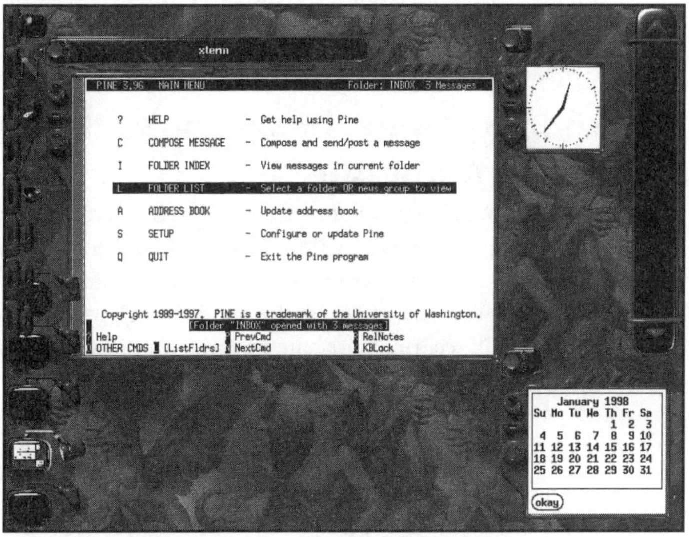

Figure 8.4.
The Enlightenment window manager provides a unique, futuristic X Window System desktop, with many unusual controls.

TIME SAVER

Be patient—there may be a significant delay before the desktop displays on your monitor after you start X because of the way Enlightenment loads its configuration files, found under the themes directory in the enlightenment directory. Enlightenment uses "*themeballs*," or gzipped tar archives to contain window elements and desktop configurations. If you want Enlightenment to start faster, you can decompress and unarchive Enlightenment's themes with the `gunzip` and `tar` commands. See Enlightenment's documentation for details.

To install this window manager, you'll need a library of graphic routines called `imlib`. Download this library from the following site:

```
ftp://ftp.mandrake.net/pub/imlib
```

After you download and install this software library (it needs about 12 megabytes of disk space after being decompressed), you must then download, compile, and install the Enlightenment software distribution. You can obtain a copy of the software from:

```
http://www.rasterman.com
http://mandrake.net/e
```

Uncompress and dearchive the Enlightenment software (it needs about three megabytes of hard drive space), then build and install the software according to the included instructions. You can then insert the Enlightenment command in your `.xinitrc` file in your home directory.

Emulating Other Desktops with the mlvwm Window Manager

If you miss your old system after migrating to Linux from another computer operating system (the one from Cupertino, California, not the one from Redmond, Washington!), you can feel comfortable again by using the mlvwm window manager. This simple window manager uses the Apple Macintosh desktop theme. Although not all menus work from the Finder's desktop, you'll feel right at home with this window manager (see Figure 8.5).

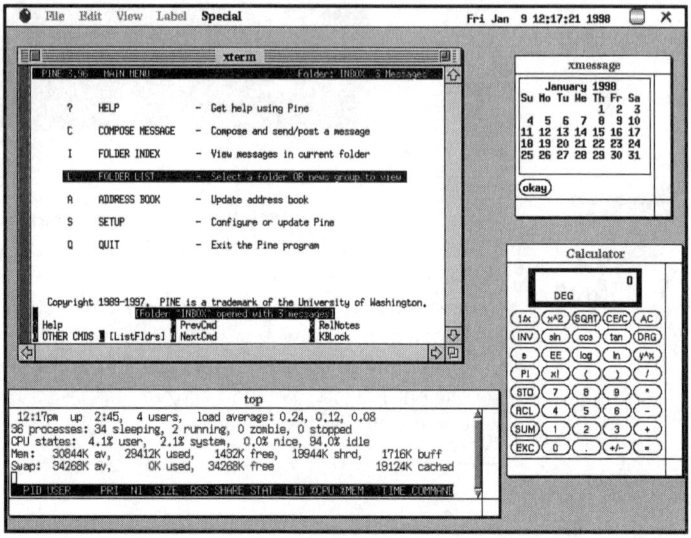

Figure 8.5.
The mlvwm window manager for X11 emulates appearance of the Apple Macintosh desktop.

Download this window manager, by Takashi Hasegawa, through the `www.plig.org` Web pages, or you can try obtaining it from the following site:

```
http://www.biole.nuee.nagoya-u.ac.jp/member/tak/mlvwm.html
```

Download the software package, then uncompress and dearchive the mlvwm sources. Edit the file `configure.h` and type the following:

```
# xmkmf
# make install
```

Once finished, you should copy the file `Mlvwmrc` from the `sample_rc` directory to a file named `.mlvwmrc` in your home directory. You can edit this file and make changes to allow mlvwm to use icons installed on your system. Mlvwm comes with some computer-translated documentation in its source package, but it also has detailed man pages in English that you can read for configuration details.

Using the Simplest Window Manager, wm2

If you don't want to fill your hard drive with countless configuration files or fiddle with complex X11 desktop settings, but still want to use X11 and a window manager, use Chris Cannam's wm2 window manager. This window manager has the bare minimum of features you'll need in a window manager. Its best feature is the list of features it doesn't have:

- no desktop icons
- no pager, or virtual desktops
- no root menus
- no complicated configuration files

Unlike other window managers discussed in this hour, wm2 requires only 65,000 bytes of hard drive space, which makes this window manager an ideal candidate for installation on Linux X11 laptops, especially where hard drive space is at a premium. Because there are no configuration files, customizing must be done when you build the program (see Figure 8.6).

Compiling and installing this window manager is a snap, with the exception of one minor glitch (you'll read about the fix in a minute). Download the source, `wm2-4.tar.gz`, then uncompress and dearchive the file:

```
# gunzip wm2-4.tar.gz
# tar xf wm2-4.tar
# cd wm2-4
# make
gcc -c -O2 Border.C
gcc -c -O2 Buttons.C
gcc -c -O2 Client.C
gcc -c -O2 Events.C
```

```
gcc -c -O2 Main.C
gcc -c -O2 Manager.C
gcc -c -O2 Rotated.C
mv -f wm2 wm2.old >& /dev/null || true
gcc -o wm2 Border.o Buttons.o Client.o Events.o Main.o Manager.o
Rotated.o -L/usr/X11/lib -lXext -lX11 -lXmu -lm
/usr/i486-linux-libc5/lib/libXt.so.6: undefined reference to `_Xsetlocale'
make: *** [wm2] Error 1
```

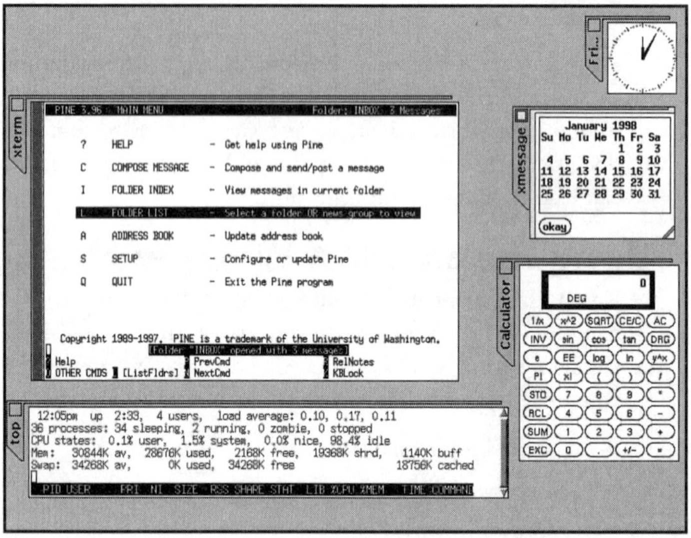

Figure 8.6.
The wm2 window manager is compact, efficient, and space-saving—ideal for running X11 on laptops with little hard drive space.

As you can see, wm2 compiles well enough, but the linker barfs on a missing subroutine and the build aborts. This error shows that when the various compiled components of wm2 were linked against your installed X11 software libraries, under the /usr/X11R6/lib directory, an X11 software routine was missing. To fix this error, open wm2's `Makefile` with your text editor and look at the beginning of the file for the linker option line:

```
LIBS    =  -L/usr/X11/lib -lXext -lX11 -lXmu -lm
```

Change this line to add the X11 Xt library to the list of X11 libraries to be linked:

```
LIBS    =  -L/usr/X11/lib -lXext -lX11 -lXmu -lXt -lm
```

Use the `make` command again, and wm2 links properly. When done, make sure you're the root operator and copy wm2 into your `/usr/X11R6/bin` directory. If you'd like to use wm2 as your window manager, insert wm2 into the `.xinitrc` file in your home directory.

PART III

Connecting to the Outside World

Hour

PART III

Hour 9

Using Communications Programs

In this hour, you'll learn about communicating with the outside world by using programs installed from this book's CD-ROM. You'll learn how to set up your serial port or modem, configure and use two communication programs, and send and receive faxes with Linux.

Although your CD-ROM contains all the software you'll need to run Linux communications programs, you'll need a serial communications port and modem to dial out with your Linux system. I assume that you're familiar with modems; communication terms such as baud rate, parity, or stop bits; and how to connect your modem to your computer.

Setting Up and Testing Your Modem

Your first task is to find your spare serial port. You should be able to find the port on the back of your computer, and it will most likely have 9 or 25 pins. If you're using a laptop, you may have a 9-pin male serial port, an RJ-11 telephone jack for an internal modem, or a PCMCIA modem card with an RJ-11 telephone jack.

You'll find your serial port in Linux by looking in the `device` or `/dev` directory. Many devices are defined there, such as hard drives, floppies, and printers, but you should look for devices of type cua or tty—for example,

```
# ls /dev/cua* /dev/ttyS*
/dev/cua0    /dev/cua2    /dev/ttyS0    /dev/ttyS2
/dev/cua1    /dev/cua3    /dev/ttyS1    /dev/ttyS
```

These devices correspond to the traditionally defined DOS serial ports, as shown in Table 9.1.

Table 9.1. DOS and Linux serial ports.

DOS Port	Linux Device
COM1	`/dev/cua0, /dev/ttyS0`
COM2	`/dev/cua1, /dev/ttyS1`
COM3	`/dev/cua2, /dev/ttyS2`
COM4	`/dev/cua3, /dev/ttyS3`

If you have a laptop with a PCMCIA modem card, you won't be able to use your modem (or any other PCMCIA devices) until you enable those services and tell Linux to look for PCMCIA devices when it starts. To enable your PC card modem, make sure that you're logged in as the root operator and edit the file named `pcmcia` in the `/etc/sysconfig` directory, to look like the following:

```
PCMCIA=yes
PCIC=i82365
PCIC_OPTS=
CORE_OPTS=
```

This tells Linux to install PCMCIA services. Save the file, and then reboot Linux. Your PC card modem (and other PC cards, if installed) should be recognized during the reboot.

Just a Minute

> If you have trouble with PCMCIA devices, read David Hinds' PCMCIA-HOWTO, which you'll find under the `/usr/doc` directory. If you want the latest information, you can also browse to
>
> `http://hyper.stanford.edu/HyperNews/get/pcmcia/home.html`
>
> If you have trouble with setting up your serial ports, read Greg Hankins' Serial-HOWTO, also under the `/usr/doc` directory. You'll find a complete discussion on setting up your serial ports and troubleshooting installation.

You can check to make sure that your serial ports are enabled by checking portions of the Linux startup message, `dmesg`, which is found under the `/var/log` directory. You can use the `dmesg` command, found under the `/bin` directory, to read this startup log—for example,

```
# dmesg
...
Serial driver version 4.13 with no serial options enabled
tty00 at 0x03f8 (irq = 4) is a 16550A
tty03 at 0x02e8 (irq = 3) is a 16550A
...
```

A portion of the `dmesg` file is reproduced here, so you can see what to look for. If you don't see a serial driver, or serial port listing, you must make sure that serial-line support is enabled for your Linux kernel.

To test your modem, make sure that you're running as the root operator, make sure that your modem is on and connected, and then try

```
# echo "ATDTXXX-XXXX/n" >/dev/cuaN
```

The number represented as XXX-XXXX is your phone number; N is the serial port you want to test. Wait at least 30 seconds or so and you should hear a dial tone, followed by the dialing, and then a busy signal. This can also be a handy way, when you have your modem working, to get the current time (albeit spoken in the tinny voice of your modem's speaker). Just insert the phone number for your local phone company's time-of-day service, save the command line in a file, and make it executable. Here's an example:

```
# cat > dotime
echo "ATDT373-0660/n" >/dev/cua1
# chmod +x dotime
# ./dotime
```

This creates the file with the `cat` command (after you type the command line, press Ctrl and the D key to save it). The `chmod` command then makes the file executable so you can run it with the final command line. If you want to test your modem interactively, you can try the `minicom` program discussed in the section "Dialing Out with Communications Programs."

Creating `/dev/modem` with the `modemtool` Command

You can also use the Red Hat X11 control-panel client to set up your modem. Make sure that you're running as the root operator, and then run the control-panel client. When you click the `modemtool` command in the control panel, the program `modemtool`, found under the `/usr/bin/` directory, will run and present a list of serial ports. Select one, and then click OK.

This program makes a symbolic link (discussed in Hour 5, "Manipulation and Searching Commands") from the selected device to a file called `/dev/modem`. You can do the same thing from the command line by using the `ln` command to create the symbolic link yourself. For example, if you have your modem connected to COM2, make sure that you're running as root, and enter

```
# ln -s /dev/cua1 /dev/modem
```

This will create a symbolic link, `/dev/modem`, which points to the serial port connected to your modem.

Dialing Out with Communications Programs

This section covers two communications programs that come with your Linux distribution: `minicom` and `seyon`. The `minicom` program can be used with or without running X11. The `seyon` program must be used while you're running the X Window System.

You'll also find an old communications program, called `cu`, under the `/usr/bin` directory. This program isn't as friendly as `minicom` or `seyon`, but if you're interested in setting up and trying this program, read the `cu` man page, and definitely read the `uucp` software documentation under the `/usr/doc` directory.

Setting Up and Calling Out with `minicom`

The `minicom` program, by Miquel van Smoorenburg and located under the `/usr/bin` directory, is a friendly communication program you can use to dial out and connect with other computers or BBSs. You can use `minicom` without running X11, but if you're running X11, you should use the `xminicom` script, also located under the `/usr/bin` directory.

The first time you use `minicom`, make sure that you're running as the root operator so you can set up and save `minicom`'s default file, `minirc.dfl`, which will be created and saved in the `/etc` directory. Assuming that you're using X11, you can start `minicom` with

```
# xminicom &
```

This command will run the `xminicom` script and start `minicom` in an X11 terminal window. To get help on how to use `minicom`, you can hold down the Alt key and press the Z key. Figure 9.1 shows the `minicom` help screen.

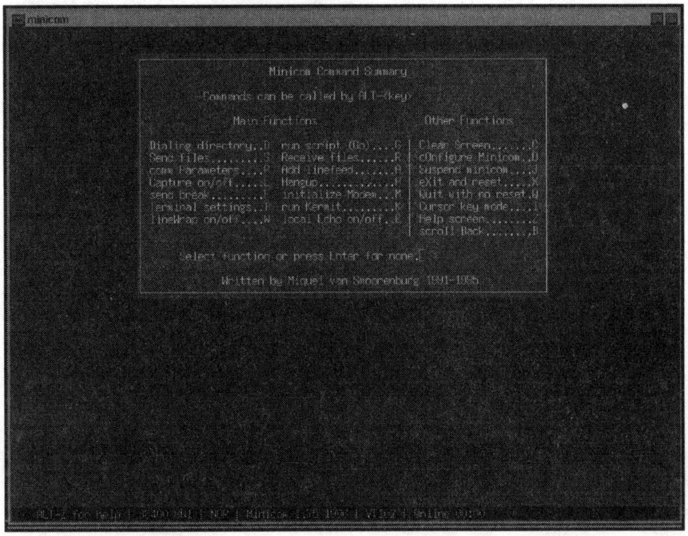

Figure 9.1.
The `minicom` *communications program features built-in help for the user.*

To configure `minicom`, hold down the Alt key and press the O key to get to the configure screen. Scroll down, select Serial Port Setup, and press the Enter key. You then can type in the Serial Device by pressing the A key. Type in the device your modem is connected to, such as `/dev/cua1`, or the symbolic link, `/dev/modem`, if you've created the link. Figure 9.2 details the serial port setup screen.

Finally, press the Enter key, select Save setup as dfl, and press the Enter key again, followed by the Escape key. Your system defaults should be set. You can then try to call out with

```
ATDTXXX-XXXX
```

If you press Enter after dialing, this should make your modem dial the phone number represented by XXX-XXXX. If you have a number of phone numbers of other computers to call, you can enter them in `minicom`'s phone directory. You can also set up `minicom` to send or retrieve files by using different file transfer programs. For details about these and other features, read the `minicom` manual page. You'll also find documentation under the `/usr/doc` directory, which contains extensive details of using other features of this program.

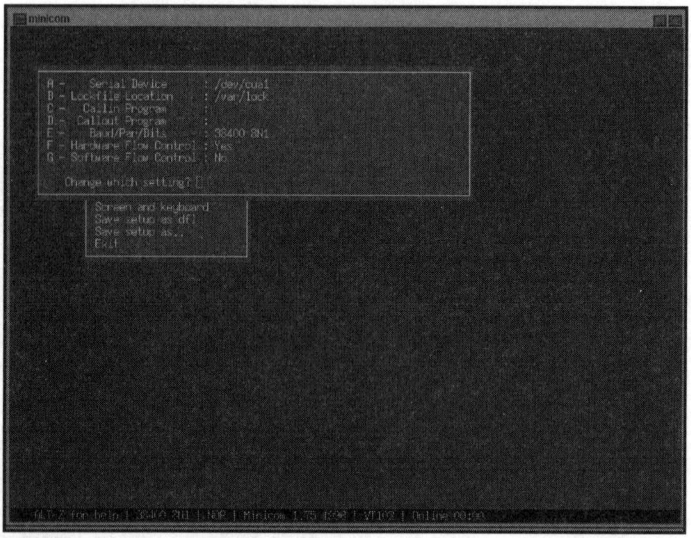

Figure 9.2.
Configuring the serial port for `minicom`.

Setting Up and Calling Out with the `seyon` X11 Client

The `seyon` communications program, by Muhammad M. Saggaf, runs only under the X Window System, and has an extensive list of features. Although `seyon` isn't as simple or initially friendly as `minicom`, it does have

- Built-in help
- A built-in telecommunications scripting language to automate calling up and logging into other computer systems
- A built-in text editor for writing telecommunications scripts
- A command-line shell dialog for running commands, which displays output in the main communication window
- Buttons to set up modem speed, parity, and stop bits

If you've created a symbolic link to `/dev/modem`, the `seyon` program will automatically recognize and work with your modem. All you have to do to call out and connect with another computer is to type your AT command string with the phone number to dial out and connect.

If you need to tell the `seyon` client the specific device for your modem, click the Set button in the Seyon Command Center window to bring up the Settings window. Click the Port button in the Settings window and type in the name of the device, `/dev/cua1` for example, in the Values? window. Figure 9.3 shows `seyon` and its settings windows.

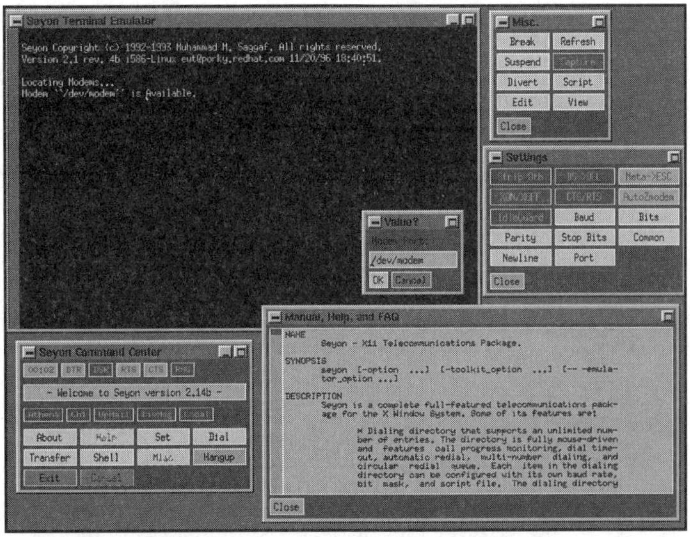

Figure 9.3.
The seyon *X11 client has point-and-click convenience for modem setup.*

Now click OK and click the Close button of the Settings window. If you'd like to start the seyon program with a default modem speed, number of bits, or parity, edit the file called startup in the .seyon directory in your home directory. This directory is installed automatically when you install the seyon program. You can make changes to the following lines in the startup file:

```
...

# set baud
set baud 19200

# can be 5, 6, 7, or 8
# set bits 8
set bits 8

# can be 0 (= no parity), 1 (= odd parity), or 2 (= even parity)
# set parity 0
set parity 0

# can be 1 or 2
# set stopBits 1
set stopBits 1
...
```

If you need help when using the seyon program, you can click the Help button in the seyon Command Center window. A window will pop up with the seyon manual page, and you can scroll through the text for help.

Setting Up Your Linux System for Dialing In

You can also set up your Linux system so that your computer's modem answers the phone and allows you to log in. You can then run a bulletin board system (BBS), word processors, spreadsheet programs, and even dial out on another line if you have at least two modems connected to your computer and two phone lines in your home.

You'll find most of the details, and custom configurations, in the Serial-HOWTO under the `/usr/doc` directory, but the three basic steps outlined here should work for nearly any modem.

> **CAUTION**
>
> Setting up your Linux system to accept incoming calls involves editing the `/etc/inittab` file and could potentially hang your system if you make an error. Always have a backup boot disk handy and make a copy of the `/etc/inittab` file before you make changes.

First, run `minicom`, and use the AT command `&V` to display your modem's profile, or default setup—for example,

```
AT&V
ACTIVE PROFILE:
B1 E1 L1 M1 N1 Q0 T V1 W0 X4 Y0 &C1 &D2 &G0 &J0 &K3 &Q5 &R1 &S0 &T5 &X0 &Y0 ~Z0
S00:000 S01:000 S02:043 S03:013 S04:010 S05:008 S06:004 S07:045 S08:002 S09:006
S10:014 S11:095 S12:050 S18:000 S25:005 S26:001 S36:007 S37:000 S38:020 S44:020
S46:138 S48:007 S51:012 S52:012 S53:010 S54:010 S95:000
```

You may see other values, but you need to make sure that your modem is at least set to the following:

```
E1 Q0 V1 S0=0 &C1 &S0
```

You can set your modem to these values by using the AT command—for example,

```
ATE1Q0V1S0=0&C1&S0&W
OK
```

Note that at the end of the AT command string, I've used the `&W` AT command to save the modem configuration as a default. You should also see the OK prompt echoed from your modem after entering the string.

The second step is to create a file called `/etc/conf.uugetty.ttySX`, where the X matches the serial port or device number of your serial port. In this example, the modem is connected to the DOS COM2 port, or `/dev/cua1` or `/dev/ttyS1`, so you'll create `conf.uugetty.ttyS1` as your file. Make sure that you're logged in as root and enter the following into the file:

```
ALTLOCK=cua1
ALTLINE=cua1
# line to initialize
```

```
INITLINE=cua1
# timeout in seconds before disconnect
TIMEOUT=60
# initialize modem
INIT="" AT\r OK\r\n
WAITFOR=RING
# modem connect
CONNECT="" ATA\r CONNECT\s\A
# delay in seconds before sending contents of /etc/issue
DELAY=1
```

Change the values for `ALTLOCK`, `ALTLINE`, and `INITLINE` to match your file's name and serial port. The `TIMEOUT` value is the amount of time in seconds your modem will wait for a carriage return from the caller before it disconnects. The `INIT` string initializes your modem (note that you could also put the previous AT command string in here, too), and the `CONNECT` string contains the AT command to answer the phone. The `DELAY` is the amount of time in seconds before the contents of the file `/etc/issue`, the login banner, is sent to the screen.

Just a Minute

> You should be familiar with the contents of the `/etc/issue` file, because it contains the text printed on your display right before the login prompt. This file is created by the startup script `rc.local` in the `/etc/rc.d` directory every time you start Linux as part of the booting process. You can customize the `rc.local` script if you'd like a different login banner.

The third step involves a one-line edit of the `/etc/inittab`, or initialization table, file. If you look in this file, you should see these lines:

```
# cat /etc/inittab
...
# Run gettys in standard runlevels
1:12345:respawn:/sbin/mingetty tty1
2:2345:respawn:/sbin/mingetty tty2
3:2345:respawn:/sbin/mingetty tty3
4:2345:respawn:/sbin/mingetty tty4
5:2345:respawn:/sbin/mingetty tty5
6:2345:respawn:/sbin/mingetty tty6
...
```

Each line represents a different Linux runlevel, documented at the beginning of the `/etc/inittab` file. This discussion doesn't cover runlevels or the details of how Linux boots, but all you have to do to enable dial-in logins for your Linux system is to change the following line:

```
3:2345:respawn:/sbin/mingetty tty3
```

to

```
3:2345:respawn:/sbin/uugetty -d /etc/conf.uugetty.ttyS1 ttyS1 38400 vt100
```

You should then save the file and restart your system. This line tells Linux to start the `uugetty` command and have `uugetty` monitor your `/dev/ttyS1` serial port for incoming calls. If you call into your Linux system, the modem will synchronize with your calling modem's speed, wait for a carriage return (or Enter keystroke), and then present a login prompt.

TIME SAVER

> If you've set up your system to accept incoming calls, you should run `minicom` as the root operator and make sure that the serial device listed under serial port setup in the configuration menu is the name of your modem's actual device, such as `/dev/cua1`, and not a symbolic link such as `/dev/modem`.

Sending and Receiving Faxes

If your modem supports fax protocols, chances are that you can send and receive faxes with Linux. Sending and receiving faxes under Linux involves graphics translation of received files and files you want to send. Your Linux distribution on the CD-ROM contains the `efax` family of fax software and documentation. You should have your modem's documentation on hand and read the `efax` manual pages and documentation under the `/usr/doc` directory carefully before you start.

Faxing with the `efax` System

The `efax` system, by Ed Casas, is a simple and easy-to-use fax system, best suited, according to its documentation, to a single-user, standalone Linux system. This software consists of a series of programs and scripts, and supports Class 1 and 2 fax modems.

The system is made up of the following programs:

- `/usr/bin/efax`—The faxing program
- `/usr/bin/efix`—A graphics conversion program used to prepare text files for faxing or converting files to different graphics formats
- `/usr/bin/fax`—A shell script used to create, send, receive, display, or print fax files

If you want to preview or fax PostScript graphics files, you'll also need to have the `gs` PostScript interpreter and the companion viewer, `ghostview`, installed on your system. For viewing received faxes, you can use the X11 clients `xv`, `xloadimage`, or `xwud`.

CAUTION

> Before you make changes to the `/usr/bin/fax` shell script, make a copy first. If you make errors or delete the file, you'll need to reinstall the `efax` software.

Before you start sending or receiving faxes, you should take a look at the `/usr/bin/fax` shell script. This program is the main way you'll send or receive faxes, but you'll need to check several sections in the file to make sure that the script is configured properly. For example, the first section lists the names of the `efax` programs:

```
FAX=/usr/bin/fax
EFAX=/usr/bin/efax
EFIX=/usr/bin/efix
```

These shouldn't pose a problem, because the programs are installed in the correct place when you installed the software. The next section lists your modem:

```
DEV=modem
```

You can use the word modem if you've created a symbolic link. However, if you have Linux set up to answer incoming calls for logins, you should use the actual name of the device—for example, `cua1`. The next section to check is the type of faxing your modem supports:

```
# CLASS=1
CLASS=2
# CLASS=2.0
```

Comment or uncomment the proper support by using the octothorpe, or pound character (#), but make sure that only one CLASS is listed. After this, you'll want to customize your faxes with your phone number:

```
# Use only digits, spaces, and the "+" character.
FROM="0 000 000 0000"
# Your name as it should appear on the page header.
NAME="from a Red Hat Linux system"
```

Enter your phone number, such as "1 202 555 1212," and name, such as "Catherine Taulbee," into the these strings. Finally, you'll want to set the default page size for faxing—for example,

```
 PAGE=letter
# PAGE=legal
# PAGE=a4
```

Comment or uncomment the different page sizes, but use only one. After you finish making your changes, you should try the fax command to test your configuration and modem by using the test command-line option—for example,

```
# fax test
------------------------------------

Please wait, this will take a minute...

------------------------------------
-- /usr/bin/fax --

FAX=/usr/bin/fax
EFAX=/usr/bin/efax
EFIX=/usr/bin/efix
DEV=cua1
CLASS=2
...
```

You'll get a three-page listing of information about your configuration, and your modem's response to the fax script's queries. If you'd like to see this information at your leisure, redirect the output of the text to a file—for example,

```
# fax test > faxtest.txt
```

You can then read about any error messages or problems with missing software. Assuming that everything is OK, you can then try faxing a document by using the `fax` command:

```
# fax send -l 12025551212 faxtest.txt
```

This tells the `fax` program to send a low-resolution, or 98 lines per inch, fax by using the fax testing information you created. To send a high-resolution fax, no option is needed—for example,

```
# fax send 7201945 faxtest.txt
faxtest.txt is text...
/usr/bin/efax: Thu Dec 04 16:29:14 1997 efax v 0.8a Copyright 1996 Ed Casas
efax: 29:14 opened /dev/cua1
efax: 29:16 dialing T7201945
efax: 29:52 connected
efax: 29:59 session 196lpi  9600bps 8.5"/215mm 11"/A4 1D    -     -  0ms
efax: 29:59 header:[97/12/04 16:29  William H. Ball (+657 0210)
➥--> 7201945  p. 1/4]
efax: 30:32 sent 20+2156 lines, 38848+0 bytes, 33 s  9417 bps
efax: 30:35 sent -> faxtest.txt.001
efax: 30:36 header:[97/12/04 16:29  William H. Ball (+657 0210)
➥--> 7201945  p. 2/4]
efax: 30:54 sent 20+2156 lines, 20854+0 bytes, 18 s  9268 bps
efax: 30:57 sent -> faxtest.txt.002
efax: 30:58 header:[97/12/04 16:29  William H. Ball (+657 0210)
```

```
➥--> 7201945 p. 3/4]
efax: 31:24 sent 20+2156 lines, 30948+0 bytes, 26 s  9522 bps
efax: 31:27 sent -> faxtest.txt.003
efax: 31:28 header:[97/12/04 16:29  William H. Ball (+657 0210)
➥--> 7201945 p. 4/4]
efax: 31:36 sent 20+2156 lines, 9023+0 bytes, 8 s  9023 bps
efax: 31:41 sent -> faxtest.txt.004
efax: 31:42 done, returning 0
```

As you can see, the fax script automatically recognized that your file was a text file because of the extension. To set your computer to automatically wait for incoming faxes, you can use the fax script's `wait` command-line option—for example,

```
# fax wait
running /usr/bin/fax answer
/usr/bin/efax: Thu Dec 04 16:42:22 1997 efax v 0.8a Copyright 1996 Ed Casas
```

You could also use the background operator to put the shell script into the background. You can check on the status of your Linux fax machine with the `status` command-line option—for example,

```
# fax status
USER       PID %CPU %MEM  SIZE   RSS TTY STAT START   TIME COMMAND
root      2304  0.3  1.3  1072   420  p3 S < 16:48   0:00 /usr/bin/efax
➥-d/dev/cua1 -v  -v chewmainrxtf

from: /var/spool/fax/cua1.2304

efax: 48:56 opened /dev/cua1
efax: 48:58 waiting for activity
```

This shows that the `efax` command is waiting on the `/dev/cua1` serial port for incoming faxes. To check whether you've received any faxes, you can use the `fax` command's `queue` command-line option—for example,

```
# fax queue

Fax files in /var/spool/fax :

-rw-r--r--   1 root     root        24090 Dec  4 16:47 1204164646.001
-rw-r--r--   1 root     root        40151 Dec  4 16:47 1204164646.002
-rw-r--r--   1 root     root        22157 Dec  4 16:48 1204164646.003
-rw-r--r--   1 root     root        32255 Dec  4 16:48 1204164646.004
-rw-r--r--   1 root     root        10325 Dec  4 16:48 1204164646.005
```

This output shows that a five-page fax is waiting in the `/var/spool/fax` directory (created automatically when you first run the `fax` command with the `wait` command-line option). You can tell that the five files are pages of the same fax by the filenames, which are the date and time, followed by the page number as an extension.

To view a fax, you can use the `fax` command's `view` option. Figure 9.4 shows the fax views—for example,

```
# fax view 1204164646*
/var/spool/fax/1204164646.001
/var/spool/fax/1204164646.002
/var/spool/fax/1204164646.003
/var/spool/fax/1204164646.004
/var/spool/fax/1204164646.005
1204164646.001 ...
1204164646.002 ...
1204164646.003 ...
1204164646.004 ...
1204164646.005 ...
```

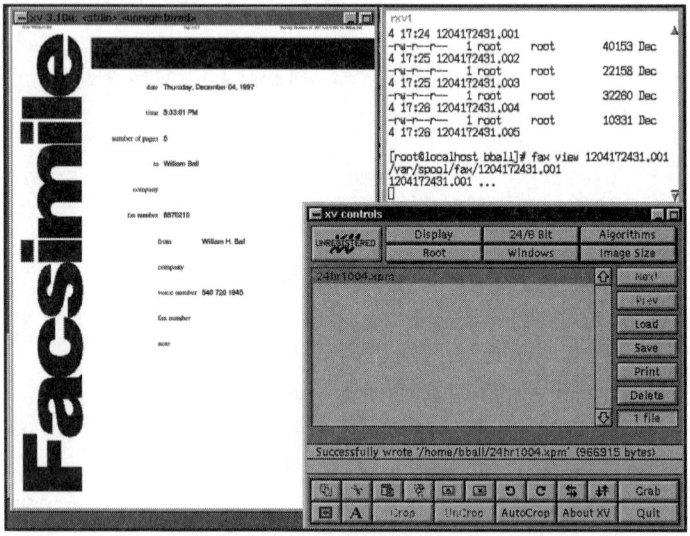

Figure 9.4.
The `fax` command automatically runs an X11 graphic program to view or print your incoming faxes.

The `fax` program will cycle through the files and display each page with a viewer you've specified in the `fax` shell script. You can use the X11 `xv` client to print your faxes, or you can try the `fax` command's `print` command-line option to print your faxes—for example,

```
# fax print 1204164646.001
/var/spool/fax/1204164646.001
1204164646.001 ...
```

This prints the first page of the incoming fax. You can print all the pages with

```
# fax print 1204164646*
```

If you want to delete a fax, you can use the `fax` command's `rm` command-line option—for example,

```
# fax rm 120417243*
/var/spool/fax/1204172431.001   /var/spool/fax/1204172431.004
/var/spool/fax/1204172431.002   /var/spool/fax/1204172431.005
/var/spool/fax/1204172431.003
deleted 1204172431.001
deleted 1204172431.002
deleted 1204172431.003
deleted 1204172431.004
deleted 1204172431.005
```

CAUTION

> The `fax` command's `rm` command-line option is potentially dangerous and may delete files in the current directory, especially if you just use a plain asterisk (*) as a filename. You should specify the fax filenames explicitly when using this command-line option.

The `efax` family of commands is a simple and versatile way to send and receive faxes with Linux. The `fax` command has more commands than are documented in the manual page, including support for voice modems and creating cover pages. Read the `fax` command itself for more details.

Sending Fax Documents with `mgetty+sendfax`

The `mgetty+sendfax` is a package of software, using the `mgetty` command, which you install in `/etc/inittab` much like the `uugetty` example shown previously, and the `sendfax` program, which is used to send faxes. The installation and configuration of this software is a little more complicated than setting up `efax`. This section shows you how to set up, configure, and use this software to send and receive fax documents with your modem.

This package of software includes many files (too many to list here). The examples in this section concentrate on the important ones, and first show you how to configure the `sendfax` software and quickly send a fax. Your first step is to make sure that you're logged in as the root operator. You'll need to change directory to the `mgetty+sendfax` directory under the `/etc/` directory. You'll see a number of files there, such as the following:

```
# ls -A
dialin.config   fax.deny     faxrunq.config  mgetty.config   voice.conf
fax.allow       faxheader    login.config    sendfax.config
```

Your first job is to create the `fax.allow` and `fax.deny` files if they don't exist. In the `fax.allow` file, enter the names of users you'd like to allow to have fax service. You should enter at least two names: root and your username.

Next, you should edit the `faxheader` file, and enter your name and phone in the sample header line—for example,

```
FAX  FROM:  John H. Doe 1 202 555 1212     TO: @T@    PAGE: @P@ OF @M@
```

TIME SAVER

> You should use the comment character, `#`, when you make changes to the `sendfax` configuration files, and retype your changes on a new line. This will save you trouble if you make mistakes and need to return the file back to its original state.

The sample header line will appear across the top of your faxed pages on the receiving fax machine. Next, you should edit the `sendfax.config` file, and first change the name of the device your modem is attached to (for example, `/dev/ttyS1` for COM2)—for example,

```
# which devices to use for outgoing faxes
#fax-devices tty4c:tty4d
fax-devices ttyS1
```

This tells the `sendfax` programs that your fax modem is attached to `/dev/ttyS1`. Next, enter the fax number (yours), which will be sent to the remote fax machine—for example,

```
# which fax number to transmit to the receiving station
#fax-id 49 89 xxxxxxxx
fax-id 1 202 555-1212
```

This will identify your fax machine to the remote fax. You'll also need to enter the type of dialing you'd like to use when sending a fax—for example,

```
# which command is used to dial out? (Could be ATD, ATDP, ATX3D0W...)
#dial-prefix ATD
ATDT
```

This tells the `sendfax` software that you'd like to dial out by using tone dialing. At this point, you're almost ready to start sending faxes. Unfortunately, though, a file named `pbm2g3` is missing from the `sendfax` distribution. You'll need this file if you want to create fax-format graphics files from text files you'd like to send.

You'll find this file in the source distribution of the `mgetty+sendfax` package at

```
http://sunsite.unc.edu/pub/Linux/system/serial/getty/mgetty+sendfax-1.0.0.tar.gz
```

Download the file, decompress and unarchive it, and change directory to the `tools` directory in the source folder, `mgetty-1.0.0`. Then, type **`make`**. After the various programs build, you can copy the program `pbm2g3` to the `/usr/bin` directory. After you do this, the `sendfax` program will work.

To send a one-page fax by using the sendfax program, you must first convert a text file into the Group 3 fax format. You can do this by using the graphics conversion program pbmtext, found under the /usr/bin directory with the pbm2g3 program—for example,

```
# cat myfile.txt ¦ pbmtext ¦ pbm2g3 > myfile.g3
```

This pipes the file myfile.txt through the pbmtext command, which outputs a portable bitmap graphics format into the pbm2g3 command, which then converts the piped stream of characters into the fax graphic format. After you do this, you can send the file (assuming that you're the root operator) with

```
# /usr/sbin/sendfax -v -l ttyS1 -C cls2 -r 5551212 myfile.g3
Trying fax device '/dev/ttyS1'... OK.
Dialing 5551212... OK.
sending 'myfile.g3'...
```

This runs the sendfax program. The -v command-line option tells sendfax to give some feedback during the faxing operation. I've specified the ttyS1 serial port with the -l option, and sent the fax through a Class 2 fax modem with -C cls2 command-line option. The phone number 555-1212 was specified with the -r option, and the file, myfile.g3, was the file you created with the preceding command-line pipe.

If you would rather use a simpler approach, try the faxspool program, which automatically converts your text file, and places it in the fax spool directory under the /var/spool/fax directory—for example,

```
# faxspool 5551212 myfile.txt
spooling to /var/spool/fax/outgoing/F000010...
spooling myfile.txt...
myfile.txt is format: ascii
Aladdin Ghostscript 3.33 (4/10/1995)
Copyright (C) 1995 Aladdin Enterprises, Menlo Park, CA.  All rights reserved.
This software comes with NO WARRANTY: see the file COPYING for details.
Loading NimbusMonL-Bold font from /usr/share/ghostscript/fonts/n022004l.pfb...
➥1750128 436826 1320152 28679 0 done.
Printing myfile.txt
Page height = 67.
\nPutting Header lines on top of pages...
\nFax queued successfully. Will be sent at next ''faxrunq'' run.\n
```

The faxspool program requires only a phone number and filename, and has the advantage of handling multiple pages easily. You can see the number of faxes awaiting in the fax queue with the faxq command—for example,

```
#  faxq
F000010/JOB: queued by bball. 1 page(s) to 5551212
```

The faxq command reports on the number of jobs you've created, the number of pages, and the phone number of the remote fax machine. You can remove the waiting fax by using the faxrm command, as in the following example:

```
# faxrm F000010
```

The waiting faxes may be sent by the root operator by running the `faxrunq` command—for example,

```
# faxrunq
processing F000011/JOB...
/usr/sbin/sendfax -v 5551212 f1.g3
Trying fax device '/dev/ttyS1'... OK.
Dialing 5551212... OK.
sending 'f1.g3'...
command exited with status 0
    send mail to bball...
```

This shows that the `faxrunq` command uses the `sendfax` program to look at the fax queue in the `/var/spool/fax` directory, connects with the modem, dials out, and then sends the fax. One nice feature of the `sendfax` software package is that a mail message is automatically mailed to the fax sender to verify the faxing, as in the following example:

```
...
Subject: OK: your fax to 5551212

Your fax has been sent successfully at: \c
Thu Dec  4 23:45:26 EST 1997
\n\nJob / Log file:
phone 5551212
user bball
input myfile.txt
pages  f1.g3
Status Thu Dec 4 23:45:26 EST 1997 successfully sent
\nSending succeeded after 0 unsuccessful tries.
```

You can also set up your Linux system to automatically receive incoming faxes with the `mgetty` program. Used much like the `uugetty` program, `mgetty` also requires at least one change to its configuration file in the `/etc/mgetty+sendfax` directory. The change you can make (as the root operator) is to edit the phone identification entry in the file `mgetty.config`—for example,

```
# set the local fax station id
#fax-id 49 89 xxxxxxxx
fax-id 1 202 555 1212
```

This sets the local fax machine phone number. After you do this, you should edit the `/etc/inittab` file as described earlier, and use `mgetty` to listen to the serial port—for example,

```
3:2345:respawn:/sbin/mgetty -s 38400 ttyS1
```

CAUTION

As mentioned before, any edits of the `/etc/inittab` file are potentially hazardous. Always have a spare boot disk and make a backup of the file first.

After you make this change, save the file and reboot the computer. Now, not only can you receive faxes, but you also can dial in from an outside line and run Linux programs. To see if any faxes have arrived, you'll have to explicitly look at the `/var/spool/fax/incoming` directory—for example,

```
# ls -A /var/spool/fax/incoming
fn4878f9aS1-_IBM-APTIVA-M61-_.01   fn4878f9aS1-_IBM-APTIVA-M61-_.02
```

This shows that a two-page fax awaits reading. You can read the faxes by first converting them to the portable bitmap file format—for example,

```
# cat /var/spool/fax/incoming/*.01 ¦ g32pbm > faxpage1.pbm
```

After you convert these fax files to the portable bitmap format, you can then use the X11 `xv` client or the ImageMagick display X11 program to read or print your faxes.

As you can see, you'll have several choices of faxing documents with Linux. The `sendfax` program, like the `efax` family of programs, also accepts other types of files to fax, and has many other options. Read the documentation for this program to find out the details.

PART III

Hour 10

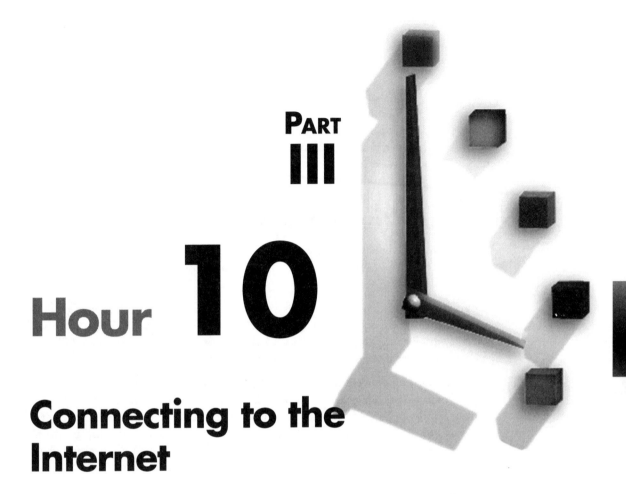

Connecting to the Internet

In this hour, you'll learn how to set up your Linux system to connect to the Internet by using the serial line Point-to-Point Protocol, known as PPP. After following the directions in this lesson, you should be able to connect to the Internet through your Internet service provider (ISP) to do email, Web browsing, or file transfers. This hour's lesson not only shows you how to do this in the simplest, most basic way possible, but also points you to sources of information for more details so that you can troubleshoot or fine-tune your connection.

I'm recommending that you use a PPP connection for several reasons:

- Although it's complex, it's easy to set up.
- You'll find documentation and details on the protocol.
- You can read the `comp.protocols.ppp` newsgroup for information.
- It offers security on both ends of the connection.
- It's a common protocol supported by nearly all ISPs.
- It's flexible enough to accommodate different types of connections.

This hour starts by listing some of the hardware and software prerequisites for Linux, and then asking you for some necessary information you'll need from your ISP. With that information, you'll create a set of customized scripts you can use to start or stop your connection. You'll also learn about some handy utilities you can use to diagnose your connection, and some other programs you can use to monitor your sessions.

Hardware You'll Need

You probably already have all the hardware you need: a modem, a modem cable if your modem is external, and a phone line. But there are other considerations, such as your serial port or modem speed.

One great thing about Linux is that it runs well, even on older computers. Although graphics-intensive applications such as X can tax the capabilities of older, slower PCs, you don't need X, a fancy display monitor, or a 16MB VRAM accelerated 3D video card to use PPP. You will, however, need a serial card to support First-In-First-Out serial buffering.

If you can use your modem under Linux to dial out and connect by using the `minicom` program or C-Kermit, chances are you won't have any problems. If you're using a PC Card modem, and the `cardmgr` PCMCIA device manager recognizes and initializes your modem, you should be OK. One way to check is to use the `dmesg` program, which displays the file `/var/log/dmesg` created when you start Linux. Run the `dmesg` program (piped through the `less` command), and look for lines in the output similar to the following:

```
# dmesg ¦ less
....
tty00 at 0x03f8 (irq = 4) is a 16550A
tty01 at 0x02f8 (irq = 5) is a 16550A
tty03 at 0x02e8 (irq = 3) is a 16550A
....
```

Another consideration is your modem's speed. Some of you may remember when 2400 or 9600-baud modems were the greatest innovation since touch-tone dialing. If you're still using a 9600 or 14.4 modem, and refuse to upgrade to the newer 56K modems until the industry protocols shake out and model prices drop to $25, you can still connect to the Internet with PPP, as your modem will autosynchronize with the newer models lodged in your ISP's modem bank.

If you want to listen to radio stations, watch live video, or upgrade your Red Hat Linux system through your phone connection, you'll want the fastest modem you can afford. Although I don't advocate that you try to get any work done through a 1200 or (shudder) 300-baud connection (which borders on masochism, but can be done, as ATM machines prove), you can use email, FTP, and text-only Web browsing at 9600 speeds.

It's up to you—besides, isn't freedom of choice what Linux is all about?

Linux Software You'll Need

To set up your PPP connection, you need to make sure that your Linux kernel supports PPP. You may have PPP support compiled into the kernel or loaded as a module when you start Linux. One way to check to see whether PPP support exists on your system is to again use dmesg:

```
# dmesg ¦ less
...
PPP: version 2.2.0 (dynamic channel allocation)
TCP compression code copyright 1989 Regents of the University of California
PPP Dynamic channel allocation code copyright 1995 Caldera, Inc.
PPP line discipline registered.
...
```

You should see similar lines. If you don't, you must recompile the kernel with built-in PPP support, or build the PPP module and use the insmod command to load the driver. You'll also need networking support enabled, especially TCP/IP.

Another piece of software you'll need is the chat program, found under the /usr/sbin directory, and part of the pppd daemon software package. The chat program is used during the dialing process to dial out and connect to your ISP's modem. Along with chat, you need the pppd daemon, also installed in the /usr/sbin/ directory. If pppd is installed, you should find a ppp directory under the /etc directory containing some or all of the following files:

```
# ls /etc/ppp
chap-secrets      options          ppp-on-dialer
connect-errors    pap-secrets      ppp-on
ip-up             ppp-off
```

If you don't see the ppp-on or ppp-on-dialer files, you can copy them from the /usr/doc/ppp-2.2.0f-3/scripts directory.

The setup you'll learn during this hour will require you to make changes to the ppp-on file, which is an executable script. Next, you may want to check to see if the file resolv.conf exists under the /etc directory. If it doesn't, don't worry, because it's a short file containing one or two lines.

Finally, you may want to see if you have the ifconfig, minicom, netstat, ping, or route commands on your system. You'll use these later to run some tests on your connection.

Information You'll Need from Your ISP

To connect to the Internet by using PPP through your ISP, you should first, obviously, have a PPP account. When you sign up for your service, your ISP account representative will most likely assume that you want a setup and software for a Windows or Macintosh system. If you say "Neither. I'm using Linux," and the response you get is a blank stare, dead air on the phone, or "What's Linux?" don't panic!

You may get lucky. As Linux grows in popularity, many ISPs in the U.S. and around the world recognize and support Linux users. If your ISP is aware of Linux, ask for the minimum system requirements, any setup guides, or install tips. The CD-ROM with this book contains the latest, stable releases of the software you need, so you won't have to worry anyway.

Assuming that your ISP doesn't know about Linux, here's what you need from your ISP:

- Your account information: username (login name) and password, so you can log into your ISP's computer.
- Your ISP's modem connect number(s), so you can connect.
- Whether your ISP assigns you a static Internet Protocol (IP) address, or assigns your IP address dynamically (the examples in this hour assume dynamic addresses, but show you where you can make changes for a static IP address).
- The IP addresses and names of your ISP's primary Domain Name Server and secondary domain name server. This information will go into the `/etc/resolv.conf` file (as explained in the section "Editing the `resolv.conf` File").

  These addresses will be in the form of four 8-bit numbers, and will look something like: 205.198.114.1 or 205.198.114.20. These will be the address or addresses of the servers used or maintained by your ISP that (among other things) translate hostnames, such as sunsite.unc.edu, into numeric IP addresses, so you can connect, query, or address other computers and users around the world. This section doesn't go into the details about the mechanics of IP addressing, and this book doesn't cover all aspects of networking under Linux.
- The name or IP address of your ISP's mailserver, so you can send and retrieve mail. You'll need this information in Hour 11, "Configuring Internet Email."
- The name or IP address of your ISP's news server, so you can read Usenet news and subscribe to newsgroups. You'll need this information in Hour 12, "Configuring Internet News."

Finally, ask for the Uniform Resource Locator, or URL, of your ISP's World Wide Web home page, if it exists. You may find technical bulletins, help files, or other information that may help in troubleshooting connections.

Setting Up a PPP Connection

Armed with this information, you'll now learn how to specify your ISP's DNS server and how to create or edit your connection script, `ppp-on`. Although specifying your ISP's DNS server(s) isn't necessary to initiate or maintain your connection, you'll need this information in place during the next hour, when you learn about Internet email.

Editing the `resolv.conf` File

This is a simple process. First, make sure that you're logged in as the operator. Then look in the `/etc` directory for a file called `resolv.conf`. If it's there, open it with your favorite text editor (see Hour 14, "Text Processing") and add the IP addresses of your ISP's DNS servers. If your ISP has only one, that's okay. If your ISP has more than one, that's okay, too. Enter the lines, using this format:

```
nameserver 205.198.114.1
nameserver 205.198.114.20
```

Then close the file. That's all there is to do! Next, you'll create or edit a script you can use to start a PPP connection.

Editing the PPP Connection Scripts

Before you start, you should know that using this script is only one way to start a PPP connection. You can use this approach, which requires you to be logged in as the root operator; a much simpler approach, which I'll show you later; or other, more complex approaches, using wrapper programs or setting options in `pppd`'s `/etc/ppp/options` file (which is parsed when the `pppd` daemon first starts).

I won't go into the detailed methods, because I want to outline the simplest approaches for you and get you on line quickly. But when you get a working connection, I suggest that you look at `pppd`'s manual pages, Robert Hart's PPP-HOWTO under the `/usr/doc/HOWTO` directory, Al Longyear's PPP-FAQ under the `/usr/doc/FAQ` directory, or pertinent sections in the *Linux Network Administrators Guide*.

The first thing you should do is to make sure that you're logged in as the root operator. Then, look in the `/etc/ppp` directory for a file called `ppp-on`. If it's there, make a copy (you can call it anything you want), or rename `ppp-on` to `ppp-on.org`. If `ppp-on` isn't there, copy it from the `/usr/doc/ppp-2.20f-3/scripts` directory. Listing 10.1 shows you parts of the script, written by Al Longyear:

Listing 10.1. The `ppp-on` connection script.

```
...
TELEPHONE=555-1212       # The telephone number for the connection
ACCOUNT=username           # The account name for logon (as in 'George Burns')
PASSWORD=password        # The password for this account (and 'Gracie Allen')
LOCAL_IP=0.0.0.0        # Local IP address if known. Dynamic = 0.0.0.0
REMOTE_IP=0.0.0.0        # Remote IP address if desired. Normally 0.0.0.0
...
DIALER_SCRIPT=/etc/ppp/ppp-on-dialer
...
exec /usr/sbin/pppd lock modem crtscts /dev/modem 57600 \
     asyncmap 20A0000 escape FF $LOCAL_IP:$REMOTE_IP \
     noipdefault netmask $NETMASK defaultroute connect \
        $DIALER_SCRIPT &
```

You need to change several parts of this script. For the most part, you need to make only a few changes. Some of the critical elements are

- `TELEPHONE`—Enter your ISP's modem connect number here.
- `ACCOUNT`—Enter your username or login name (usually assigned by your ISP).
- `PASSWORD`—Enter your password here (usually assigned by your ISP).
- `DIALER_SCRIPT`—The complete pathname of your dialing script, which uses the `pppd` daemon's companion `chat` program. The `chat` program does the dialing, connecting, and login for you. If you can't find a copy of this script, which is called `ppp-on-dialer`, look under the `/usr/doc/ppp-2.2.0f-3/scripts` directory. (Listing 10.2 shows the `ppp-on-dialer` script.) Note that if your ISP's computer doesn't present a `login:` and `password:` prompt, you'll have to change the `login:` and `password:` strings in this script to match the ones from your ISP.

Listing 10.2. The `ppp-on-dialer` dialing script.

```
...
exec chat -v                                                  \
        TIMEOUT          3                                    \
        ABORT            '\nBUSY\r'                           \
        ABORT            '\nNO ANSWER\r'                      \
        ABORT            '\nRINGING\r\n\r\nRINGING\r'         \
        ''               \rAT                                 \
        'OK-+++\c-OK'    ATH0                                 \
        TIMEOUT          30                                   \
        OK               ATDT$TELEPHONE                       \
        CONNECT          ''                                   \
        login:            $ACCOUNT                            \
        password:        $PASSWORD
```

Next, examine the `pppd` command line in the `ppp-on` script, and change `/dev/modem` to match the device your modem is connected to. If you want, you can use the approach outlined in Hour 9, "Using Communications Programs," to make a symbolic link from your modem's serial port to `/dev/modem`. Here's a tip: If you have a 14.4 modem, use 19200 as the numeric value; if you have a 28.8 or 33.6 modem, try 57600. You may be able to connect at a faster speed, especially with newer modems.

TIME SAVER

> If your ISP assigns IP addresses automatically (dynamic IP addresses, or addresses that may be different each time you log in), you're all set. But if you must connect to a specific (static, or fixed) IP address, you'll need to remove the `noipdefault` option from the `pppd` command line, and change the `$REMOTE_IP` string to the IP address provided by your ISP (you can do this in the `pppd` command line or further up in the script in the `$REMOTE_IP` variable).

Finally, make sure that the `ppp-on` and `ppp-on-dialer` scripts are executable by checking with `ls -l`, or modifying with the `chmod` program:

```
# chmod +x /etc/ppp/ppp-on*
```

You're now ready, assuming that your modem is connected to your computer, and your phone line is connected to your modem, to try a connection.

Starting and Stopping PPP Connections

This section shows you how to connect to your ISP and start your Internet session. There are several ways to do this. The first way you'll see is the most basic, simplest way to connect with the `minicom` program without using the scripts you just created. Then you'll learn how to use your PPP connection script, `ppp-on`.

JUST A MINUTE

> The `minicom` program, discussed in Hour 9, is a communications program you can use to dial out and connect to other computers or information services, such as bulletin board systems, or BBSs. See the `minicom` manual page for more information.

Using `minicom` to Connect

Using `minicom` to connect with your ISP has an advantage because your account information and password aren't recorded in the system logs under the `/var/log` directory. You can use `minicom` each time you want to use the Internet, but you may find the process tedious. I'm showing you this approach first, because you may find it useful in verifying that the login and password entries you've specified in your `ppp-on-dialer` script will work.

Here is the step-by-step method. You can do this because `minicom` can quit without resetting your modem. This means you can use `minicom` to dial out, connect, and then quit, allowing you to start your PPP session with the `pppd` daemon. Here's how:

1. Run `minicom`.
2. Type **ATDT**, followed by your ISP's modem number.
3. Wait for the connection, your ISP's prompt, then log in with your username and password. Note whether the login and password prompts are different. If so, write them down so you'll have the information you need to edit the `chat` program options in your `ppp-on-dialer` script.
4. Press Ctrl+Q to exit `minicom` without a modem reset.
5. From the command line, type the following:

```
# pppd -d detach /dev/modem &
```

After a second or so, you're connected! (Well, you should check first—try some of the programs discussed later.)

Using Your `ppp-on` Script to Connect

Using the `ppp-on` script to establish your PPP connection is easy. Make sure that you're logged in as root, and type the following to start the connection:

```
# /etc/ppp/ppp-on
```

You'll notice that you have to type the entire pathname to the script. If you find your connection works, you can move the script to the `/usr/local/bin` directory, or make a symbolic link to the script with (you can call it whatever you want; just don't use `pppd`)

```
# ln -s /etc/ppp/ppp-on /usr/local/bin/start-ppp
```

After you start the script, you should hear your modem connect to your phone line, dial out, then connect with your ISP's modem. After several seconds, you should be connected!

Just a Minute

> If you don't like the sound of your modem or find it disruptive (especially if you have to work in a quiet environment), use your modem's AT command set to turn off the modem's speaker. Run `minicom`, type **`ATM0`**, press Enter, type **`AT&W`**, and then press Enter again to save the settings. Now you can start stealth PPP connections!

Stopping the PPP Connection

To stop your PPP session, use the `ppp-off` script, found in the `/etc/ppp` directory. To use it, type

```
# /etc/ppp/ppp-off
```

This script works by finding your network interface, `ppp0`, which you can test by using some of the programs in the next section and then using the `kill` command to kill the process ID of `ppp0` (the `kill` command is discussed in the next hour).

Just a Minute

> If you're interested in the details on setting up other serial-line connections, such as Serial-Line IP, or SLIP, look under the `/usr/doc/slip-login-2.1.0.6` directory.

Checking the Connection

You can diagnose, troubleshoot, or get more information about your PPP connection in a number of ways. You can use networking utility programs during your connection to test, time, and diagnose the `ppp0` interface. You can also examine system logs to look for any problems occurring during startup, connecting, and disconnecting.

This section introduces you to a few of these networking programs, and shows you where to look in your system logs for more information.

Using the `ifconfig` Command

Although the `ifconfig` command, found under the `/sbin` directory, is generally used in network administration by the root operator to configure network interfaces (a skill not covered in this book; see the *Linux Network Administrators Guide*), you can use `ifconfig` to see the status of your PPP connection.

This command can also be helpful when you're running programs, such as newsreaders, which may appear "frozen," but are actually sending and receiving data, but not displaying updates on your screen. To use `ifconfig`, just enter

```
# ifconfig
lo        Link encap:Local Loopback
          inet addr:127.0.0.1  Bcast:127.255.255.255  Mask:255.0.0.0
          UP BROADCAST LOOPBACK RUNNING  MTU:3584  Metric:1
          RX packets:17257 errors:0 dropped:0 overruns:0
          TX packets:17257 errors:0 dropped:0 overruns:0

ppp0      Link encap:Point-Point Protocol
          inet addr:207.226.80.52  P-t-P:207.226.80.4
Mask:255.255.255.0
          UP POINTOPOINT RUNNING  MTU:1500  Metric:1
          RX packets:676 errors:0 dropped:0 overruns:0
          TX packets:545 errors:0 dropped:0 overruns:0
```

The command will list the current, active network interfaces. Look at the `ppp0` listing and you can see the number of bytes received and transmitted (in the form of packets) over your PPP interface. Calling the program intermittently from another console or terminal window under X will show you the progress of data being sent and received.

Using the `netstat` Command

The `netstat` command is the definitive command for checking your network activity, connections, routing tables, and other network messages and statistics. You'll want to try this command if you're interested in a flexible listing of what's going on. For example, you can try (the following example output is abbreviated):

```
# netstat
Active Internet connections (w/o servers)
Proto Recv-Q Send-Q Local Address           Foreign Address         State
tcp        1      0 localhost:1644          localhost:1322          CLOSE_WAIT
tcp        0      0 localhost:2579          localhost:6000          ESTABLISHED
...
tcp        0      0 serial52.staffnet.:4216 megan.staffnet.com:pop  ESTABLISHED
Active UNIX domain sockets (w/o servers)
Proto RefCnt Flags       Type       State         I-Node Path
unix  2      [ ]         STREAM     CONNECTED     417
...
unix  2      [ ]         STREAM                   419    /dev/log
unix  2      [ ]         STREAM     CONNECTED     1982
unix  2      [ ]         STREAM                   1983   /dev/log
```

The `netstat` command has more than a dozen different command-line options. See the `netstat` manual page for more information.

Using the ping Command

The `ping` command is useful for verifying that your ISP's IP addresses are valid and for testing the response times of your ISP's host servers. `Ping` sends test packets of data and measures the time it takes for the host to send back the information—for example:

```
# ping staffnet.com
PING staffnet.com (207.226.80.1): 56 data bytes
64 bytes from 207.226.80.1: icmp_seq=0 ttl=254 time=176.9 ms
64 bytes from 207.226.80.1: icmp_seq=1 ttl=254 time=180.0 ms
64 bytes from 207.226.80.1: icmp_seq=2 ttl=254 time=170.0 ms
64 bytes from 207.226.80.1: icmp_seq=3 ttl=254 time=170.0 ms
64 bytes from 207.226.80.1: icmp_seq=4 ttl=254 time=170.0 ms
64 bytes from 207.226.80.1: icmp_seq=5 ttl=254 time=170.0 ms
64 bytes from 207.226.80.1: icmp_seq=6 ttl=254 time=169.7 ms
...

-- staffnet.com ping statistics --
7 packets transmitted, 7 packets received, 0% packet loss
round-trip min/avg/max = 169.7/172.3/180.0 ms
```

By default, `ping` will continue to send and receive information until you tell it to quit with a Ctrl+C. You should also know that using the `-f`, or `flood`, option isn't a nice thing to do to your ISP (or any other host computer for that matter), as it creates network overhead and unnecessary network traffic.

Using the route Command

The `route` command, generally used to set up or delete networking routes for interfaces, may also be useful in showing you what's going on with your `ppp0` interface. You can try the following:

```
# /sbin/route
Kernel IP routing table
Destination     Gateway         Genmask         Flags Metric Ref    Use Iface
pm2.staffnet.co *               255.255.255.255 UH    0      0        0 ppp0
127.0.0.0       *               255.0.0.0       U     0      0        2 lo
default         pm2.staffnet.co 0.0.0.0         UG    0      0        3 ppp0
```

For more details about the `route` command, see its manual page.

Reading Your System Log

If you'd like to read in detail about what's going on while your scripts are executing, take a look through your system log, a file called `messages`, under the `/var/log` directory. Try

```
# less /var/log/messages
```

Look for the start of the `pppd` daemon in the `ppp-on` script. Notice that your dialer script uses the `chat` program, which does most of the work and then quits, followed by `pppd` getting and setting the network IP addresses.

```
...
Nov  5 16:29:49 localhost pppd[370]: pppd 2.2.0 started by root, uid 0
Nov  5 16:29:51 localhost chat[371]: timeout set to 3 seconds
Nov  5 16:29:51 localhost chat[371]: abort on (\nBUSY\r)
Nov  5 16:29:51 localhost chat[371]: abort on (\nNO ANSWER\r)
Nov  5 16:29:51 localhost chat[371]: abort on (\nRINGING\r\n\r\nRINGING\r)
Nov  5 16:29:51 localhost chat[371]: send (rAT^M)
Nov  5 16:29:51 localhost chat[371]: expect (OK)
Nov  5 16:29:51 localhost chat[371]: rAT^M^M
Nov  5 16:29:51 localhost chat[371]: OK -- got it
Nov  5 16:29:51 localhost chat[371]: send (ATH0^M)
Nov  5 16:29:51 localhost chat[371]: timeout set to 30 seconds
Nov  5 16:29:51 localhost chat[371]: expect (OK)
Nov  5 16:29:51 localhost chat[371]: ^M
Nov  5 16:29:51 localhost chat[371]: ATH0^M^M
Nov  5 16:29:51 localhost chat[371]: OK -- got it
Nov  5 16:29:51 localhost chat[371]: send (ATDT659-9041^M)
Nov  5 16:29:51 localhost chat[371]: expect (CONNECT)
Nov  5 16:29:51 localhost chat[371]: ^M
Nov  5 16:30:10 localhost chat[371]: ATDT659-9041^M^M
Nov  5 16:30:10 localhost chat[371]: CONNECT -- got it
Nov  5 16:30:10 localhost chat[371]: send (^M)
Nov  5 16:30:10 localhost chat[371]: expect (ogin:)
Nov  5 16:30:10 localhost chat[371]:  57600^M
Nov  5 16:30:12 localhost chat[371]: ^M
Nov  5 16:30:12 localhost chat[371]: ^M
Nov  5 16:30:12 localhost chat[371]: Staffnet PM0 login: -- got it
Nov  5 16:30:12 localhost chat[371]: send (username^M)
Nov  5 16:30:12 localhost chat[371]: expect (assword:)
Nov  5 16:30:12 localhost chat[371]: username^M
Nov  5 16:30:12 localhost chat[371]: Password: -- got it
Nov  5 16:30:12 localhost chat[371]: send (password^M)
Nov  5 16:30:12 localhost pppd[370]: Serial connection established.
Nov  5 16:30:13 localhost pppd[370]: Using interface ppp0
Nov  5 16:30:13 localhost pppd[370]: Connect: ppp0 <--> /dev/modem
Nov  5 16:30:16 localhost pppd[370]: local  IP address 207.226.80.171
Nov  5 16:30:16 localhost pppd[370]: remote IP address 207.226.80.214
...
```

You can look at portions of your log to troubleshoot whether your modem is working, or your ISP's modems are working. Hopefully everything will go well, but if you have a hard time connecting or setting up your scripts, take the time to read the `chat` and `pppd` manual pages, along with the PPP-HOWTO and PPP-FAQ.

Just a Minute

> If you're still having trouble, be sure to read Robert Hart's PPP-HOWTO, along with Al Longyear's PPP-FAQ, which go into much more detail about setting up PPP connections. You'll find a lot of handy hints about setting up, testing, and troubleshooting your connection. If security is a big issue for you, be sure to read these documents. You should also check with the `comp.os.linux.networking`, `comp.os.linux.setup`, or `comp.protocols.ppp` Usenet newsgroups for specific information or tips on using PPP.

The next two hours show you how to set up your email and newsreader programs so you can send and receive email, and read some favorite Usenet newsgroups.

PART III

Hour 11

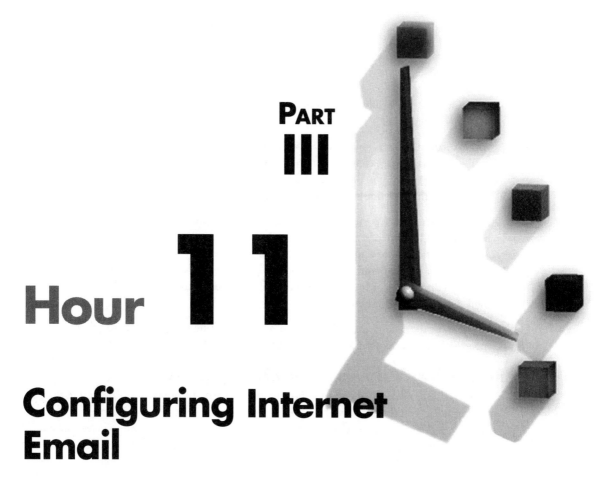

Configuring Internet Email

This hour shows you how to set up your Linux system to handle electronic mail. You'll also explore various programs you can use to read and send mail.

First you'll learn to set up your system to send and receive mail, building on your experience in setting up and connecting with your ISP using PPP.

Setting Up and Getting Your Email

There's not really much to do to set up your system to send and receive mail, although configuring the main mail daemon, `sendmail`, is complex enough to be considered a black art, suitable only for UNIX wizards. You shouldn't be intimidated though, because you can use email right after you install Linux and create other users.

I can't discuss all of the details about UNIX mail in this hour, but you should understand how electronic mail works in general. The main programs involved in email are, in technical terms, transport agents and user agents. A *transport agent* is a program, usually a daemon, which sends mail files from one computer to the next automatically. A *user agent* is a program, also called a mail reader, which you use to manage messages.

After you install Linux, you'll find all of the programs you need to compose, send, and receive mail. The transport agent used in Linux is `sendmail`, and it is configured and run automatically when you boot the operating system. As far as user agents go, you have your choice, and they are discussed later in the hour.

Because you're connecting to the Internet with a PPP connection, the general approach to handling mail outlined in this hour is to log in and connect, retrieve mail, and then disconnect (or stay connected for a few quick replies). If you've experimented with free email account programs for other operating systems, you know the general approach is to minimize connect time by composing and replying to mail offline, then connecting, sending and retrieving mail, followed by logging off.

If you want the details about Linux mail handling, along with pointers to other sources of information, read Vince Skahan's Mail-HOWTO under the `/usr/doc/HOWTO` directory.

Retrieving Your Email with `popclient`

By now you're probably wondering how to get your email from your ISP. If you recall from the last hour, you should have the IP address or name of your ISP's mail server. To get your mail, you'll need the `popclient` program, found in the `/usr/bin` directory. You'll also need to know what Post Office Protocol, or POP, your ISP uses, along with your username and password. Most ISPs support either POP2 or POP3, which are simple protocols for retrieving your messages.

Put all this information together, connect to your ISP, and then grab all your waiting email with one command line:

```
# /etc/ppp/ppp-on
# popclient -3 -u username -p password mailserver.yourisp.com
```

You can also put this command line into a text file, use `chmod +x`, and call it as follows:

```
# domail
QUALCOMM Pop server derived from UCB (version 2.1.4-R3) at megan starting.
3 messages in folder
reading message 1.
reading message 2.
reading message 3......
```

The `popclient` program is designed to work only one way; it retrieves your mail from your ISP's mail server, then tells your ISP's mail server to delete your mail after it is received. You can also use other options, such as telling your ISP's mail server to keep copies of your mail even after you retrieve, or to put your retrieved mail into an optional directory on your system.

By default, your mail will go into a single file with your username under the `/var/spool/mail` directory. See the `popclient` manual page for more options.

Using `fetchmail` as an Alternative

If you'd like to try an another program instead of `popclient` to retrieve your mail, you may want to try `fetchmail`. This program offers a few more features, and can run in daemon mode, checking to see if you have mail while you're connected to your ISP. Using `fetchmail` is easy, for example:

```
# fetchmail -p POP3  staffnet.com
Enter password for bball@staffnet.com:
1 message from bball@staffnet.com.
reading message 1 (581 bytes)  flushed
```

`fetchmail` will prompt for your password (so you can gain access to your ISP's mail server), then retrieves your mail and flushes (or deletes) your mail from your ISP's mail server. `fetchmail` also has a nifty option, `-c`, which unlike `popclient`'s `-c` option, will merely check to see if you have mail waiting, and report the number of messages. See `fetchmail`'s manual page for more information.

Now that you've retrieved your mail, how do you read it, or reply to messages? This is where user agents, or mail-reading programs, come in.

Sending Mail with Mail Programs

This section introduces you to three basic mail programs you can use under Linux. The explanations start with one of the oldest, the `mail` program, then follow with two screen-oriented programs, `pine` and `elm`.

Using the `mail` Program

The `mail` program, found under the `/bin` directory, is the simplest mail program you can use, but it is not screen-oriented. `mail` can send and receive mail, but you're limited to working on a line-by-line basis. This program is handy for quick messages and is easy to use. For example, to create a quick message, call `mail` with an address on the command line:

```
# mail bball@staffnet.com
Subject: Using the mail Program
This is how to use the mail program!
Have fun, and enjoy.
.
EOT
```

The `mail` program will respond by asking for a Subject: line. Enter your text, and then press the Enter key. Then, type each line of text, and when you're done, put a period (.) on a line by itself. The `mail` program will then send the message. Retrieving your messages is easy. After you connect to your ISP, and retrieve your mail using either `popclient` or `fetchmail`, you can simply type `mail` on the command line, for example:

```
# mail
Mail version 5.5-kw 5/30/95.  Type ? for help.
"/var/spool/mail/bball": 2 messages
>   1 mwc@savoynet.com      Tue Nov 18 10:43  38/2126  "Save on Inkjet /Laser"
    2 bball@staffnet.com    Tue Nov 18 11:27  24/701   "test"
&
```

The `mail` program will retrieve your mail from the `/var/spool/mail` directory, print its version, then list each message, and present the ampersand (`&`) as a prompt. Note that the current message is preceded by a right angle bracket (greater-than sign). The basic `mail` commands are

- `t`—Type, or list, the current message
- `n`—Go to the next message and list it
- `+`—Move to next message and list it
- `-`—Move backward to previous message and list it
- `h`—Reprint list of messages (after listing a message)
- `d`—Delete current message
- `R`—Reply to sender
- `r`—Reply to sender and all recipients
- `q`—Quit, saving messages in the default mailbox, `mbox`
- `x`—Quit, don't save messages in `mbox`

One handy way to send a long message quickly is to use the command-line redirection operator of your shell. For example, if you have composed a long message in your favorite text editor, you can send the message with

```
# mail -s "How is it going?" myfriend@somewhere.com < mymessage.txt
```

Using this approach, the `mail` program will create a message with a subject you specify with the `-s` option (note that you must enclose the text with quote marks), and then put the file `mymessage.txt` into the body of the message. Be careful, though, because the message will be sent right away without asking you if you really want to send it.

There are many more commands and different ways to use the `mail` program, and you may find it useful. See the `mail` manual page for more information. Although using `mail` can be quick and convenient, the next two mail programs are a lot more interactive, and offer features most people have become accustomed to when they send and receive mail.

Configuring and Using the `pine` Mail Program

The `pine` mail program, which you'll find under the `/usr/bin` directory, was developed by the University of Washington as an interactive mail and news reader. This means that not only can you use `pine` for sending or reading your mail, but you can also use it to read Usenet newsgroups. Usenet and different news readers are discussed later in this hour, but this section focuses on configuring and using `pine` for mail.

The `pine` program also comes with an extremely easy-to-use editor called `pico`, which might easily become your favorite Linux text editor, because it can be used with any other program, and not just `pine`. See Hour 14, "Text Processing," for more details about the `pico` editor.

The `pine` program is easy to set up and use. Most of the work is done for you automatically when you first start the program, for example:

```
# pine
Creating subdirectory "/home/bball/mail" where Pine will store
its mail folders.
```

The `pine` program starts up and creates a directory called `mail`, along with a `.pinerc` configuration file in your home directory. Before you start composing or sending mail, you should configure `pine` to recognize your username, your ISP's mail server, and, as you'll see later on, your ISP's news server. Although you can compose mail, and use `pine`'s `postpone` feature to save your composed messages, you won't be able to send mail until you tell `pine` who you are, or the name of your ISP's mail server.

To do this, type an **s**, then a **c** to get to `pine`'s configuration screen (see Figure 11.1).

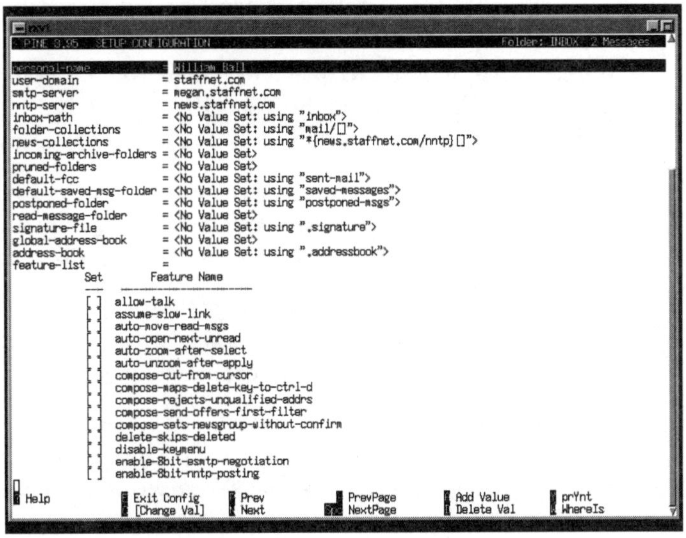

Figure 11.1.
Specifying the personal name, user domain, SMTP server, and NNTP server in the `pine` *mailer configuration screen.*

Enter your personal name, the domain of your ISP, the name of your ISP's mail server, and if you know it, the name of your ISP's news server. Then type an **e**, and `pine` will ask if you want to save the changes. Your configuration will then be saved in the `.pinerc` file in your home directory. Although you can edit this file in your favorite text editor, using `pine` is a lot easier.

To compose a message, press the **c** key, and you'll be in `pine`'s compose mode (see Figure 11.2).

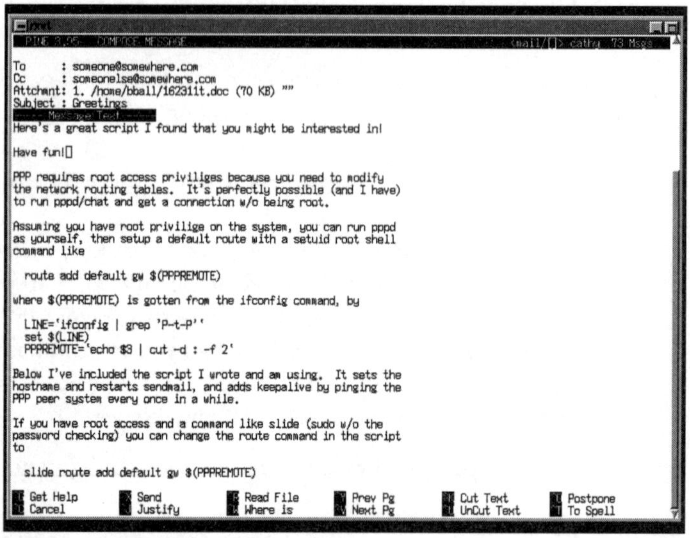

Figure 11.2.
Composing a mail message with file attachments to multiple recipients in the `pine` *compose mode.*

You can specify multiple recipients to your message by typing a comma between names. You can also send file attachments by typing the name of the file (if it is in your home directory), or the complete path of your file if it is somewhere else on your filesystem.

As you compose your message, you can use your cursor keys to move around the text, and a number of editing keys to write your text. You can also delete or undelete lines of text for cutting and pasting. For more details on editing, see the `pico` manual page.

When you're finished composing your message, you can send the message right away by using Ctrl+X, or postpone the message by using Ctrl+O. Using this approach, you can create or reply to messages while you're not connected to your ISP, and then send them later on.

When you retrieve your mail, `pine` will look in the `/var/spool/mail` directory, then extract the messages and put them into the default folder, INBOX, in the mail folder in your home directory (see Figure 11.3). You can also create other folders, and save and delete messages in different folders to organize your mail. Of course, you can also use the `procmail` approach discussed in the section "Configuring `procmail` and Writing Recipes to Fight Spam" to automate some of this process for you.

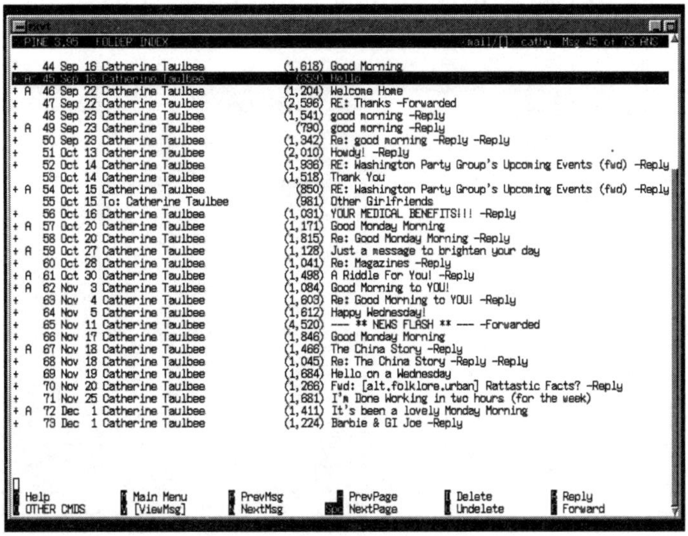

Figure 11.3.
You can select messages through `pine`*'s message list of a* `pine` *mail folder.*

The folder index of your messages is displayed in a list, and you can select messages by scrolling up and down with the cursor keys. From the main list of messages, you can delete, undelete, save, read, and export messages to your directory. To read a message, just hit the Enter key.

The `pine` program has a number of command-line options, and other features, such as built-in help, which you access with the question mark (`?`) from `pine`'s main menu. Other `pine` functions, such as reading news, are discussed later in this hour.

Configuring and Using the `elm` Mail Program

The `elm` program, which is more than 10 years old, was originally developed by Dave Taylor, and has features of the `mail` and `pine` programs. You can, as in `mail`, send a message from the command line, using the `mail` command example you saw earlier, for example:

```
# elm -s "How is it going?" bball@staffnet.com < author.msg
Sending mail...
Mail sent!
```

When you first start `elm`, you'll be asked if you want to create `elm`'s default mail folder, Mail.

```
# elm

Notice:
ELM requires the use of a folders directory to store your mail folders in.
Shall I create the directory /home/bball/Mail for you (y/n/q)? y
```

11

Unlike `pine`, `elm` must be started in a window with at least 14 rows, or it will complain and quit.

After you retrieve your mail, `elm` reads your messages and displays your messages as shown in Figure 11.4 (just as the `pine` mail program does).

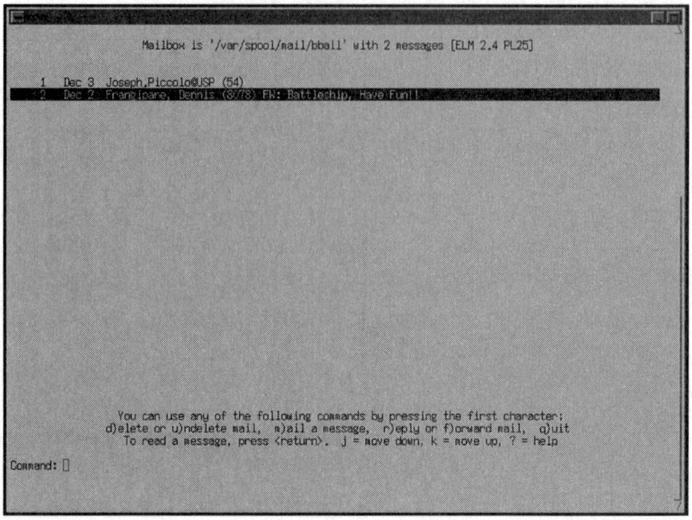

Figure 11.4.
The `elm` *mail program displays messages in a list.*

As in `pine`, you can use `elm` to delete, forward, save, or compose messages. You can customize some of its features by typing an **o** while in `elm`'s main display. These custom features are saved in an `elmrc` file under the `.elm` folder in your home directory.

This book doesn't go into all the details about the `elm` program. Make sure to read the manual page for `elm` before you start using it. If you'd like more information, you can also check

`http://www.myxa.com/elm.html`

Subscribing to Mailing Lists

Once you feel confident that your mail system is working, you may want to subscribe to a mailing list. Mailing lists are handled by automatic mail servers, and work by relaying messages generated to all members of a mailing list. One smart way to subscribe to mailing lists is to sign up for a digest version, in which the day's message traffic is condensed into a single or twice-daily mailing.

You can find out more about mailing lists by browsing to

`http://www.lsoft.com/lists/listref.html`

One query sent to a mailing list server at the University of Georgia returned:

```
Date: Tue, 18 Nov 1997 19:12:15 -0500
From: "L-Soft list server at UGA (1.8c)" <LISTSERV@UGA.CC.UGA.EDU>
To: bball@staffnet.com
Subject: Output of your job "bball"

> lists global
There are currently 14,869 public LISTSERV lists known to
LISTSERV@UGA.CC.UGA.EDU. Without a search string, the listing generated by
the LIST GLOBAL command would be over 44,500 lines long and add up to an
estimated 1486k of data. Please use a search string to limit the size of the
file that will be returned to you. For instance, "LIST GLOBAL CHEM" will
return a description of all the lists related to chemistry (lists whose name
or topic contains the string "CHEM").
```

Chances are that you'll find a mailing list that will interest you. Have fun!

Configuring `procmail` and Writing Recipes to Fight Spam

We're all used to getting junk mail or telemarketing calls. Day after day, we receive offers for credit cards, home equity loans, new long-distance service, or great deals on prime cuts of pot roast at the local food market. You can do something about unwanted postal mail, junk faxes, and telemarketing calls, but there's no current regulation regarding junk email.

You can, however, use `procmail`, which is found under the `/usr/bin` directory, to filter your incoming mail. You'll need to create a directory, create several files, write a small script, and customize how your incoming mail is handled by writing short filters, or `procmail` recipes. It will only take you a minute or so to set up your system to organize incoming mail and dispose of junk mail.

The first step is to create a text file, called `.procmailrc`, in your home directory. Then, type in the following, specifying the name of your mail directory (if you use `pine`, the directory is `mail`), the location of the `.procmail` directory (which you'll soon create), and the name of your `procmail` filter file:

```
MAILDIR=$HOME/mail
PMDIR=$HOME/.procmail
INCLUDERC=$HOME/rc.mailfilter
```

Save this file. Next, create a text file called `.forward` in your home directory. This file should contain the following line:

```
"|IFS=' ' && exec /usr/bin/procmail -f- || exit 75 #username"
```

This command line controls `procmail`, and you should use your username instead of *`username`*. Now, make your `.forward` file world-readable, and your home directory world-searchable with the chmod command. See the following example (making sure you're in your home directory):

```
# chmod 644 .forward
# chmod a+x .
```

You're almost done. Now, with the mkdir command, create a directory called .procmail, change directories into it, and create a text file called rc.mailfilter.

This file will contain your procmail filters, or recipes. While these recipes can be extremely complex (so complex in fact, that you can write your own mail delivery service), this section presents simple recipes to get you started.

First, examine a sample message's mail headers (which contain the From:, To:, or Subject: lines). The British MG sports cars digest has the following subject line in each message:

```
Subject: mgs@autox.team.net digest #905 Mon Nov 17 10:09:07 MST 1997
```

Each digest message can contain almost 100,000 characters, and is sent twice a day, so it would be nice to have all these digests go into their own mail folder, which you'll call mgdigest. So, you'll enter

```
:0:
*^Subject:.*digest
mgdigest
```

This small recipe will save any incoming message with a subject line containing the word digest into a mail file called mgdigest in your mail program's mail directory. Note that you don't have to create this mail file yourself. It will be created for you when you first retrieve mail, and procmail finds a match. You can also use another recipe to have all mail files from your friends saved to a specific folder, for example:

```
:0:
*^From:.*aol.com
AOL
```

"OK," you're asking, "but what about junk email?" Well, you know what you want to do with junk email—trash it! For Linux users, there's a special place to which you can send junk email: the old bit bucket, /dev/null. So if you get an unwanted message from a place like hotlips4u.com, you can send this type of junk to the boneyard with

```
:0:
^From:.*hotlips4u.com
/dev/null
```

The mail message won't be stored on your hard drive, and you won't have to bother with any mail from that address again. Using this approach is simplistic, however, and if you get a lot of junk mail, you may want to experiment with more complex recipes, which can filter out everything except people with whom you want to exchange mail.

If you would like to add some more features to your `procmail` service, read the `procmailrc` manual page. For a great selection of `procmail` recipes, see the `procmailex` manual page, which details numerous examples, ranging from the simple to the complex.

Want more information about `procmail`, writing `procmail` recipes, and filtering your mail? Look for Nancy McGough's Filtering Mail FAQ, which is posted regularly to the `comp.mail.misc`, `comp.mail.elm`, `comp.mail.pine`, and other newsgroups. Reading news from Usenet also happens to be the next hour's subject!

PART III

Hour 12

Configuring Internet News

This hour shows you how to set up your Linux system to handle electronic newsgroups. You'll learn about Usenet news, the world's largest international electronic bulletin board. You'll also explore various programs you can use to read, post, and respond to Usenet posts or messages.

Reading Usenet News

This section introduces you to Usenet news and shows you how to set up and use the `tin` and `slrn` newsreader programs during your PPP connection. Reading news can be an endless source of amusement, help, and even frustration (especially if the "signal-to-noise" ratio is low).

Usenet newsgroups are organized in a hierarchy, usually by topic or type of discussion. For example, the Linux newsgroups are generally organized under the `comp` topic. Here is a partial list of Linux newsgroups:

```
comp.os.linux.announce
comp.os.linux.hardware
comp.os.linux.misc
```

```
comp.os.linux.networking
comp.os.linux.setup
comp.os.linux.x
```

This shows that Linux subjects, such as setup, hardware, and X11 are organized under the topics of computers, operating systems, and Linux. You'll find many other subjects organized the same way.

Although there's no guarantee you'll find the exact subject you're looking for, chances are you'll easily find a newsgroup discussing a subject you're interested in.

Today, there are dozens of different Usenet software transport programs and newsreaders, and more than 30,000 different newsgroups.

All newsreaders offer the basic functions of

- Subscribing or unsubscribing to newsgroups
- Browsing messages and reading follow-up messages (threads)
- Directly mailing a reply to the author of a message
- Posting a follow-up message to a newsgroup message
- Saving the contents of a message (usually to a directory called `News` in your home directory)

Both `tin` and `slrn` read a newsgroup index file called `.newsrc`, which is normally located in your home directory. Although you can start both `tin` and `slrn`, and tell the programs to retrieve a complete list of active newsgroups from your ISP's news server, you'll waste lots of time while the programs retrieve the list (nearly 30,000 at the time of this writing). Instead, create the `.newsrc` file with your favorite text editor, and then enter the newsgroups you want to browse, for example:

```
news.announce.newusers:
comp.os.linux.announce:
comp.os.linux.development.apps:
comp.os.linux.development.system:
comp.os.linux.hardware:
comp.os.linux.misc:
comp.os.linux.networking:
comp.os.linux.setup:
comp.os.linux.x:
comp.windows.x:
comp.windows.x.i386unix:
rec.autos.antique:
alt.humor.best-of-usenet:
rec.humor:
```

Notice that the list does not have to be in alphabetical order. You must have a colon following the newsgroup. If you type in a newsgroup not supported by your ISP, both `tin` and `slrn` will ignore the name, and both programs will display the list of newsgroups in the same order in which you typed them in the `.newsrc` file.

Developing your own list of newsgroups will speed up your newsreading considerably. Read on to learn more about `tin` and `slrn`.

Reading Usenet News with the `tin` Newsreader

Iain Lea's news reader, `tin`, which is found under the `/usr/bin` directory, is a full-screen newsreader that reads a list of newsgroups from the `.newsrc` file in your home directory. The `tin` reader is easy to use (see Figure 12.1). You can navigate through its display with cursor keys, read messages with the Enter key, and reply with a single keystroke.

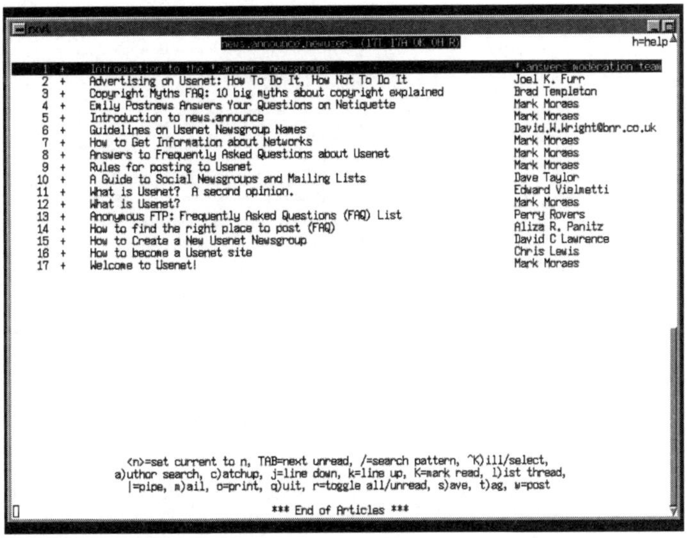

Figure 12.1.
The `tin` newsreader displays newsgroup messages in a cursor-driven list.

In order to read Usenet news with `tin`, you must tell the program the name of your ISP's NNTP, or news server. You should have received this information when you signed up for service. Once you have the name, you can tell `tin` the NNTP server name in at least two ways, one of which will work with `tin` and `slrn`.

First, make sure you're logged in as root. Then, using a text editor, either edit or create a file called `nntpserver` under the `/etc` directory. There's no special format to the file, and all you have to do is put in the name of the news server, for example:

```
# cat /etc/nntpserver
news.staffnet.com
```

Then, connect with your ISP, and call `tin` with this command line:

```
# tin -nqr
```

12

This tells the `tin` program that you want it to only load newsgroups from your `.newsrc` file, do a quick start without checking for any new newsgroups, and finally, to read your news remotely from your ISP's NNTP server. Once `tin` reads the groups, and gathers any new news, it will display the groups (see Figure 12.2). You can read a group by using the cursor to select a group, and hitting the Enter key.

Figure 12.2.
Reading a newsgroup's messages with the `tin` *newsreader.*

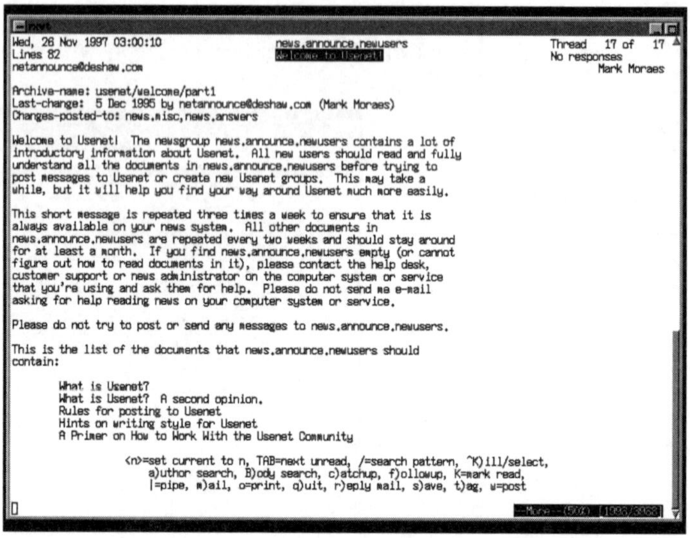

You can also tell `tin` your ISP's NNTP server by using an environment variable, `NNTPSERVER`. Creating environment variables is discussed in Hour 6, "Using the Shell." One way to create the `NNTPSERVER` variable, if you always use the bash shell, is to log in as root, then edit a file named `profile` in the `/etc` directory. Enter the following into the file, and make sure the `NNTPSERVER` variable is placed in the `export` statement, for example:

```
NNTPSERVER='news.staffnet.com'
export NNTPSERVER
```

You can then try to read the variable into your environment with

```
# source /etc/profile
```

After trying to source this file, you can check for the `NNTPSERVER` variable by using the `printenv` command, or you can log out and log back in, and check again. Once you've defined `NNTPSERVER`, this will work for `tin` and `slrn`.

You can configure other aspects of `tin`, such as the default editor to use while posting or replying to messages. See the `tinrc` file under the `.tin` directory in your home directory for details, and read the `tin` manual page for the options.

Reading Usenet News with the `slrn` Newsreader

The `slrn` newsreader, by John E. Davis, found under the `/usr/bin` directory, is a newsreader like `tin`. But `slrn` has some nifty features not supported by the `tin` program:

- Message headers and messages are displayed at the same time.
- Extensive custom colorization of different parts of the display and messages is available.
- Mouse-cursor–aware mode
- Different NNTP servers may be specified on the command line.

Figure 12.3 shows the `slrn` screen.

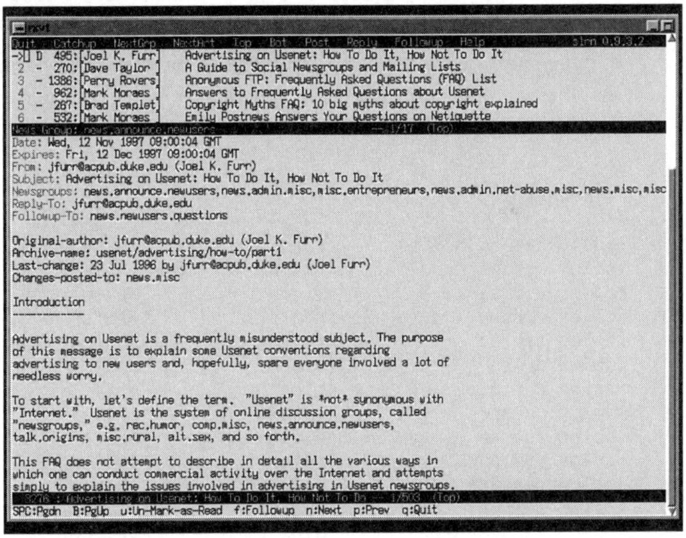

Figure 12.3.
The `slrn` newsreader features mouse-aware menus and split-screen viewing of messages and message contents.

The `slrn` program features a split display once you're reading messages in a newsgroup. You can also run `slrn` without specifying an `NNTPSERVER` variable with the `-h` command-line option, for example:

```
# slrn -h news.staffnet.com
```

12

You'll also be able to browse quickly once you learn most of its keystroke commands.

> **Just a Minute**
>
> Here's a tip on an undocumented feature you won't find in the `slrn` manual page: You can scroll up and down through messages by using the left or right mouse buttons of your mouse. You can also use `slrn` in a menu-driven mode by enabling mouse support. This is handy if you run `slrn` in an `xterm` or `rxvt` window under X11.

When you start `slrn`, the program will look under the `/usr/lib/slrn` directory for a file called `slrn.rc`, which contains system wide defaults for the program. You should copy this program as `.slrnrc` to your home directory, and make your changes to this file. Although there are many different customizations you can perform, a few are covered here to get you started.

To enable mouse support, look in your `.slrnrc` file for

```
% Enable xterm mouse support: 1 to enable, 0 to disable
  set mouse 0
```

Change `set mouse 0` to `set mouse 1` to enable menu- and mouse-driven modes in `slrn`. Another change you may want to make is how `slrn` displays messages and menus. Look for the Colors section of the `.slrnrc` file:

```
%---------------------------------------------------
% Colors
%---------------------------------------------------
color header_number     "black"         "white"
color header_name       "black"         "white"
color normal            "black"         "white"
color error             "red"           "white"
color status            "yellow"        "blue"
color group             "blue"          "white"
color article           "blue"          "white"
color cursor            "black"         "white"
color author            "blue"          "white"
color subject           "black"         "white"
color headers           "black"         "white"
color menu              "yellow"        "blue"
color menu_press        "blue"          "yellow"
color tree              "red"           "white"
color quotes            "red"           "white"
color thread_number     "blue"          "white"
color high_score        "red"           "white"
color signature         "red"           "white"
color description       "blue"          "white"
color tilde             "black"         "white"
```

These lines are in the format of display item, foreground color, and background color.

According to the slrn manual page, these colors can be

```
black          gray
red            brightred
green          brightgreen
brown          yellow
blue           brightblue
magenta        brightmagenta
cyan           brightcyan
lightgray      white
```

With a little bit of work, you can devise your own display. The slrn newsreader is a flexible, customizable program.

JUST A MINUTE

The pine program is almost two programs in one. Although most people will use pine primarily as a mail handler, pine can be an efficient way to read news, and can save you disk space if you don't have much room on your hard drive for other programs (especially if you're using a laptop computer).

You've already seen how you specify your ISP's news server in the .pinerc file, or through pine's setup and config commands. To read news, make sure you're connected to your ISP, then run pine. Cursor to the folder list view, press the Enter key, then cursor down to the news collection expanded list and tap the Enter key.

Part III

Hour 13

Internet Downloading and Browsing

This hour introduces you to programs you'll use to get information and programs from the Internet. I'll assume that you have signed up with an Internet Service Provider (ISP) and that you have configured your Linux system to start and stop Point-to-Point Protocol network connections.

JUST A MINUTE

> If you already have an account with a local ISP, but have not configured your Linux system to connect to the Internet, read Hour 10, "Connecting to the Internet," for instructions.

I'll first introduce you to two Internet file transfer programs, and then cover some of the many World Wide Web browsers you'll find for Linux.

Using File Transfer Protocol Programs to Get Files

There are several ways to retrieve files from other computers on the Internet. You can use email or a Web browser, but if you're interested in just getting files into your computer, you can use the `ftp` (file transfer) program. The `ftp` program is one of the oldest programs to support the standard File Transfer Protocol, or FTP, and was the original program designed to transfer files. The FTP protocol lets you send and receive files interactively with the `get` and `put` commands.

The next section shows you how to use two FTP transfer programs, `ftp` and `ncftp`.

Retrieving Files with the `ftp` Command

The `ftp` command, found under the `/usr/bin` directory, has five different command-line options, but is most often used with a hostname, or name of remote computer, for example:

```
# ftp ftp.mcp.com
```

This command line specifies that you want to connect to the `ftp` server at Macmillan Publishing. You don't have to specify a hostname on the command line, because you can run the `ftp` program interactively, repeatedly connecting and disconnecting to different computers. The `ftp` command has more than 70 different built-in commands, including a help facility. This hour doesn't cover all the different commands, but you can get more information about these commands by reading the `ftp` program's manual page, or by using the built-in `help` command.

Some of the commands you'll most likely use, especially when all you want to do is retrieve some programs or source code from Linux sites, are

`!`—Prompt for and run a shell command. This is a handy way to view the contents of files, delete files you've just downloaded, or check on how much hard drive space you have left.

`ascii`—Download any specified files in text form.

`binary`—Download any specified files in binary form. You must use this command before downloading most compressed Linux files.

`bye`—Close any open connection, and exit the `ftp` program.

`cd`—Change directories, for example:

```
> cd ..
```

`close`—Close the current connection.

`get`—Download a specific file from the current directory to your current directory, for example:

```
> get killbarney.tgz
```

`ls`—List files or directories in the current directory.

`mget`—Download several files, one after another, that match a specified pattern, for example:

```
> mget kill*.tgz
```

`open`—Opens a connection to a specified host, for example:

```
> open ftp.mcp.com
```

For example, to run the `ftp` command interactively, all you have to do is type

```
# ftp
ftp> help
Commands may be abbreviated.  Commands are:

!               debug           mdir            sendport        site
$               dir             mget            put             size
account         disconnect      mkdir           pwd             status
append          exit            mls             quit            struct
ascii           form            mode            quote           system
bell            get             modtime         recv            sunique
binary          glob            mput            reget           tenex
bye             hash            newer           rstatus         tick
case            help            nmap            rhelp           trace
cd              idle            nlist           rename          type
cdup            image           ntrans          reset           user
chmod           lcd             open            restart         umask
close           ls              prompt          rmdir           verbose
cr              macdef          passive         runique         ?
delete          mdelete         proxy           send
ftp> help exit
exit            terminate ftp session and exit
ftp> help bye
bye             terminate ftp session and exit
ftp> bye
#
```

CAUTION

> If you have enforced disk quotas for users of your Linux system, users can easily exceed the quota you've enforced, especially when downloading large files. One way to help users on a quota-enforced system is to tell them to first change directory to the `/tmp` directory if using `ftp`, and to then open a connection to download any large files. The `/tmp` directory will be cleaned out by your housekeeping `crontab` routines later on to make more room on your hard drive, but your users will be able to download large files without hitting hard limits on their quotas.

To demonstrate the `ftp` program in action, I'll show you a sample session:

```
# ftp ftp.mcp.com
Connected to ftp.mcp.com.
220 iq-mcp FTP server (Version wu-2.4(3) Thu Jun 12 14:38:11 EST 1997) ready.
Name (ftp.mcp.com:bball): anonymous
331 Guest login ok, send your complete e-mail address as password.
Password:
230 Guest login ok, access restrictions apply.
Remote system type is UNIX.
Using binary mode to transfer files.
ftp> ls
200 PORT command successful.
150 Opening ASCII mode data connection for /bin/ls.
total 14
drwxr-xr-x   7 root     other        512 Dec  4 20:01 .
drwxr-xr-x   7 root     other        512 Dec  4 20:01 ..
d--x--x--x   3 root     other        512 Dec  4 18:44 bin
dr-xr-xr-x   2 root     other        512 Dec  4 18:44 dev
d--x--x--x   2 root     other        512 Dec  4 21:13 etc
drwxr-xr-x  31 672      anon-ftp    1024 Dec  8 14:17 pub
dr-xr-xr-x   3 root     other        512 Dec  4 20:01 usr
226 Transfer complete.
ftp> cd pub
250 CWD command successful.
ftp> cd software
250 CWD command successful.
ftp> ls
200 PORT command successful.
150 Opening ASCII mode data connection for /bin/ls.
total 168
drwxrwxr-x  24 232      19          1024 Dec  4 19:40 .
drwxr-xr-x  31 672      anon-ftp    1024 Dec  8 14:17 ..
drwxrwxr-x   3 232      19           512 Dec  4 19:34 CAD
drwxrwxr-x   3 232      19          1024 Dec  4 19:36 Internet
-rw-rw-r--   1 232      19          7570 Jul  9 14:58 MANUALIN.TXT
drwxrwxr-x   2 232      19           512 Dec  4 19:36 WordProc
-rwxrwxr-x   1 232      19         47981 Jun 29  1995 aaplay.exe
drwxrwxr-x   2 232      19           512 Dec  4 19:40 adstuff
drwxrwxr-x   2 232      19           512 Dec  4 19:40 brady
drwxrwxr-x   2 232      19          1536 Dec  4 19:36 database
```

```
-rwxr-xr-x   1 19       19            42 Dec 20  1996 erp
drwxrwxr-x   2 232      19          1024 Dec  4 19:37 games
drwxrwxr-x   4 232      19           512 Dec  4 19:37 general
drwxrwxr-x   2 232      19          1024 Dec  4 19:37 graphics-dtp
drwxrwxr-x   2 232      19           512 Dec  4 19:37 macintosh
drwxrwxr-x   2 232      19           512 Dec  4 19:40 mlr
drwxrwxr-x   3 232      19           512 Dec  4 19:37 multimedia
lrwxrwxrwx   1 root     other         13 Dec  4 19:34 net-cd -> ../que/net-cd
drwxrwxr-x   2 232      19           512 Dec  4 19:37 network-comms
drwxrwxr-x   2 232      19          1024 Dec  4 19:37 news-releases
drwxrwxr-x   2 232      19           512 Dec  4 19:38 operating-sys
drwxrwxr-x  35 232      19          2560 Dec  4 19:39 programming
drwxrwxr-x   2 232      19           512 Dec  4 19:39 spreadsheet
drwxrwxr-x   2 232      19           512 Dec  4 19:40 temp
drwxrwxr-x   2 232      19          1024 Dec  4 19:39 utilities
drwxrwxr-x   2 232      19           512 Dec  4 19:40 vrml
drwxrwxr-x   2 232      19           512 Dec  4 19:40 windows-95
drwxrwxr-x   9 232      19           512 Dec  4 19:40 windows-utilities
226 Transfer complete.
ftp> cd operating-sys
250 CWD command successful.
ftp> ls
200 PORT command successful.
150 Opening ASCII mode data connection for /bin/ls.
total 21836
drwxrwxr-x   2 232      19           512 Dec  4 19:38 .
drwxrwxr-x  24 232      19          1024 Dec  4 19:40 ..
-rw-rw-r--   1 232      19       1061074 Jun  5  1997 bjsa200.exe
-rw-rw-r--   1 232      19           660 Jun  5  1997 bjsa200.txt
-rwxr-xr-x   1 19       19       1228592 Apr 22  1997 diskeepr.zip
-rw-rw-r--   1 232      19        308263 Aug 21 20:26 err6000.exe
-rw-r--r--   1 232      19         35930 Dec 20  1994 inidoc.zip
-rw-r--r--   1 232      19        301250 Dec 20  1994 iniexe.zip
-rw-rw-r--   1 232      19        491792 Jul  1 19:37 oleaut32.dll
-rw-rw-r--   1 232      19         47616 Nov 21  1995 os2errat.doc
-rw-rw-r--   1 232      19       1990677 Jun  5  1997 patch.zip
-rwxr-xr-x   1 19       19         29660 Apr 22  1997 pg.exe
-rw-r--r--   1 232      19         15583 Dec 20  1994 shutdo.zip
-rwxr-xr-x   1 19       19          5265 Apr 22  1997 stub.exe
-rwxr-xr-x   1 19       19       1406264 Apr 22  1997 tapedisk.exe
-rw-rw-r--   1 232      19         12968 Apr 23  1996 uslinux.txt
-rwxr-xr-x   1 19       19       4139587 Apr 22  1997 website.exe
226 Transfer complete.
ftp> ascii
200 Type set to A.
ftp> get uslinux.txt
local: uslinux.txt remote: uslinux.txt
200 PORT command successful.
150 Opening ASCII mode data connection for uslinux.txt (12968 bytes).
226 Transfer complete.
13294 bytes received in 5.86 secs (2.2 Kbytes/sec)
ftp>
ftp> bye
221 Goodbye.
#
```

This sample session shows that I specified the `ftp` server at Macmillan as the host computer I wanted to connect to and retrieve files. By convention, many system administrators create and maintain a user called `ftp`, and a directory called `ftp`, which, although it does not require no password, does require you to enter a mail address in the form of `user@somewhere.com`. The location of the `ftp` directory may differ, but if you examine the `/etc/passwd` file for your Linux system, you'll find an `ftp` user with a directory under the `/home` directory, for example:

```
ftp:*:14:50:FTP User:/home/ftp:
```

This `/etc/passwd` entry shows that people can connect to your system (if you're on a network or have enabled user dial-in logins). By convention, when you use the `ftp` program to connect to other computers, you enter your username at the Name: prompt as `anonymous`, followed by your email address as the password.

You can see that, after I logged in, I first listed the current directory, then changed directory to the `pub` directory. After listing that directory, I changed to the `software` directory, then changed directories to the `operating-sys` directory. If I had known the full path to the file I wanted, I could have specified that pathname in a single `cd` command, for example:

```
> cd pub/software/operating-sys
```

I then enabled the `ftp` command's ASCII transfer mode, retrieved the file `uslinux.txt` with the `get` command, and then logged off and exited the `ftp` program with the `bye` command. As you can see, using the `ftp` command is not hard and is an easy way to retrieve files.

You can also open an anonymous `ftp` connection to your own computer to demonstrate how `ftp` works without having an Internet connection available. You can specify the hostname of your computer, which you can get with the `hostname` command, or by using your computer's Internet Protocol address, for example:

```
# hostname
localhost.localdomain
# ftp localhost
Connected to localhost.
220 localhost FTP server (Version wu-2.4.2-academ[BETA-12]
➥(1) Wed Mar 5 12:37:21 EST 1997) ready.
Name (localhost:bball): anonymous
331 Guest login ok, send your complete e-mail address as password.
Password:
230 Guest login ok, access restrictions apply.
Remote system type is UNIX.
Using binary mode to transfer files.
ftp> ls
200 PORT command successful.
150 Opening ASCII mode data connection for /bin/ls.
total 6
drwxr-xr-x   6 root     root          1024 Nov 28 21:25 .
drwxr-xr-x   6 root     root          1024 Nov 28 21:25 ..
d--x--x--x   2 root     root          1024 Nov 28 21:25 bin
```

```
d--x--x--x   2 root     root          1024 Nov 28 21:25 etc
drwxr-xr-x   2 root     root          1024 Nov 28 21:25 lib
dr-xr-sr-x   2 root     ftp           1024 Mar  3  1997 pub
226 Transfer complete.
ftp > bye
221 Goodbye.
#
```

You can also log into other computers using an assigned username and password, but for this example, I'll use my own system:

```
# ftp 127.0.0.0
Connected to 127.0.0.0.
220 localhost FTP server (Version wu-2.4.2-academ[BETA-12](1)
➥ Wed Mar 5 12:37:21 EST 1997) ready.
Name (127.0.0.0:bball): bball
331 Password required for bball.
Password:
230 User bball logged in.
Remote system type is UNIX.
Using binary mode to transfer files.
ftp> ls documents
200 PORT command successful.
150 Opening ASCII mode data connection for /bin/ls.
total 62
drwxrwxr-x   2 bball    bball         1024 Dec 11 08:46 .
drwxrwxr-x  14 bball    bball         2048 Dec 11 13:39 ..
-rw-rw-r--   1 bball    bball         5289 Oct 23 12:46 FCFCU102397.aw
-rw-rw-r--   1 bball    bball         5381 Nov 24 15:00 IRS112497.aw
-rw-rw-r--   1 bball    bball         4693 Dec  3 20:37 book.as
-rw-rw-r--   1 bball    bball         5852 Oct 30 10:13 compound.as
-rw-r--r--   1 bball    bball        14820 Dec 11 08:46 invest.as
-rw-r--r--   1 bball    bball         6288 Dec  7 20:39 invest.dif
-rw-r--r--   1 bball    bball         2883 Dec  7 20:40 invest.txt
-rw-rw-r--   1 bball    bball         9436 Dec  7 20:41 sc.txt
226 Transfer complete.
ftp> bye
221 Goodbye.
#
```

In this example, after logging in with my system username and password, I ended up in my home directory, instead of the default `ftp` directory. If you have an open PPP connection with your ISP, and other users know your computer's IP address, you and other users can access your system's files and upload and download files.

13

Downloading with the `ncftp` Command

The `ncftp` command, found under the `/usr/bin` directory, is much like the original `ftp` command, but features some unique improvements, such as

- A visual mode, with colors
- A status bar, with separate command line and scrolling window

- Visual status of downloading—a progress meter to show elapsed and remaining time for file downloads
- Bookmarks and a bookmark editor, so you can use abbreviated hostnames of computers

Like the `ftp` command, `ncftp` also has built-in help. The `ncftp` command, by Mike Gleason of NCEMRSoft, also sports a number of interesting command-line options. If you know the hostname of the computer and the complete path to a desired file, you can retrieve the file with a single command line, for example:

```
# ncftp -a ftp://ftp.mcp.com/pub/software/operating-sys/uslinux.txt
# nctp -a ftp.mcp.com:/pub/software/operating-sys/uslinux.txt
```

Both command lines will FTP to the `ftp.mcp.com` host, log in anonymously, then retrieve the `uslinux.txt` file. This is a handy way to retrieve known files from remote computers. These command lines may also be used in shell scripts, or combined with pipes to other commands to process the incoming files. You can, for example, automatically translate incoming graphics files and save them in a specified directory:

```
# ncftp -c ftp.wx.com:/pub/wxmaps/east/1230.gif | gif2tiff
➥ >/home/ftp/pub/wxmaps/today.tiff
```

This example (using a fictional `ftp` server) downloads a `.GIF` format graphic, then translates the graphic into `.TIFF` format and puts it into your system's `ftp` area. You can use this approach to download files automatically, especially when used in a `crontab` file. (For details about using `crontab`, see Hours 24, "Scheduling," and 18, "Personal Productivity Tools.")

You'll also find the `ncftp` status bar helpful when interactively downloading files. Although I can't show you the animation of the progress meter, when you use `ncftp` to download files, you'll get information on how the downloading is going, for example:

```
wustl> get app-defaults.color

Receiving file: app-defaults.color
100%  0 ==================================> 6583 bytes. ETA:  0:00
app-defaults.color:  6583 bytes received in 5.77 seconds, 1.11 kB/s.
ftp.wustl.edu   /packages/NCSA/Web/Mosaic/Unix/binaries/app-defaults
wustl>
```

This shows a completed download of the X11 application defaults file for the Mosaic Web browser. If you'd like to get the latest version of the `ncftp` command, you'll find it at `ftp.probe.net`, in the `/pub/ncftp` directory.

Browsing the World Wide Web with Linux Browsers

This section introduces you to half a dozen Web browsers for Linux. You'll find two of these browsers on the CD-ROM included with this book. The other four, Red Baron, Grail, Mosaic, and Netscape Communicator, must be retrieved from their home sites on the Internet.

This book doesn't have enough room to cover these browsers in detail. If you're interested in learning about Web browsers or writing your own Web pages, I suggest you look at the following books:

HTML by Example, by Todd Staufer, Que

Using HTML, by Mark Brown, John Jung, and Tom Savola, Que

Fast Browsing with the Lynx Command

The Lynx browser, sponsored by the University of Kansas, does not support graphics, sound, or any of the other plug-in features of today's modern Web browsers. You'll really like Lynx anyway because it's fast, efficient, and does not take up a lot of disk space.

Lynx was designed to run on regular displays, or terminals, so you don't need to run the X Window System in order to use it. This program is ideal for quickly browsing Web pages to get the information you need without the "World Wide Wait" of too-large graphics, or animations that just waste bandwidth.

The Lynx browser has 66 different command-line options, but it's easy to use. If you've properly set up your system, and have started your PPP connection, you can start browsing by specifying a Uniform Resource Locator (Web address) on the command line, for example:

```
# lynx http://www.mcp.com
```

Figure 13.1 shows the Lynx browser.

If you need to fine-tune some of the ways the `lynx` command works, you can edit its configuration file, `lynx.cfg`, in the `/usr/lib` directory. I suggest that you make a copy of this file, and copy it to your home directory with `.lynxrc` as the filename. In this file, you can set a number of Lynx features. For example, if you specify the name of your ISP's news server, you can read news:

```
NNTPSERVER:your.ISPnewserver.com
```

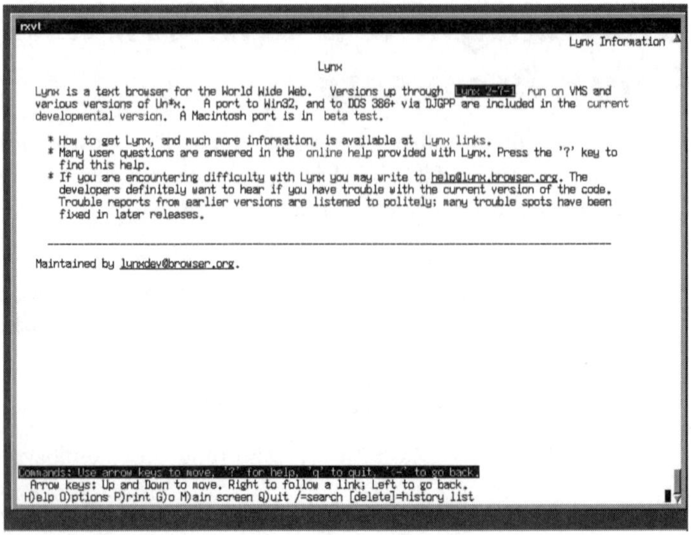

Figure 13.1.
The Lynx text-only Web browser is a compact, efficient program you can use to quickly browse Web pages without waiting for graphics loading.

After you make this change, you can try to browse news with

```
# lynx news://your.ISPnewserver.com
```

You can also use the Lynx browser to retrieve files without browsing. By using this approach, you can automatically research or get information on a regular basis.

```
# lynx http://www.yahoo.com/headlines/news/summary.html -dump >news.raw
```

Lynx will also download files just like other browsers if you press the Enter key while your cursor has a file or link highlighted. The basic navigation keys for this browser are the cursor and the Enter and Tab keys.

For more information about the Lynx browser, see its manual page.

Browsing with the Arena Browser

The Arena browser, found under the `/usr/X11R6/bin` directory, is an X Window System browser now supported by Yggdrasil Computing. New versions of this browser may be found at

```
ftp://ftp.Yggdrasil.com/pub/dist/web/arena
```

The Arena browser unfortunately does not obey any X11 Toolkit options. You can, however, load local HTML files, or specify a Web address on the command line, for example:

```
# arena index.htm
# arena http://www.mcp.com
```

Browsing with the Red Baron Browser

The Red Baron browser is a Web browser from Red Hat Software, Inc. and has most of the features you expect in a browser. You'll need to run the X Window System in order to use this browser.

You can use this browser to display, view, save, and print different Web pages. As with other browsers, you can also download files. However, unlike the Grail and Netscape browsers, Red Baron does not obey X11 Toolkit geometry settings.

If you need help while you're working with Red Baron, you can press the F1 function key on your keyboard. Red Baron will then read in its help files, which are found in the `help` directory under the `/usr/lib/redbaron` directory on your system.

If you find Red Baron similar to Mosaic, that's because it is a variant of the Mosaic browser, compiled to run on Linux systems without Motif libraries present.

Exploring Unique Features of the Grail Browser

The Grail browser is unique among Linux browsers. This browser is written using the `python` language, and comes with the full source code.

JUST A MINUTE

> The Grail browser, from the Corporation for National Research Initiatives, is made up of 27,000 lines of interpreted `python` language source code. This browser, like the Lynx browser, is compact and efficient, and takes up only one-tenth of the hard drive space of other browsers such as Red Baron, Mosaic, or Netscape, but offers full HTML 2.0 compatibility, including forms, `python` language applets, graphics, and frames. For more information about the increasingly popular `python` language, browse to
>
> `http://www.python.org`

You can use Grail like any other browser. You can simply type

```
# grail
```

to start the program, which will cause Grail to load, and then try to connect to its home page, `http://grail.cnri.reston.va.us/grail`. If the Grail browser takes up too much of your display, you can use X11 Toolkit geometry settings to have the browser create a smaller window, for example:

```
# grail -g 640x480+0+0
```

This will start the browser in a 640×480 window at the upper-left portion of your screen. You can also specify an initial page to load from the command line, for example:

```
# grail http://www.mcp.com
```

If you would like to set Grail to load a different home page when it starts, you can use the General item of its Preferences menu to set this value, along with eight other default actions.

If you want more information about Grail, browse to the Grail home page.

Getting the Mosaic Browser

The Mosaic browser, from the National Center for Supercomputing Applications, is one of the original Web browsers, and has helped spawn the variety of browsers in use today. If you'd like to explore this browser, you can get the full source code, in which case you'll need to also purchase and install the X11 Motif libraries, and then compile, or build, the browser for Linux. You'll find copies at

```
ftp://ftp.ncsa.uiuc.edu/Mosaic
```

If you don't have Motif, a commercial graphical interface library for the X Window System, you can download a binary, or precompiled, version that doesn't require Motif. You can find a copy at

```
ftp://ftp.wustl.edu/packages/NCSA/Web/Mosaic/Unix/binaries/2.7b
```

Look for the file `Mosaic-linux-static-2.7b5.gz`, which contains everything you need in one 3.2MB compressed file. Once you decompress the file and make it executable, you can run it, for example:

```
# gunzip Mosaic-linux-static-2.7b5.gz
# chmod +x Mosaic-linux-static-2.7b5
# ./Mosaic-linux-static-2.7b5
```

The Mosaic browser will start by creating several resource files in your home directory. You may also use several X11 Toolkit options to start the browser, such as geometry settings, for example:

```
# Mosaic -geometry 640x480
```

This command line will start the Mosaic browser in a 640×480-pixel window on your display. By default, Mosaic will try to automatically load its home page:

```
http://www.ncsa.uiuc.edu/SDG/Software/Xmosaic
```

Although the Mosaic browser is a single, self-contained program, all of its help files are loaded from the Mosaic home page at `www.ncsa.uiuc.edu`.

Setting Up and Downloading with Netscape Communicator

The Netscape Communicator Web browser, by Netscape Communications, is one of the most popular browsers for all computer systems. You can get a copy specifically designed for Linux by navigating to the Netscape home page, `home.netscape.com`, filling out various queries and menus, and downloading the file.

Be prepared for a long wait, however. The current version of the browser, Netscape Communicator 4.03, is more than 10 megabytes in compressed form, and features several additional built-in components, such as mail, composer, and discussions (for reading Usenet news). After you have downloaded the file into a temporary directory, decompress the Netscape package by using the `gunzip` command, and then type

```
# ./ns-install
```

The installation script, `ns-install`, will extract the required files, create any necessary directories, and then install the browser. By default, Netscape and all of its files are installed into a directory called `netscape` under the `/opt` directory. You'll want to take a look at the README file in the `netscape` directory for information on release notes, features, or known problems.

If you'd like to run Netscape from the command line, you can specify its full path, for example:

```
# /opt/netscape/netscape
```

This will run the browser, but a better way to set up Netscape is to create a symbolic link to a more often recognized directory, such as `/usr/local/bin`, for example:

```
# ln -s /opt/netscape/netscape /usr/local/bin/netscape
```

This will create the symbolic link, `netscape`, in a binary directory usually recognized by your `PATH` environment variable.

Netscape, like most well-behaved X11 clients, can also use several X11 Toolkit options. If you don't like the large initial window, you can specify a smaller starting window using geometry settings. You can get a list of Netscape's initial command-line options with the `-help` option.

You'll find several of these options useful. For example, as I've pointed out in this hour, the geometry settings can help reduce the initial window size of your browser. A much better option, especially for laptop users with little screen real estate, is the `-component-bar` option, for example:

```
# netscape -component-bar &
```

This command will run Netscape, but the application, and its additional components, which include mail, discussions, and composer, will appear in a short vertical floating window you can put off to one side of the screen. You can then run the desired component by clicking on one of the icons in the small window.

There's not enough room in this hour to discuss all of the various components and the differences between different versions of Netscape Communicator, but you can find a lot of information by using Netscape's Help menu information system. Unlike Mosaic and other browsers, Netscape installs all of the help files you need to get started on your hard drive. You'll find information about each component, and how to set up and use them, along with a full discussion of HTML page composition.

Figure 13.2 shows the Netscape Communicator browser.

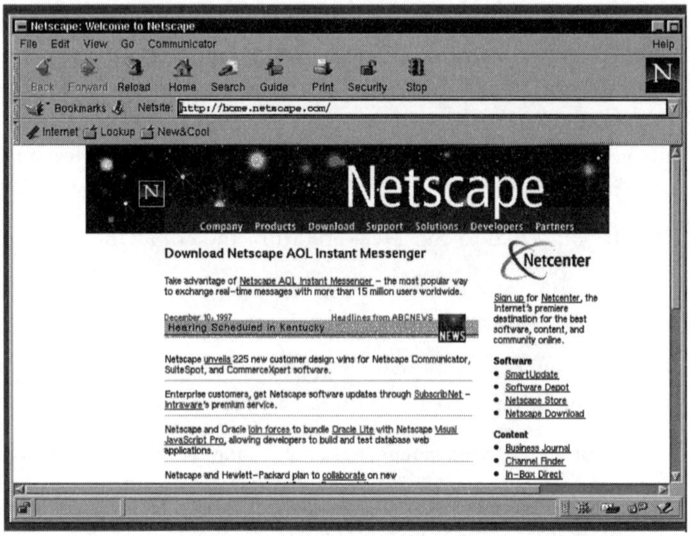

Figure 13.2.
The Netscape Communicator browser, one of the most popular Web browsers, comes in a Linux version and supports most of the popular Netscape plug-ins.

TIME SAVER

> Interestingly enough, Netscape's installation script does not create the required directories or links for Netscape's built-in help files by default. This will result in an error message when you try to use Help for the first time. You can fix this by creating the required link with:
>
> ```
> # ln -s /opt/netscape /usr/local/lib/netscape
> ```
>
> After you've created this symbolically linked directory, you'll be able to use the Help menu in Navigator.

The Linux version of Netscape Communicator also supports many different plug-ins, or additional programs that add features to this browser. Some of these plug-ins allow you to listen to live radio or watch recorded and live video. For more information about using plug-ins with Netscape, browse to

```
http://cgi.netscape.com/eng/mozilla/2.0/extensions/info.cgi
```

For more information about getting the latest audio and video, or RealPlayer, plug-in, browse to

```
http://www.real.com/50/index.html
```

Chatting with Internet Relay Chat

The `irc` (Internet relay chat) command, found under the `/usr/bin` directory, is a program you can use to converse with other people on the Internet. When you run `irc`, you can use the built-in `irc` commands to connect to chat servers, see who is chatting, and set many other options.

The `irc` command has built-in help on more than 110 different commands and topics, many of which have further subtopic help. In order to use this program, you should have an active Internet connection. By default, the `irc` program will try to connect to several default chat servers (other computers supporting IRC). Once you're connected, the screen will split into two parts, with ongoing discussions and responses in the upper portion of the screen. You can use the lower portion of the screen to enter commands to the `irc` program, or send keyboard sentences as messages to different active discussions.

Using IRC is much different from reading and responding to Usenet newsgroups. Discussions and comments are read and sent as you type. You should first browse through the `irc` command's help facility, and read all the available introductory information about the following topics: basics, commands, etiquette, expressions, intro, ircII, menus, news, newuser, and rules.

You can get a list of the help topics by using the `irc /HELP` command, for example:

```
> /HELP newuser
> /HELP etiquette
```

To find out more about participating in `irc` chat sessions, read the built-in help files, and see the documentation for `irc` under the `/usr/doc` directory.

Connecting with Other Computers with the `telnet` Command

You can use the `telnet` command to log in to remote computers to run programs, view files, or download data. The `telnet` command has a number of options, but is generally used with a hostname, or remote computer system's name, on the command line to start a telnet session, for example:

```
# telnet computer.somewhere.com
```

This command will connect you to the remote computer, and you'll receive a login prompt. You'll generally need to have a username and password in order to enter the remote system. For security reasons, few computer systems allow unknown users anonymous access. You may be able to find a list of computer systems providing access by using your favorite search engines, such as through a Web search site.

TIME SAVER

If you've "telnetted" to a remote computer system through an active Internet connection, or through a shell account through a direct dial-in to the computer, you can easily transfer programs using the `sz` and `rz` (send and receive) programs (if those programs are resident on the remote computer). After you've dialed in to a remote computer directly through the phone line, you can transfer files to your computer with: `sz -w 2048 filename.tgz`.

This command will send the file `filename.tgz` using the ZMODEM communications protocol. Your communications program should automatically start receiving the file using this protocol (most communications programs, anyway). If you're connected through an Internet connection, the companion program, `rz`, should be automatically started to receive the file. If not, you can start the `rz` program manually. See the `sz` and `rz` manual pages for more information.

You may also run the `telnet` command in an interactive mode, opening and closing sessions to different remote computers. Like the `ftp` command, the `telnet` command has built-in help. If you'd like to get a list of available help topics, you can use the question mark (`?`), for example:

```
# telnet
telnet> ?
Commands may be abbreviated.  Commands are:

close           close current connection
logout          forcibly logout remote user and close the connection
```

```
display         display operating parameters
mode            try to enter line or character mode ('mode ?' for more)
open            connect to a site
quit            exit telnet
send            transmit special characters ('send ?' for more)
set             set operating parameters ('set ?' for more)
unset           unset operating parameters ('unset ?' for more)
status          print status information
toggle          toggle operating parameters ('toggle ?' for more)
slc             change state of special charaters ('slc ?' for more)
auth            turn on (off) authentication ('auth ?' for more)
z               suspend telnet
environ         change environment variables ('environ ?' for more)
?               print help information
telnet>
```

If you'd like to experiment with this command without an active Internet connection, you can telnet to your own computer from a terminal window under X11, or through the console. As with the `ftp` command, you should first determine the hostname of your computer with the `hostname` command, then either specify the hostname on the `telnet` command line, or run `telnet`, and use its `open` command to start the session, for example:

```
#  hostname
localhost.localdomain
# telnet localhost
Trying 127.0.0.1...
Connected to localhost.
Escape character is '^]'.

Welcome to Red Hat Linux!
Kernel 2.0.31 on an i586
login: bball
Password:
Last login: Fri Dec 12 16:51:44 on tty1
#
```

As you can see, after entering the username and password at the login prompt, you'll be presented with the shell prompt command line.

PART IV

Using Linux Productively

Hour

PART
IV

Hour 14

Text Processing

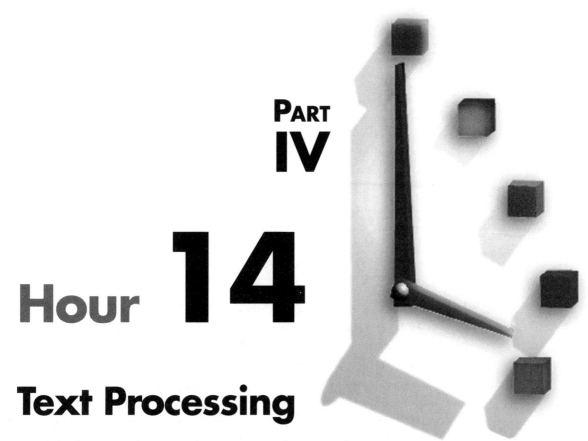

This hour provides you with an overview of some word processing, or text editing, tools for Linux. There's not enough time to cover all of the 100 or more Linux text editors, but this hour provides you with highlights of the features of the tools you'll find on your CD-ROM. It also shows you the basics of using these editors to get you started.

Word Processors in the Linux Environment

Text editors are used by many different types of people. Casual users, writers, programmers, and system administrators will all use a text editor at one time or another in Linux. You'll definitely need to know how to change text files to configure Linux to work the way you want. What follows is an introduction to different word processors, text editors, and text tools you can use during your Linux sessions.

Although how you use a computer dictates what type of software is important and should be installed, most people agree that more than half our time when using a computer is spent using a text editor or word processor. This will change, of course, as computer software interfaces evolve and network communication becomes more integrated into our work environment, but in general, if you're using Linux on your computer at home you're probably going to be word processing or editing files a lot of the time.

The tools in this hour are interactive programs that allow you to enter text, move a cursor, or drop a menu. These programs and related files vary in size from nearly 20 megabytes to less than 200,000 characters. However, there are more than two dozen text tools, including line editors such as the `ed` or `ex` commands, for Linux, that while not interactive, enable you to change, manipulate, or rearrange text.

Features of the emacs Environment

What do you call a text editor that edits text, reads Usenet news, acts as a personal calendar and diary, sends electronic mail, is a programming language interpreter, plays games, is a Linux shell, and more? Why, emacs, of course!

emacs, which stands for editing macros, was originally developed by Richard Stallman, who founded the Free Software Foundation, or FSF. The emacs editor is distributed by the FSF as part of the GNU, or GNU's Not UNIX project. Without a doubt, emacs is the most widely available and fully featured free editor, and runs on more computer systems than any other text editor.

There isn't enough time in this hour (or this book!) to cover all the features of this program. Look at Table 14.1 to find most of the keyboard commands you can use to get started.

Table 14.1. Basic emacs commands and keystroke combinations.

Action	Key Combination
	C-b=hold down Ctrl key, press b
	M-v=hold down Alt key, press v
Cursor backward	C-b
Cursor forward	C-f
Cursor up	C-p
Cursor down	C-n
Go to beginning of line	C-a
Go to end of line	C-e
Page down	C-v

Action	Key Combination
Page up	M-v
Go to end of file	M->
Go to beginning of file	M-<
Delete character	C-d
Delete word	M-d
Delete line	C-k
Undo	C-_
Open File	C-x C-f
Save File	C-x C-s
Save As	C-x C-w
Help	C-h
Tutorial	C-h t
Quit	C-x C-c

emacs has 22 different command-line options, but is easy to start. To run emacs and open a text file for editing, just specify the file's name on the command line. For example,

```
# emacs myfile.txt
```

This loads the editor and opens your file. If you just specify emacs on the command line by itself, the program starts, displays an opening screen, and clears when you touch the keyboard. Starting the emacs tutorial is highly recommended if you're a beginner. Hold down the Ctrl key and press the h key. You'll see a prompt on the emacs command line at the bottom of the screen. Press the t key, and then press Enter to start the tutorial.

If you enter this command at the shell prompt of an X11 terminal window, the X11 version of emacs with mouse and menu support automatically starts (see Figure 14.1). But what if you want to run the console, or non-X11 version of emacs instead? In this case, use a different name for emacs, emacs-nox, or use the `-nw`, or no-window command-line option:

```
# emacs-nox myfile.txt
# emacs -nw myfile.txt
```

Both commands run emacs in your X11 terminal window, although you'll still see a menu bar across the top of the terminal screen. emacs also obeys most X11 Toolkit options, such as geometry settings. Some of the X11 options you may find helpful include the following:

- `geometry 80x24+400+200`—Start in a window 80 characters wide by 24 lines, at screen position X (400) Y (200)
- `fg color`—Set foreground to color

- `bg color`—Set background to color
- `cr color`—Set text cursor to color
- `ms color`—Set mouse cursor to color

Use these options, and others, to customize how emacs looks when started in X11:

```
# emacs -geometry 80x24 -fg black -bg white blue -cr red
```

This starts emacs in a window 80 characters wide by 24 lines high. The text is black, with a white background. The cursor is red, and the mouse cursor is blue. emacs also has 13 different X resource settings you can configure and enter into your `.Xresources` file in your home directory. You also can save editor defaults (such as word wrapping, or fill-mode on) in a file called `.emacs` in your home directory. See the emacs manual page for details.

Figure 14.1.
The emacs editor features split windows, built-in help, a tutorial, and other tools to help you be more productive.

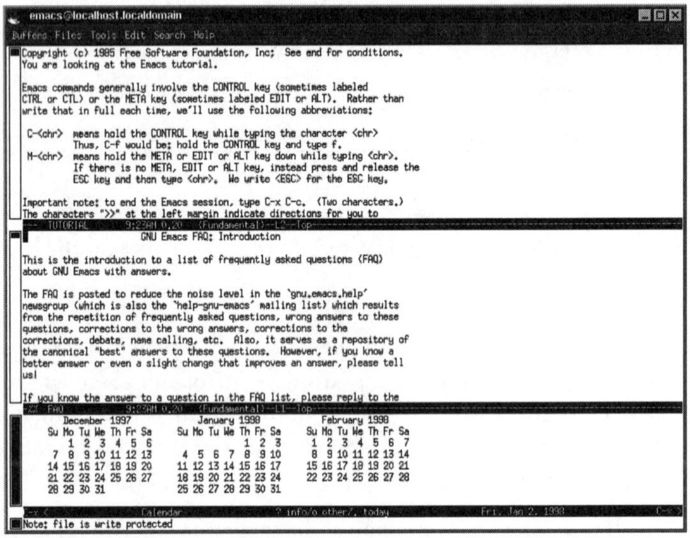

The emacs program for Red Hat Linux comes in four different packages containing various files and utilities. If you install everything, emacs requires more than 35 megabytes of disk space. You can, however, save 15 megabytes if you don't install the Emacs-d package, which is the source for emacs functions, modes, and utilities. If you don't use the X Window system, you can save another 2.5 megabytes by not installing the Emacs-X11 package.

You'll find documentation for emacs under the `/usr/doc`, `/usr/share/emacs/20.2/etc`, and `/usr/info` directory. You also can read the emacs manual page for an overview.

Variants of the Visual Editor Improved—vim

The vim editor, by Bram Moolenaar, is a text editor compatible with the original Berkeley Software Distribution vi editor by Bill Joy. An X11 version is called gvim and sports multiple scrolling windows and menus.

TIME SAVER

> Although the vim `:version` command shows that the systemwide vimrc and gvimrc resource files are located under the `/usr/share/vim` directory, this is not true; you won't find these files installed with the vim package. However, you can create your own resource file after making changes to vim while running the editor, and then using the `:mkvimrc` command. A resource file called `.vimrc` (which you can copy to `.gvimrc`) is created in your home directory, and contains your changes. You can then edit and add your own commands, configurations, and menus to these files.

Several symbolic links are created on your system when you install the vim package from your CD-ROM:

- `/bin/ex -> /bin/vim`
- `/usr/bin/ex -> /bin/vim`
- `/usr/bin/vi -> /bin/vim`
- `/bin/vi -> /bin/vim`
- `/bin/view -> /bin/vim`
- `/usr/X11R6/bin/vimx ->/usr/X11R6/bin/gvim`

The vim editor is used as a replacement for the ex, vi, and view editors (see Figure 14.2). Although vim is a visual editor, supporting features such as cursor movement, when invoked as ex, the vim editor emulates the ex script editor.

The vim editor features a number of improvements over the traditional vi editor, and has 23 different command-line options. In vim you'll find built-in help, split-screen windows, block moves, command-line editing, horizontal scrolling, and word wrap for word processing.

The gvim version of vim, used under the X Window System, has custom colors, window sizes, scrollbars, and menus. You can create your own set of menus containing specific vim commands, and generate different versions of vim by saving your features in different gvim resource files. You can then use the `-u` command-line option to load a custom version.

Creating new menus for gvim is easy. You can, for example, group related macros or custom commands you've created into a separate menu. For details about building custom menus, read the files `vim_menu.txt` and `vim_gui.txt` under the `/usr/share/vim` directory.

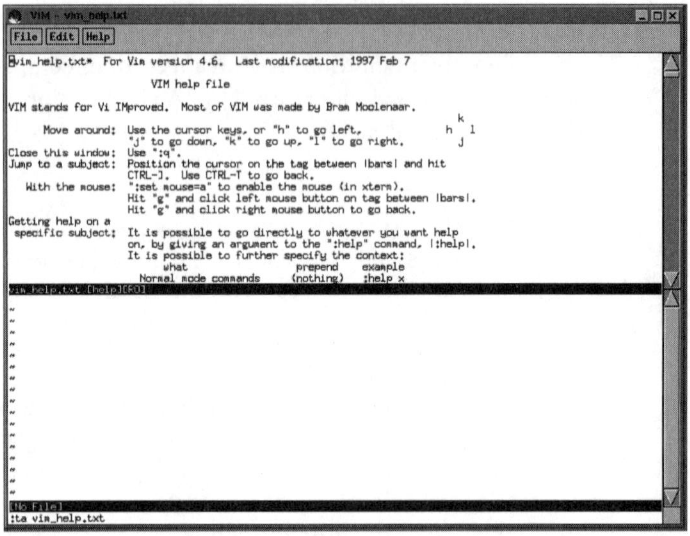

Figure 14.2.
The X11 version of the vim editor, gvim, features split scrollable windows, along with menus you can customize.

Most of the documentation for vim is contained in its built-in help, and there are 21 text files containing extensive instructions in the `/usr/share/vim` directory.

Features of Pine's pico Editor

The pico editor, included with the University of Washington's pine electronic mail program, is a compact, efficient, and easy-to-use editor usually used to compose or reply to e-mail messages. This editor is a nifty replacement for all your editing needs, and is especially handy if you need a reliable text editor, but don't have a lot of hard drive space (for example, on a laptop).

Despite its relatively small size, the pico editor has most of the features you'd expect in a word processor, including

- Word wrap
- Built-in help
- Word search
- Paragraph justification
- Text block move, copy, and delete
- Mouse support
- Spell checking

The pico editor has 16 different command-line options and rudimentary crash protection (see Figure 14.3). It attempts to save any work in progress before exiting, saving your file with a name ending in `.save`, or if unsaved, in a file named `pico.save`.

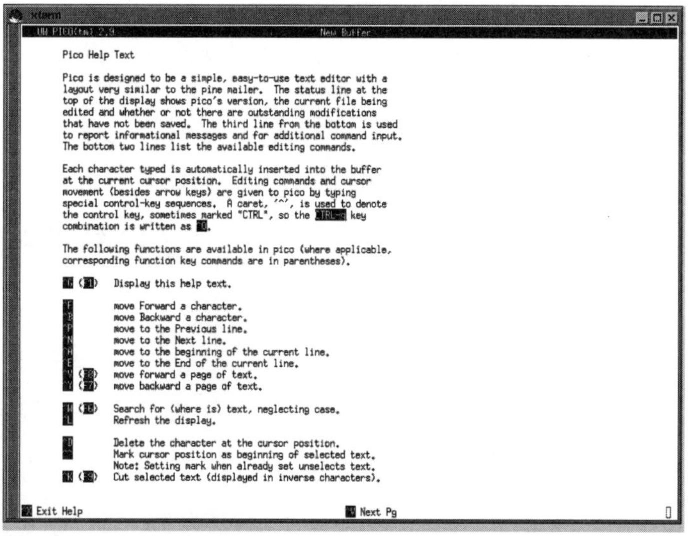

Figure 14.3.
The pico editor, part of the pine electronic mail program distribution, is a compact and easy-to-use editor with nearly all of the basic features of a text editor.

This editor is an excellent choice for your `$EDITOR` environment variable, as it is much friendlier and easier to learn than the default `$EDITOR` variable, which points to the `vi` command. As the root operator, set the `$EDITOR` variable for all users by editing the `/etc/profile` file, and inserting the following line:

```
EDITOR=/usr/bin/pico
```

Also, make sure that the following line contains the word `EDITOR`:

```
export USERNAME ENV PATH EDITOR
```

Save the file, and then enter the following to use the new `$EDITOR` variable:

```
# source /etc/profile
```

After you do this, any Linux command requiring a default system editor will use pico. Also use these changes in the `.bash_profile` file in your home directory.

You'll find documentation for pico in its manual page, or you can use the lynx Web browser to read the pine and pico technical documentation with the following:

```
# lynx /usr/doc/pine-3.96/tech-notes/index.html
```

Five Editors in One—joe

The joe editor, by Joseph H. Allen, comes in five different versions: jmacs, joe, jpico, jstar, and rjoe (see Figure 14.4). The jmacs version emulates the emacs editor. The jpico version emulates the pine mailer's pico text editor. The jstar version uses WordStar-compatible keyboard commands, while the rjoe program is a restricted editor.

joe's configuration files are found under the `/usr/lib/joe` directory. Copy the file called `joerc` to your home directory, save it with the `.joerc` filename, and then edit this file to change joe's help menus, display, and keyboard commands.

You'll find documentation for the joe editor in its manual page (which needs to be spell checked), and by using its built-in help.

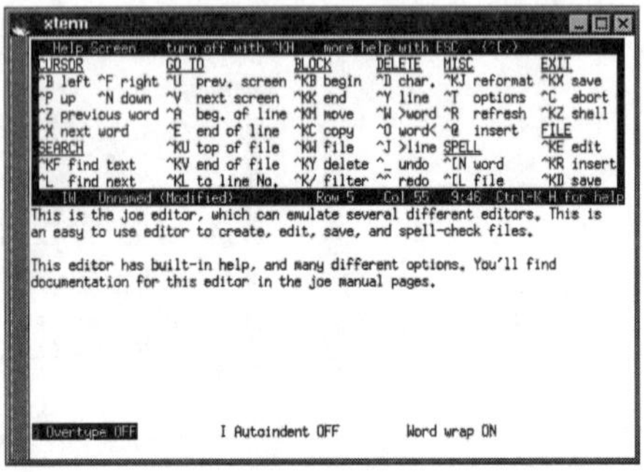

Figure 14.4.
The joe editor comes in five versions, and can emulate the keyboard commands of several different editors, such as pico and emacs.

There is a bug in the version of joe on your CD-ROM that involves proper resizing of the editor in consoles or X11 windows greater than 80 characters by 25 lines in size. Upgrade to the newer version by obtaining and installing the `joe-2.8-10.i386.rpm` file. You can get this file from Red Hat Software by browsing to the following site:

`ftp://ftp.redhat.com/pub/redhat/updates/5.0/i386/`

Configuring the jed Editor

The jed editor, by John E. Davis, comes in two versions: one for the console, and the other tailored for the X Window System (see Figure 14.5).

jed's main configuration files may be found under the `/usr/lib/jed/lib` directory, and you may customize how jed runs by placing preferences in a `.jedrc` file in your home directory. Copy the file `jed.rc` from the `/usr/lib/jed/lib` directory to your home directory as `.jedrc`, and then edit to your taste.

The jed editor has built-in help, but you'll find information about jed under the `/usr/doc` directory, in its manual page, and in info files under the `/usr/lib/jed/info` directory.

Changing Text with sed and Other Filters

Until now, this hour has discussed interactive editors featuring cursor movement, menus, or other keyboard commands. There are several other programs, such as text filters, or stream editors, included with your system that can edit text.

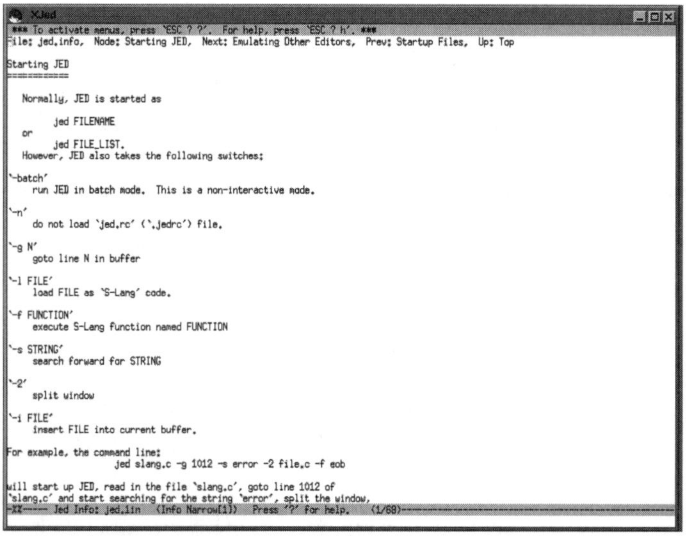

Figure 14.5.
The jed editor has built-in help and text menus you can use as a shortcut to keyboard commands.

If you've read the discussion in Hour 6, "Using the Shell," you'll recall that many Linux programs can use your shell's standard input and standard output. By using shell operators such as pipes or redirection operators, you can use Linux commands to filter text through pipelines to manipulate or change the text stream. There also are several other programs, such as ex and sed, that are specifically designed to edit filtered text, and are called stream editors.

Thanks to the FSF folks, the GNU text-utils package of two dozen text utilities is also installed on your system. This collection includes: cat, cksum, comm, csplit, cut, expand, fmt, fold, head, join, md5sum, nl, od, paste, pr, sort, split, sum, tac, tail, tr, unexpand, uniq, and wc.

Some of these formatting commands, such as fmt and pr, are discussed in the next hour, "Preparing Documents," but this section shows you how you can use several others to manipulate text. For example, the `tr`, or transliterate command, can be used to work on streams of text to translate, squeeze, or delete characters.

The `tr` command works by taking sets, or lists of characters on the command line, and using these sets to translate input text. If you have a document in upper- and lowercase, but would like to change the text to all uppercase, you can tell the `tr` command to do this by specifying the two sets of characters. A public domain software license (found in the `/usr/doc/shadow-utils` directory) is used in the following example.

```
# cat LICENSE
...
1.  You may make and give away verbatim copies of the source form of the
Standard Version of this Package without restriction, provided that you
```

```
duplicate all of the original copyright notices and associated
disclaimers.

2.  You may apply bug fixes, portability fixes and other modifications
derived from the Public Domain or from the Copyright Holder.  A Package
modified in such a way shall still be considered the Standard Version.
...
```

You can change this document to all uppercase with the following:

```
# cat LICENSE ¦ tr a-z A-Z
...
1.  YOU MAY MAKE AND GIVE AWAY VERBATIM COPIES OF THE SOURCE FORM OF THE
STANDARD VERSION OF THIS PACKAGE WITHOUT RESTRICTION, PROVIDED THAT YOU
DUPLICATE ALL OF THE ORIGINAL COPYRIGHT NOTICES AND ASSOCIATED
DISCLAIMERS.

2.  YOU MAY APPLY BUG FIXES, PORTABILITY FIXES AND OTHER MODIFICATIONS
DERIVED FROM THE PUBLIC DOMAIN OR FROM THE COPYRIGHT HOLDER.  A PACKAGE
MODIFIED IN SUCH A WAY SHALL STILL BE CONSIDERED THE STANDARD VERSION.
...
```

The document has been piped, using the `cat` command, through the `tr` command, specifying that you'd like the set of lowercase letters, from a to z, to be translated to uppercase, or A to Z. The `tr` command can also be used to translate individual characters. For example, you'll notice that two spaces are used following each number and a period in the example text. You can replace multiple occurrences of characters with a single character by using the `-s`, or squeeze command-line option:

```
# cat COPYING ¦ tr -s " "
...
1. You may make and give away verbatim copies of the source form of the
Standard Version of this Package without restriction, provided that you
duplicate all of the original copyright notices and associated
disclaimers.
...
```

As you can see, the two spaces have been replaced with a single space. The `tr` command also filters input to other commands, such as `cut`, to quickly generate custom reports. For example, if you don't need all the information from the `ls` command's `-l`, or long format listing, and only want certain columns of the output, you can get any column you want by filtering the listing through several pipes:

```
# ls -l
...
-rw-r--r--   1 root     root         4244 May  5  1997 CENSORSHIP
-rw-r--r--   1 root     root         3315 Jun  2  1997 CHARSETS
-rw-r--r--   1 root     root        12794 Jun  2  1997 CODINGS
-rw-r--r--   1 root     root         4976 Jun  9  1993 COOKIES
-rw-r--r--   1 root     root        17989 Sep 19 22:01 COPYING
-rw-r--r--   1 root     root         5595 Jun 18  1995 DEBUG
-r--r--r--   1 root     root         5633 Sep 19 22:01 DISTRIB
```

```
-rw-r--r--    1 root     root       955298 Nov  7 10:33 DOC-20.2.1
-rw-r--r--    1 root     root       131199 May 17  1997 FAQ
-r--r--r--    1 root     root        11494 Sep 19 22:01 FTP
...
```

This is a lot of information, but if you only want the permissions, size, and name of each file, you can quickly generate a custom listing with the following:

```
# ls -l | tr -s " " | cut -d" " -f1,8,9
...
-rw-r--r-- 4244 CENSORSHIP
-rw-r--r-- 3315 CHARSETS
-rw-r--r-- 12794 CODINGS
-rw-r--r-- 4976 COOKIES
-rw-r--r-- 17989 COPYING
-rw-r--r-- 5595 DEBUG
-r--r--r-- 5633 DISTRIB
-rw-r--r-- 955298 DOC-20.2.1
-rw-r--r-- 131199 FAQ
-r--r--r-- 11494 FTP
...
```

The listing now only shows the first, eighth, and ninth columns of the original listing, because the `tr` command squeezed multiple spaces into a single space. The output is then piped through the `cut` command, specifying a field delimiter, using the `-d` option (in this case, a space). Notice that although the first and second columns look okay, the third is a little ragged. If this still isn't what you want, clean it up by again using the `tr` command to replace the space delimiter with a tab:

```
# ls -l | tr -s " " | cut -d" " -f1,5,9 | tr " " '\t'
...
-rw-r--r--      4244    CENSORSHIP
-rw-r--r--      3315    CHARSETS
-rw-r--r--      12794   CODINGS
-rw-r--r--      4976    COOKIES
-rw-r--r--      17989   COPYING
-rw-r--r--      5595    DEBUG
-r--r--r--      5633    DISTRIB
-rw-r--r--      955298  DOC-20.2.1
-rw-r--r--      131199  FAQ
-r--r--r--      11494   FTP
...
```

You can use these filters to change text in your documents, but stream editors, such as the `sed` command, offer more capable approaches to editing text from the command line. For example, the sample license document uses the phrase *this Package* to describe a software package. If you're the software developer of a new game, *Nano-Warrior*, and need to save time writing copyright licenses, you can change all occurrences of *this Package* to *Nano-Warrior* easily and quickly without using a text editor:


```
# cat LICENSE | sed 's/this Package/Nano-Warrior(TM)/g'
...
1.  You may make and give away verbatim copies of the source form of the
```

```
Standard Version of Nano-Warrior(TM) without restriction, provided that you
duplicate all of the original copyright notices and associated
disclaimers.
...
```

The `sed` `s`, or substitute command, is used to search for all instances of the first string, and to replace each instance with the second because of the `g`, or global, command. The original text file is not changed, and you can save a new version by redirecting the output.

The `sed` command also is designed to work using editing scripts. To make numerous, regular changes to files, create an editing script and use your script to edit files. Use the `sed` command's `-f`, or script file command-line option to use the script:

```
# sed -f myscipt.sed < form.ltr >output.ltr
```

JUST A MINUTE

> There are too many text filters included with your Linux distribution to discuss in this hour; see the manual pages for the filter commands listed near the beginning of this section. You also may want to experiment with the wc, or word count, program, which reports the number of characters, words, and lines in your text documents.

Applix Words

There are many other Linux word processing programs besides the text editors installed on your system. These programs may be in the public domain, distributed as shareware, or sold commercially. One word processor, Applix Words by Applix, Inc., sold by Red Hat Software, deserves special mention because it

- Is an integrated part of the Applixware suite of office tools, and includes a spreadsheet, graphics, mail, and presentation program, and supports frames, linked objects, and pasted graphics
- Provides a WYSIWYG view of your documents, and comes with two dozen fonts
- Imports and exports 20 different word processing file formats
- Supports extensive editing macros
- Includes a spelling dictionary and thesaurus
- Includes extensive built-in and context-sensitive help
- Creates and edits hypertext markup language, or HTML documents
- May be completely customized with new menus or keyboard commands
- Builds indexes, tables, tables of contents, and glossaries
- Was used to write this book!

Applix Words requires the X Window System (see Figure 14.6). The Applixware suite needs about 135 megabytes of your hard drive space, and 16 megabytes of your computer's memory to run comfortably. Once installed, run Applix Words with the following:

```
# applix -wp
```

This command line starts the word processor. Applix Words also has a tutorial, like emacs. To start learning, select the Help menu, and then pull down the Tutorial menu item (you also can hold down the Alt key, then press h, followed by the t key).

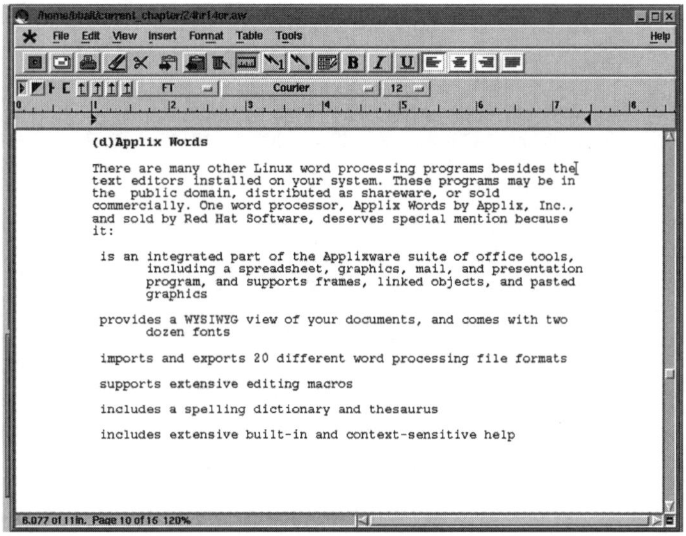

Figure 14.6.
The Applix Words program from Applix, Inc. is part of Red Hat Software's Applixware suite of office tools and is a WYSIWYG word processor with many different features, including a customizable interface and professional editing tools for writers.

Find out more about Applix Words by browsing to the following site:

```
http://www.redhat.com
```

Spell Checking Your Documents

Misspelled words in your documents can be embarrassing, especially if other people read your text. Correct spelling is an important part of writing and word processing. Just as errors in syntax can cause programming errors, spelling errors can cause problems in miscommunication, and loss of a potential job, customer, or the respect of a supervisor.

Fortunately, your Linux distribution comes with the ispell spelling checker, so you won't have to suffer the embarrassment of misspelling! This section shows you how to correct documents and fix your spelling errors.

Correcting Documents with the `ispell` Command

The `ispell` command, found under the `/usr/bin` directory, is an interactive spelling program you can use alone or with your text editor to correct spelling mistakes. Several editors included with your Linux distribution, such as emacs and pico, are set up to automatically use this program for spell checking, but using ispell by itself is easy. For example, to check the spelling of the file `myfile.txt`, use

```
# ispell myfile.txt
```

The ispell program loads the text, and then displays the first found error in context, along with a single or several suggested replacements:

```
MERCHANTIBILITY              File: LICENSE

WARRANTIES, INCLUDING, WITHOUT LIMITATION, THE IMPLIED WARRANTIES OF
MERCHANTIBILITY AND FITNESS FOR A PARTICULAR PURPOSE.

 0: MERCHANTABILITY



[SP] <number> R)epl A)ccept I)nsert L)ookup U)ncap Q)uit e(X)it or ? for help
```

Correct the spelling by either typing 0, the number of the suggested replacement word, or R, to replace the word by retyping it. Look up other words with `L`, the lookup command, which searches the system dictionary, called words, located under the `/usr/dict` directory. If you use the `I`, or insert command, ispell creates a personal dictionary in your home directory, using `.ispell_english` as a filename.

You also can specify multiple documents on the ispell command line:

```
# ispell *.txt
```

This command line causes ispell to load each file ending in `.txt` for spell checking. If you'd prefer to use ispell as the more traditional UNIX spell command, which reads a document then prints out a list of suspected words, use ispell's `-l`, or list option, on the command line:

```
# ispell -l < LICENSE
...
Julianne
Haugh
uunet
uu
MERCHANTIBILITY
...
```

Note that the < redirection operator has been used because in the `-l` mode, the `ispell` command acts as a spelling filter, checking the input text stream against its dictionary (located under the `/usr/lib/ispell` directory). You can-redirect this list to a file, or use ispell's `-f` command-line option:

```
# ispell -l -f errors -a <LICENSE
```

This sends all misspelled words to the file called `errors`. The ispell program has 15 different command-line options. Use the `-L` option to change the amount of context, or text displayed before and after a suspected error. The `-b` option creates a backup file of your original document, which is a good idea if you make a mistake and enter a wrong correction (this is the default for your version of ispell).

The ispell package includes nine other programs you can use to build your own dictionaries, or add lists of words from your personal dictionary into ispell's dictionaries. For details about these programs, see the ispell manual page. For details about building your own dictionaries, read the ispell manual page under the `/usr/man/man4` directory. You can do this with the following command:

```
# man 4 ispell
```

Documentation for ispell is in its two manual pages and under the `/usr/doc` directory.

Single Word Lookup and Other Tricks

When all you need is quick confirmation of the spelling of a single word, you don't have to run your word processor or text editor to get the answer, because you can use the `look` command, found under the `/usr/bin/`directory.

Although the `look` command is normally used to search files and print all lines matching a given string pattern, the `look` command quickly looks up a word in the system dictionary. If you don't specify a file to search on the `look` command line, `look` automatically searches the system dictionary, called words, which is located in the `/usr/dict` directory. See the following example:

```
# look consci
conscience
consciences
conscientious
conscientiously
conscious
consciously
consciousness
```

JUST A MINUTE

> The system dictionary, words, is a symbolic link to the file called `linux.words`, also located in the `/usr/dict` directory. This dictionary, a 400,000-character, plain ASCII list of sorted words, contains 45,402 words. You can find an even larger dictionary, called web2, which is more than two megabytes, and contains more than 100,000 words, by searching your favorite Linux Internet sites (try `sunsite.unc.edu`).

All you have to do is type several characters of the beginning of a word and the `look` command prints any matches found in the system dictionary. You also can use the ispell command's

-a command-line option to check spelling interactively, or quickly look up a single word, or several words at the keyboard. Lookups are performed on ispell's dictionary, not the system dictionary. See the following example:

```
# ispell -a
@(#) International Ispell Version 3.1.20 10/10/95
seperate
& seperate 1 0: separate

mispell
& mispell 3 0: dispell, ispell, misspell

mississippi
& mississippi 1 0: Mississippi

truncate
*
[Ctrl-d]
#
```

Notice that ispell starts, prints a short version message, and then waits for your input. When you enter a misspelled word, ispell echoes the word back, and if a suggested replacement is found, prints the replacement with a number. Also note that ispell even corrects words spelled correctly, but not properly capitalized. Finally, if you enter a correct word, ispell merely echoes back an asterisk. To quit, enter an end of text character by holding down the Ctrl key and pressing d.

PART IV

Hour 15

Preparing Documents

Hour 14, "Text Processing," discussed text editing tools and programs used to create, edit, and save documents. This hour introduces you to programs and utilities used to format and print your text documents. It starts off with a discussion of different text formatting programs, and shows you how to easily format your documents for printing without using complicated formatting commands. It then shows you how to use more complex programs by using simple commands.

The hour concludes with a discussion of the basics of document printing under Linux, as well as detailed information about how to configure your printer to get the best possible output.

Formatting Text

While you can do basic formatting of text documents using a text editor or word processor, most of these programs for Linux lack the necessary features to add page numbering, boldfacing, font changes, indenting, or other fancy text layout.

Producing nicely typeset documents by using the programs included with your Linux distribution is usually a three-step process. First, you create the document with a text editor. You intersperse your text with typesetting commands to create a certain effect when you filter your document through a formatting program. The second step is to process your document through the typesetting program to produce formatted output. The third step is to either check your formatting by previewing the document, or if you're confident about your formatting, to print the document.

This section shows you how to use typesetting programs to produce nicely typeset documents. It also discusses the basic syntax, or commands, that these programs recognize.

Formatting Text Using Text Filters

In Hour 14 you were introduced to some text filters to change the output of different programs or the contents of a document. These filters can help you format your documents if you don't want to learn a complex formatting program or use complicated typesetting commands, and are useful for quickly building formatted documents with headers, footers, margins, and page numbers.

Sending directory listings or short text files directly to your printer without formatting may be okay, but printing larger text files usually requires nicer formatting. One command you can use is the `pr` command, found under the `/usr/bin` directory. The `pr` command has 19 different command-line options to format documents. Look at the following example:

```
# pr +4 -h "Draft Number 1" -o 8 <mydocument.txt >output.txt
```

This command line formats the file `mydocument.txt`, starting at page 4, with a header containing the date, time, page number, and the words "Draft Number 1," with a left margin of 8 spaces. Using the > redirection operator, the formatted output is then saved to a file called `output.txt`, which you can print at a later time.

The pr program also formats selected streams of text. One handy use is to create formatted columns. For example, if you have a paragraph, you can quickly create columns of text by combining several filter programs and then formatting the text with the `-COLUMN` command-line option.

```
# cat cities.txt
Cinncinati, San Francisco, Philadelphia, Austin, Washington
D.C., Albany, Indianapolis, Raleigh, Chicago, Miami,
Norfolk, Savannah, Seattle, Pittsburgh, St. Louis, Phoenix,
Nashville, Las Vegas, Atlantic City
# cat cities.txt | sed 's/, /#/g' | tr "#" '\n' | sort | pr -l 1 -3
Albany                Atlantic City         Chicago
Indianapolis          Las Vegas             Miami
Nashville             Norfolk               Phoenix
Pittsburgh            Raleigh               Savannah
Seattle               St. Louis             Washington
```

The preceding example is a list of cities, separated by commas. By using several filters, including the `pr` command, the text has been formatted into a readable list, sorted alphabetically. This command line works by first using the sed stream editor (discussed in Hour 14) to change each comma and space to a pound (#) sign. The pound sign is then translated to a carriage return, by the `tr` command (also discussed in Hour 14) and the text, now a list of words, one per line, is fed into the `sort` command. The sorted text is then fed into the `pr` command to produce three columns of text (the `-l`, or page length option, with a value of 1 has been used to inhibit the page header).

You also can use the `fmt` command with the `pr` command, to change the word wrap, or width of your text documents. The following example is part of a public-domain software license (found under the `/usr/doc/shadow-utils` directory).

```
# cat LICENSE
...
1.  You may make and give away verbatim copies of the source form of the
Standard Version of this Package without restriction, provided that you
duplicate all of the original copyright notices and associated
disclaimers.

2.  You may apply bug fixes, portability fixes and other modifications
derived from the Public Domain or from the Copyright Holder.  A Package
modified in such a way shall still be considered the Standard Version.
...
```

While this text may be okay when printed on the screen, or by using the default settings with the `pr` command, the text overruns lines if you use a left-hand margin of 10 spaces. Look at the following example,

```
# pr -o 10 < <LICENSE
...
          1.  You may make and give away verbatim copies of the source form of
the
          Standard Version of this Package without restriction, provided that
you
          duplicate all of the original copyright notices and associated
          disclaimers.

          2.  You may apply bug fixes, portability fixes and other modifications
          derived from the Public Domain or from the Copyright Holder.  A Packag
e
          modified in such a way shall still be considered the Standard Version.
...
```

The preceding certainly won't look nice when printed! To fix it, use the `fmt` command to format the text into a smaller line width before formatting with the `pr` command:

```
# cat LICENSE ¦ fmt -w 60 ¦ pr -o 10
...
          1.  You may make and give away verbatim copies of the
          source form of the Standard Version of this Package
```

```
        without restriction, provided that you duplicate all of
        the original copyright notices and associated disclaimers.

        2.  You may apply bug fixes, portability fixes and other
        modifications derived from the Public Domain or from the
        Copyright Holder.  A Package modified in such a way shall
        still be considered the Standard Version.
...
```

As you can see, the text now fits nicely on your page when printed. But what if you want to save paper and would like to see at least two pages of output on a single page? In this case, use the `mpage`, or multiple page command to print several sheets of paper on a single page. Look at the following example:

```
# mpage -2 myfile.txt >myfile.ps
```

This command line uses the `mpage` command, found under the `/usr/bin` directory, to create a PostScript file you can later print, which contains the contents of the `myfile.txt` document as two side-by-side pages on each sheet of paper.

JUST A MINUTE

> You can use the `mpage` command's `-O`, `-E`, or `-R` options to print full-duplex, or back-to-back documents. This can be handy for producing small booklets using letter-size paper with a printer that's not capable of printing on both sides of each sheet. You also can set different margins, fonts, and order of printed pages. See the `mpage` manual page for details.

By using the `fmt`, `pr`, or `mpage` commands, along with other text filters, you can perform quick and dirty rudimentary text formatting. If you want to try more complex formatting, use a text formatting program.

Formatting Text with the `groff` Formatter

If you've used Linux for the past several hours and have read some of its manual pages, you should be familiar with at least one complex formatting program: `groff`. When you read a manual page with

```
# man ls
```

it is equivalent to the following:

```
# nroff -man /usr/man/man1/ls.1 | less
```

Notice that the `nroff` command is used on the command line instead of groff. This is because the `nroff` command installed on your system is a shell script, written to use the GNU groff formatting program to emulate the `nroff` command. All Linux manual pages are written using a special set of `nroff` commands called man macros. You also can tell the `groff` command to use man macros to format manual pages. For example, if you create a manual page for a new game called nw, the manual page, called nw.6, may look like the following:

```
# cat nw.6
.TH Nano-Warrior 6  Games 1/1/98 Linux
.SH NAME
nw - play Nano-Warrior
.SH SYNOPSIS
nw
.B -d
.PP
-d = play deathmatch mode
.SH DESCRIPTION
.PP
The nw command is used to play a game of Nano-Warrior on your Linux
console. Play continues until you are wiped out by hordes of alien
invaders swarming down the screen.
.PP
Don't give up the fight!
.SH FILES
/usr/games/nw
.PP
$HOME/.nw_scores
.SH BUGS
Probably too many.
```

You can process this manual page and send it to your display with the following:

```
# groff -Tascii -man nw.6
Nano-Warrior(6)                Linux                Nano-Warrior(6)


NAME
       nw - play Nano-Warrior

SYNOPSIS
       nw -d

       -d = play deathmatch mode

DESCRIPTION
       The  nw  command is used to play a game of Nano-Warrior on
       your Linux console. Play continues until you are wiped out
       by hordes of alien invaders swarming down the screen.

       Don't give up the fight!

FILES
       /usr/games/nw

       $HOME/.nw_scores

BUGS
       Probably too many.
```

Notice that the man page macros have boldfaced the sections and formatted the following text automatically. A list of these and other manual page macros are found in the man.7 manual page under the `/usr/man/man7` directory. You can read this manual page with the following:

```
# man 7 man
```

The `groff` formatting program also comes with other sets of typesetting macros, such as the me, mm, or ms manuscript macros used to format text files. You'll generally need to specify the macro set on the `groff` command line if you use these commands:

```
# groff -Tascii -mm myfile.txt
```

Documentation for several of these macros are in various `groff`-related manual pages. One of the best documented sets included with your Linux distribution is the mm manuscript macros in the `groff_mm` manual page. Table 15.1 lists some common macros you can use to produce formatted documents.

Table 15.1. Common `groff_mm` macros.

Action	Macro Name
Center justify	.ds C
End text box	.b2
Justification off	.sa 0
Justification on	.sa 1
Line fill off	.ds N
Line fill on	.ds F
New paragraph with x indent	.p x
No indents	.ds L
Right justify	.ds R
Start bold text	.b
Start text box	.b1
Use columns	.mc
Use one column	.1c
Use two columns	.2c

Some of the more common commands that don't require a macro set are listed in Table 15.2. Experiment with them to see their effect on your documents before printing.

Table 15.2. Common groff typesetting commands.

Action	Command Name
Begin new page	`.bp`
Begin new paragraph	`.pp`
Center next x lines	`.ce x`
Center text x	`.ce x`
Insert (space) x inches down	`.sp xi`
Insert x inches down	`.sv xi`
Set font bold	`.ft B`
Set font roman	`.ft R`
Set line spacing to x	`.ls x`
Temporary indent x inches	`.ti xi`
Turn off line fill	`.nf`
Turn on centering	`.ce`
Turn on indenting x inches	`.in xi`
Turn on line fill	`.fi`
Underline next x lines	`.ul x`

When you're ready to produce a formatted document, use the `groff` command's `-T` command-line option to produce a document in several different formats. The `groff` formatter produces PostScript, TeX dvi (discussed next), text, HP printer-control language, or PCL, formats. Look at the following example:

```
# groff -Tascii -mm myfile.txt >myfile.txt
# groff -Tps -mm myfile.txt >myfile.ps
# groff -Tdvi -mm myfile.txt >myfile.dvi
```

You can preview these documents before printing by using several different programs, such as ghostview for PostScript, or xdvi, for dvi files.

Formatting Text with TeX

The TeX typesetting system, originally by Donald E. Knuth, is a collection of programs and other utilities used to produce professionally formatted documents. It is a much more sophisticated system than the `groff` distribution, and includes more than 65 programs, along with related support files, such as libraries, macros, fonts, and documentation.

If you install TeX on your system, you'll need at least 30 megabytes for the main distribution, 10 megabytes for a series of related macros called LaTeX, and eight megabytes for 50 different fonts. Obviously, describing the entire system and how to use each different program in the TeX system is beyond this hour. But this section shows you how to get started with a sample document.

CAUTION

> Previewing TeX dvi documents requires a preprocessing step that can take several minutes before the pages are even displayed. Files must first be processed by the MakeTeXPK program, and related processes can eat up your system resources. A much better approach is to convert the file to PostScript with the `dvips` command, found under the `/usr/bin` directory, with: `dvips -f < texdoc.dvi >tex.ps`, and to then use the ghostview program with `ghostview tex.ps` to read the file.

You'll find documentation for TeX in a variety of places. You can read the manual pages for related files, check the `/usr/info` directory for TeX info files, and browse to the `/usr/lib/texmf/texmf/doc` directory. There are 10 different directories of documentation files, but the easiest way to read about your TeX distribution is to use the lynx Web browser with the following:

```
# lynx /usr/lib/texmf/texmf/doc/index.html
```

The TeX distribution files are displayed in an organized list, and you can browse through the list to download sample files and guides directly to your home directory. Beginning users should definitely read the TeX Frequently Asked Questions document.

Like the `groff` program, TeX uses formatting commands inserted in your text files to manipulate how your file looks when printed. You'll create your file, insert appropriate commands or macros to format text, and then process your document through TeX to create an output file, usually in dvi format, that you can preview or print.

To see a sample of TeX using the LaTeX macros, try processing an example file in the TeX directories:

```
# latex  /usr/lib/texmf/texmf/doc/generic/pstricks/samples.tex
```

This creates a file called `samples.dvi`. You should convert the file to PostScript first, then preview the document with the ghostscript program:

```
# dvips -f <samples.dvi >samples.ps
# ghostview samples.ps
```

You'll see that you can use TeX to produce complex diagrams and text. But you'll have to make the effort to learn TeX first!

JUST A MINUTE

> There are many different macros and macro sets included with the TeX formatting system. Covering the details of complex formatting is beyond the scope of this book, but you're encouraged to experiment, starting with simple commands to get a feel for typesetting documents. There are nearly 100 books on using TeX on the market. If you're serious about learning how to use TeX, a good book is indispensable.

Printing Text Documents

After you've finished formatting your text files, using either a series of filters or inserted typesetting commands, you'll want to print your file to produce a typeset document. In order to control the printing of your documents, you need to understand how Linux handles printing, and how to start, stop, cancel, or control the printing process.

There are several printing commands you'll use to control the printing process on your system. This section first shows you how your printer is described under Linux, and where the important printer files are located.

Printers are known as character mode devices, and are listed under the `/dev` directory. Look at the following example:

```
# ls /dev/lp*
/dev/lp0 /dev/lp1 /dev/lp2
```

This shows the three parallel printer devices installed on your system by default. Chances are good that you have a parallel printer attached to your computer, so this hour's discussion is limited to parallel printers. Once set up, you'll find little difference between how parallel and serial printers are handled by Linux.

TIME SAVER

> Serial printers are serial devices, and have names such as /dev/ttySX, where X is a number from 0 to 3, similar to your modem ports. Read the `setserial` command's manual page to learn how to set your serial port to the fastest baud rate your printer supports.

To determine if your printer is working, first make sure your printer is plugged in, attached to your computer's parallel port, and turned on. Then try sending a directory listing to your printer with the following:

```
# ls >/dev/lp1
```

If you've specified the right printer device, your printer should activate and print the current directory list. If nothing happens, try the following:

```
# cat /proc/devices
```

to see if the printer device driver was loaded or compiled into your kernel. You should see something like the following:

```
Character devices:
 1 mem
 2 pty
 3 ttyp
 4 ttyp
 5 cua
 6 lp
 7 vcs
10 misc
14 sound
127 pcmcia

Block devices:
 1 ramdisk
 2 fd
 3 ide0
 9 md
22 ide1
```

If you don't see an lp device listed, make sure that parallel printing is either compiled into your kernel, or installed using the lp.o module, located under the `/lib/modules/2.0.31/misc` directory (see Hour 1, "Preparing to Install Linux," for kernel configuration details).

Printing Documents with the lpr Printing System

If you've installed a printer during the initial Linux installation process, you'll find your printer defined in the `/etc/printcap` file. This file is an ASCII database of your system's local and networked printers, and describes the capabilities of each printer.

You can have different entries for your printer to handle color or black-and-white documents, or different paper sizes. Look at the following example:

```
##PRINTTOOL3## LOCAL cdj500 300x300 letter {} DeskJet500 1 1
lp:\
     :sd=/var/spool/lpd/lp:\
     :mx#0:\
     :sh:\
     :lp=/dev/lp1:\
     :if=/var/spool/lpd/lp/filter:
##PRINTTOOL3## LOCAL cdj500 300x300 letter {} DeskJet500 3 1
lpcolor:\
     :sd=/var/spool/lpd/lp0:\
     :mx#0:\
     :sh:\
     :lp=/dev/lp1:\
```

15

```
    :if=/var/spool/lpd/lp0/filter:
##PRINTTOOL3## LOCAL cdj500 300x300 letter {} DeskJet500 8 1
lpgray:\
    :sd=/var/spool/lpd/lp0:\
    :mx#0:\
    :sh:\
    :lp=/dev/lp1:\
    :if=/var/spool/lpd/lp0/filter:
##PRINTTOOL3## LOCAL cdj500 300x300 letter {} DeskJet500 24 1
lpcolorbest:\
    :sd=/var/spool/lpd/lp0:\
    :mx#0:\
    :sh:\
    :lp=/dev/lp1:\
    :if=/var/spool/lpd/lp0/filter:
```

This `printcap` file contains definitions (created with the `printtool` command, discussed in the following section, "Defining Printers with the `printtool` Command") for the lp, lpcolor, lpgray, and lpcolorbest printers, but all describe the same printer. These names are handy as reminders when you want to print different documents (or if you need to change print cartridges to use color).

Linux uses a line printer spooling system. When you first boot, Linux starts lpd, the line printer daemon. The lpd program runs in the background, waiting for print requests. You start a print request with the `lpr` command:

```
# lpr mydocument.txt
# lpr myfile.ps
```

This command line spools, or sends your documents to a file in the `/var/spool/` directory. You also can use the `lpr` command as a printing filter to print outgoing streams of formatted text:

```
# groff -Tascii -mm myfile.txt ¦ lpr
```

This command line sends the output of the `groff` formatting program through the line printer spooler. You also can spool multiple files, then track your requests by using the `lpq` command. See the following example:

```
# lpr mes.txt
# lpr test.txt
# lpq
lp is ready and printing
Rank   Owner      Job  Files                                     Total Size
active bball      16   mes.txt                                   368 bytes
1st    bball      17   test.txt                                  359 bytes
```

To stop either of these print jobs, use the `lprm` command:

```
# lprm 17
```

This command stops the printing of job 17, the file `test.txt`. You also can (as the root operator) disable or enable printers, or reorder jobs with the `lpc` command. See the lpc man page for details.

Defining Printers with the `printtool` Command

Installing, changing, or deleting local printers with your Linux system is a snap, thanks to the Red Hat `printtool` program, located under the `/usr/bin` directory. This program, used with the X Window System, is a printer setup program you can run from the command line, or through the X11 control-panel program.

Because these programs run under X11, you'll have to start X, then, making sure you're the root operator, type the following in a terminal window:

```
# control-panel
```

or

```
# printtool
```

If you run the control-panel program, select the `printtool` button. `Printtool`'s main window appears and lists all printers defined in the /etc/printcap database. From here, you can add, delete, or edit existing printer entries. To add a printer, click the Add button. You'll be asked to select a local, remote, or LAN manager printer. For the sake of example, assume that you want to set up a printer attached to your computer. Press the local button, then click the OK button.

The `printtool` program then shows which parallel printer devices have been detected (see Figure 15.1). Note that one of the devices, /dev/lp0, /dev/lp1, or /dev/lp2, should be detected. If not, your printer is not on, or printing support hasn't been enabled.

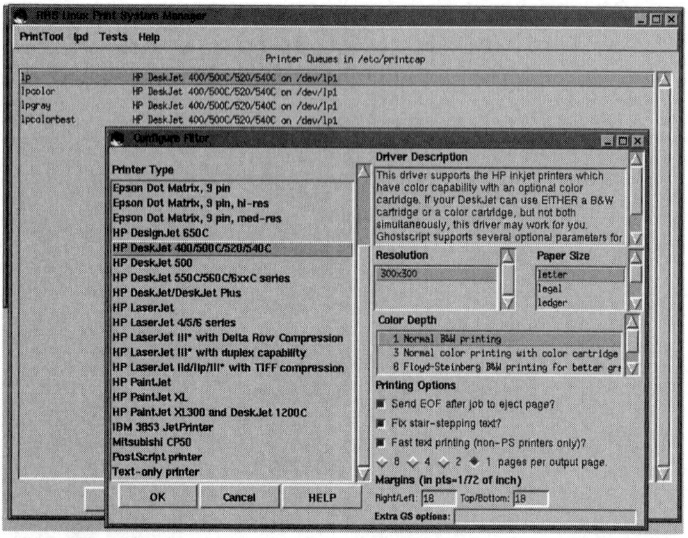

Figure 15.1.
The Red Hat `printtool` *program provides an easy-to-use interface when you need to configure a printer for Linux.*

Next, click the OK button. You can give your printer a unique name by typing it in the names field of the dialog box. Press the Select button next to the input filter dialog box entry. A large window called Configure Filter appears, listing 26 printers. Select your printer, or a printer similar to yours. Also select your printer's resolution, paper size, color depth, or other options, and then press the OK button.

Press the next OK button and the printer you've defined will be in the list of Printer Queues. Select your printer, then try an ASCII or PostScript test from the Tests menu.

PART IV

Hour 16

Graphics Tools

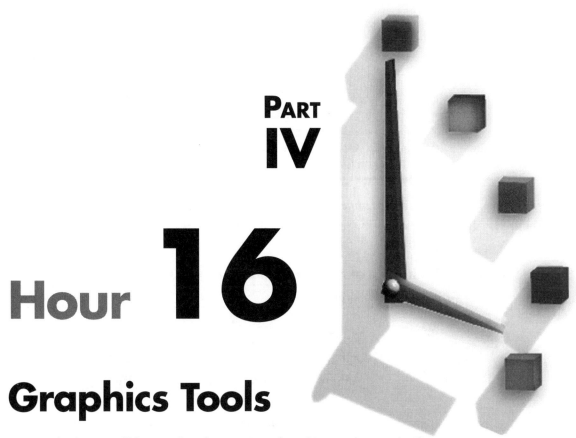

In this hour you'll be introduced to a variety of graphics programs and utilities for Linux. This hour starts with a short discussion of different graphics formats you'll find on your system, then shows you how to convert graphics using filter programs and other graphic utilities. These programs are useful for creating, editing, and translating graphics imported from other computer systems.

You'll find a treasure trove of great graphics programs on this book's CD-ROM, and you're likely to be impressed with their usefulness and versatility. You'll be able to translate nearly any type of graphic, and will be able to perform sophisticated operations to transform your graphics files.

Understand Linux Graphics File Formats

There are many different types of graphics file formats, and examples of several types are installed in your system. You may already be familiar with several different formats, especially if you've used other computer operating systems. However, when you use Linux, expect to run into graphics files in formats you've never seen before.

Many files can be recognized by the filename's extension, or letters following a period in the filename. For example, you may recognize .GIF, .PCX, .TIF, or .JPG as common extensions. In Linux, you'll also find files in formats such as .xbm or .xpm installed on your system. The `/usr/X11R6/include/X11/bitmaps` directory contains nearly 100 different bitmap files, and the `/usr/X11R6/lib/X11/xfm` directory contains more than 100 black-and-white bitmap icons, as well as more than 110 color pixmap icons.

Table 16.1 is a list of some of the graphics formats, along with relevant conversion programs you'll find on your system. To convert a graphic image from one format to another, see the manual page for the relevant conversion program.

Table 16.1. Linux graphics formats and conversion programs.

Format	Type	Conversion Program
.10x	Gemini 10X	pbmto10x
.3d	Red/Blue 3D pixmap	ppm3d
.asc	ASCII text	pbmtoascii
.atk	Andrew Toolkit raster	atktopbm
		pbmtoatk
.bg	BBN BitGraph graphic	pbmtobg
.bmp	Windows, OS/2 bitmap	bmptoppm
		ppmtobmp
.brush	Xerox doodle brush	brushtopbm
.cmu	CMU window manager bitmap	cmuwmtopbm
		pbmtocmuwm
.ddif	DDIF image	pnmtoddif
.dxb	AutoCAD database file	ppmtoacad
		sldtoppm
.dvi	TeX printer file	dvips
		dvilj4
		dvilj4l
		dvilj2p
		dvilj
.epsi	PostScript preview bitmap	pbmtoepsi
.epson	Epson printer graphic	pbmtoepson

Format	Type	Conversion Program
.fits	FITS file	fitstopnm
		pnmtofits
.g3	Group 3 fax file	g3topbm
		pbmtog3
.gif	Graphics Interchange	giftopnm
		gif2tiff
		ppmtogif
.go	Compressed GraphOn	pbmtogo
.gould	Gould scanner file	gouldtoppm
.icn	Sun icon	icontopbm
		pbmtoicon
.ilbm	IFF ILBM file	ilbmtoppm
		ppmtoilbm
.img	GEM image file	gemtopbm
		pbmtogem
		imgtoppm
.icr	NCSA ICR raster	ppmtoicr
.jpeg	JPEG	cjpeg
		djpeg
		jpegtran
.lj	HP LaserJet data	pbmtolj
.ln03	DEC LN03+ Sixel output	pbmtoln03
.mgr	MGR bitmap	mgrtopbm
		pbmtomgr
.mitsu	Mitsubishi S340-10 file	ppmtomitsu
.mtv	MTV ray tracer	mtvtoppm
.pbm	Portable bitmap	pbm*
.pcl	HP PaintJet PCL	ppmtopjxl
.pcx	PCX graphic	pcxtoppm
		ppmtopcx

continues

Table 16.1. continued

Format	Type	Conversion Program
.pgm	Portable graymap	pbmtopgm
		pgmtoppm
		ppmtopgm
.pi1	Atari Degas file	pi1toppm
		ppmtopi1
.pi3	Atari Degas file	pbmtopi3
		pi3topbm
.pict	Macintosh PICT file	picttoppm
		ppmtopict
.pj	HP PaintJet file	pjtoppm
		ppmtopj
.pk	PK format font	pbmtopk
		pktopbm
.plot	UNIX plot file	pbmtoplot
.png	Portable Network Graphic	pngtopnm
		pnmtopng
.pnm	Portable anymap	pnm*
.pnt	MacPaint file	macptopbm
		pbmtomacp
.ppm	Portable pixmap	ppm*
.ps	PostScript (lines)	pbmtolps
		pnmtops
.ptx	Printronix printer graphic	pbmtoptx
.qrt	QRT ray tracer	qrttoppm
.ras	Sun rasterfile	pnmtorast
		rasttopnm
.sgi	Silicon Graphics image	pnmtosgi
		sgitopnm

Format	Type	Conversion Program
.sir	Solitaire graphic	pnmtosir
		sirtopnm
.sixel	DEC sixel format	ppmtosixel
.spc	Atari Spectrum file	spctoppm
.spu	Atari Spectrum file	sputoppm
.tga	TrueVision Targa file	ppmtotga
		tgatoppm
.tiff	Tagged File Format	pnmtotiff
		tifftopnm
		ppmtotiff
		tiff2ps
.txt	text file bitmap	pbmtext
.uil	Motif UIL icon	ppmtouil
.upc	Universal Product Code	pbmupc
.x10bm	X10 bitmap	pbmtox10bm
.xbm	X11 bitmap	pbmtoxbm
		xbmtopbm
.xim	Xim file	ximtoppm
.xpm	X11 pixmap	ppmtoxpm
		xpmtoppm
.xv	xv thumbnail	xvminitoppm
.xvpic	xv thumbnail file	xvpictoppm
.xwd	X11 Window Dump	pnmtoxwd
		xwdtopnm
.ybm	Bennet Yee face file	pbmtoybm
		ybmtopbm
.yuv	Abekas YUV file	ppmtoyuv
		yuvtoppm
.zeiss	Zeiss confocal file	zeisstopnm
.zinc	Zinc bitmap	pbmtozinc

Converting and Viewing Graphics

There are a number of ways to convert graphics files to different formats using the programs you'll find installed on your system. A number of painting or drawing programs discussed in this hour translate graphics. Many programs in Table 16.1 also work as filters in piped commands (see Hour 6, "Using the Shell," for details) to translate graphics.

You can use different combinations of these commands to convert files. The resulting files, which may display and print the same, usually aren't the same file size, so a side benefit of converting graphics may be to save disk space. Look at the following example:

```
# xwd >graphic.xwd
# xwdtopnm <graphic.xwd ¦ pnmtotiff >graphic2.tiff
xwdtopnm: writing PPM file
pnmtotiff: computing colormap...
pnmtotiff: 6 colors found
# ls -l graphic.xwd graphic2.tiff
-rw-rw-r--   1 bball    bball      240380 Jan  5 15:15 graphic.xwd
-rw-rw-r--   1 bball    bball       15278 Jan  5 16:51 graphic2.tiff
```

The first command line uses the xwd client to create an X11 window dump graphic (after you select a window and press your left mouse button). Then the window dump file is converted to a portable anymap format, and this stream is fed into the `pnmtotiff` command to create a .tiff graphic. As you can see, the .tiff graphic file format is nearly 16 times smaller than the X11 window dump graphic.

There are also many graphics programs not listed in Table 16.1 that can be used to alter graphic images. For example, the `pnmrotate`, `pnmsmooth`, or `pnmscale` commands rotate, smooth, and resize graphic images. You can use a variety of these programs to not only convert graphics, but change their appearance or orientation.

If you're using pipes to convert a graphic, you also can change the image on the fly by applying these filter programs. The previous example, now has a filter inserted during the conversion:

```
# xwd >graphic.xwd
# xwdtopnm <graphic.xwd ¦ pnmflip -topbottom ¦ pnmtotiff >graphic.tiff
xwdtopnm: writing PPM file
pnmtotiff: computing colormap...
pnmtotiff: 6 colors found
```

Here a window dump is created, and then, using the pnmflip program, it is turned upside down and backwards before creating the .tiff version. Combinations of different filters achieve different effects.

TIME SAVER

> Not all graphics conversion programs included with your Linux distribution read the standard input and write to the standard output. Read the manual pages for any desired conversion programs before experimenting with pipes on the command line. Also, be cautious: preview or print the results of your conversions before discarding original files to make sure you achieve the effect you want, and that the resulting graphic does not suffer loss of image quality.

If you don't want to experiment with complex pipes, you may want to try using the `convert` command, one of seven programs in the ImageMagick package (discussed later in the section, "Graphics Editing with ImageMagick"). Using the `convert` command is an alternative way to translate files. Found under the `/usr/bin` directory, this command translates more than 75 different graphics file formats (even some not listed in Table 16.1). The convert program works by recognizing different file extensions on the command line, as shown in the following example.

```
# xwd >graphic.xwd
# convert graphic.xwd graphic.tiff
```

Again the xwd client is used to create an X11 window dump graphic. Then the `convert` command is made to create a .tiff file by specifying the .tiff extension on the second, or output file on the command line. For details about using the convert command, see the ImageMagick and convert command manual pages.

Graphic Editing with GIMP

Although you can change or manipulate graphics from the command line, if you use X11, it can be a lot more fun to interactively work with files using an image processing program. One of the best and newest graphics tools for Linux is GIMP, the GNU Image Manipulation Program by Spencer Kimball and Peter Mattis (see Figure 16.1).

This is a capable and complex program with many features. If you've worked with image-editing programs on other operating systems, you'll appreciate the tools and filters included with this program. The GIMP features

- 9 program operation menus
- 21 different editing tools
- 109 different plug-in filters and tools to create image effects or perform operations
- Multiple image windows, handy for cutting and pasting or multiple views of a file

- Multiple layers for each image, so that effects may be superimposed
- Six floating windows and dialog boxes for selecting tools, brushes, colors, or patterns
- Multiple undo levels, handy if you make mistakes!
- Import and export of 24 different graphics formats

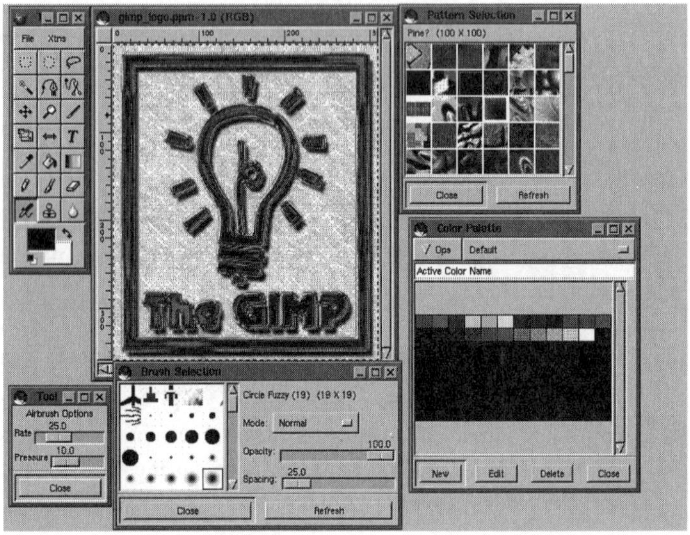

Figure 16.1
The GIMP image editor is an impressive X11 client with many professional features, including nearly 100 different filters for manipulating graphics.

You'll need nearly 23 megabytes of hard drive space to install GIMP, its software libraries, support files, and related directories. The main GIMP files are installed under the `/usr/share/gimp/X.XX` directory, where `X.XX` is the current version. A library of GIMP plug-ins is located under the `/usr/lib/gimp/X.XX/plug-ins` directory, where `X.XX` is the current version. Plug-ins are compiled modules, or programs run by GIMP from different menus.

This program has 11 different command-line options, but does not support X11 Toolkit options such as geometry settings. You can specify a graphic file on the command line. GIMP attempts to load and interpret the file according to the file's extension. Starting GIMP is easy; simply type the following.

```
# gimp &
```

When you first start GIMP, you'll be presented with a large window that provides details about various GIMP resource files. You'll be asked to confirm installation of a directory called `.gimp` in your home directory. This directory contains seven different files and subdirectories that specify how GIMP works, and lists your preferences for tools, brushes, and plug-ins.

The file `gimprc` under your `.gimp` directory contains settings, such as default brushes, patterns, palettes, and temporary directories you can customize. You also can specify the type of measurement to be used in your rulers, such as pixels, inches, or centimeters, and whether or not GIMP performs auto-saving of your image files as you work.

CAUTION

> The version of GIMP installed on your system lacks documentation, but you should know that if you edit large image files, you may quickly run out of disk space because GIMP creates large temporary files during editing sessions (this is not unusual, as even commercial image editing applications typically require swap storage three times larger than system memory). If you have a separate hard drive with a lot of room, change the swap-path (not the same as your Linux swap partition!) setting in the `gimprc` file to point to a directory on that drive. If you're really tight on memory and hard drive space, you can uncomment the `stingy-memory-use` option. On the other hand, if you have a lot of system memory, change the tile-cache size to force GIMP to use less swap space (and run faster).

Once GIMP is running, you can tear off different dialog boxes and windows by using the dialog menu item under the GIMP File menu. If you have an active image window, access the complete GIMP menu system by pressing your right mouse button while the cursor is over your image. The various menus will cascade, and you can select the file, edit, or other menu operations by dragging your cursor through the menus.

GIMP does not come with a manual page, but you'll find some documentation under the `/usr/doc/gimp` directory. For the latest news and details about this program, browse to the following site:

```
http://www.gimp.org
```

You'll find copies of the latest GIMP and links to GIMP Frequently Asked Questions lists, a GIMP tutorial, and new plug-ins.

Graphics Editing with ImageMagick

The ImageMagick package, by John Cristy, is a collection of seven programs you'll find installed on your system. Some of these commands require the X Window System, while others may be used from the command line. The `convert` command has already been discussed in this hour, but you may find some of the other utilities useful when you want to manipulate graphics:

- animate Displays a series of graphics; requires X11
- combine Combine, overlay multiple images into a single image

- convert Convert or changes graphic files
- display Display program with menus for manipulating images; requires X11
- import Window capture utility; requires X11
- mogrify Convert or change, then overwrite multiple graphic files
- montage combines several graphics into a larger graphic

You'll really like ImageMagick's `display` command, which has more than 75 different features and effects you can use to edit or change graphic images. One interesting feature is the ability to load images into a visual directory so you can see thumbnails of all images in a directory. Using the `display` command is easy, but you must be running the X Window System. From a terminal command line, type the following:

```
# display &
```

This starts the program. To see a visual directory of your graphics, type the following:

```
# display 'vid:*.gif' &
```

This command line loads all .gif graphics in the current directory. Once the program starts, access its menus by pressing the left mouse button when your cursor is over the images window. The `display` command imports and exports 58 different graphics formats. The program features built-in help, and also can create slide shows of graphics (see Figure 16.2).

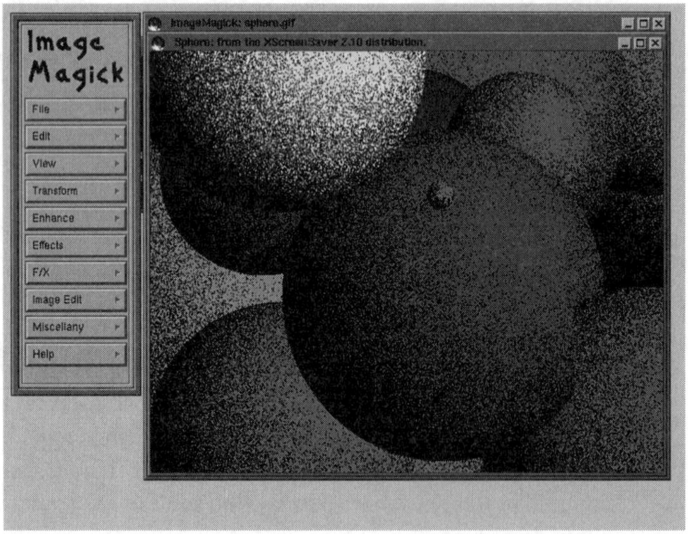

Figure 16.2
The display X11 client, included with the ImageMagick software package, can be used to make changes to many different types of graphics.

For more information about ImageMagick, see its manual page, and the manual pages for the other programs in the distribution. Comprehensive hypertext documentation is under the `/usr/doc/ImageMagick` directory.

Using the `xv` Command to View Graphics

The `xv` command is a handy previewer used to review, crop, scale, edit, or convert graphics. This command offers many sophisticated sizing and color controls, and you also can use `xv`, found under the `/usr/X11R6/bin` directory, to capture windows of your X11 session (you must run X11 in order to use the `xv` command).

The `xv` command loads a single file or series of graphics if you specify the files on the command line:

```
# xv *.jpg
```

This command line loads all files ending in .jpg in the current directory. After the files are loaded, scroll through a list of files to make your changes, or use a graphic directory to select your files (see Figure 16.3).

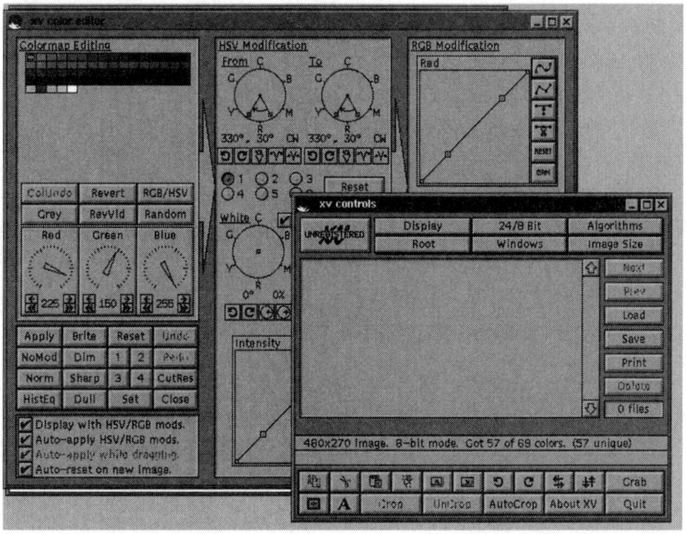

Figure 16.3
The `xv` command is an X11 client that loads, edits, captures, saves, or prints images, and features sophisticated color controls.

The `xv` command can import and export 18 different graphics file formats, and also prints graphics. For more information about using `xv`, see its manual page, or read the definitive documentation (128 pages in PostScript format, nearly as many as the `xv` command's 107 command-line options!) found under the `/usr/doc/xv` directory.

Using the gv Command to View PostScript Files

The `gv` command is a PostScript previewer used to examine or read PostScript graphics or documents before printing. You must run the X Window System to use this program. The `gv` command, found under the `/usr/X11R6/bin` directory, is a much-improved previewer by Johannes Plass, and is based on the previous ghostview program by Tim Theilson (you'll find a symbolic link under `/usr/X11R6/bin` called ghostview, which points to `gv`).

The `gv` command has more than 36 different command-line options, and uses a number of X11 Toolkit options, such as geometry settings. You can start `gv` by itself, or specify a file on the command line, along with its options:

```
# gv -geometry 640x480 myfile.ps
```

This command line starts the `gv` command in a 640 by 480 pixel window with the file `myfile.ps` displayed. Another great feature of the `gv` command is that it reads portable document format, or .pdf files (see Figure 16.4). This is a handy way to read .pdf documents without installing an additional .pdf reader, such as Adobe Acrobat.

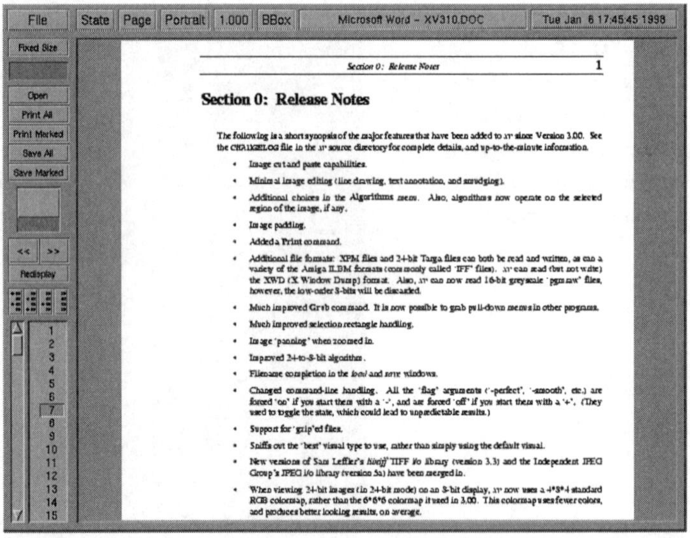

Figure 16.4
The gv X11 client displays PostScript or PDF documents and graphics, and provides an easy-to-use interface to previewing files before printing.

The `gv` command also uses a unique scrolling mechanism; instead of scrollbars alongside or below the document window, a rectangular button controls the document viewing area. You also can print whole documents or selected pages by using different commands.

You'll find a comprehensive manual page, along with a hypertext series of .html files under the `/usr/doc/gv` directory.

Painting and Drawing with xpaint and xfig

If you need to create or edit simple bitmap graphics, use David Koblas' xpaint program, found under the `/usr/X11R6/bin` directory. For technical drawing, you'll also find the xfig program, which uses drawing objects (with handles), rather than a flat canvas.

The xpaint program features a floating control window with tools, and a separate canvas window with color palettes for selecting or mixing colors. The xpaint program has several different command-line options, and also can use a resource file, called `.Xpaintrc` (located in your home directory), to customize colors and patterns. You can load graphics from the command line:

```
# xpaint mygraphic.bmp
```

The xpaint program starts, presents the image in an editing window, and displays a floating window of tools (see Figure 16.5). Xpaint imports eight and exports 10 different file formats. You also may have multiple windows with different images waiting to be edited.

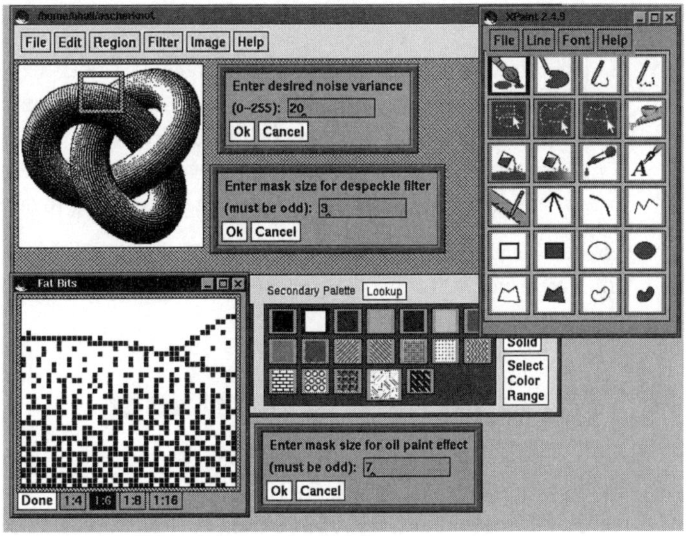

Figure 16.5
The xpaint X11 client is a simple bitmap editing program with a fatbits mode, multiple windows, and image filters.

If you'd rather work with a drawing program, try the xfig program (see Figure 16.6). Like xpaint, you must run X11 in order to use this program. You should have an X11 display of at least 1024 pixels high by 768 pixels wide in order to use this program (although you can use it with an 800-by-600 display, you'll miss some tools on the xfig window).

Starting the xfig program is easy, and you can control the initial size of its drawing area by using the `-ph` and `-pw` command-line options. For example,

```
# xfig -ph 6 -pw 8 &
```

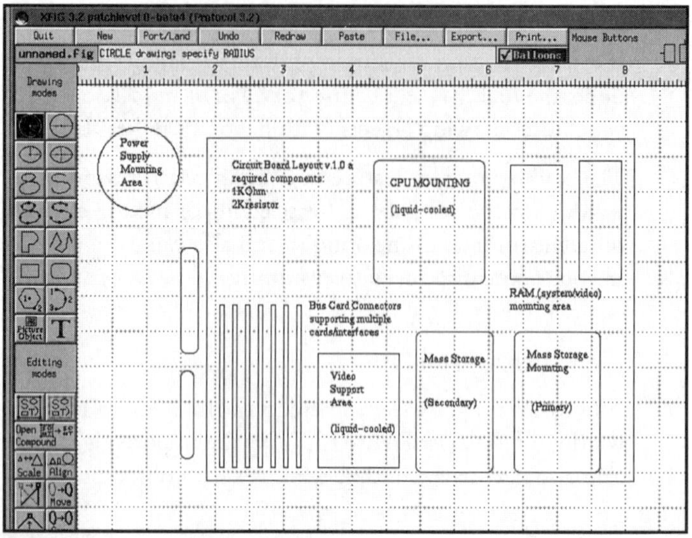

Figure 16.6
The xfig drawing program, which runs under X11, requires a 1024x768 window, and can be used to produce technical drawings or other illustrations.

This command line starts the xfig program with a canvas six inches high by eight inches wide. The xfig program features pop-up balloon help for its menus. You can use this program to draw intricate drawings or other illustrations you can later include in documents or graphics. The xfig program can import .gif, .jpeg, .pcx, .xpm and PostScript documents. One interesting feature is its ability to spell check any text in your drawings.

Customize xfig's default colors or keyboard commands by editing the files `Fig-color` and `Fig` under the `/usr/X11/lib/X11/app-defaults` directory. For more details about how to use xfig, see its manual page.

A Word About Scanners

Although Linux runs on many different computers and supports many different hardware devices, the state of scanner support is still in its infancy. Before you buy a scanner with the express purpose of using it with Linux, carefully check all Linux Internet sites for different scanning software, and then carefully read the documentation.

You'll find scanner support for many models from Nikon, Epson, Genius, Hewlett Packard, and Mustek. Although most scanners for Linux require a small computer system interface, or SCSI interface, you'll find support for the Connectix series of QuickCams using your computer's parallel port. But there are variations between models of scanners even from the same manufacturer, and not all models in a particular series of scanners may be supported.

One place to look for scanner software, documentation, and support is in the small collection of graphic application capture software packages at the following site:

```
http://www.sunsite.unc.edu/pub/Linux/apps/graphic/capture
```

For QuickCam support, try the following site:

```
http://www.quickcam.com/developer.html
```

If you'd like to scan documents using the xv X11 client, look for the xvscan software at the following site:

```
http://www.tummy.com
```

PART IV

Hour 17

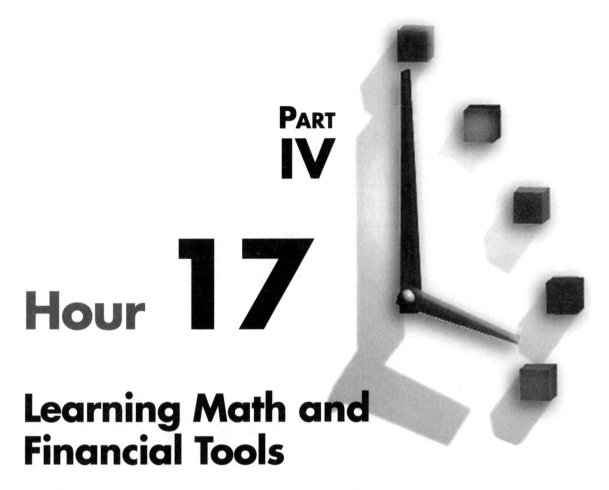

Learning Math and Financial Tools

This lesson is an introduction to some of the mathematical and financial tools available for Linux. This hour shows you calculators, spreadsheets, and graphic modeling programs, and points you to sources where you can find even more programs. Whether you're only interested in setting up simple single-screen spreadsheets, or would rather plot detailed maps using 200 megabytes of cartographic data from the U.S. Geologic Survey, you'll find Linux tools to help you get started.

The hour begins with a discussion of some calculators and calculating languages, and introduces you to just some of the Linux spreadsheet programs, followed by a discussion of modeling programs, such as `gnuplot`. This hour can't cover all the of the more than 1,500 scientific applications for Linux, but if you have an interest in other fields such as artificial intelligence, astronomy, biology, chemistry, database systems, electronics, linear algebra, physics, or raytracing, you can find tools for Linux to help you.

Calculators

This section introduces you to several Linux calculators. You'll find some of these handy when you pay bills, cook, or even travel. Some of these calculators work from the command line, and others run under the X Window System.

Doing Desk Calculations with the dc Command

The dc (desk calculator) command is a command-line calculator that uses reverse Polish notation, or RPN, to perform calculations, and has more than 30 different operators and internal commands.

The dc command, found under the /usr/bin directory, is easy to use:

```
# dc
44
55
+
p
99
q
```

The example shows that to add two numbers, you first enter the numbers, then enter the operator, then use the p command to print the value placed on the stack by the addition operator. The q command quits the dc program. This method of performing calculations is not as inconvenient as you may think. For example, suppose that you're going through the checks you've written during the month, and you want to check your written calculations. Using the dc command, you can enter

```
# dc
2500.00
49.95
-
p
2450.05
32.18
-
p
2417.87
q
```

You started by entering a $2500.00 balance, then entered $49.95 as the first check, followed by the subtraction operator, or minus sign. The p command prints the result, and the next current balance of $2450.05 is maintained on the stack. You can also use the dc command to read files of calculations instead of typing commands at your terminal, and it has 256 different registers, or temporary storage areas for your calculations. See the dc command's manual page for more information and other features.

Calculating with the X11 `xcalc` Client

The `xcalc` client is one of the more familiar graphic calculators (see Figure 17.1), and comes with the XFree86 X Window System. The `xcalc` command, found under the `/usr/X11R6/bin` directory, has only two command-line options, `-stipple`, and `-rpn`. The `-stipple` option merely colors the background of `xcalc`'s face, whereas the `-rpn` option tells the `xcalc` command to use `rpn` for doing calculations, and changes its appearance.

You must be running X11 in order to use the `xcalc` command. You can use your mouse or the keyboard to enter numbers and perform calculations. To use it in its normal mode with the `-stipple` option, type

```
# xcalc -stipple &
```

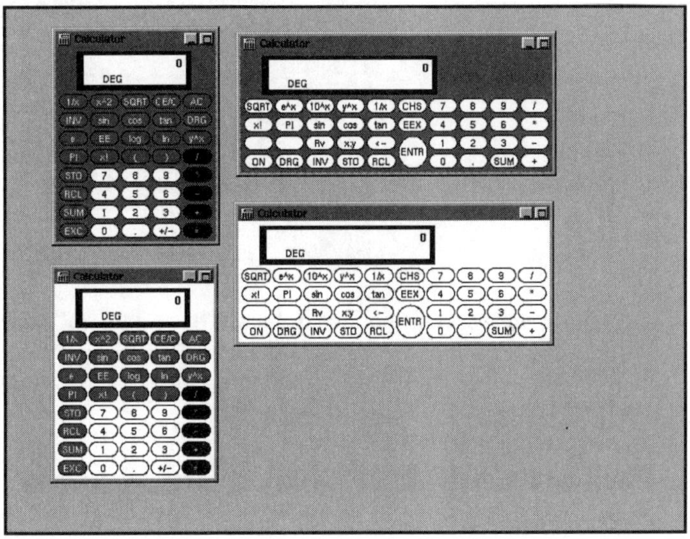

Figure 17.1.
The `xcalc` *calculator.*

To use the `xcalc` command as an `rpn` calculator, type

```
# xcalc -rpn -stipple &
```

You can customize nearly any aspect of `xcalc` by editing its defaults file, `Xcalc`, which is found under the `/usr/X11R6/lib/X11/app-defaults` directory. See the `xcalc` manual page for more information.

Three Calculators in One: `dtcalc`

The `dtcalc` calculator, part of Red Hat Software, Inc.'s Common Desktop Environment, or CDE (see Hour 8, "Exploring Other X11 Window Managers"), offers a variety of features and can emulate a logical, scientific, or financial calculator. Although `dtcalc` does not have as much register storage as the `dc` command, you can use your mouse or keyboard to enter data, just as you can with `xcalc`. Figure 17.2 shows the `dtcalc` calculator.

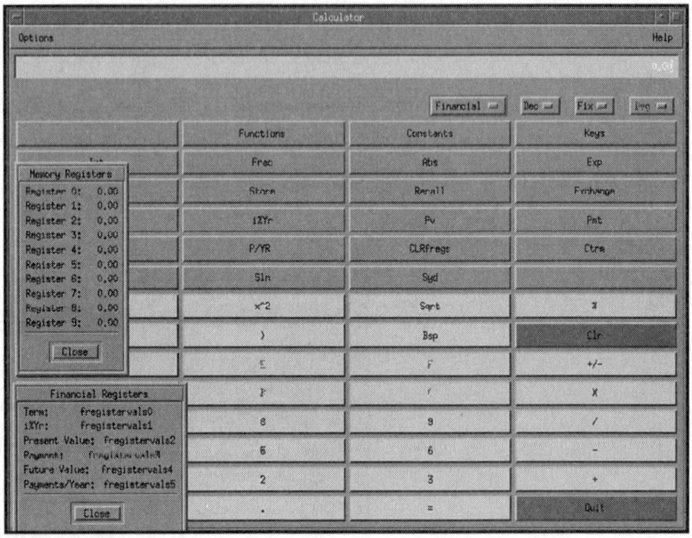

Figure 17.2.
The `dtcalc` *calculator, part of the Common Desktop Environment for the X Window System, can emulate three different calculators.*

You can perform calculations in binary (base 2), octal (base 8), decimal, and hexadecimal (base 16). You can also define your own functions and constants. Like most other CDE applications, `dtcalc` has extensive and context-sensitive help. For more information about CDE, see Hour 6, "Using the Shell."

Performing Unit Conversions with the `units` Command

If you've ever had trouble remembering the formulas to convert miles to meters, or cups to gallons, you'll really like Adrian Mariano's `units` command, which you'll find under the `/usr/bin` directory. Want to know how many furlongs per mile? How about how many acres in a square mile?

One way to use the `units` command is from the command line, for example:

```
# units floz gallon
        * 0.0078125
        / 128
```

This simple example shows how to find out how many fluid ounces are in a gallon. You see that there are 128, and that a fluid ounce is less than one-hundredth of a gallon. Although using the command line is handy for quick conversions, you can also run a series of queries as follows:

```
# units
501 units, 41 prefixes

You have: mile*mile
You want: acre
        * 640
        / 0.0015625
You have: mile2
You want: acre
        * 640
        / 0.0015625
You have: mile^2
You want: acre
        * 640
        / 0.0015625
You have: mile
You want: furlong
        * 8
        / 0.125
You have: 100 fathoms
You want: feet
        * 600
        / 0.0016666667
...
```


In the interactive mode, you can ask `units` for any number of conversions. The `units` command works by reading its library of conversions from the file `units.lib` under the `/usr/lib` directory. As you can see, you can use different notations to indicate amounts to be converted. Another interesting feature is that `units` can also perform currency conversions, for example:

```
# units dollar yen
        * 107.52688
        / 0.0093
```

Note that this may not be entirely true, as currency values change daily. You can edit the `units.lib` file and insert not only current currency values, but also prices for gold, silver, platinum, or pork bellies. See the `units` manual page for more information.

Programming Calculators with the bc Language Interpreter

The `bc` command is an interpreter for a calculator language. You can use this command, by Philip Nelson, to write calculator programs while `bc` is running, or have `bc` run the program after it starts. The `bc` language has nearly 40 operators, functions, and programming logic keywords. Although this section doesn't go into how to program in `bc`, it shows you how a simple checkbook balancing program (from `bc`'s manual page) can work like the earlier example for the `dc` command. If you'd like to try this program, see the `bc` manual page, then type the program into a file using your favorite text editor. You can run it with

```
# bc nameofyourfile
```

The bc command will start by reading in its program, and present the following:

```
...
Initial balance? 2500.00

current balance = 2500.00
transaction? 49.95
current balance = 2450.05
transaction? 32.18
current balance = 2417.87
transaction?
...
```

This is only one way to use the bc command's language. With a little effort, you can write your own. But if you'd rather use more complex programs to perform calculations, you know that you should use a spreadsheet application. The next section discusses the variety of spreadsheets for Linux.

Spreadsheets

Spreadsheet programs offer a convenient way to store and manipulate financial or scientific data. You can use these programs to help manage your home or a business. Typical uses involve personal finance, such as tracking loans and investments, or running business inventory control, personnel worksheets, or accounting tasks.

You can also use these programs to do forecasting, or "what if" calculations. This can help you create estimates you can use for home mortgages, auto loans, and even home construction. You're limited only in your imagination with most of these programs, and many not only offer the ability to work as a whiz-bang calculator, but will also create graphic charts so you can graph your data visually.

Although you won't find any of these programs on your CD-ROM, once you've connected to your ISP (see Hour 10, "Connecting to the Internet"), you can use the lynx Web browser or your downloaded copy of Netscape to get copies or more information about them. If you need to have a spreadsheet program to use with Linux, you're in luck, because at least a dozen are available, and nearly half come with source code so you can make changes, add features, or fix problems.

Using the Public Domain sc Spreadsheet

The sc (spreadsheet calculator) command (see Figure 17.3) is a freely available, public domain spreadsheet program. This program is a collective work of nearly 60 programmers, and runs on many different UNIX systems. With a little effort in learning its commands, you'll be able to build very capable spreadsheets. The sc program is free, and it comes with source code. A short tutorial and manual page documenting its features is included.

This program is especially handy if you're running Linux on a small hard drive and disk space is at a premium. The sc program requires only about 120 kilobytes of disk space, but provides a lot of features.

Using the sc program is easy. You can load programs from the command line when you start it, or you can load and save programs while it's running. You can run this program as follows:

```
# sc
```

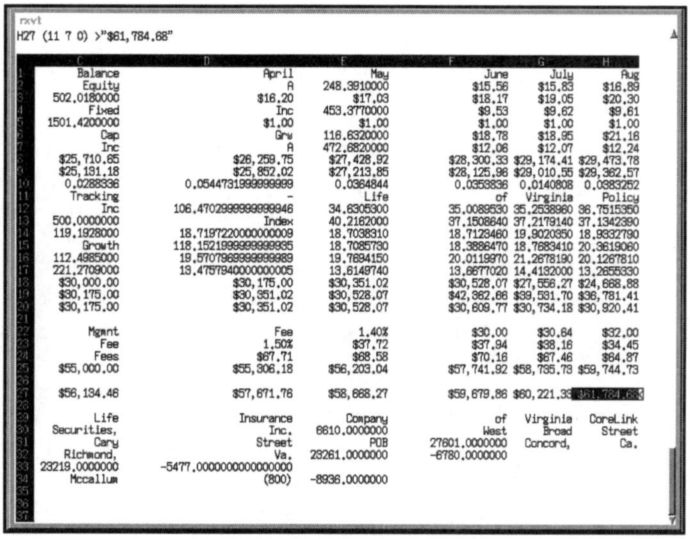

Figure 17.3.
The sc *spreadsheet calculator works with or without the X Window System, and it comes with a short tutorial.*

If you'd like a quick reference to the sc commands, use the sc companion command (included with the source code), the scqref command, and pipe the output through the nroff and less commands. Then either read at your leisure, or redirect to a file you can edit and print, for example:

```
# scqref ¦ nroff -man ¦ less > scref.txt
```

To learn how to use the sc spreadsheet program, load the sc program's tutorial, which you'll find under the /usr/lib/sc directory:

```
# sc /usr/lib/sc/tutorial.sc
```

This will run sc and load the tutorial. An included program, called psc, can help you import text-only data files by converting word processor or other spreadsheet program files. The sc program has more than 60 built-in functions, and because you get the source code, you can add your own. One place to find the source code to the sc spreadsheet is

http://www.cdrom.com/pub/linux/slackware_source/ap/sc

Plotting Graphics with the X11 xspread Spreadsheet

If you like the sc spreadsheet program, but would like updated menus and features, you may want to try the xspread program, by software engineering teams at the University of Wisconsin-Milwaukee. This program requires that you're running X11, but offers these additional features:

- An improved program menu
- Mouse support to run program features
- The ability to import Lotus 1-2-3 format files
- Support to generate and display line, bar, stacked-bar, and pie chart graphics from spreadsheet data

The xspread program works the same way as the sc spreadsheet program. You can use this program with any sc spreadsheets you've devised. Along with the sc tutorial, you'll find an expanded manual detailing the xspread improvements.

You can also generate graphics with the xspread program. By selecting Graph, then defining a label range of cells, and a data range of cells, you can quickly generate visual representations of your data. To print your charts, capture the chart window with the xv command (see Hour 16, "Graphics Tools").

Unlike sc, this program appears to be distributed under the GNU General Public License, even though its manual page states that xspread is in the public domain. This means that the software is free, and you can make any changes you want, but you cannot claim the program as your own. One source of the xspread spreadsheet package is at this location:

```
http://www.cdrom.com/pub/linux/slackware_source/xap/xspread
```

Finding and Using the teapot Spreadsheet

As an alternative to the sc program, you might want to try the teapot (table editor and planner) spreadsheet program by Michael Haardt. This spreadsheet works under X11 or your console. The program's menu appears at the bottom of your screen, where you'll find nearly all of the features of sc and xspread. The teapot program also has these features:

- Import of sc and .WK1 spreadsheet files
- Export of CSV, HTML, LaTeX, or ASCII file formats
- Three-dimensional spreadsheets
- Extensive and customized support of keyboard function keys
- Availability in German, English, or Dutch language versions

Although the teapot program does not have the graphics features of the xspread version of the sc spreadsheet, you'll find that the teapot spreadsheet has much better documentation, including example programs, and an extensive tutorial that takes you from the concept of spreadsheet programs and how they work to a step-by-step guide on how to use teapot.

Like sc and xspread, the teapot spreadsheet is a space-saving way to handle spreadsheet data on your computer. You can find a copy of the teapot spreadsheet at

ftp://cantor.informatik.rwth-aachen.de/pub/unix/teapot-0.9.tar.gz

If you'd just like a little information about teapot, browse to

http://cantor.informatik.rwth-aachen.de/~michael/projects/teapot-en.html

Finding and Using the Shareware Wingz Spreadsheet

The Wingz spreadsheet, from Investment Intelligence Systems Corporation, is a shareware program you can evaluate, use for 45 days, and then pay a registration fee, or discard. Unlike many shareware programs, this is as capable a spreadsheet program as many commercial offerings.

Also, unlike sc, xspread, or teapot, this program requires about six megabytes of hard drive space when installed. You'll find nearly any feature you could need in a spreadsheet program, including a built-in scripting language called HyperScript. You can use HyperScript to build custom interfaces and programs to present your spreadsheet data. You won't find much documentation, but there are some impressive example sheets you can load and examine, and Wingz has built-in, context-sensitive help.

After you install Wingz, you can run the program after first defining the environment variable, WINGZ. To do this you can define the program at the command line with

```
# WINGZ=/pathwhereWingzisinstalled/Wingz ; export WINGZ
# $WINGZ/bin/Wingz
```

The first line defines the WINGZ environment variable to point to the Wingz directory, and the second runs the spreadsheet program. The actual application, Wingz, is found in the bin directory under the Wingz directory. You can also run one of two shell scripts included in the Wingz distribution to temporarily set the WINGZ variable.

The Wingz spreadsheet (see Figure 17.4) imports and exports a variety of well-known spreadsheet file formats, such as Lotus 1.a and 2.0, DIF, text, and SYLK.

You can generate many different types of 3D graphics, and spreadsheets may be linked, or previewed before printing. To read more about Wingz, or to get a copy, browse to

http://wingz.iisckc.com

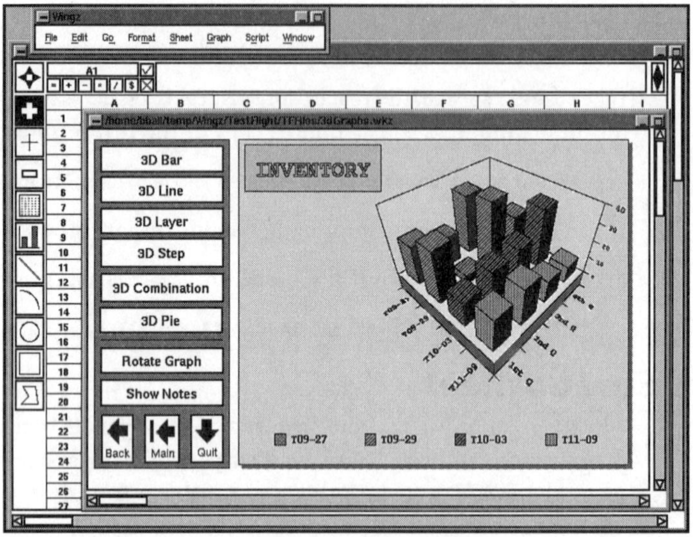

Figure 17.4.
The `Wingz` *spreadsheet offers graphics and desktop publishing capability for Linux.*

Commercial Features of the Applixware Spreadsheet Program

The Applixware spreadsheet program (see Figure 17.5) is part of the commercial Applixware suite of 10 programs for Linux (see Hour 14, "Text Processing" for more information). This spreadsheet program is integrated with the other Applixware programs using linked objects. This means that if you change the data in your spreadsheet file, the data or chart used in a word processing document will also change.

As you might expect with a commercial program, this spreadsheet offers all of the features of competing titles. Besides such features as integration with the other programs in its suite, print previews, or 3D graphics, this spreadsheet program has drag-and-drop cell movement, multiple views, and numerous database functions.

You can import and export many different types of spreadsheet formats, as shown in Table 17.1.

Table 17.1. Applixware spreadsheet import and export formats.

Import	Export
XLS	XLS3, XLS4, XLS5
WKS, WK1, WK3, WK4	WK1, WK3
DIF, XDIF	DIF
CSV	CSV
SYLK	SYLK
text	text

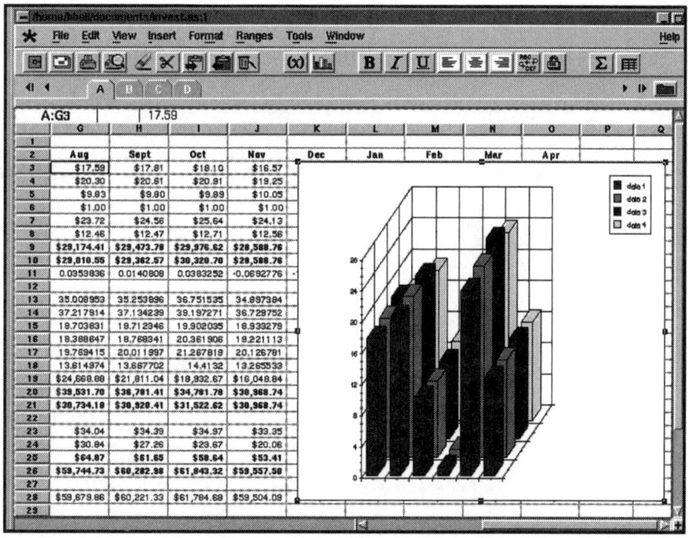

Figure 17.5.
The Applixware spreadsheet has mouse-driven toolbars, style sheets, and supports multiple graphics.

You can find out more about the Applix spreadsheet program by browsing to

`http://www.redhat.com`

Using `gnuplot` to Graph Mathematical Formulas

This section shows you how to use `gnuplot`, an interactive plotting program by Thomas Williams and Colin Kelley. This program supports nearly 40 different printers and output devices, although you'll probably want to experiment with `gnuplot` using the X Window System, and print your graphics using PostScript (see Hour 15, "Preparing Documents," for more information on how to do this).

Although `gnuplot` (no relation to GNU software, but supported and distributed by the Free Software Foundation under the GNU General Public License) is not the only mathematical modeling and plotting program available for Linux, it is included on your CD-ROM. You'll find the `gnuplot` program under the `/usr/bin` directory.

The `gnuplot` program (see Figure 17.6) is a complete, interactive plotting program, and was originally designed to graph math functions and data. In this regard it is somewhat similar to other commercial formula-interpretation and plotting programs. It can read and save files, and has built-in help, so you can query the program while you use it.

Using `gnuplot` is simple. The program has five different command-line options, but many aspects of the program may be controlled interactively or as commands in a loaded `gnuplot` data file. One common use of the command-line option may be to control the point size (in pixels) of drawing lines using the `-pointsize` option, as in the following example:

```
# gnuplot -pointsize 2
```

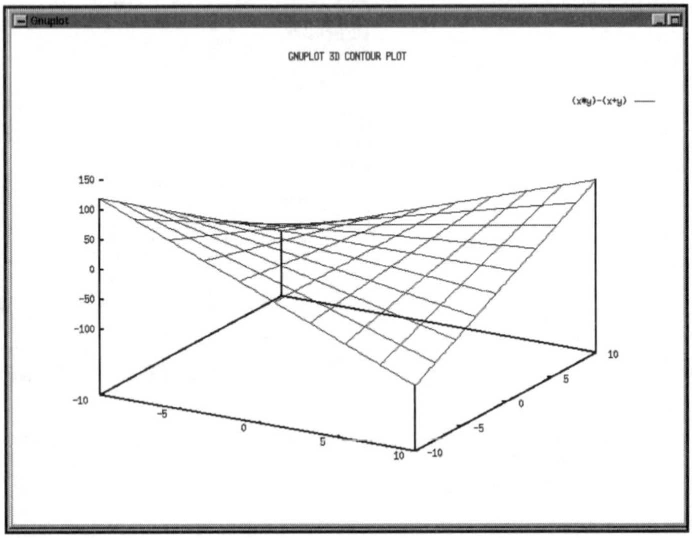

Figure 17.6.
The `gnuplot` *program can help you visualize mathematical formulas or spreadsheet data.*

You can use and plot many types of mathematical expressions, and according to the `gnuplot` documentation, any C, Pascal, FORTRAN, or BASIC language mathematical statement may be used. For example, Figure 17.6 shows a graphic plot of the expression (x*y)-(x+y). Once you have finished, type `quit` to exit the program.

You can find more documentation, the `gnuplot` FAQ, and updates to the `gnuplot` program at

`http://www.cs.dartmouth.edu/gnuplot_info.html`

Tips

Many, many different financial and math applications are available for Linux. This hour has barely scratched the surface. You'll find financial applications that can help you manage investment portfolios, track stock prices, or aid in developing cost estimates for construction projects. You'll also find hundreds of specialized programs you can use in solving special computing needs for other sciences. One of the best sites for perusing some of the best of these applications is

`http://SAL.KachinaTech.COM/`

You'll also find a number of financial tools for Linux, along with source code, at

`http://sunsite.unc.edu/pub/Linux/apps/financial`

Part IV

Hour 18

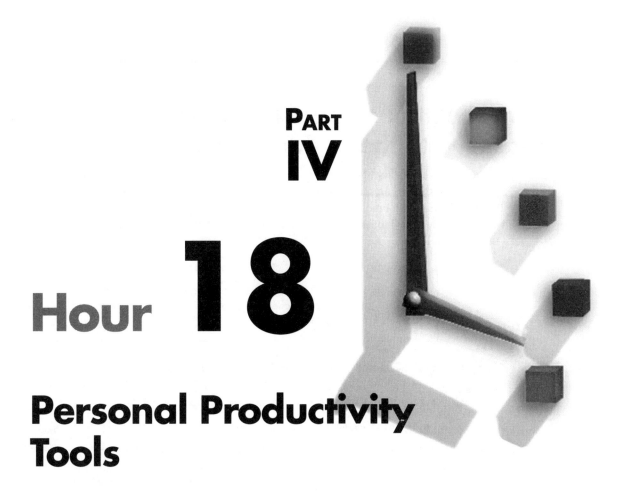

Personal Productivity Tools

This hour shows you some calendars, commands, and X11 clients you can use to help your personal productivity. Whether it's keeping a diary or creating reminders, you'll learn how to use these tools under Linux to keep you on track and on schedule with your life.

Each program or technique discussed in this hour can be accomplished with software you'll find on the CD-ROM that came with your book. After reading this discussion, you'll find additional ways to use these programs to craft your own set of tools and techniques for personal productivity.

Scheduling Personal Reminders and Tasks with the `at` Command

If you need to keep track of important schedules, set reminders, or run programs unattended, you can use the `at` command. This command, found under the `/usr/bin` directory, will schedule commands, or jobs, to be run at a time you specify. For example, if you're working on a project but need to remember to catch your car pool, you can enter a quick `at` job from the command line.

> **TIME SAVER**
>
> Your system should allow you to use the `at` commands by default. If it does not, see Hour 24, "Scheduling," on how to enable `at` command facilities for your system.

The following shows the `at` command for the car pool example:

```
# at 16:15
xmessage -display :0.0 "The car pool is leaving in 15 minutes."
EOT
Job 4 will be executed using /bin/sh
```

This will tell the `at` command to run the `xmessage` program to display the text of your message about your car pool on the specified X11 display. The `-display` command-line option will tell the `xmessage` command which screen to show the message on, usually 0.0, which you can find with

```
# printenv ¦ fgrep DISPLAY
```

This command line searches a listing of your environment variables (discussed in Hour 6, "Using the Shell") and prints the value of the `DISPLAY` variable. The end-of-text in the listing means that you should press Ctrl-D to close the command and then enter the job. If you make a mistake in the syntax of the command, you'll receive a mail message at the scheduled time.

You can also use the `at` command to provide a visual reminder, if you're using X11, by controlling the color of your desktop, for example:

```
# at 16:15
xsetroot -display :0.0 -solid Red
xmessage -display :0.0 "The car pool is leaving in 15 minutes."
EOT
Job 8 will be executed using /bin/sh
```

This will turn your desktop a solid red color at the appointed time, then display your message. As you can see, you can combine multiple commands to do a number of things at once. If you find this approach convenient, you can also type these commands into a text file called `carpool` and run the commands with the following:

```
# at 16:15 -f carpool
```

As a further convenience, you can place this command line in your `.xintrc` script in your home directory to schedule the job after you start X11 at the beginning of the day. You can see a list of scheduled jobs with the `atq` command, for example:

```
# atq
Date                   Owner   Queue   Job#
17:00:00 12/07/97      bball   c       15
18:00:00 12/07/97      bball   c       16
19:00:00 12/07/97      bball   c       17
16:00:00 12/25/97      bball   c       18
```

This shows that three jobs are scheduled for December 7, with another scheduled for December 25. When you schedule jobs with the `at` command, a shell script containing your commands is created in the `/var/spool/at` directory. The `atq` command looks in this directory for your jobs, then prints them to your display.

You can use the `at` command to schedule a job minutes, hours, days, weeks, or even years in advance. If you want to run your carpool reminder file in three hours, you can use the `at` command's plus sign (+) command-line option, for example:

```
# at +3 hours -f carpool
```

This would run your job three hours from the current system time. If you want to remove one or two jobs, you can use the `atrm` command. For example, using your job queue from the earlier example, you would type

```
# atrm 16 18
```

This would remove jobs 16 and 18, but leave the other two intact. Using the `at` command is a handy way to program one-time reminders for specific times. In the next section, I'll show you how to schedule other jobs to run at regular intervals.

JUST A MINUTE

> You can also use Rob Nation's X11 client, rclock, to schedule reminders or run programs at a selected day or time. To build a reminder, create a file called `.rclock` in your home directory and enter reminder command lines—for example: `11:30 mtwtf Time for lunch!`
>
> This displays a reminder for lunch during the week.

Scheduling Regular Reminders with the `crontab` Command

Although the at command is helpful for scheduling one-time jobs, you'll want to use Paul Vixie's `crontab` command if you need regular tasks completed at regular intervals. The `crontab` command, found under the `/usr/bin` directory, is used to enter your desired times and commands into a personal file.

The `crontab` command works by looking for `crontab` schedules, by username, in the `/var/spool/cron` directory. The `crontab` file for your Linux system is called `crontab` and is located in the `/etc` directory. The program that runs the system and user `cron` schedules is the `cron` daemon, which is started when you boot Linux, and which wakes up each minute to check the system and user files.

To create your own `crontab` file, you must use the command's `-e` option, for example:

```
# crontab -e
```

TIME SAVER

> Make sure you've enabled `crontab` use for your system. See Hour 24 for details on how to do this. You'll also want to define the default `EDITOR` environment variable to your favorite text editor when you create or edit your `crontab` files. See Hour 6 for information on how to set environment variables.

This command will launch the default text editor, defined in your shell's `EDITOR` environment variable, so you can create or edit your personal `crontab` file. If your default editor is vi, and you either don't want to use vi, or would like to use a different editor, you can temporarily change the `$EDITOR` variable using your shell. For example, if you're using the bash shell, and want to use the pico text editor, you can use

```
# EDITOR /usr/bin/pico; export EDITOR
```

This will set the default editor to the pico editor. You can confirm this by searching your environment variables, for example:

```
# printenv | fgrep EDITOR
EDITOR=/usr/bin/pico
```

Whichever editor you use, you'll initially be presented an empty file if you've never created a `crontab` file. You can then enter `crontab` settings. Before you can enter your own schedule, you should know how to format a `crontab` request. You'll find the format of `crontab` requests and some sample entries in the crontab manual page under the /usr/man/man5 directory. You can read this manual page as follows:

```
# man 5 crontab
```

Your crontab file should contain settings to start programs you want to run at regular and even not-so-regular times, for example:

```
* * * * * somecommand
0,15,30,45 * * * * somecommand
0 * * * * somecommand
```

The first example shows you'd like to run a program every minute. The second crontab entry runs a program every 15 minutes. The third example shows you'd like to run a program once an hour, on the hour.

If you'd like to run a program once a day at an appointed time, you can use:

```
30 7 * * * somecommand
30 0  * * * somecommand
15 16 * * * somecommand
```

The first example runs at 7:30 a.m. The second example runs at 30 minutes past midnight. The third example runs at 4:15 p.m. each day. You can also run a program on a specific day of the month or the week, for example:

```
30 16 1 * * somecommand
30 15 * * mon somecommand
```

The first example runs at 4:30 p.m. on the first day of each month, and the second runs at 3:30 p.m. each Monday. To round out these examples, you can also specify a particular month, or example:

```
30 7 25 12 * somecommand
```

This command runs the command at 7:30 a.m. on each December 25. The commands you specify can also be system utilities or even your own shell scripts. You can use the crontab command's -l (list) option to print your cron settings, for example:

```
# crontab -l
# DO NOT EDIT THIS FILE - edit the master and reinstall.
# (/tmp/crontab.1911 installed on Mon Dec  8 18:52:52 1997)
# (Cron version -- $Id: crontab.c,v 2.13 1994/01/17 03:20:37 vixie Exp $)
0,30 * * * * /usr/local/bin/saytime
0 8 * * * * /usr/local/bin/ppp on
3 8 * * * * /usr/local/bin/popclient -u bball -p mypasswd staffnet.com
```

This shows a crontab file that speaks the time every half hour, starts a PPP connection at 8 a.m. every day, and downloads the day's mail three minutes after the PPP connection has started. You can remove your crontab file with the crontab command's -r (remove) option, for example:

```
# crontab -r
```

Using the `crontab` command is an easy way to create, run, and manage regular tasks. Even though you can create your own reminders, you'll want to use a calendar for short- or long-range planning.

Creating Appointment Reminders with the X11 ical Client

You can use Sanjay Ghemawt's ical calendar to store appointments and reminders in a personal calendar. The ical client, found under the `/usr/X11R6/bin` directory, has a number of unique features and improvements over the cal or gcal calendar printing programs:

- Custom graphical X11 interface with menus, dialogs, sliding controls, and buttons
- Copy and paste, drag-and-drop notes, and appointments
- Alarms for upcoming events
- Multiple calendar views
- Import, export, and autosaving of calendar files
- Group sharing of calendar files
- Printing of different calendars
- `cron`-type scheduling of appointments, notes, or reminders
- To-do checklists
- Built-in help

When you first run ical, the program shows the current month, set to the current day, along with a note, or appointment entry list on the right. The ical client also uses many of the standard X Toolkit command-line options, so you can change geometry settings to set the initial calendar size, or start the ical client as an icon, for example:

```
# ical -iconic
```

or

```
# ical -geometry 800x600
```

Figure 18.1 shows the ical client.

Notices are created by selecting a day, then clicking on and typing in the box below the calendar. Appointments for the day are created by clicking on a specific time, and typing in the name of the appointment. You can drag appointments anywhere during the day to rearrange your schedule by holding down the middle mouse button (or both left and right mouse buttons if you're using a two-button mouse).

Figure 18.1.
The ical X11 client features notices, appointments, to-do lists, and reminder alarms.

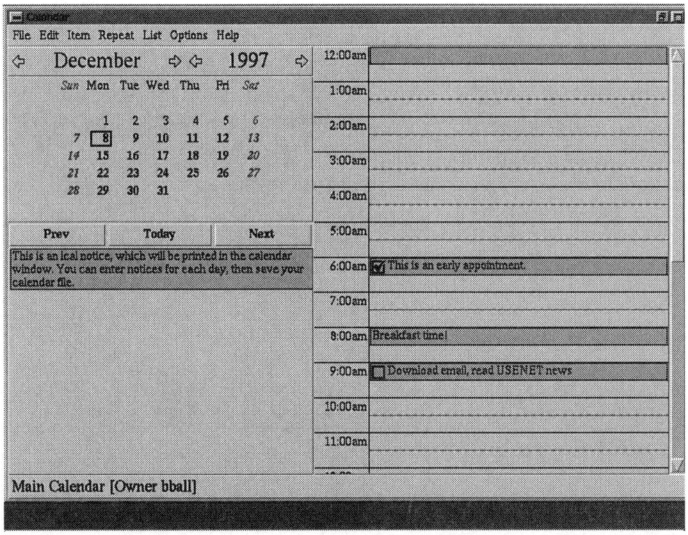

After you have set your notice or appointments, you can also set an alarm to have the ical client warn you of an upcoming event. To set a reminder alarm, first click on the appointment, then select the Item menu's Properties item to set an alarm for an appointment. You can also just double-click on the appointment to bring up the alarm dialog.

You can tell ical to remind you from 1 to 15 days in advance, with up to 60 warnings the hour before an appointment. The ical alarm notice window will pop up at the preselected times as a reminder.

Time Saver

> The ical client must be running in order to receive alarms. You can, however, use the `ical` command and its `-popup` command-line option in a `crontab` entry. If you use `-popup`, ical will list all of the day's appointments in a window, then exit after you press the Okay button.

Figure 18.2 shows the ical client's alarm dialog.

If you select an appointment or notice, you can also make it repeat daily, weekly, monthly, or annually by selecting the pertinent Repeat menu item. When you cause an item to repeat, it will automatically be duplicated in your calendar.

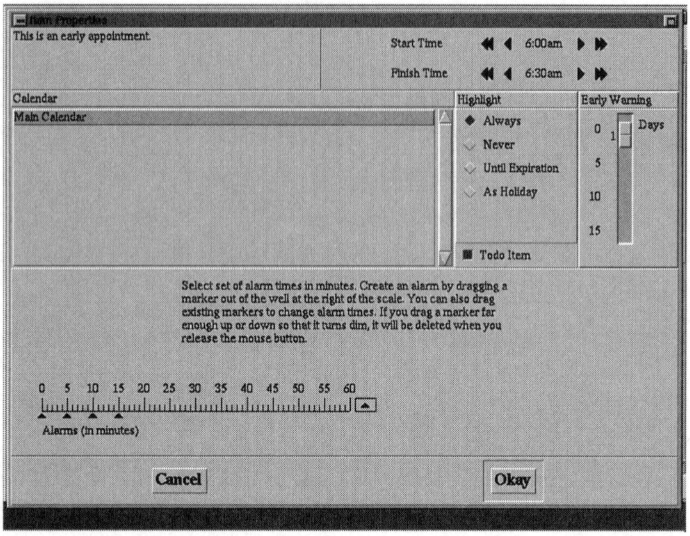

Figure 18.2.
The ical client's alarm dialog features multiple, cascading alarms, with drag-and-drop controls.

Appointments can also be made to-do items, by clicking on the appointment, then selecting Todo from ical's Item menu. A box will appear at the beginning of the text. Until you complete the item by clicking in the box with your left mouse button to place a check mark, the to-do item will reappear on the next day's list of appointments.

You can list your appointments and notices by using ical's List menu. If you'd like hard copy of your calendar, you can print six different built-in calendar formats, or specify a range of days. Before you print, you can also preview your calendar.

The ical client is a convenient way to organize personal or group tasks. You'll also want to take a look at some of ical's companion shell scripts and programs under the `/usr/lib/ical/contrib` directory, to find tips and hints on how to customize ical to suit your needs.

Checking the Calendar and Keeping Appointments with emacs

The emacs text editor, more fully discussed in Hour 14, "Text Processing," has a number of features that can help your personal productivity or even keep you amused. You can check the current calendar, see a list of holidays (and more), and keep a diary with appointment reminders.

If you're using X11, you'll automatically run the X11 version of emacs unless you specify the `emacs-nox` version on the command line to run emacs in your terminal window, for example:

```
# emacs-nox
```

After you start the X11 version of emacs, you can view a calendar of the previous, current, and next month through the Display Calendar item on the Tools menu. You can also use the non-X11 emacs command, `ESC-x-calendar`. Press the Esc key, type an **`x`**, then enter the word **`calendar`**, and press the Enter key.

Figure 18.3 shows the emacs editor.

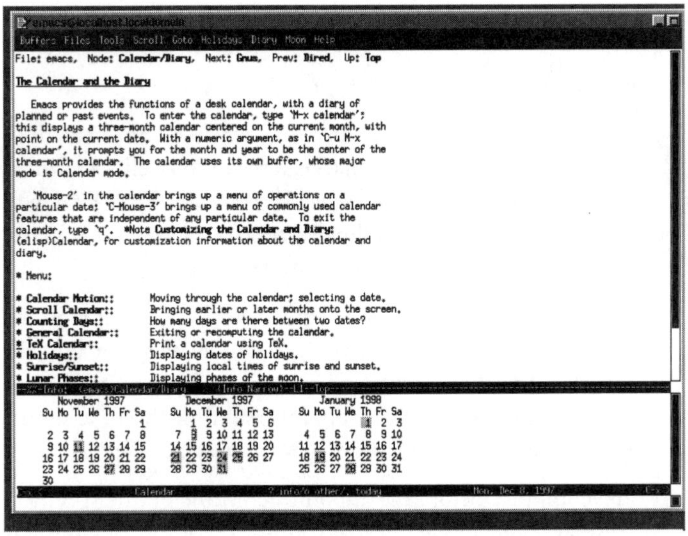

Figure 18.3.
The emacs editor features a built-in calendar with an assortment of calendar tools, including a diary and appointment reminder.

You can get help on using emacs' calendar tools by typing the question mark after clicking in the calendar window. A help menu of calendar items will appear. You'll also notice that when you click in the calendar window, the emacs menu bar will change, and offer you a Goto, Holidays, Diary, and Moon menu. You can use the Goto menu to advance the calendar forwards or backwards, or jump to nearly 20 different types of calendars, such as Julian, and even Mayan!

The Holidays menu will either list all the holidays for a range or days or months displayed by the calendar listing at the bottom of the screen, or will mark the holidays by highlighting days of the calendar listing. The Moon menu will list the different phases of the moon.

18

TIME SAVER

More than 100 different calendar commands are available in emacs. You should also know that in order to receive appointment reminders, emacs must be running. For more information, first try calendar's help, and then use the *apropos* command from emacs' Help menu to get more detailed information.

You can also use emacs to remind you of important events by using Neil Mager's emacs appointment commands. To set appointment reminders, you must first create an `.emacs` file in your home directory containing the following:

```
(setq view-diary-entries-initially t)
(setq appt-issue-message t)
(display-time)
(add-hook 'diary-hook 'appt-make-list)
```

Use the File menu to save this file. Then create an emacs diary by starting the calendar mode. After you've enabled the emacs calendar mode, click in the calendar window on a specific day, go to the Diary menu, and select Insert Daily. Your scratch buffer will change to "diary," and you'll find your cursor following text containing the selected date. Make some diary entries, then save the buffer, and exit and restart emacs.

After you restart emacs, you can enter appointment reminders in your diary with the emacs `appt-add` command. First enter the calendar mode, and click your left mouse button on a specific day. Next, press and release the Esc key, type an **`x`**, then type **`appt-add`**, and press Enter. You'll be asked for appointment time (hours and minutes). Enter the time. After you press Enter, you'll be prompted for a message. Type in your reminder and press Enter again.

Five minutes before the appointment time on the specified day, emacs will beep and then display a new mode line, informing you of the appointment. Two minutes later, the same thing will happen. You can also manually add reminders to your diary file, for example:

```
 8:00am Jogging with dog
12:00am Lunch with Cathy
15:00pm Check with car repair shop
```

You can save these reminders following each date in your diary files. If you want to delete appointments, use the `appt-delete` command after selecting a specific day. You'll be asked interactively to delete various appointments from your diary.

By using the emacs calendar mode and appointment functions, you can build a history of your appointments in your personal diary. Experiment with different modes, and read the emacs info files for more information.

Part IV

Hour 19

Playing Linux Games

It's time to sit back, relax, and have some fun. Chances are that you've skipped the rest of the book and are reading this chapter first. Well, that's okay, because we all know the real reason we bought our computers, right? To zap hordes of alien invaders streaming across our screen!

In this hour you'll learn about two music CD players and some of the more than 70 games you can install on your system. This hour starts with an overview of the CD players, then moves on to information about playing games at the console and with the X Window System.

Playing Music CDs with the `cpd` and `xplaycd` Commands

Using your computer as a stereo system may seem a bit extravagant, but it's nice to be able to listen to music while you work. In order to do this, Linux must be configured to use your sound card.

TIME SAVER

> If you have not configured Linux to support sound, stop! In order to use your CD-ROM drive to play music CDs, you must have sound support installed in your kernel. See Hour 22, "Red Hat Tools."

If your sound card works with Linux, great! You can start playing music CDs right away. If you're not using X11, you can play music CDs with Sariel Har-Peled's `cdp` command, found under the `/usr/bin` directory. This command is a text-mode program. To use it, put a music CD in your CD-ROM drive and type the command:

```
# cdp
```

If nothing happens, make sure have a symbolic link, called `/dev/cdrom`, that points to your CD-ROM device—for example,

```
# ls -l /dev/cdrom
lrwxrwxrwx    1 root     root            3 Dec 22 08:19 /dev/cdrom -> hdb
```

You can create a symbolic link with the `ln` command. Make sure you're logged in as the root operator and type the following:

```
# ln -s /dev/XXX /dev/cdrom
```

This creates the symbolic link, `/dev/cdrom`, which points to your CD-ROM drive device XXX (hdb, sdb, scd, and so on). If you're not the root operator when you run first run `cdp`, you may get an error message:

```
# cdp
As root, please run
chmod 666 /dev/cdrom
to give yourself permission to access the CD-ROM device.
```

By default, CD-ROM devices are created with a file permission of 660, and the `cdp` command requires your device to be readable by anyone on your system. To fix this, use the `chmod` command (discussed in Hour 21, "Handling Files"):

```
# chmod 666 /dev/cdrom
```

Now run the cdp command. When it starts, you'll see a list of the tracks on your CD. You should then turn on the NumLock key of your keyboard to control how you'd like to play your CD. Table 19.1 lists the controls for playing CDs from your keyboard's keypad.

Table 19.1. The cdp command keypad controls.

Action	Keypad Key
Soft exit (music continues)	0
Help	.
Back 15 seconds	1
Hard abort (eject CD)	2
Forward 15 seconds	3
Previous Track	4
Replay CD	5
Next Track	6
Stop	7
Toggle Pause/Resume	8
Play	9

The cdp command has a number of command-line options. A symbolic link, called cdplay, can be used to play music without the cdp command's interactive screen. You can tell cdplay to start playing music at a certain track with the play option, followed by a track number:

```
# cdplay play 3
```

This command line starts the cdp program, and your music CD starts playing from the third track. For more details about using the cdp command, see its manual page. The cdp command is handy for playing CDs from your console or the command line of an X11 terminal window, but if you use X11 all the time, you may want to use the xplaycd command, found under the /usr/X11R6/bin directory.

The xplaycd command, by Olav Woelfelschneider, is an X11 client you can use to play music CDs. The program appears in a small window with the standard music CD controls, along with horizontal stereo volume bars and a list of buttons representing the tracks on the CD. You can raise or lower your music's volume by clicking your left mouse button ahead of or behind the horizontal bars.

One great feature of this program is the ability to reorder tracks, and even play a track multiple times (see Figure 19.1). By clicking a track number and dragging, you can rearrange the play sequence of the tracks on your CD. To play a track multiple times, click a track number with your mouse's middle button and drag the track along the CD track sequence. When you release your mouse button, the track number is duplicated.

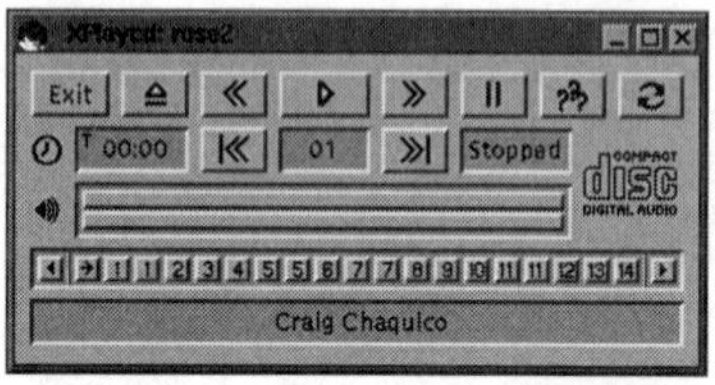

Figure 19.1.
The xplaycd X11 client offers standard music CD controls, along with track re-ordering and volume control.

The xplaycd also supports a music CD database, so you can create playlists of tracks for your favorite CDs. If you press your right mouse button anywhere on the xplaycd window, a menu of editing commands pops up. Use this menu to create and save your CD's play list. The database will be saved in the `/var/lib/cddb`, or CD database directory. You also can save CDs into different categories, such as jazz, new age, and so on. For details about using the `xplaycd` command, read its manual page, or the more detailed documentation under the `/usr/doc/` multimedia directory.

Games for the Console

If you don't use X11, you also can have fun at the console, because you'll find an assortment of 43 classic games you can play. Some of the games, like DOOM, have impressive graphics. Others use simple cursor movements and characters on your display.

Install the Berkeley Software Distribution, or BSD games, and you'll find: arithmetic, atc, backgammon, battlestar, bog, caesar, canfield, cribbage, factor, fish, hangman, mille, monop, paranoia, robots, trek, wargames, worm, and wump.

If you like text-based adventure games, try the `scottfree` command. This game interpreter comes with 11 adventures. Play an adventure by specifying its name on the command line.

```
# scottfree 6_circus
Scott Free, A Scott Adams game driver in C.
Release 1.14, (c) 1993,1994,1995 Swansea University Computer Society.
Distributed under the GNU software license

Roll up! Roll up!

The CIRCUS is in town!

Tell me what to do ?
```

This command line starts a circus text adventure. For more information about playing these games, read the files in the `/usr/doc/scottfree` and `/usr/doc/mysterious` directories.

Want the challenge of a good chess game? Try the gnuchess program, which plays an extremely strong game of chess. You'll find several versions of this game installed on your system. The gnuchess version uses cursor addressing to provide a basic graphic display. The gnuchessr version scrolls each board after successive moves, and uses reverse video and cursor addressing for a fancier display.

Moves are entered by specifying the column and row as a letter and number. For example,

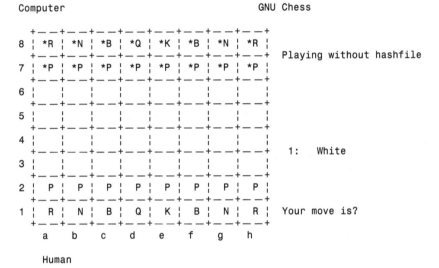

```
Computer                                        GNU Chess

  +---+---+---+---+---+---+---+---+
8 | *R | *N | *B | *Q | *K | *B | *N | *R |
  +---+---+---+---+---+---+---+---+  Playing without hashfile
7 | *P | *P | *P | *P | *P | *P | *P | *P |
  +---+---+---+---+---+---+---+---+
6 |    |    |    |    |    |    |    |    |
  +---+---+---+---+---+---+---+---+
5 |    |    |    |    |    |    |    |    |
  +---+---+---+---+---+---+---+---+
4 |    |    |    |    |    |    |    |    |
  +---+---+---+---+---+---+---+---+   1:    White
3 |    |    |    |    |    |    |    |    |
  +---+---+---+---+---+---+---+---+
2 |  P |  P |  P |  P |  P |  P |  P |  P |
  +---+---+---+---+---+---+---+---+
1 |  R |  N |  B |  Q |  K |  B |  N |  R |  Your move is?
  +---+---+---+---+---+---+---+---+
    a    b    c    d    e    f    g    h

    Human
```

To move the pawn up two squares from the lower rank, enter e2, and press the Enter key. The computer then makes its move, and new piece positions are updated on your display. The gnuchess program has more than 23 command-line options, and features display play modes, hints, and timed games. For more information, see the gnuchess manual page.

19

Playing Emacs Games

The venerable emacs editor (discussed in Hour 14, "Text Processing") not only edits text, reads mail, and handles your appointments, but also comes with 18 wacky games and modes that you can use to pass the time, such as doctor, dunnet, psychoanalyze-pinhead, and yow.

Start an emacs game by holding down the Alt key, then pressing the x key on your keyboard. In the command prompt at the bottom of your emacs screen type in one of the following, and then press the Enter key: blackbox, cookie1, dissociate, doctor, dunnet, hanoi, life, mpuz, solitaire, spook, or yow.

The best way to play dunnet, a text adventure, is to use emacs from the command line:

```
# emacs -batch -l dunnet
Dead end
You are at a dead end of a dirt road.  The road goes to the east.
In the distance you can see that it will eventually fork off.  The
trees here are very tall royal palms, and they are spaced equidistant
from each other.
There is a shovel here.
>
```

This command line starts the game. At the > prompt, enter commands such as `inventory`, `look`, or `go east`. To end the adventure, enter the word `quit`. You'll find more games for emacs in the `/usr/share/emacs/20.2/lisp/play` directory. For more details, you also can peruse the source code for the games by installing emacs' LISP source.

Games for the X Window System

In this section you'll be introduced to several games for X11. There are more than two dozen you can play, but rather than discussing them all, the following pages highlight several of the best games for strategy and action.

If you like playing board games, you're in luck! There are several good board games for the X Window System on this book's CD-ROM. Want more action? Try some of the video arcade games—you're sure to find some you like. The following is a list of just a few arcade games:

- acm—Aerial combat simulator for X11
- paradise—A networked combat game
- xbill—Quash a familiar face before "another" operating system is installed on your computer
- xchomp—Classic Pac-Man-like game
- xdemineuer—Minesweep-type game
- xjewel, xtrojka, cxhextris, xbl—Tetris-like games
- xlander—A lunar lander game
- xpilot—Networked combat game
- xpuzzles—A series of puzzle games for X11

Playing Chess with the xboard Client

Chess is a classic game, and one of the major challenges you can face is playing chess against your computer. To play chess in X11, use the xboard client. This program can use the GNU chess engine, and play chess over the Internet or through electronic mail (see Figure 19.2).

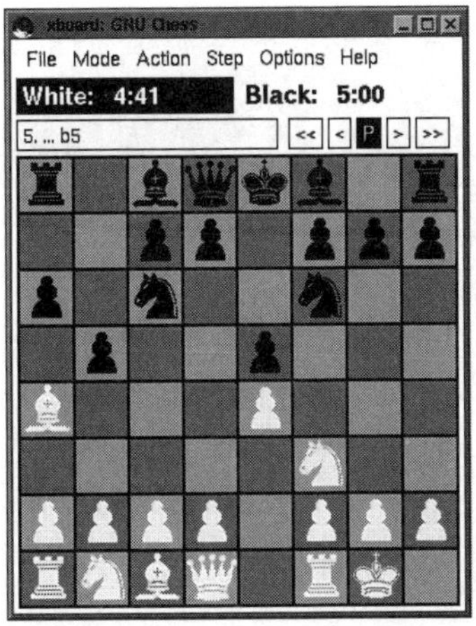

Figure 19.2.
The xboard X11 client plays chess on your display, over the Internet, or through electronic mail.

The xboard client recognizes many X11 Toolkit options, such as geometry settings, and has 54 different command-line options. If you have a display less than 1024×768 pixels, you should use the `-size` or `-boardSize small` command-line option to fit the board on your screen:

```
# xboard -size small &
```

This command line starts xboard using smaller chess pieces. For more details about using xboard, see the xboard and gnuchess manual pages.

Playing X11 Solitaire

If you enjoy playing card solitaire games, you'll like the xpat2 X11 client. This program features 14 different solitaire games with scoring, hints, built-in help, and sound (see Figure 19.3).

The xpat2 game, by Heiko Eissfeldt and Michael Bischoff, is found under the `/usr/X11R6/bin` directory. For more details, read the xpat2 manual page.

Playing Backgammon for X11

For backgammon fanatics, the xgammon game will produce hours of fun and practice. This game, by Lambert Klasen and Detlef Steuer, requires the X Window System, and runs comfortably on an 800×600 pixel display (see Figure 19.4).

The xgammon client has 21 different command-line options. For an interesting variation, try watching your computer play itself:

```
# xgammon -g cvc &
```

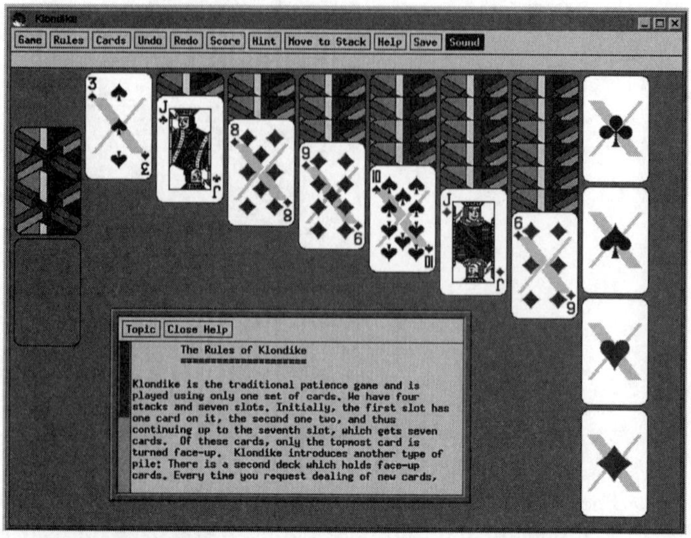

Figure 19.3.
The xpat2 solitaire game for X11 features 14 different card games.

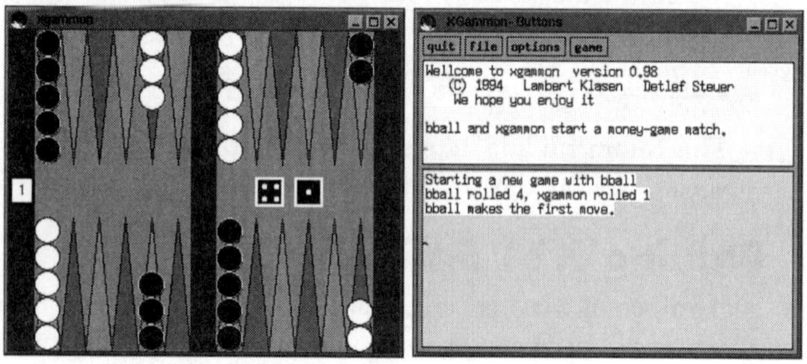

Figure 19.4.
The xgammon game for X11 features several types of play, such as computer against human, and provides a challenging game.

This starts the xgammon game so you can watch the action. You also can create your own challenging games by editing the board and placing backgammon stones in different positions before play. For details about xgammon, read its manual page.

Playing Galaga for X11

Video action arcade games can be a lot of fun, especially if they have great graphics and sound. If you like shoot-em-ups, you'll love the xgal game by Joe Rumsey. This X11 client features a spiffy interface, and can be played by using your mouse or keyboard.

The xgal program has six different command-line options, but you can start the program without any at a terminal window by typing the following:

```
# xgal &
```

To start playing, press your spacebar. Use the right and left cursor keys to move your ship across the screen, and your spacebar to fire. For more information, see the README file under the `/usr/doc/xgalaga` directory.

Breakout the Fun with the X11 Client Xboing

Xboing, by Justin C. Kibell, is a fast-paced, arcade-quality paddle and ball game for the X Window System. This game sports great graphics and sound, and provides hours of fun. You can start the xboing program from the command line of a terminal window. You'll need a display of at least 1024×768 pixels to play.

By default, xboing does not use sound, so if you want to hear sounds when you play, you must use the `-sound` command-line option. Set the speed of the ball's action after playing a game to fine-tune xboing's challenge by using the `-speed` option.

```
# xboing -sound -speed 7
```

This command line starts xboing with sound enabled, and a very fast ball speed. Another good option to use is `-grab`, which keeps your cursor within xboing's X11 window, preventing you from accidentally activating other windows and missing any action. For more details about playing this game, see the xboing manual page.

Playing DOOM for X Window

DOOM, by id Software, is one of the most popular arcade games to hit the personal computer scene in recent years. You'll find a copy on this book's CD-ROM, and you can play DOOM from the console or from an X11 terminal window.

If you start DOOM from the command line as a regular user, you may experience permission errors. If so, use the `su` command to start the game as the root operator:

```
# su -c "rundoom"
```

You'll be asked if your computer can support sound. Type a `y` or `n`, then press the Enter key to start the game. If you start DOOM from an X11 terminal window, the game starts in a small, floating window. Some documentation for running DOOM may be found under the `/usr/doc/doom` directory.

Part V

Administering Your System

Hour

Hour 20

Basic System Administration

This hour introduces you to the basics of system administration. You'll learn how to use the su command, get information about your system, how to manage other users, and how to use file tools to keep Linux running in top form. Although much of what's discussed in this hour consists of commonsense guidelines, you'll also get some valuable tips on squeezing the best performance out of Linux. You'll also use this knowledge in the next four hours, which cover handling files, the Red Hat control panel, archiving, and scheduling.

Even if you're the only person who uses your computer, you should still learn basic system administration, or sysadmin, skills, for at least some of the following reasons:

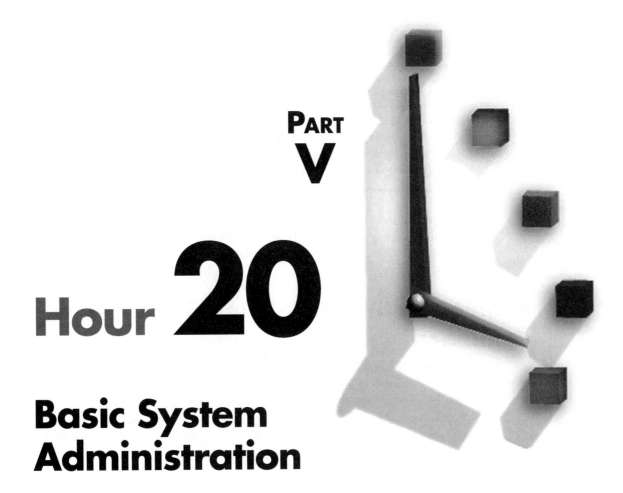

- To back up or restore your system, or at the least, important files
- To conserve disk space
- To install new software or upgrade your Linux system
- To teach someone else about Linux, such as a coworker, friend, spouse, or child
- To troubleshoot problems

Here's a good reason that you should never run your system as the root operator: Always running as root can be dangerous because you have access to all files on the system, and can delete, move, or copy them all. You can wipe out your system (remember the warning in Hour 5, "Manipulation and Searching Commands," about the rm command) with this command:

```
# rm -fr /*
```

If you run Linux from your own account, this problem won't happen, because rm will complain with "Permission denied," and quit. But what if you're logged in under a user other than root, and you need to do things to your system as the root operator? This is where the su command comes into play.

Running as the Root Operator with the su Command

The su command, although commonly called the superuser command, allows you to run a command as any user on your system. Found under the /bin directory, su has seven different command-line options. Several of the most common are covered here. Although you'll most likely use su to become root, this command can be handy if you want to become another user and troubleshoot such problems as email or printing. Using the su command is easy, for example:

```
# su
Password:
su: incorrect password
```

By default, the su command will allow you to become the root operator if you call it without a username. You'll be asked to enter a password, and su will complain and quit if you enter the wrong one. If you enter the right password, you'll be logged in as root. To return to your shell, use your shell's exit command, as follows:

```
$ su
Password:
# whoami
root
# exit
exit
$ whoami
bball
```

This shows that after you execute the exit command, you're returned to your normal user status. Another handy feature of the su command is the -s command-line option to run a different shell. If you want to try a different shell without using the chsh command to permanently change your shell, you can use the following:

```
$ printenv ¦ SHELL
```

```
SHELL=/bin/bash
$ su -s /bin/ksh
Password:
# printenv ¦ fgrep SHELL
SHELL=/bin/ksh
# exit
$
```

This shows that although the default shell is bash, you can temporarily use the pdksh, or public domain Korn shell. But unless you specify your own username, you'll run the new shell as the root operator. A better approach is

```
$ su -s /bin/ksh yourusername
```

Finally, you can also use the `su` command to execute a command when you use the `-c` command-line option. This can be handy to do tasks only permitted to the root operator, for example:

```
# su -c "mount -t msdos /dev/hdc1 /mnt/flash"
Password:
```

This command line mounts the `/dev/hdc1` device, a SunDisk flash card with a DOS filesystem, at the `/mnt/flash` directory mount point. If you need to temporarily mount or unmount diskettes, CD-ROMs, or other devices, you'll find this a convenient approach. Hour 21, "Handling Files," covers mounting and unmounting other filesystems.

If you're using Linux in the console mode (not running X11), you can use the console keys (Alt-F1 and so on), to run a virtual console as the root operator to do root operator tasks. But this is a bad convenience, as you may be tempted to run as root all the time. At least using the `su` command makes you think about why you're running as root. Be careful!

The next section introduces you to tools you can use to determine how your system is working.

Getting Disk Space Information

When you installed Linux, you installed your system onto a partition, designated by a specific device, such as `/dev/hda1`, `/dev/sdb1`, and so on. Hopefully, you made the partition large enough to accommodate your present and future needs. But how do you check to see how much room you have left on disk, or for that matter, how many disks you have? Although Linux can support up to 4 terabytes, and maximum file sizes up to 2 gigabytes, not many of us are wealthy enough to own, or even need, that much storage. Even though disk storage is getting cheaper, it is still at a premium when you have a lot of software installed or need the work space.

Getting Filesystem Statistics with the df Command

The df (free disk space) command will gather and summarize some important statistics about all currently mounted filesystems. The df command is easy to use, for example:

```
# df
Filesystem          1024-blocks   Used Available Capacity Mounted on
/dev/hda3               497699  443871     28124      94%   /
/dev/hda1               509856  469632     40224      92%   /mnt/dos
/dev/hdc1                 3868    2596      1272      67%   /mnt/flash
/dev/hdb                644324  644324         0     100%   /mnt/cdrom
```

This output shows four different filesystems on three different devices mounted under Linux. The first is the root partition at the / directory on /dev/hda3; the second is a DOS partition under /mnt/dos on /dev/hda1; the third is a flashcard under /mnt/flash on /dev/hdc1; and the fourth is a CD-ROM, mounted under /mnt/cdrom on /dev/dev/hdb. The df command also lists the size of the storage device, how much has been used, how much is available, and the current capacity of the device. Notice that the CD-ROM has no space left. This is because it is mounted read-only, meaning you can't save or delete files on this device. The command shown in the next example will let you know.

One handy way to find out about the different filesystems you have mounted is to use the mount command. This command is usually used during startup, and by the root operator to mount and unmount filesystems, but you can use mount to show what type of filesystems are in use, and how the filesystems are mounted, for example:

```
# mount
/dev/hda3 on / type ext2 (rw)
/dev/hda1 on /mnt/dos type msdos (rw)
none on /proc type proc (rw)
/dev/hdc1 on /mnt/flash type msdos (rw)
/dev/hdb on /mnt/cdrom type iso9660 (ro)
```

This shows that your root partition, on the / directory, is a Linux ext2 filesystem mounted read-write, whereas /mnt/dos and /mnt/flash contain DOS partitions, also read-write. (The /proc filesystem is a special directory Linux uses for process reporting, such as running applications, system state, and so on.) Finally, mount reports that your CD-ROM is mounted as a read-only iso9660 filesystem.

You can use this information from mount to get specific information with the df command, by using the df command's -t, or filesystem, option, as follows:

```
# df -t ext2
Filesystem          1024-blocks   Used Available Capacity Mounted on
/dev/hda3               497699  443873     28122      94%   /
```

This tells df to just show information about any mounted Linux filesystems. You can get a list of valid filesystems to specify with the df command by looking at the mount manual page.

The `mount` command is covered in more detail in Hour 21, "Handling Files." You can see that by using the `df` and `mount` command, you can get reports on the type of mounted devices, how the devices are mounted, and how much room you have left on each.

Getting Filesystem Disk Usage with the du Command

The `du` (disk usage) command conveniently summarizes how your disk is being used, by reporting the amount of space required by each directory or specified path. Although the `du` command has more than 20 command-line options, this section presents some of the common ones, and leaves it up to you to experiment. You can use the `du` command by itself, or specify a directory or path, for example:

```
# du
904     ./book
12080   ./mail
1       ././.tin/.mailidx
1       ././.tin/.index
10      ././.tin
...
589     ./News
9       ././.index
7       ././.procmail
5       ././.ncftp
418     ./reading
778     ./documents
27199   .
```

This report (for brevity, not all the directories are listed) shows the contents of a home directory, with a total for 27,199 1-kilobyte blocks. If you find this hard to understand, you can have `du` report the size in bytes, for example:

```
# du -b
897606  ./book
12294410        ./mail
1024    ././.tin/.mailidx
1024    ././.tin/.index
9382    ././.tin
561715  ./News
4033    ././.index
4139    ././.procmail
2791    ././.ncftp
424037  ./reading
784216  ./documents
26785752        .
```

If this is too much information for you, then you can use the `--summarize` option to get the total in either kilobytes or bytes, as follows:

```
# du -b --summarize
26786903        .
```

20

The du command can also help you keep track of directories which, unattended, sometimes grow out of control or use a lot of disk space. If you specify a path, du will report on the different size of the directories, pinpointing any that may contain too much information, for example:

```
# du --summarize -b /var/* ¦ sort -nr
6474535 /var/lib
2336494 /var/log
868163  /var/catman
76362   /var/spool
14591   /var/dt
2385    /var/run
2048    /var/lock
2048    /var/local
1024    /var/tmp
1024    /var/preserve
1024    /var/nis
```

Here I've combined the du command, which has been instructed to summarize the number of bytes in each directory, with the sort command, which has been set to use a numerical sort in reverse order. This one-liner, which uses pipes (discussed in Hour 6, "Using the Shell"), will automatically print the largest directories at the top of the output list. You can see that the /var/log directory is getting pretty big. The /var/lib directory will be large because it contains the rpm databases (rpm is discussed in Hour 22, "Red Hat Tools").

Although the du command does not, like the df command, have a -t option to specify which filesystem to report on, you can use the -x option to exclude other filesystems. Or, you can have du report on other filesystems by specifying a usage report at the mount point. For example, du will merrily chug along and summarize how much room your Windows directories take up:

```
# du -b --summarize /mnt/dos/* ¦ sort -nr
129486405       /mnt/dos/windows
23929345        /mnt/dos/msoffice
20811654        /mnt/dos/photoenf
7744046 /mnt/dos/tranxit
6828902 /mnt/dos/org2
6647520 /mnt/dos/laplink
5556496 /mnt/dos/acrobat3
4041127 /mnt/dos/pcdr
3753962 /mnt/dos/psp
3603469 /mnt/dos/insync
3176769 /mnt/dos/antvirus
2669335 /mnt/dos/airlite
2408920 /mnt/dos/winfax
...
```

This (shortened) report shows that next to the operating system, the largest space is taken up by certain applications. This information can be helpful in making a decision on what applications to uninstall if you need more disk space.

Checking Symbolic Links with the `stat` Command

The `stat` command will give you a lot of information about a file or directory. Much of this information is technical, but you may find the `stat` command useful for checking symbolic links. The `stat` command does not have any command-line options, but you can specify directories or filenames, for example:

```
# stat .
  File: "."
  Size: 2048         Filetype: Directory
  Mode: (0775/drwxrwxr-x)         Uid: (  500/   bball)  Gid: (  500/   bball)
Device:  3,3   Inode: 91932      Links: 19
Access: Wed Nov 19 17:29:42 1997(00000.00:04:46)
Modify: Wed Nov 19 16:52:12 1997(00000.00:42:16)
Change: Wed Nov 19 16:52:12 1997(00000.00:42:16)
```

You can see that the `stat` command shows who the file or directory belongs to, along with permissions, and other information. If you want to use `stat` to check symbolic links, you can try

```
# touch file1
# ln -s file1 file2
# rm file1
rm: remove `file1'? y
# stat file2
Can't stat file2
```

As a beginning sysadmin, you can use this knowledge to devise an even better approach to help `stat` look at file directories recursively. There are a number of ways to do this. Here's one handy command line you can use to check all the symbolic links in your Linux filesystem:

```
# find / -xdev | xargs stat | fgrep "Can't stat"
```

This command line uses the `find` command to feed pathnames to the `stat` command (through the `xargs` command), and then the `fgrep` command to print all matches when `stat` can't find a symbolic link. As you become a more proficient sysadmin, you'll devise your own bag of tricks to help diagnose your system.

Saving Disk Space

This section gives you some tips on saving disk space. Part of being a sysadmin is maintaining the health of your filesystem, and performing cleanup operations occasionally to free up disk space. Once you've found some techniques or approaches that work for your system and the way you work on your system, you'll find that you can routinely trim and recover megabytes of disk space.

One good way to save disk space is not to install a lot of software. For example, how many different word processors do you need? How many graphics programs do you need? If you find a capable program, delete others that do the same thing. Make sure to read Hour 22 to see how the `rpm` command can help you free up disk space and customize your Linux installation by deleting packages of programs and supporting software.

You can often trim the size of your directories by looking for less often used programs, or collections of graphics or text you don't need. You've already seen one way to find directories that may be candidates for cleanup. But you should also consider some other file types that may more obviously be deleted.

For example, some Linux programs create backup files with the tilde prefix. You can search for these as follows:

```
# find / -name ~* -xdev
```

Once you feel comfortable with the results, you can pipe the filenames into the `rm` command, using the `xargs` command to build a cleanup command line (although you can also use the `find` command's `-exec` command-line option):

```
# find / -name ~* -xdev | xargs rm -f
```

You should also search for files named `core`. These are *core dumps*, or dumps of program memory created if a program abnormally aborts. Some of these files can be huge, for example:

```
# ls -l /usr/lib/rhs/glint/core
-rw-------    1 root     root      10768384 Sep 16 15:26 /usr/lib/rhs/glint/core
```

You can use the bash or pdksh shells' `ulimit` command to limit the size of these core files. To see the current allowable size of core files, use the `ulimit` command's `-c` option, for example:

```
# ulimit -c
1000000
```

This doesn't mean that core dumps are limited to 1MB, but 1,000,000 512-byte blocks! You can limit the size of core files with the `-c` option, as in

```
# ulimit -c 1000
```

This sets the maximum size of core files to 512,000 bytes. If you're using the csh shell, use

```
# limit coredumpsize 1000
```

Limiting the size of these files is one way to can save disk space in the future. Other candidates for removal include

`*.bak, *.BAK`	Backup files
`*.o`	Compiled object files from compiling operations
`#*`	Backup files
`*.1, *.2, *.3`	File extensions for system log files under the `/var/log` directory. Some logs can grow quite large, and unless you really need them, they should be deleted.

CAUTION

> Be careful about deleting files with file-number extensions, such as `.1`, across your system: you will delete a lot of libraries and manual pages if you automate a search-and-destroy mission starting at the root, or /, directory!

If you feel uncomfortable with letting the `find` command run through your file system and deleting files, just have the command generate a report of candidate files as follows:

```
# find / \( -name core -o -name *.o \) -xdev > deletelist.txt
```

Note that you can also set this command to run unattended, at regular intervals, and have the report emailed to you as an automatic reminder. See Hour 24, "Scheduling," for details.

If you experiment with your own combination of commands, you'll soon come up with your own customized reports and cleanup actions. You now know how to get information about your drive space. You'll also learn about managing disk space, using quotas (software limits on hard drive usage) in the "Managing User Access" section. For now, you'll learn how to find out more about what's going on in your computer's memory when you run Linux.

Getting Memory Information

Although the industry trend has been to offer more hard drive space and more memory for less money, many people don't like to outlay more cash to expand their systems. The good news is that Linux is very efficient at using memory, because even a 16MB system provides enough room (with an equal amount of swap space) to run X11 and most programs well. The bad news is that programs are getting larger all the time, especially with *feature creep*, in which more and more functions creep into programs. This section introduces you to some programs you may find helpful in understanding your system's memory, and gives you some tips on conserving memory.

Memory Reporting with the `free` Command

The `free` command shows breakdowns of the amounts and totals of free and used memory, including your swapfile usage. This command has several command-line options, but is easy to run and understand, for example:

```
# free
             total       used       free     shared    buffers     cached
Mem:         30892      28004       2888      14132       3104      10444
-/+ buffers:            14456      16436
Swap:        34268       7964      26304
```

This shows a 32MB system with 34MB swap space. Notice that nearly all the system memory is being used, and nearly 8MB of swap space has been used.

By default, the `free` command displays memory in kilobytes, or 1024-byte notation. You can use the `-b` option to display your memory in bytes, or the `-m` option to display memory in megabytes. You can also use the `free` command to constantly monitor how much memory is being used through the `-s` command. This is handy as a real-time monitor if you specify a .01-second update and run the `free` command in a terminal window under X11.

Virtual Memory Reporting with the `vmstat` Command

The `vmstat` is a general-purpose monitoring program, which offers real-time display of not only memory usage, virtual memory statistics, but disk activity, system usage, and central processing unit (CPU) activity. If you call `vmstat` without any command-line options, you'll get a one-time snapshot, for example:

```
# vmstat
 procs                      memory    swap        io     system         cpu
 r b w   swpd   free   buff cache  si  so    bi    bo   in    cs  us  sy  id
 0 0 0   7468   1060   4288 10552   1   1    10     1  134    68   3   2  96
```

If you specify a time interval in seconds on the `vmstat` command line, you'll get a continuously scrolling report. Having a constant display of what is going on with your computer can help you if you're trying to find out why your computer suddenly slows down, or why there's a lot of disk activity.

Viewing Your Shell's "Ulimit"ations

You've already seen how you can limit the size of core dump files previously in this hour. There are other settings you can set in your shell. If you're using the bash or pdksh (ksh) shell, you can use the `ulimit` command's `-a` option to print your current settings, for example:

```
# ulimit -a
core file size (blocks)  1000000
data seg size (kbytes)   unlimited
file size (blocks)       unlimited
max memory size (kbytes) unlimited
stack size (kbytes)      8192
cpu time (seconds)       unlimited
max user processes       256
pipe size (512 bytes)    8
open files               256
virtual memory (kbytes)  2105343
```

If you're using the tcsh or csh shell, you can use the `limit` command to list the current settings:

```
$ limit
cputime         unlimited
filesize        unlimited
```

```
datasize        unlimited
stacksize       8192 kbytes
coredumpsize    1000000 kbytes
memoryuse       unlimited
descriptors     256
memorylocked    unlimited
maxproc         256
```

These limits are different from limits for the root operator. The limits shown in this example are known as *soft limits*. To view the shell's hard limits, log in as the root operator, and use the `-a` limit option (use `-Ha` for bash or ksh's `ulimit` command), for example:

```
$ su
Password:
# limit -h
cputime         unlimited
filesize        unlimited
datasize        unlimited
stacksize       8192 kbytes
coredumpsize    unlimited
memoryuse       unlimited
descriptors     256
memorylocked    unlimited
maxproc         256
```

As you can see, viewing the limits as the root operator in the tcsh shell shows a much different situation. This is another good reason not to run as the root operator! As a sysadmin, you can use these settings to limit the amount of memory or number of processes available to each user. This is extremely handy if you have a number of people working on your computer at the same time, and you want to conserve system memory. For using Linux on a standalone computer under your normal login and working conditions, you'll find the default limits quite reasonable.

Reclaiming Memory with the `kill` Command

As a desperate measure if you need to quickly reclaim memory, you can stop running programs by using the `kill` command. In order to kill a specific program, you should use the `ps` command to list current running processes, and then stop any or all of them with the `kill` command. By default, the `ps` command lists processes you own and which you can kill, for example:


```
# ps
  PID TTY STAT  TIME COMMAND
  367  p0 S    0:00 bash
  581  p0 S    0:01 rxvt
  582  p1 S    0:00 (bash)
  747  p0 S    0:00 (applix)
  809  p0 S    0:18 netscape index.html
  810  p0 S    0:00 (dns helper)
  945  p0 R    0:00 ps
```

The ps command will list the currently running programs and the program's process number, or PID. You can use this information to kill a process with

```
# kill -9 809
```

However, if you need to reclaim memory efficiently, you should use the ps command's -m option, which also lists the memory usage of each process, for example:

```
# ps -m
  PID TTY MAJFLT MINFLT  TRS   DRS  SIZE  SWAP   RSS  SHRD   LIB  DT COMMAND
  747  p0      0      3   16   208   364   140   224   224     0   0 (applix)
  582  p1    151    274  124   184   436   128   308   268     0  10 (bash)
  959  p0     89     20   28   376   404     0   404   320     0  21 ps -m
  367  p0    305    826  220   316   600    64   536   428     0  27 bash
  810  p0    313     38  164   696   968   108   860   596     0  47 (dns helpe
  581  p0    212    508   28   960  1280   292   988   304     0 171 rxvt
  809  p0   2615   1205 3900  3692  8684  1092  7592  4644     0 699 netscape
```

By using this information, you can see that if you want to reclaim the most memory, you should stop the Netscape Web browser, as it is using nearly 9MB of system memory. Although you wouldn't normally use the kill command to stop programs, the kill command can be helpful to stop runaway, or nonresponsive, programs. The kill command works by sending a signal to the Linux kernel, along with the PID, so the kernel can act on the process. There are various signals you can use, although, as I've pointed out, the -9, or SIGKILL option is the most abrupt and drastic. You can see a list of different signals by using the kill command's -l option, for example:

```
# kill -l
 1) SIGHUP       2) SIGINT       3) SIGQUIT      4) SIGILL
 5) SIGTRAP      6) SIGIOT       7) SIGBUS       8) SIGFPE
 9) SIGKILL     10) SIGUSR1     11) SIGSEGV     12) SIGUSR2
13) SIGPIPE     14) SIGALRM     15) SIGTERM     17) SIGCHLD
18) SIGCONT     19) SIGSTOP     20) SIGTSTP     21) SIGTTIN
22) SIGTTOU     23) SIGURG      24) SIGXCPU     25) SIGXFSZ
26) SIGVTALRM   27) SIGPROF     28) SIGWINCH    29) SIGIO
30) SIGPWR
```

For more details on these signals, and the kill command, see its manual page.

The ps command has nearly two dozen command-line options, and you can also list all running processes. See the ps manual page for more information. You can also use the top command, discussed next, to find and kill processes.

Getting System Load Information with the top and xload Commands

The top command, found under the /usr/bin directory, is a system monitor that displays statistical information about how Linux is currently handling your memory, swap file, and processes. The top program also shows how long your system has been running, the status of your CPU, the size of each process, and more. You'll typically use the `top` command by running it on a spare console, or separate X11 terminal window (see Figure 20.1).

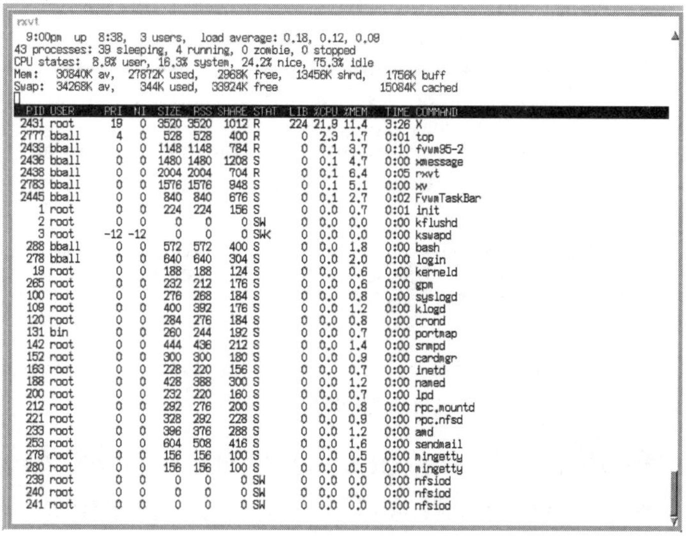

Figure 20.1
The `top` command provides an ongoing display of your system.

The `top` command also has a number of interactive controls, including a help screen, accessed with the question mark or the H key. You can also toggle various modes of the display, such as listing processes by memory usage or limiting the number of processes displayed. This can be helpful if you would like to monitor only the top five processes that require the greatest amount of your system's memory, and it can help you diagnose problems if your computer starts unusual disk or swap file activity.

You can also use `top` to interactively kill processes, using the K key, or change a process's priority (how much time the CPU devotes to a task) with the R key. The `top` program has 19 different interactive commands, and you can customize its display by adding or removing different information fields and lengthening or shortening the number of processes. See its manual page for more information.

The `xload` command, used under X11, provides a running graph of your system's load, instead of the `top` command's statistics. System loads vary from computer to computer, but you can generally tell when your system is overloaded by inordinate disk activity, as processes are swapped back and forth from your swap file. The `xload` command can help give you a visual warning if you're running too many programs, and may be especially helpful if you're running X11 on a 8MB or 16MB Linux system.

The `xload` command has eight different command-line options, and you can customize the color of the moving graphic, scale lines, or background.

Determining How Long Linux Has Been Running with the uptime and w Commands

The `uptime` command shows you how long Linux has been running, how many users are on, and three system load averages, for example:

```
# uptime
 12:44am  up  8:16,  3 users,  load average: 0.11, 0.10, 0.04
```

If this is too little information for you, try the `w` command, which first shows the same information as the `uptime` command, and then lists what currently logged-in users are doing:

```
# w
 12:48am  up  8:20,  3 users,  load average: 0.14, 0.09, 0.05
USER     TTY      FROM              LOGIN@  IDLE   JCPU   PCPU  WHAT
bball    ttyp0    localhost.locald  9:47pm 15.00s  0.38s  0.16s  bash
bball    ttyp2    localhost.locald 12:48am  0.00s  0.16s  0.08s  w
```

The `w` command gives a little more information, and it is especially helpful if you would like to monitor a busy system with a number of users.

Getting Network and Mail Information with the pppstats and mailstat Commands

The `pppstats` command, found under the `/usr/sbin` directory, will give you a running statistical display on the status and activity of your PPP connection. The information is similar to the output of the `ifconfig` command. To use the `pppstats` program, specify the PPP interface (usually 0) on the command after you have connected to your ISP:

```
# /usr/sbin/pppstats 0
    in   pack   comp uncomp     err  |    out   pack   comp uncomp     ip
 24791     93     74      5       0  |   1922     72     54      4     14
    78      4      3      0       0  |     80      4      3      0      1
   129      2      0      0       0  |    160      3      0      1      2
  1169     23     21      1       0  |    842     23     20      2      1
 12748     28     27      1       0  |    730     27     18      9      0
  9582     18     13      5       0  |    375     13      6      7      0
  9399     18     16      2       0  |    268     12      8      4      0
    71      3      2      0       0  |     80      4      3      0      1
...
```

This shows the `pppstats` command in action after displaying a line of statistics every five seconds, during startup of a newsreading session.

The `mailstat` program, a shell script written by S.R. van den Berg, found under the `/usr/bin` directory, is useful to check whether there's incoming mail, and can be used to generate reports about your mail usage.

```
# mailstat /var/log/maillog
No mail arrived since Nov 19 16:27
```

Monitoring Your Serial Ports with the `statserial` Command

The `statserial` program, originally by Jeff Tranter, can be used to show the status of your serial ports, and can be a lifesaver if you need to troubleshoot modems or serial ports. To use `statserial`, you must specify the device on the program's command line. You can, for example, tell `statserial` to monitor your modem by specifying its symbolic link:

```
# ln -s /dev/cua1 /dev/modem
# statserial /dev/modem
Device: /dev/modem

Signal  Pin  Pin  Direction  Status  Full
Name    (25) (9)  (computer)         Name
----    ---  ---  ---------- ------  ----
FG       1    -      -          -    Frame Ground
TxD      2    3      out        -    Transmit Data
RxD      3    2      in         -    Receive  Data
RTS      4    7      out        1    Request To Send
CTS      5    8      in         1    Clear To Send
DSR      6    6      in         0    Data Set Ready
GND      7    5      -          -    Signal Ground
DCD      8    1      in         0    Data Carrier Detect
DTR     20    4      out        1    Data Terminal Ready
RI      22    9      in         0    Ring Indicator
```

Time Saver

> You must be the root operator to use the `statserial` program.

Managing User Access

One of your main jobs as a sysadmin is to manage the users on your system. This involves creating accounts for new users, assigning home directories, specifying an initial shell for the user, and possibly restricting how much disk space, memory, or how many processes each person can use. This section shows you how to use different command-line programs to manage users. You should also read Hour 22, "Red Hat Tools," if you'd like to see how you can do these and other tasks with graphical utilities while running the X Window System.

Creating Users with the `adduser` Command

One of the first things you should do after installing Linux is to create a user account for yourself. You'll want to do all your work in Linux through this account, and do your system management using the `su` command. There are several ways to create new users in Linux, but this section shows you the easy way, using a trio of commands: `adduser`, `passwd`, and `chfn`.

The first step in creating a new user is to use the adduser command, found under the /usr/sbin directory. You must be the root operator to run this program:

```
# adduser
Only root may add users to the system.
```

The adduser program also requires you to specify a user name on the command line, for example:

```
# adduser cloobie

Looking for first available UID... 502
Looking for first available GID... 502

Adding login: cloobie...done.
Creating home directory: /home/cloobie...done.
Creating mailbox: /var/spool/mail/cloobie...done.

Don't forget to set the password.
```

The command will create an account, assign a user identification (UID), a group identification (GID), and then create a directory called cloobie under the /home directory. As a reminder, the adduser program tells you to set a password for your new user.

Changing Passwords in /etc/passwd with the passwd Command

After creating your new user, you must assign a password with the passwd command. This command will create an entry in the passwd text database in the /etc directory. To show you how this works, the following example shows you the passwd file, creates a password for your new user, and then shows you the password file so you can see the new entry.

```
# cat /etc/passwd
root:syvolaPd3M4QE:0:0:root:/root:/bin/bash
bin:*:1:1:bin:/bin:
daemon:*:2:2:daemon:/sbin:
adm:*:3:4:adm:/var/adm:
lp:*:4:7:lp:/var/spool/lpd:
sync:*:5:0:sync:/sbin:/bin/sync
shutdown:*:6:0:shutdown:/sbin:/sbin/shutdown
halt:*:7:0:halt:/sbin:/sbin/halt
mail:*:8:12:mail:/var/spool/mail:
news:*:9:13:news:/var/spool/news:
uucp:*:10:14:uucp:/var/spool/uucp:
operator:*:11:0:operator:/root:
games:*:12:100:games:/usr/games:
gopher:*:13:30:gopher:/usr/lib/gopher-data:
ftp:*:14:50:FTP User:/home/ftp:
nobody:*:99:99:Nobody:/:
bball:ODyJ5x09iRgNQ:500:500:Billy Ball,,,,:/home/bball:/bin/bash
cloobie:*:502:502:RHS Linux User:/home/cloobie:/bin/bash
```

You can see that although an account has been created, and contains a username, UID, PID, name, directory, and default shell, there's no password. To add a password, type the command, along with the new user's name:

```
# passwd cloobie
New UNIX password:
Retype new UNIX password:
passwd: all authentication tokens updated successfully
```

You'll be asked for a password, and then asked to retype it to verify. If all goes well, the password will be recorded in `/etc/passwd`, for example:

```
cloobie:9Qa4.uFMhmInA:502:502:RHS Linux User:/home/cloobie:/bin/bash
```

Later on, users can change their own password by using the `passwd` command, and you should encourage frequent password changes.

CAUTION

> As the sysadmin, you can change anyone's password if they forget it. Don't forget yours!

Finally, you'll also want to use the `chfn` command to enter formal information about users, or have your users enter this information. The `chfn` command will ask

```
# chfn cloobie
Changing finger information for cloobie.
Name [RHS Linux User]: Mr. Cloobie Doo
Office []: 400 Pennsylvania Ave.
Office Phone []: 202-555-1212
Home Phone []: 202-555-4000

Finger information changed.
```

If you now examine the `/etc/passwd` entry, you'll see

```
cloobie:9Qa4.uFMhmInA:502:502:Mr. Cloobie Doo,400 Pennsylvania Ave.,
202-555-1212,202-555-4000,:/home/cloobie:/bin/bash
```

This information is used by the `finger` command. The formal name may also be used along with the user name in mail messages, for example:

```
#  finger cloobie
Login: cloobie                          Name: Mr. Cloobie Doo
Directory: /home/cloobie                Shell: /bin/bash
Office: 400 Pennsylvania Ave.           Office Phone: 202-555-1212
Home Phone: 202-555-4000
Never logged in.
No mail.
No Plan.
```

The `finger` command will extract the user's information from the `/etc/passwd` file and print it in a nice format. One of the other things you should note in a user's `/etc/passwd` entry is the name of a shell at the end. This can be a unique way to not only specify the type of shell used (your Linux system is set up to assign the bash shell by default), but to restrict the user to a particular program.

Restricting Logins

Your users normally can change the shell used after login through the `chsh` command. You can list the currently available shells by using the `chsh` command's `-l` (list shells) option, for example:

```
# chsh -l
/bin/ash
/bin/bsh
/bin/bash
/bin/sh
/bin/csh
/bin/ksh
/bin/tcsh
```

The `chsh` command looks in a file called `shells` under the `/etc` directory, and prints a list. This does not mean that these shells are available, just "acceptable." You can edit this file, adding or removing shells that can be specified by your users. You should make sure that the shells listed in this file are available on your system. To change shells, you can type

```
# chsh -s /bin/ksh
Changing shell for root.
Shell changed.
```

You can also use the `chsh` command to specify a program, other than a shell, to use as the program run when the user logs in, for example:

```
# chsh -s /usr/bin/pico cloobie
Changing shell for cloobie.
Warning: "/usr/bin/pico" is not listed as a valid shell.
Shell changed.
```

The `chsh` program will complain if the program is not listed as a shell in the `/etc/shells` file. Then check to see if the change was made:

```
# cat /etc/passwd
...
cloobie:9Qa4.uFMhmInA:502:502:Mr. Cloobie Doo,400 Pennsylvania Ave.,
202-555-1212,202-555-4000,:/home/cloobie:/usr/bin/pico
```

The preceding example specified the text editor pico, which would allow a user to do word processing, printing, or spell-checking of documents, but that's all! As soon as the user logs into Linux, the user is right in the text editor. After quitting the text editor, the user is logged out. This is a handy technique you can use to restrict users, especially children, if you only want them to play a game.

There are other restrictions you can put in place. The next section shows you how you can limit how much of your system's hard drive can be used.

Setting Disk Quotas

On large, multiuser systems, disk quotas are not only a way of life, but a necessity. You can impose disk quotas on your Linux system, and you should, especially if you worry about your disk space, or if you're afraid the users will create huge files and overrun your hard drive. You can also use disk quotas as a warning device (and maybe justification for a new hard drive?). This section explains how to start, set, and stop disk quotas.

Quota Manipulation with the `quota`, `quotaon`, and `quotaoff` Commands

Disk quotas limit the amount of hard drive space in several ways. You can set quotas for a group of users, by using the GID, or impose limits on individual users. To manage disk quotas, you'll use some or all of these commands:

`quota`	To report on disk quotas
`quotaon`	To turn on and set disk quotas for users
`quotaoff`	To turn off disk quotas for users
`repquot`	Also reports on quotas
`edquota`	Edits user quotas
`quotacheck`	Checks filesystem on quota usage

This book won't go into all the details of these programs (read the manual pages), but this section shows you how to set a disk quota for the new user you created. The first thing you must do is to enable quotas for your Linux filesystem. This involves editing the filesystem table, `fstab`, in the `/etc/` directory. Be careful! You must make sure you don't make any other changes, or you could cause boot problems. You have been warned!

Make sure you're logged in as root, then use your favorite text editor to open the `fstab` file, and edit the line containing the entry for your Linux partition, for example:

```
# <device>    <mountpoint>  <filesystemtype> <options> <dump> <fsckorder>
/dev/hda3                /                             ext2   defaults 1 1
```

Now add a command and the word `usrquota` to the word default, for example:

```
/dev/hda3                /                             ext2   defaults,usrquota 1 1
```

Save the `/etc/fstab` file. Next, use the `touch` command to create a file called `quota.user`, and make the file read-write enabled, for example:

```
# touch /quota.user
# chmod 600 /quota.user
```

After you have done this, reboot your computer by using the `shutdown` command with the `-r`, or restart, option. Log back in as root, and use the `edquota` command, found under the `/usr/sbin` directory, along with the `-u` option, to edit quotas for your new user, for example:

```
# edquota -u cloobie
```

The `edquota` command will read in the `user.quota` file under your `root`, or `/`, directory. This file is normally a binary file, but `edquota` will open the file using the text editor defined in your `EDITOR` environment variable. If you don't like the default editor, you can first specify your own temporarily as follows:

```
# EDITOR=/usr/bin/pico;export EDITOR
```

This will make the `edquota` command use the pico text editor. When `edquota` runs, you'll end up in your editor with the following text:

```
Quotas for user cloobie:
/dev/hda3: blocks in use: 58, limits (soft = 0, hard = 0)
        inodes in use: 41, limits (soft = 0, hard = 0)
```

Although it is not important to understand all the information here (see Albert M.C. Tam's mini-HOWTO, Quota, under the `/usr/doc/HOWTO/mini` for details), you can easily set both the maximum number of files and the maximum size of your user's directory. To set limits to 3–5MB for disk space, and between 500 and 1000 files, use

```
Quotas for user cloobie:
/dev/hda3: blocks in use: 58, limits (soft = 3000, hard = 5000)
        inodes in use: 41, limits (soft = 500, hard = 1000
```

Save the file. Then, as a last step, you must set a grace period using `edquota` again, but this time with the `-t` option. Your new user will be warned if the lower, or "soft," limit is exceeded, for example:

```
# edquota -t cloobie
```

You can then set the grace-period warnings for either exceeding the number of files or disk use, for example:

```
Time units may be: days, hours, minutes, or seconds
Grace period before enforcing soft limits for users:
/dev/hda3: block grace period: 1 days, file grace period: 1 days
```

If you want to warn your user right away, use a grace period of one day (you can also use minutes or seconds). Finally, you can use the `quota` command to check the new quota, for example:

```
# quota cloobie
Disk quotas for user cloobie (uid 502):
     Filesystem  blocks    quota    limit    grace    files    quota    limit    grace
      /dev/hda3      58     3000     5000                41      500     1000
```

Using disk quotas may sometimes be necessary. If your disk space is at a premium, this could be one way to manage your hard drive resources.

PART V

Hour 21

Handling Files

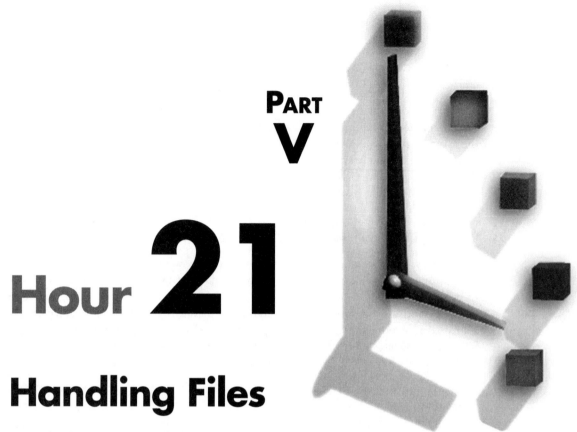

This hour continues with the basics of system administration and introduces you to handling files under Linux. You'll learn how to mount filesystems, manage the filesystem table (`fstab`), and format floppies. You'll see how you can protect files and directories.

You will use this knowledge to help you administer your Linux system. Knowing how to manage file ownership is an important Linux skill and can help you overcome problems later on.

One great reason to get up to speed about file access and ownership has to do with security. There are some important files in your Linux system that, as root operator, you don't want all users to have access to. If you've set up your system to handle dial-in calls, you'll want to make sure that important files, and even other mounted filesystems, such as DOS or Windows, are protected. If you share your computer, you normally wouldn't want other users to have access to your files, but on the other hand, you might want to share files with other people, but don't know how.

This hour starts with a discussion of the Linux file system.

There's a difference between a file system and a filesystem. A *file system* is the layout of the directories and hierarchy of files on a partition. A *filesystem* is the layout of the lower-level format of a storage device. Linux recognizes a number of filesystems. You can find a list in the `fstab`, or filesystem table, manual page under the `/usr/man/man5` directory, but it's best to look at the current list of supported systems in the `mount` command manual page. Why? Because the `mount` command is used to mount the filesystem at a mount point, or a path you specify. For now, take a look at the Linux file system.

How Linux Is Organized

The software that comes with the Linux kernel is from a variety of different UNIX systems. Some programs, utilities, and commands, like mail or printing, come from a UNIX distribution, called the Berkeley Software Distribution, or BSD. Other programs and methods of organizing software, such as startup scripts and organization of files used during startup, come from either AT&T System V UNIX or later variants. Because of this mixed heritage, Linux has a mix of directories, and although most pundits say Linux leans towards being System V-ish, you'll find elements of BSD and System V.

To give you a better idea, Listin 21.1 contains an edited directory listing, courtesy of the `tree` command.

Listing 21.1. The basic Linux file system, or directory tree.

```
/ - the root directory
|-- bin - programs considered necessary
|-- boot - Linux boot image
|-- dev - devices, like serial ports, printers, hard drives
|-- etc - configuration files for network, X11, mail, etc.
|-- home - where users live (including sysadmin)
|-- lib - software libraries
|-- lost+found - recovered files (from e2fsck)
|-- mnt - where you mount other filesystems
|   |-- cdrom
|   |-- dos
|   |-- flash
|   `-- floppy
|-- proc - kernel, device, process status files
|-- root - where the sysadmin works, but doesn't live
|-- sbin - system binaries (many root-only)
|-- tmp - temp files stored, deleted from here
|-- usr - hosts much, much software, libraries
|   |-- X11R6 - X Window System software
|   |-- bin - more software
|   |-- dict - dictionaries
|   |-- doc - FAQs, HOW-TOs, software documentation
|   |-- etc - software configuration files
```

```
|    |-- games - fun, fun, fun!
|    |-- i486-linuxaout
|    |-- include - header files for programming
|    |-- info - GNU information
|    |-- lib - more software libraries
|    |-- libexec
|    |-- local - programs not on CD-ROM
|    |   |-- bin
|    |   |-- doc
|    |   |-- etc
|    |   |-- games
|    |   |-- info
|    |   |-- lib
|    |   |-- man
|    |   |-- sbin
|    |   `-- src - source code to programs
|    |-- man - manual pages
|    |   |-- man1..9n
|    |-- sbin
|    |-- share
|    |-- src - source for Linux!!!
|    |   |-- linux -> linux-2.0.30
|    |   |-- linux-2.0.30
|    `-- tmp -> ../var/tmp
`-- var - system logs, compressed manual pages
```

As you can see, the main directory structure is not that complicated. What is important to understand here is that you should know where you are as you navigate the file system. When you install software, especially without the benefit of using Red Hat's `rpm` package-management command (which you'll learn about in Hour 22, "Red Hat Tools"), you should know where different software should reside on your system. Many programs will also require different software components to be installed in different parts of the directory.

If you look at the file system listing, you'll see a `/mnt`, or `mount`, directory. Although you don't have to use this directory as a gateway to other filesystems, this is traditionally where other systems are mounted. The next section discusses how to have these other systems appear under the mount directory.

Using the `mount` Command to Access Other Filesystems

The `mount` command, found under the `/bin` directory, is an essential program used not only by sysadmins, but also by Linux during startup and shutdown. This command is used to mount filesystems and make them available in the directory tree. During startup, the primary Linux partition, an `ext2` filesystem, is mounted at the root filesystem, or `/`, directory.

You can also have other filesystems automatically mounted when Linux starts, or you mount and unmount filesystems, using the `mount` and the `umount` commands, while you work. The Linux `mount` command recognizes and will mount (depending on how your kernel is configured) more than a dozen different filesystems. This section concentrates on the most common, such as `ext2` for Linux, `msdos` for DOS or Windows, and `iso9660` for CD-ROMs.

Understanding the Filesystem Table, /etc/fstab

When you start Linux, one of the first scripts to run is the `rc.sysinit` script under the `/etc/rc.d` directory. This script mounts your Linux partition as read-write after it checks the partition for errors. Then, if everything is OK, it will mount all filesystems described in the filesystem table, `fstab`, under the `/etc` directory with the following command:

```
# mount -a -t nonfs
```

This mounts all filesystems described in the `/etc/fstab` (except for NFS filesystems; see the `mount` command manual page for details). The `/etc/fstab` file is a short text file:

```
# <device>     <mountpoint>   <filesystemtype> <options> <dump> <fsckorder>

/dev/hda3       /                    ext2   defaults,usrquota 1 1
/dev/hdb        /mnt/cdrom           ignore 0 0 0
/dev/cdrom      /mnt/cdrom           iso9660 noauto,ro 0 0
/dev/hda1       /mnt/dos             msdos  defaults 0 0
/dev/hdc1       /mnt/flash           msdos  defaults 0 0
/dev/fd0        /mnt/floppy          ext2   noauto 0 0

none            /proc                proc   defaults
/dev/hda2       none                 swap   sw
```

The `fstab` columns show the device, where the filesystem will be mounted, the type of filesystem, any `mount` options, whether or not the `dump` command (discussed in Hour 23, "Archiving") needs to check for files to be archived, and the order in which the filesystem is checked during reboot.

The `fstab` rows show a Linux `ext2` filesystem, which you configured to support quotas in the last hour; two CD-ROM devices (`/dev/cdrom` is a symbolic link to `/dev/hdb`); a DOS filesystem partition on the same hard drive as the Linux `ext2` partition; a DOS filesystem on a flash RAM card; the floppy drive; the `/proc` directory (used internally by the Linux kernel); and finally, the Linux swap filesystem.

CAUTION

> You should know that editing the filesystem table by hand is inherently dangerous. You learned to add quotas in Hour 20, "Basic System Administration," but generally you should not edit this file by hand. Instead, use Red Hat's graphical filesystem configuration tool, `fstool`, discussed in Hour 22. Use this tool if you need to add a hard drive, new partitions, and so on. Although you can edit the `fstab` file, before you do, make sure you have a backup boot disk on hand, and make a copy of the `fstab` file before you edit it.

Normally the root operator mounts and unmounts filesystems. But if you take my advice and don't run Linux as root all the time, you'll have to use the `su` command to mount and unmount filesystems. By using the `user` option of the `mount` command, you won't have to use the `su` command to mount CD-ROMs. You can, for example, change the original `fstab` entries to

```
/dev/cdrom      /mnt/cdrom            iso9660 noauto,ro,user 0 0
/dev/hdb        /mnt/cdrom            iso9660 noauto,ro,user 0 0
```

You'll now be able to mount CD-ROMs without having to be the root operator, by using

```
# mount /dev/cdrom
```

or

```
# mount /mnt/cdrom
```

This will automatically mount your CD-ROM's filesystem at the `/mnt/cdrom` path. You'll also be able to switch your disks with the `umount` command, for example:

```
# umount /dev/cdrom
```

or

```
# umount /mnt/cdrom
```

Although you should enable this type of convenience only if you're using Linux on a standalone computer, and only for certain types of filesystems, such as CD-ROMs, it is convenient, especially for removable filesystems. Another type of removable filesystem is the venerable floppy drive. The next section discusses floppy drives, and is followed by a discussion of a package of floppy utilities that can make life easier when dealing with floppies under Linux.

Formatting a Floppy

This section introduces you to three programs you might need to format a floppy under Linux and takes you step-by-step through the process. You might find this information useful if you want to back up files or use the floppy to install and test new software. You'll also learn how to format and then mount your floppy in Linux native format using the `ext2` filesystem (used for your Linux partition, and the root, or `/`, directory).

The floppy devices are located under the `/dev` directory, and there are quite a few of them. You'll find a device corresponding to just about any type of floppy device ever made. You can look at the `/dev` directory for floppy devices as follows:

```
# ls /dev/fd*
/dev/fd0          /dev/fd0H1722     /dev/fd0h1600     /dev/fd1E3200     /dev/fd1H830
/dev/fd0CompaQ    /dev/fd0H1743     /dev/fd0h360      /dev/fd1E3520     /dev/fd1d360
/dev/fd0D1040     /dev/fd0H1760     /dev/fd0h410      /dev/fd1E3840     /dev/fd1h1200
/dev/fd0D1120     /dev/fd0H1840     /dev/fd0h420      /dev/fd1H1440     /dev/fd1h1440
/dev/fd0D360      /dev/fd0H1920     /dev/fd0h720      /dev/fd1H1600     /dev/fd1h1476
/dev/fd0D720      /dev/fd0H360      /dev/fd0h880      /dev/fd1H1680     /dev/fd1h1494
/dev/fd0D800      /dev/fd0H720      /dev/fd1          /dev/fd1H1722     /dev/fd1h1600
/dev/fd0E2880     /dev/fd0H820      /dev/fd1CompaQ    /dev/fd1H1743     /dev/fd1h360
/dev/fd0E3200     /dev/fd0H830      /dev/fd1D1040     /dev/fd1H1760     /dev/fd1h410
/dev/fd0E3520     /dev/fd0d360      /dev/fd1D1120     /dev/fd1H1840     /dev/fd1h420
/dev/fd0E3840     /dev/fd0h1200     /dev/fd1D360      /dev/fd1H1920     /dev/fd1h720
/dev/fd0H1440     /dev/fd0h1440     /dev/fd1D720      /dev/fd1H360      /dev/fd1h880
/dev/fd0H1600     /dev/fd0h1476     /dev/fd1D800      /dev/fd1H720
/dev/fd0H1680     /dev/fd0h1494     /dev/fd1E2880     /dev/fd1H820
```

This section concentrates on the more common device for 3.5-inch, 1.44MB floppies. These are

`/dev/fd0`—Drive A

`/dev/fd1`—Drive B

A number of supported floppy formats are listed in the `fdprm`, or floppy drive parameter file, under the `/etc/` directory. Take a look at a portion of the file:

```
# /etc/fdprm  -  floppy disk parameter table

# Common disk formats. Names are of the form
#  actual media capacity/maximum drive capacity
# (Note: although 5.25" HD drives can format disks at 1.44M, they're listed
#        as 1200 because that's the common maximum size.)

#               size sec/t hds trk stre gap  rate spec1 fmt_gap
360/360          720     9   2  40    0 0x2A 0x02 0xDF     0x50
1200/1200       2400    15   2  80    0 0x1B 0x00 0xDF     0x54
360/720          720     9   2  40    1 0x2A 0x02 0xDF     0x50
720/720         1440     9   2  80    0 0x2A 0x02 0xDF     0x50
720/1440        1440     9   2  80    0 0x2A 0x02 0xDF     0x50
360/1200         720     9   2  40    1 0x23 0x01 0xDF     0x50
720/1200        1440     9   2  80    0 0x23 0x01 0xDF     0x50
1440/1440       2880    18   2  80    0 0x1B 0x00 0xCF     0x6C
...
```

The format you'll most likely be interested in is the 1440/1440 description of today's 3.5-inch high-density drives. Using this name, you'll use the `setfdprm` (set floppy disk parameter) command (found under the `/usr/bin` directory), to associate your drive A: floppy with its device, `/dev/fd0`, as follows:

```
# setfdprm -p /dev/fd0 1440/1440
```

After that, you can proceed with a low-level format of your drive. To do this, you'll use the `fdformat` (floppy disk formatting) command (found under the `/usr/bin` directory). Insert a blank disk in your drive and then use

```
# fdformat /dev/fd0
Double-sided, 80 tracks, 18 sec/track. Total capacity 1440 kB.
Formatting ... done
Verifying ... done
```

Here, you've told the `fdformat` command to do a low-level format of the `/dev/fd0` device. Be careful! Make sure to specify the correct device.

TIME SAVER

You should also know that you can alternatively use a specific floppy device to do the low-level format, for example:

```
# fdformat /dev/fd0H1440
```

This tells `fdformat` to use the specific floppy device for high-density drives, in this case, the A: drive.

The next step is to create a filesystem on the floppy. You'll use the `mke2fs` command to make a Linux second extended filesystem on the floppy. The `mke2fs` command, found under the `/sbin` directory, has at least two dozen command-line options, but you'll only use a few, for example:

```
# mke2fs -c -v -L "Linux1" /dev/fd0
mke2fs 1.10, 24-Apr-97 for EXT2 FS 0.5b, 95/08/09
Linux ext2 filesystem format
Filesystem label=Linux1
360 inodes, 1440 blocks
72 blocks (5.00%) reserved for the super user
First data block=1
Block size=1024 (log=0)
Fragment size=1024 (log=0)
1 block group
8192 blocks per group, 8192 fragments per group
360 inodes per group

Running command: badblocks -s /dev/fd0 1440
Checking for bad blocks (read-only test): done
Writing inode tables: done
Writing superblocks and filesystem accounting information: done
```

The preceding example used the -c option to check the disk for any bad blocks, and the -L option to give the floppy a name. In order to see what's going on, it also used the -v (verbose mode) option. The mke2fs command will automatically determine the size of your floppy, check it using the badblocks command, found under the /sbin directory, and then create your Linux filesystem. You might also want to use the -m option with a value of 0 to have the most room available, and specify the high-density floppy device (by default, mke2fs will reserve five percent of the filesystem for the root operator), as follows:

```
# mke2fs -m 0 /dev/fd0H1440 1440
```

As a final step, you can mount the floppy, using the mount command, and then check the floppy's size, for example:

```
# mount -t ext2 /dev/fd0 /mnt/floppy
#  df /dev/fd0
Filesystem         1024-blocks  Used Available Capacity Mounted on
/dev/fd0                1390      13      1377       1%   /mnt/floppy
```

Knowing how to format floppy drives is important. If you're only interested in DOS floppies, you'll want to explore the mtools package, discussed next.

The mtools Package

The mtools package is a set of programs you can use in just about any operation on MS-DOS floppies. These utilities include

- mattrib—Change file attributes
- mbadblocks—Floppy testing program
- mcd—Change directory command
- mcheck—Check a floppy
- mcopy—Copy files to and from disk
- mdel—Delete files on disk
- mdeltree—Recursively delete files and directories
- mdir—List contents of a floppy
- mformat—Format a floppy
- minfo—Categorize, print floppy characteristics
- mkmanifest—Restore Linux filenames from floppy
- mlabel—Label a floppy
- mmd—Create subdirectory
- mmount—Mount floppy

- mmove—mv command for floppy files, directories
- mpartition—Make DOS filesystem as partition
- mrd—Delete directories
- mren—Rename a file
- mtoolstest—Test mtools package installation
- mtype—Types a file
- mzip—Zip/Jaz drive utility
- xcopy—Copy one directory to another

This hour doesn't cover all these utilities, but from the list, you should be able to see that the most often used will be the mformat, mdir, mcopy, and mdel commands. The mformat command will format nearly any type of floppy device. One nice feature of this package of software is that you don't have to remember the specific names of floppy devices, such as /dev/fd0, and can use the (possibly) familiar A: or B: drive designators. For example, to format a floppy in your drive A:, you would use

```
# mformat a:
```

This will automatically format your disk. After the mformat command has finished, you can copy files to and from the disk with the mcopy command, for example:

```
# mcopy *.txt a:
```

This will copy all files ending in .txt to your disk. To copy files from your disk, just reverse the arguments (in DOS form) to the mcopy command:

```
# mcopy a:*.txt
```

This will copy all files ending in .txt to the current directory, or a directory you specify. To see what is on the disk, use the mdir command, for example:

```
# mdir a:x*.*
 Volume in drive A has no label
 Directory for A:/

xena     msg      8708 11-21-1997  12:14p xena.msg
xgames   msg      2798 11-21-1997  12:14p xgames.msg
xrpm     msg      3624 11-21-1997  12:14p xrpm.msg
       3 file(s)           15 130 bytes
                        1 067 008 bytes free
```

To label the disk, you can use the mlabel command, for example:

```
# mlabel a:
 Volume has no label
Enter the new volume label : LINUX
```

To delete files on your disk, use the `mdel` command:

```
# mdel a:*.txt
```

This will delete all files ending in `.txt` on the disk in the a: drive. You've learned the basic operations, but you can also mount your disk. For details, see the `mmount` manual page, along with the `mount` command manual page. Now that you know how to manage different filesystems, the next section covers how to manage your files.

Managing File Ownership and Permissions

Managing files in Linux means more than moving files around the file system or keeping files grouped by similar behavior or topic. You can change which user or group owns a file or directory, and whether or not you, your group, or others can read, write, or execute (run) your files.

The `chmod` (change access permissions) command, found under the `/bin` directory, is used to give or take away permission of groups or others to your files. Before you can begin to use the `chmod` program, you should understand Linux files and how Linux handles file permissions. In Hour 4, "Reading and Navigation Commands," you learned how to get a long-format directory listing using the `-l` option with the `ls` (list) command. This option shows the mode and permissions flags of files, for example:

```
# ls -l book/*doc
-rw-r--r--   1 bball    bball        78073 Nov 16 19:58 book/24hr06or.doc
-rw-r--r--   1 bball    bball        52287 Nov 16 19:57 book/24hr11or.doc
```

The mode and permissions flags for directories and files is listed in the first column, and consists of a sequence of 10 letters. The first letter tells you the type of file.

Understanding Linux File Types

There are at least eight file types in Linux, but these are the four most common ones:

- `b`—Block device
- `c`—Character device
- `d`—Directory
- `l`—Symbolic link

You'll usually find block and character devices under the `/dev` directory. Your modem or printer port on your PC will probably be a character device, whereas your floppy drive is a block device, for example:

```
# ls -l /dev/lp0 /dev/cua1 /dev/fd0
```

```
crw-rw----    1 root     uucp        5,  65 Dec 31  1979 /dev/cua1
brw-rw----    1 root     disk        2,   0 Sep 15 23:48 /dev/fd0
crw-rw----    1 root     daemon      6,   0 Sep 15 23:48 /dev/lp0
```

As you can see, the different devices have either `c` or `b` in front of the permissions flags. You can also use the `ls` command to list the permissions of a directory, using the `-d` (directory) option, for example:

```
# ls -ld book
drwxrwxr-x   2 bball    bball        1024 Nov 18 19:35 book
```

The `d` denotes a directory. Symbolic links will also have a designated type in the `ls -l` listing, for example:

```
# touch file1
# ln -s file1 file2
# ls -l file2
lrwxrwxrwx   1 bball    bball           5 Nov 23 11:14 file2 -> file1
```

Now that you understand some of the basic file types, the next section shows you how to read the permissions flags.

Reading File Permissions Flags

Although the permissions sequence of letters might seem cryptic and mysterious at first, you can easily decipher what these mean. To do this, break the sequence of nine characters into three groups of three. Each group of characters represents (from left to right):

`r`—The file can be read.

`w`—The file can be written to.

`x`—The file can be executed, or run, or in the case of a directory, searched.

The first group of three characters is for the owner. If you create the file, you can change any of these permissions. The next group of three characters is for the group. If you recall the discussion of the `/etc/passwd` file in Hour 20, you know that by default, you are assigned to two groups when your account is first created, one with your name and the other to the group users. As the system administrator, or sysadmin, you can organize users on your system by assigning users to different groups.

You'll find a list of groups for your Linux system in the group file under the `/etc` directory. This file contains a text database of groups. Here are a few sample entries:

```
root::0:root
bin::1:root,bin,daemon
daemon::2:root,bin,daemon
sys::3:root,bin,adm
adm::4:root,adm,daemon
...
users::100:bball,cloobie
bball::500:bball
cloobie::502:cloobie
```

The format of the `/etc/group` file is: group, password, group number, and a comma-delimited list of users who belong to the group. This means that you can assign read, write, or execute permissions to your group, and allow or deny access to your files. As the root operator, or sysadmin, you can organize your users into different groups. This is important, and one of the reasons you might need to use the `chown` (change ownership) command, as you'll see later on in this hour.

The final set of three characters denotes the read, write, and execution permissions you grant all other users. Now that you know how to read the permissions, take a look at some examples before moving on to the `chmod` program.

When you create a file, by default, you and the members of your group have read and write permissions on that file. You can change the default of file creation permissions with your shell's `umask` command (see your shell's manual page for details). Here's a simple example:

```
# touch myfile
# ls -l myfile
-rw-rw-r--    1 bball     bball             0 Nov 23 12:11 myfile
```

This shows that you (`rw-`) and your group (`rw-`) can read and write the file, whereas all others (`r--`) can only read the file. If `myfile` were available to everyone on your system, the permissions would look like this:

```
-rw-rw-rw-    1 bball     bball             0 Nov 23 12:11 myfile
```

Now anyone (`rw-`) can read or write this file. If `myfile` were only available for reading and writing to you, the permissions would look like this:

```
-rw-------    1 bball     bball             0 Nov 23 12:11 myfile
```

This shows that you (`rw-`), but not your group (`---`) or others (`---`), can read the file. How do you change these settings? With the `chmod` command.

Changing File Permissions with the `chmod` Command

You can use the `chmod` command in several ways to change file or directory permissions. Learning how to use this command is not as easy as 1-2-3, but it is as easy as 4-2-1!

The `chmod` command can be used in at least two different ways. Although you can use `chmod` to create simple commands from text files, using the `+x` command-line option (as you learned in Hour 6, "Using the Shell"), you might want to set exact permissions of certain files in your home directory, or as the sysadmin, of critical files on your system. The `chmod` command uses octal, or base eight, notation in modifying file or directory permissions. The 4-2-1 sequence corresponds to the three `rwx` sequences in the permissions flags.

How does this work? Well, suppose you want to make one of your files private, so that no one else (except the root operator, of course) can read or write your file. When you first create the file, you and your group can read and write the file, while others can only read it. Knowing that 4-2-1 matches rwx, and knowing that the group and others permissions follow your permissions in the permissions flag, you can use chmod with the octal number 600 to change the permissions, for example:

```
# touch afile
# ls -l afile
-rw-rw-r--    1 bball    bball              0 Nov 23 12:34 afile
# chmod 600 afile
# ls -l afile
-rw-------    1 bball    bball              0 Nov 23 12:34 afile
```

This makes the file readable and writable only by you, because you've enabled read (4) + write (2) for yourself and no one else. To change the file permissions back to the original access permissions, you would want to enable read (4) + write (2) for you (6), your group (6), and read-only permissions for all others (4), and use the octal number 664, for example:

```
# chmod 664 afile
# ls -l afile
-rw-rw-r--    1 bball    bball              0 Nov 23 12:34 afile
```

You can also change file directory permissions, and either let other people list the contents of your directory, or have access only to the files in a directory, and not be able to list the directory contents. For example, to protect a directory from prying eyes (again, from everyone but the root operator), you can try

```
# mkdir temp
# cd temp
# touch file1 file2 file3
# cd ..
# chmod 700 temp
# ls -ld temp
drwx------    2 bball    bball          1024 Nov 23 12:51 temp
```

If anyone else tries to look into your directory, they will see

```
# ls /home/bball/temp
ls: /home/bball/temp: Permission denied
```

But what if you want to allow others to read files in the directory without being able to list the contents? To do this, you can enable execute permission of your directory, for example:

```
# chmod 701 temp
# ls -ld temp
drwx-----x    2 bball    bball          1024 Nov 23 12:51 temp
```

Now, no other users will be able to list the contents of your directory, but can read files that you tell them are within, for example:

```
# ls -ld /home/bball/temp
ls: /home/bball/temp: Permission denied
# ls -l /home/bball/temp/file1
-rw-rw-r--    1 bball    bball              0 Nov 23 12:51 /home/bball/temp/file1
```

As you can see, using the chmod command's octal notation is not that hard. What you have to decide is to whom you want to grant access, and what kind of access you'd like your files to have. The chmod command also has a command-line form as follows:

```
ugoa +-= rwxXstugo
```

This book doesn't go into all the details of this notation (you can read the chmod command's manual page for more details), but the next few examples duplicate chmod's actions using the previous examples. You can protect a file from anyone else with

```
# ls -l file1
-rw-rw-r--    1 bball    bball          0 Nov 23 13:50 file1
# chmod go-rwx file1
# ls -l file1
-rw-------    1 bball    bball          0 Nov 23 13:50 file1
```

As you can see, the file is now readable and writable only by you, because you have specified that your group (g) and others (o) do not (-) have read, write, or execute (rwx) permission. Now, you can protect your directory from prying eyes as follows:

```
# chmod go-rwx temp
```

And, to mimic the last example, to enable others to read files in the directory, but not list the directory contents, you can use

```
# chmod o+x temp
```

You're now familiar with file and directory permissions, and using the chmod command. The next section shows you how you can change ownership of files or directories using the chown command.

Changing File Ownership with the chown Command

The chown (change ownership) command, found under the /bin directory, is used to change, either permanently or temporarily, the ownership of files or directories. If you recall the previous discussion of the /etc/group file in this hour, you'll remember that your users can be assigned to different groups. Using the chown command, you can assign ownership to different users or groups.

For example, if you've created a text file, you can share it with members of your group or others with the chmod command. By using chown, you can tell Linux specifically what other users or groups can have access to your file. You can use the groups command to find out what groups you belong to, for example:

```
# groups
bball users
```

This shows that the user, bball, belongs to two groups: bball and users. As the root operator, you belong to at least seven groups, for example:

```
# groups
root bin daemon sys adm disk wheel
```

To find out who belongs to a group, look at the `/etc/group` file, or use the name of a user, for example:

```
# groups cloobie
cloobie : cloobie users
```

This shows that you and cloobie belong to at least one group, called users. To assign one of your files to the users group, and give cloobie access, you can use the `chown` command's syntax of user:group, for example:

```
# chown :users myfile
# ls -l myfile
-rw-rw-r--    1 bball    users           0 Nov 23 14:16 myfile
```

You might think that to assign specific ownership, you can use the following:

```
#  chown cloobie:users myfile
chown: myfile: Operation not permitted
```

What happened? This shows why Linux has groups. You can assign access of one of your files to a group, but unless you're the root operator, you cannot assign one of your files to appear to have been either created by or owned by another user. Make sure you're logged in as the root operator and use

```
# chown cloobie:cloobie myfile
# ls -l myfile
-rw-rw-r--    1 cloobie  cloobie         0 Nov 23 14:16 myfile
```

As you can see, even though the file `myfile` was created by the user bball, as the sysadmin, you can assign ownership to any users and any group. If you just want to change the group ownership of a file or directory, you can use the `chgrp` command; if you want to change your users or your own group, you can use the `newgrp` command.

Changing Groups and Ownerships with the `chgrp` and `newgrp` Commands

The `chgrp` (change group) command, found under the `/bin` directory, is used only to change group ownerships. In this regard, it is not as flexible as the `chown` command, which can do both. The `chgrp` command accepts a group name or group id (GID), for example:

```
# ls -l myfile
-rw-rw-r--    1 bball    bball           0 Nov 23 14:16 myfile
```

This shows that the file belongs to user bball and group bball. To change the group ownership and grant access to other members of the group, use

```
# groups bball
bball : bball users
# chgrp users myfile
# ls -l myfile
-rw-rw-r--    1 bball    users             0 Nov 23 14:16 myfile
```

Now, other members of the users group can access the file. Along with the `chgrp` command, you'll find the `newgrp` command, which is found under the `/usr/bin` directory. Although the `chgrp` command will change group ownership of one of your files or directories to a group you belong to, (or if you're the root operator, any group), you can use the `newgrp` to shift your current group membership, for example:

```
# groups
bball users
# touch file1
# ls -l file1
-rw-rw-r--    1 bball    bball             0 Nov 23 14:53 file1
# newgrp users
# groups
users bball
# touch file2
# ls -l file2
-rw-rw-r--    1 bball    users             0 Nov 23 14:54 file2
# newgrp bball
```

This shows that the user bball originally belonged to the default group bball. This was verified by creating a file showing the current user and group ownership. Next, the user bball changed to the users group, created a file, and verified that the created file has the new group's access. Finally, the user bball changed back to the original group, bball.

As you can see, Linux offers you a great deal of flexibility in assigning file ownerships and permissions. By using different combinations of directory and file ownership and permissions, you can organize your system along lines of types of work, types of users, or types of files.

PART V

Hour 22

Red Hat Tools

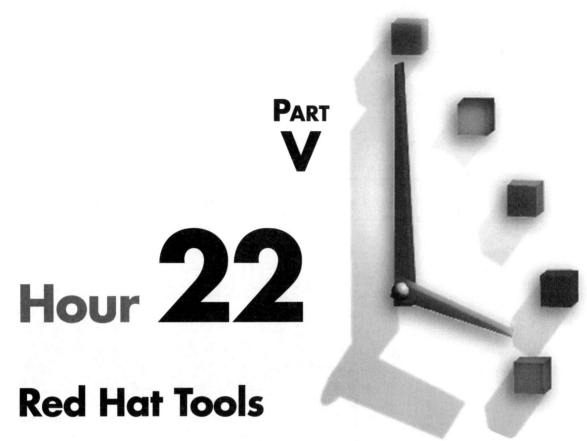

In this hour you'll learn how to use Red Hat Software's graphic system-administration utilities. These easy-to-use programs are an efficient and handy way to configure and maintain your system. You'll quickly learn why many Linux users prefer the Red Hat Linux distribution, and why several of the tools, such as the `rpm` command, or the Red Hat Package Manager, have become standard tools in the Linux system administrator's toolbox.

This collection of Red Hat tools proves that Linux system management is becoming easier, and is catching up with the graphic system administration tools provided by commercial UNIX operating systems. In fact, if you have experience with any other systems, you may find the Red Hat tools easier to use.

Configuring Your System with the Control-Panel

This section discusses Otto Hammersmith's control-panel, through which you can access eight system administrator tools. You must run the X Window System in order to use the `control-panel` command, which you'll find under the `/usr/bin` directory. You'll also need to be logged in as the root operator to use all but one of control-panel's tools.

To start the `control-panel` command, which uses files under the `/usr/lib/rhs` directory, type its name on the command line of an X11 terminal window.

```
# control-panel &
```

This command line starts the `control-panel` command. A vertical window with large buttons appears. You can select different tools by moving your cursor over a button and pressing the left mouse button. You also can change control-panel's window to display horizontally through its File menu (see Figure 22.1).

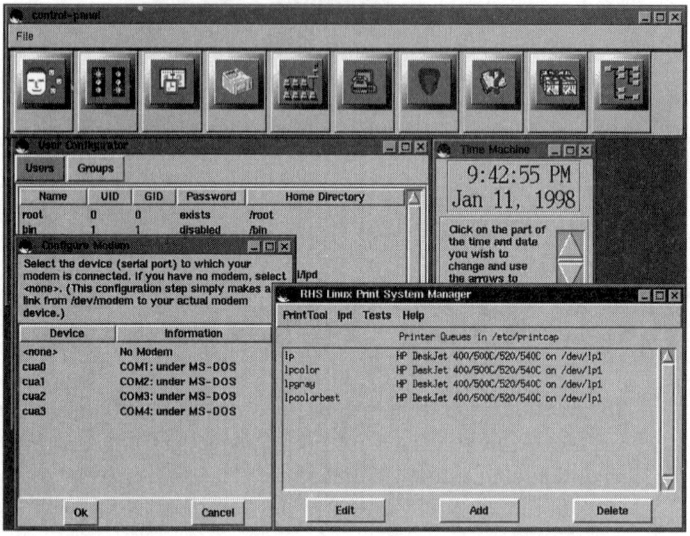

Figure 22.1.
The `control-panel` *command is used to run and display Red Hat system administration tools you can use as the root operators to manage your system.*

TIME SAVER

The fstool utility is also part of the `control-panel` command, but according to Red Hat Software, you should instead use the `cabaret` command (discussed later in this hour in the section "Maintaining Your Filesystem with the cabaret Command"). The `cabaret` command also is available through the setup utility.

Some of the control-panel tools have built-in help. For information about the `control-panel` command, read its manual page.

Creating and Maintaining Users with the `usercfg` Command

As a system administrator, you may find yourself adding, deleting, or changing users and user information. If you don't want to use the `adduser`, `passwd`, `chsh`, `chgrp`, and `chfn` commands (discussed in Hour 20, "Basic System Administration"), you can use the `usercfg` command (see Figure 22.2). This graphic tool presents a dialog box that enables you to implement the following tasks:

- Edit user and group identification information
- Change users' login shells
- Change users' passwords
- Edit users' finger information
- Add or delete system users

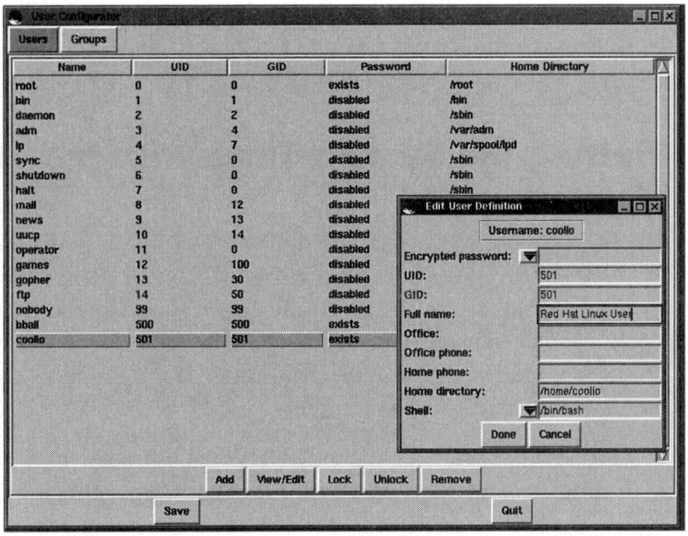

Figure 22.2.
The `usercfg` *command is a graphic interface to several command-line system administration commands.*

Run this command by clicking the usercfg button in the control-panel window, or by starting a terminal window and typing the following:

```
# usercfg
```

Managing System Services with the `tksysv` Command

The `tksysv` command, by Donnie Barnes, is a run-level editor for Linux. While you don't need to know all of the technical details about run-levels (you can find a description in the `/etc/inittab` file), you should know that this tool changes which system services are started or stopped when you log in at the console, run the X Window System, or reboot your system into the single-user mode for system maintenance.

The `tksysv` command presents a dialog box with a list of services on the left and five columns on the right, with each column representing a run level.

CAUTION

You should definitely read the `tksysv` command's built-in help, accessed through the command's Help menu. Make sure you know what you're doing, because stopping services can have a drastic effect by potentially disabling PPP connections, printing, or other system features you normally need.

Start `tksysv` by clicking on the Runlevel Editor button in the control-panel window, or by starting a terminal window and typing the following:

```
# tksysv
```

Setting the System Time with the `timetool` Command

The `timetool` command is used to set or reset your system's date and time. You also can set your system to use a 24-hour clock. When you use timetool, you'll see a dialog box that enables you to set the date and time. When you select a portion of the date or time, the portion is highlighted in red (if you're using a color monitor, of course). Change the value by clicking the up or down arrow in the dialog box. This tool can be especially handy if you live in an area using daylight savings time!

To use the `timetool` command, select the Date and Time button from the control-panel, or start the command from a terminal window by typing the following:

```
# timetool
```

Creating Printers with the `printtool` Command

Details about using the `printtool` command, used to install and set up your system's printer(s), are in Hour 15, "Preparing Documents."

Configuring your Network Services with the `netcfg` Command

The `netcfg` command is a convenient way for system administrators to easily configure networking services and devices (see Figure 22.3). It's not necessary to go into the details of network configuration, or to discuss using this command in great depth, but you should know that this command installs networking services, such as Point-to-Point Protocol or Serial Line Interface Protocol connections. This is a handy tool you can use to set the hostname of your computer, add domain nameserver addresses for connecting to your

Internet service provider, configure your system's loopback network device (necessary if you want to run the Common Desktop Environment, discussed in Hour 8, "Exploring Other X11 Window Managers"), or add other network services for your users.

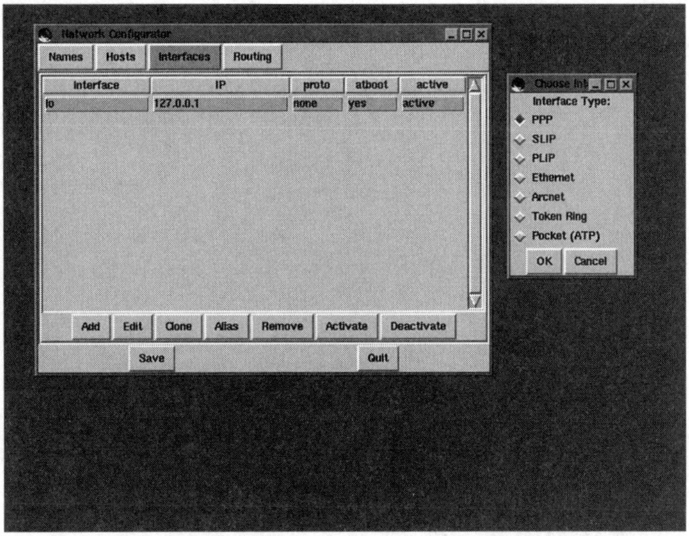

Figure 22.3.
The `netcfg` *command is used to start, stop, add, delete, change, or otherwise configure a range of network devices and services.*

Start the `netcfg` command through the control-panel, or by typing its name on the command line:

```
# netcfg &
```

Creating a Symbolic Modem Link with the `modemtool` Command

The `modemtool` command creates a symbolic link, called /dev/modem, that points to a specified serial port you select.

Run the `modemtool` command from the control-panel by clicking the Modem Configuration button, or by entering the command name on a command line:

```
# modemtool
```

Kernel Configuration with the `kernelcfg` Command

The `kernelcfg` command is a system administration tool and graphic interface to the `init`, `lsmod`, `insmod`, and `rmmod` commands (see Figure 22.4). Use this command's window to control running modules. Unlike the `tksysv` command, you won't find a help file, so be careful before removing running modules unless you're sure that's exactly what you want to do.

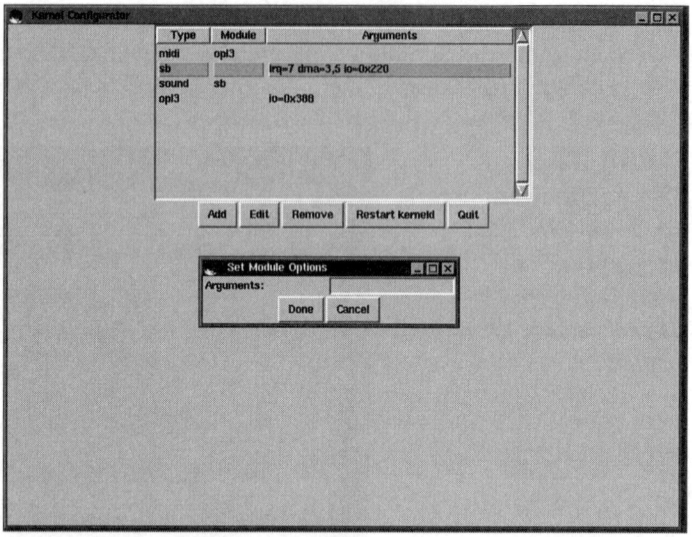

Figure 22.4.
The `kernelcfg` *command presents a window of currently loaded system modules.*

The `kernelcfg` command may be run from the control-panel by clicking the Kernel Daemon Configuration Button, or by typing the following on the command line:

```
# kernelcfg
```

Using the `glint` and `rpm` Commands

The `glint` command is a graphic representation of your system's software database, used by the Red Hat Package Manager, or `rpm` command. The `glint` command visibly demonstrates the benefits of using a combination of a graphic interface and a sophisticated software management program for system administration. The `glint` and `rpm` commands are just two of the reasons why Red Hat Linux is the easiest Linux distribution to install, maintain, and use.

Run `glint` from the control-panel by pressing the Package Management button, or by typing the following on the command line:

```
# glint &
```

When `glint` starts, it uses the `rpm` command to parse the database of the software installed on your system, found in the `/var/lib/rpm` directory. This database is then graphically displayed by different folders in an open window. You can see the software installed on your system by navigating through the various folders. You can then query, uninstall (or delete), verify, or see what other packages are available for installation.

In order to use the `glint` command's buttons, first select a software package by clicking the package's icon with your left mouse button. Then query or delete the package by pressing the appropriate `glint` button. Deleting a package with `glint` is the equivalent to using the `rpm` command with its -e option. For example,

```
# rpm -e doom-1.8-9
```

This `rpm` command deletes all software files associated with the Doom 1.8-9 package. As you can see, using the `glint` command saves you a lot of typing, and using the `rpm` command is a lot easier than searching your file system for all files related to the game Doom.

Press the Available button in the `glint` window, and the `glint` command searches for available software packages to install. If any are found, the package names are compared against your system's database of files, and a new window of folders or packages is displayed. Select a package from the new window and then press the Install button, and glint attempts to install the software (actually, the process is a bit more complicated than that, but simplicity serves here). This is the equivalent to using the `rpm` command with its `-i`, or install command-line option:

```
# rpm -i asoftwarepackage.rpm
```

This `rpm` command attempts to install the named software package. Again, you should see that using `glint` is a lot easier.

TIME SAVER

> The `glint` command normally looks in the `/mnt/cdrom/RedHat/RPMS` directory for additional software packages to install. If you have an additional hard drive, or a different directory of containing rpm files, use the `glint` command's Configure button to specify the path to the files.

Use the `glint` command to peruse the contents of your Linux software, and if necessary, to delete unneeded packages to save hard drive space. You won't find any documentation for `glint`, but you can read the rpm manual pages to find out more about the `rpm` command and managing software packages.

Finding Help with the `helptool` Command

The `helptool` command is used to search your system for related documents containing a phrase you enter into its search dialog box (see Figure 22.5). This command searches user documents, GNU info files, and manual pages for corresponding readable documents.

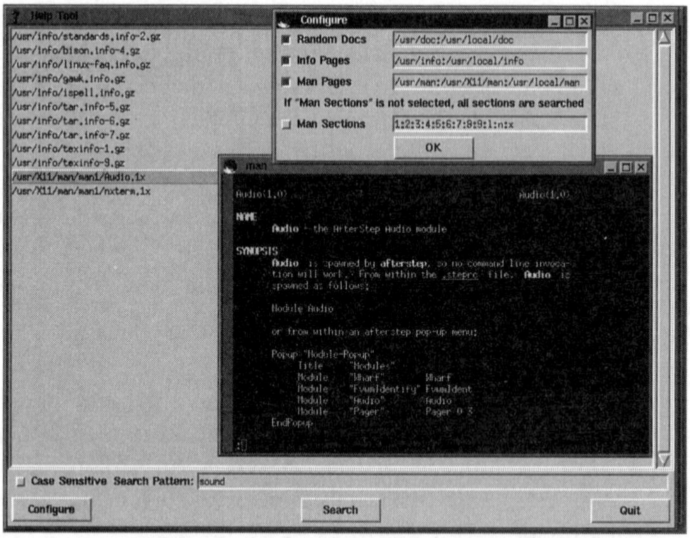

Figure 22.5.
The `helptool` *command searches your Linux system for helpful documents in response to an entered query.*

When the `helptool` has finished, get help by double-clicking with your left mouse button on the name of any listed documents. Double click a manual page filename, and a terminal window appears, using the `man` command to display the file. Double-click an info document name, and a terminal window appears, then `helptool` displays the document using the GNU `info` command.

Unlike other tools discussed in this hour, any user running the X Window System can use the `helptool` command.

Configuring Your System with the `setup` Command

This section shows you how to use the `setup` command to change or configure your Linux system's keyboard, mouse, filesystem, kernel processes, sound, or time. This set of system configuration tools may seem familiar because they use some of the windows or dialog boxes from when you first installed Linux.

The `setup` command may be started in an X11 terminal window, but you don't have to run the X Window System to use `setup` or any of its tools.

Starting the `setup` command, found under the `/usr/sbin` directory, is easy—simply type the following:

```
# setup
```

This command line runs the `setup` command, which then displays a scrolling list of tools. Move through the list with your cursor keys, stop on a program, then press the Tab key to go to the Run or Quit buttons. Run a command by pressing the F1 function key, or tabbing to the Run button and pressing the Enter key. Quit the `setup` command by tabbing to the Quit button and pressing the Enter key, or by pressing the F12 function key.

Each `setup` command recognizes your keyboard's Tab key to navigate through menus. You can quit each command with the F12 function key.

Maintaining Your Filesystem with the `cabaret` Command

The `cabaret` command is used to configure your filesystem, add new filesystems such as CD-ROMs or flash memory cards, change the type of filesystem on existing partitions, and mount or unmount hard drives or other devices. According to Red Hat Software, this command should be used instead of the control-panel's `fstool` command.

CAUTION

> Editing or changing the characteristics of Linux, DOS, or other partitions is inherently dangerous, and could cause you to lose data. Always keep a backup of your `/etc/inittab` file, which contains a database of the various filesystems available to Linux.

Use the `cabaret` command with care! Navigate through the command dialog boxes by using the Tab key. Don't press the Enter key unless you're absolutely sure you know what you're doing!

Probing Your Mouse with the `mouseconfig` Command

The `mouseconfig` command probes your system, looking for different pointing devices installed on your system. If you have a two-button mouse, you this command enables you to set your mouse to emulate three buttons.

Installing Sound Service with the `sndconfig` Command

The `sndconfig` command represents a breakthrough in sound configuration for Linux. Until `sndconfig`, you generally had to recompile the Linux kernel to add sound or support for different types of sound cards. The `sndconfig` command uses loadable modules, found under the `/lib/modules/2.0.31/misc` directory to configure your kernel to handle your sound system.

The `sndconfig` command presents a dialog box from which you can select one of five different Sound Blaster or Sound Blaster-compatible sound cards. After you select a card, press the Enter key; you can then edit the hardware's input/output value, IRQ, or DMA channels.

TIME SAVER

> Be sure to have your sound card's documentation on hand when you use the `sndconfig` command. Don't play guessing games with values for five different sound cards and 20 different settings. It's best to enter correct values and not waste time configuring Linux for sound.

The sndconfig program then tests your configuration by trying to play a sample sound, called `sample.au`, located in the `/usr/share/sndconfig` directory (if you hear the sample, you'll hear Linus Torvald's voice, and know how to pronounce the word Linux!). Tell the `sndconfig` command that you heard the sound by tabbing to the Yes button and pressing the Enter key, and the correct settings for your sound card and the kernel module, sound.o, will be written into the file `conf.modules`, found under the `/etc` directory.

Setting the System Time with the `timeconfig` Command

The `timeconfig` command is used to set the location and timezone of your computer. This command can be handy if you travel with your computer and need to tell Linux the current local time.

Configuring X11 with `Xconfigurator`

The `Xconfigurator` command is used to configure the X Window System to run on your computer's hardware. For details about configuring X11, see Hour 3, "Configuring the X Window System."

PART V

Hour 23

Archiving

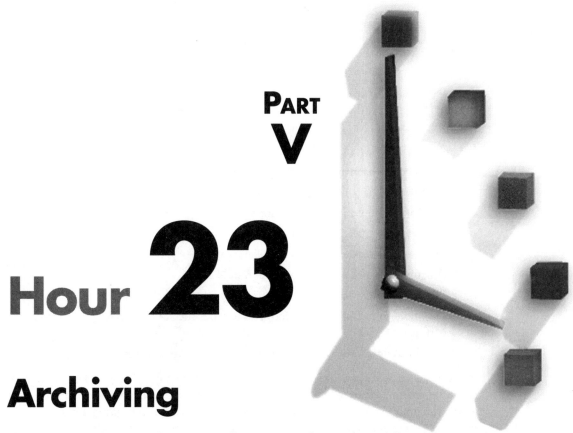

This hour continues the discussion of basic system administration skills and shows you how to back up and restore your system by using several different Linux utilities (included on your CD-ROM). With a little effort, you'll be able to easily perform these system administration tasks.

Considerations Before Performing Backups and Restores

There are several things you should consider before backing up or restoring your system. Although one ideal time to back up is after you've installed Linux and made sure all your devices (such as the sound card, graphics card, or tape drive) are working, there are other considerations. For example, if the kernel supplied on the CD-ROM works well for your system, then you can simply rely on the CD for your initial backup in case you have to do a full restore.

You should understand the difference between a backup and an archive. Backups are performed at regular intervals to save important documents, files, or complete systems.

Archives are made to save important documents, files, or complete systems for long periods of time. This means that you should first devise a backup strategy and ask yourself the following questions:

- Do I need to use a formal backup strategy?
- Do I need to back up the entire system each time?
- Do I need to back up selected files or whole directories?
- How often should I do the backup?
- How long do I need to keep my archived copies?
- Do I need reports or statistics on the backups?
- What media (such as floppy or tape) should I use?
- What software format (such as tar or dump) should the backup be in?
- Do I need to use any specialized software tools, such as backup scripts, or can I perform the backups by hand?
- Should compression, straight copying, or encryption be used?

You can answer some of these questions by looking at the way you use your Linux system. If you're just using Linux for word processing or running spreadsheets, you can probably get away with only backing up certain files or directories. If you're using Linux to learn programming, you'll want to keep not only original copies of your programs, but perhaps different versions. If you have other users on the system, you'll want to not only save copies of their directories, but the `/etc/passwd` file, or even the whole system, so that you can quickly restore the system in the event of a hard drive crash (unlikely) or system operator error (more likely).

The size of your system and the capacity of your hard drives or other storage devices may determine how to approach a backup strategy. If your Linux system is small enough (around 200MB), you can quickly back up everything to another hard drive or to a tape drive. You also can use a removable media drive, such as an Iomega Zip drive or Sysquest EZ-flyer. If you only have to save copies of a small number of small files, you may even be able to use high-density floppies for storage.

You'll probably decide on a combination of archiving and regularly scheduled full or incremental backups. You need to choose the software to use and explore how to automate as much of the process as possible, perhaps by using `crontab` entries (discussed in Hour 24, "Scheduling"). Whatever you do, when you decide on your strategy, stick to it! The worst time to create and use a backup strategy is after you run into problems or lose files.

Backing Up Your System with the `tar` Command

Although use of the `tar` command was discussed in Hour 5, "Manipulation and Searching Commands," as the system administrator, you'll want to explore some of the more complex `tar` command-line options and experiment with creating backups before implementing your backup strategy.

The `tar` command creates a tape archive. You can write the archive to your hard drive, a tape drive, or nearly any other Linux device. To create a quick backup of your users' home directories, use `tar` to create the archive. For example,

```
# tar cPfC users.tar / home
```

This command line creates the tape archive `users.tar` in the current directory. One easy way to regularly back up these directories is to save them on a different file system. If you have a DOS or Windows partition mounted (see Hour 21, "Handling Files"), automate the backup process with a `crontab` entry:

```
30 17 * * * root tar cPfC /mnt/dos/windows/desktop/users.tar / home
```

This entry, in the `/etc/crontab` file, backs up your users' directories at 5:30 p.m. each day and saves the archive in the Windows desktop folder. As you can see, automating the backup process isn't that hard, and has the benefit of working in the background without your attention; a process called an unattended backup. If you save your data on a separate file system, you can easily restore the files later by using the `tar` command's `x`, or extract, option:

```
# cd /
# tar xvf /mnt/dos/windows/desktop/users.tar
```

These command lines restore your users' directories and files, starting at the `/` or root directory. While backing up files to another file on your hard drive is easy, you also can use the `tar` command with tape drives by specifying the tape device on the `tar` command line.

JUST A MINUTE

> Unfortunately, there are no utilities to format tapes under Linux. Although you must still use a DOS or Windows utility to do this, you won't have to bother with formatting if you make sure to purchase preformatted tapes.

This hour doesn't detail all the ins and outs of installing or using different tape devices, but it does show you the general approach and some examples you may want to try. To use a tape drive with the `tar` command, you must find the tape device under the `/dev` directory. There are a number of them, but this section uses the general floppy tape driver, `/dev/ftape`, as an example.

Although most tape drives will rewind a freshly inserted tape, you can use the `mt`, or magnetic tape command to rewind or re-tension your tape. Insert the tape, then use the following:

```
# mt -f /dev/ftape rewind
```

After the tape has rewound, erase it with the `mt` command's `erase` option:

```
# mt -f /dev/ftape erase
```

After the tape has been erased, you can write a tar archive to the tape by specifying the `/dev/ftape` device:

```
# cd /
# tar cf /dev/ftape /home
```

This command creates a tape archive of all the files and directories under the `/home` directory. To restore your tape archive, you must use the `tar` command's extract, or `x` command-line option:

```
# cd /
# tar xf /dev/ftape
```

There are many more options with the `tar` command. You'll want to explore some of them, such as the `d` option to test archives, or the `z` option to compress files (and save tape space). For more information, see the tar manual page and read the ftape-HOWTO under the `/usr/doc` directory.

Using the `cpio` Command to Backup and Restore

The `cpio`, or copy in and out command, may be used in much the same way as the `tar` command, but with several differences, especially with archive creation or extraction command-line options. For example, to create a `cpio` archive, you must use the `-o`, or create, option. The `cpio` command also requires a list of filenames, with paths, to build an archive. To do this, use the `find` command which handily creates the required names for you.

For example, if you have a directory called `x11` that contains a number of files you'd like to archive, you can combine the output of the `find` command with the `cpio` command to build the archive.

```
# find x11 | cpio -ov >x11.cpio
cpio: x11: truncating inode number
x11
x11/xfree86faq.txt
x11/xappsfaq.txt
x11/x11faq.txt
x11/disaster.txt
x11/XHints1.txt
1082 blocks
```

This command line shows that the `cpio` command has been fed the names of the files inside the x11 directory, creating an archive with the `-o` option and showing you the files added with the `-v` option. The name of the archive is `x11.cpio`, and it is created using the greater than, or >, redirection operator.

To restore a `cpio` archive, use the `cpio` command's extract, or `-i` command-line option:

```
# cpio -i < x11.cpio
1082 blocks
```


This command line shows that to extract a `cpio` archive you can use the less than, or <, redirection operator in conjunction with the `-i cpio` extract option. The `cpio` program re-creates the directory and finishes by printing the number of 512-character blocks that were written to your hard drive.

You also can use the combination of the `find` command and `cpio` to create archives of any directory, or even different files on your system. To back up all files in your directory that belong to you, and are less than one day old, (or have been modified in the last day), you can use the `find` command's `-user` and `-mtime` command-line options:

```
# find /home/bball -user bball -mtime -1 -print ¦ cpio -o >today.cpio
```

This command line creates a `cpio` archive, called `today.cpio`, which contains all the files you've modified in the last 24 hours. You're only limited by your imagination in how to devise your backups, and how to back up your system. For more information on the `cpio` command, read its manual page. For more information about the `find` command, see Hour 5, or read the find manual page.

Using the `taper` Script for Tape Drive Backups and Restores

The taper program, by Yusaf Nagree, is a backup and restore program used to create compressed or uncompressed archives of selected files or directories. This program provides a nice interface to creating and maintain tape archives. You also may use other types of media to do your backups.

Using the `taper` command is easy. Specify the type of media to use with the `-T` media option. According to the latest documentation, the `taper` command supports the following:

- `ftape`—The floppy drive tape driver, used for tape drives that attach to the floppy interface (this driver is included with your Linux system).
- `zftape`—A newer floppy drive tape driver that handles additional tape formats.
- `scsi`—Driver for tape drives using a SCSI interface.
- `ide`—Driver to support IDE tape drives.
- `removeable`—Driver to support floppies, or removable hard drives.

If you don't have a tape drive, but would like to try the taper program to test a backup of a directory or two to floppy diskettes, use the `-T` command-line option with the `removable` option:

```
# taper -T removable
```

This starts the taper program, using the default floppy device, `/dev/fd0`. You'll be asked to select the files or directories before you start the backup. The taper program has too many features to discuss here, but you'll find its documentation under the `/usr/doc` directory in the file `TAPER.txt`.

Configuring the BRU Backup System for Backups and Restores

If you purchase Linux from Red Hat Software, a copy of Enhanced Software Technologies' BRU, or Backup and Restore Utility, is on your CD-ROM (see Figure 23.1). This is a complete commercial software backup application you can use to back up your system or files, using nearly any tape drive and even floppies. This section shows you some of the highlights of this software, which provides data verification, error detection, data compression, and selective backup and restores. You can use the BRU software from the command line or while using X11.

Figure 23.1.
The BRU 2000 backup and restore utility features menus and buttons to manage Linux system backups.

Install the BRU software from your CD-ROM either during the initial install, or later on, using the control-panel or glint commands (see Hour 22, "Red Hat Tools"). When you first run BRU, you must also tell BRU which device to use to back up your files.

First, go to the File menu and choose Configure BRU. The BRU Configuration Utility window appears. Click the Devices button in this window, then click New. A New Device window with a scrolling list of different devices appears. Click the down arrow to choose one (see Figure 23.2).

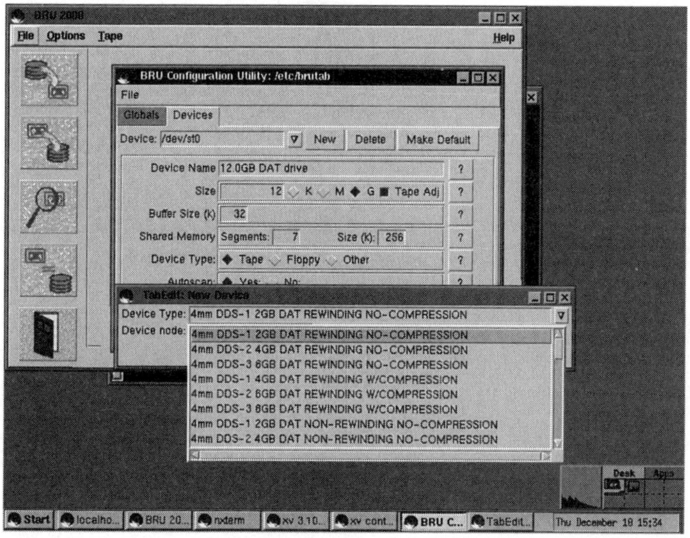

Figure 23.2.
The BRU Configuration Utility features several windows, including a tape device selection list.

There are 37 different devices listed, including floppy drives. If you don't see a device you have in the list, select the `OTHER` device option to create your own. For example, if you have an older, floppy-based tape drive that uses the QIC-80 format, select `OTHER`, then specify the tape device (most likely `/dev/rft0`, the rewinding tape device).

Once you've selected the backup device, choose Save in the BRU Configuration window. To begin a backup, insert a tape (or floppy) in your computer. The BRU program checks the floppy or tape, then tells you its status. You can then select Backup from the BRU program's File menu. You'll see a File Selection dialog box, which enables you to select whole files or directories to back up. See Figure 23.3 for a representative window. After you've finished selecting and adding the directories or files, click the Begin Backup button to start your backup.

The BRU program has many different features, including compression, scheduling, and tape archive verification. You can find out more about this program by browsing to the following site:

```
http://www.estinc.com
```

Figure 23.3.
The BRU directory and file selection dialog box offers selective backup sets for archiving directories and files.

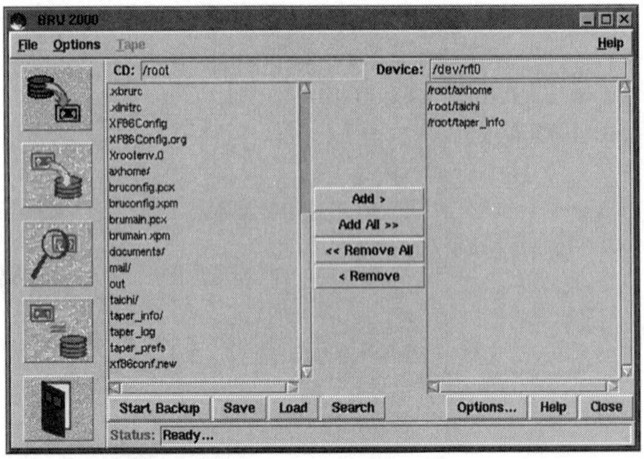

PART V

Hour 24

Scheduling

In this hour, you'll finish with learning system administration skills. By now you've learned most of the commands used by sysadmins, and should be familiar with most of the tasks you have to perform to maintain your system for yourself or other users. This hour shows you how to put all this knowledge together in order to automate these tasks using the `cron` daemon, and other Linux scheduling programs.

By using the programs and techniques outlined in this hour, you can automate many different system administration jobs and maintain a healthy, well-running system. The first topic discussed is the `cron` daemon, and then you'll learn how to administer the `at` command facilities for different users on your system.

Using the `cron` Daemon

The `cron` daemon, `crond`, is a program started after you boot Linux by the `cron.init` script in the `/etc/rc.d/init.d` directory on your system. This is done automatically, so you don't have to worry about starting the `cron` daemon every time after your boot Linux. The crond program runs in the background, and checks several files. The first is the crontab file in the /etc directory. A portion of this file reads as follows:

```
...
# run-parts
01 * * * * root run-parts /etc/cron.hourly
02 1 * * * root run-parts /etc/cron.daily
02 2 * * 0 root run-parts /etc/cron.weekly
02 3 1 * * root run-parts /etc/cron.monthly
...
```

As you can see, there is a list of files (actually, directories), which contain tasks that are run hourly, daily, weekly, and monthly. If you look at the contents of the cron.weekly directory, you'll find a file called makewhatis.cron that contains

```
#!/bin/bash

makewhatis -w
exit 0
```

You can see that this is a shell script that executes the makewhatis command to build your system's whatis database (see Hour 4, "Reading and Navigation Commands").

The cron command also searches the /var/spool/cron directory for personal crontab files with user's names. These files are created with the crontab command, found under the /usr/bin directory, and are used by users to schedule their own regular tasks. But how do you tell cron when to run these scripts? Read on to see the format of the cron commands.

Managing User cron Scheduling

Although the /etc/crontab file is for scheduling regular, system-wide tasks, you can let users on your system create their own cron schedules. If you want to enable your users to use the crontab command to create personal cron files under the /var/spool/cron directory, you should first create two files: /etc/cron.allow and /etc/cron.deny. Under the /etc/cron.allow file, insert the root operator name, root, and the names of any users you want to allow access to the cron daemon. If neither of these files exist, users may or may not have access to personal cron files. You can create files for your users with the crontab command, or users may create their own.

CAUTION

> Be careful! Always use the crontab command's -u command-line option. If you run this while running as root (after using the su command), and don't use this option, you'll edit the root operator's crontab settings instead of your own.

The next section shows you the format of the crontab file, and the difference between the format of a cron entry for your Linux system and for individual users.

Setting Schedules with the crontab Command

The format of crontab entries is detailed in the crontab manual page under section 5. To see the manual page, use

```
# man 5 crontab
```

This page provides specifications for crontab entries. However, to make things simpler, I'll give you some examples, and at the end of this hour, some samples you can use. In general, the fields of an entry are

```
minutes    hour    day of month    month    day of week    command
```

Entries are usually separated with a space. However, cron entries in the /etc/crontab file must have a username inserted between the day of week entry and the command. A username field is not needed for personal crontab entries.

As a simple example, you can have Linux tell you the time every 15 minutes by first calling the crontab command with the -e command-line option, and then adding

```
0,15,30,45 * * * * /usr/local/bin/saytime %
```

This tells the cron daemon to execute the saytime command to speak the time every fifteen minutes. You can find the saytime command at

```
http://sunsite.unc.edu/pub/Linux/sound/speech/saytime.tgz
```

If you'd like to hear the time every minute (though it might drive you crazy!), you can use

```
* * * * * /usr/local/bin/saytime %
```

Note that if you don't use a carriage-return at the end of the line in your entry, you should use a percent (%) sign. Here are some more example entries:

```
* 22 * * 1-4 /usr/bin/wall 'Time for bed! Finished your homework yet?' %
0 1 * * * /usr/bin/find / -xdev -name core -exec /bin/rm {} \; %
0,30 * * * /usr/bin/tput bel >/dev/console %
* 12 25 12 * /bin/echo 'Happy Holidays' ¦ /bin/mail -s Greetings root %
```

The first example broadcasts a gentle reminder to all your users using the wall command, at 10 p.m., Monday through Thursday. The second example runs the find command to search your system at 1 a.m. each morning for core files, and deletes any found. The third rings your terminal's bell on the hour and half hour, using the tput command to output. The last example sends a mail message at noon on December 25th.

Experiment with different tasks and times. You can also have search results for files, reports of users online, and uptime reports directed to log files, or mailed to you. You can also use cron to schedule backups when you're away, or have your system shut down at a preselected time.

Managing User Scheduling with the `atrun` Command

The `cron` daemon is useful for scheduling regularly run programs, or performing regular tasks, as you found out in Hour 18, "Personal Productivity Tools." The `at` command is useful for one-time or reminder jobs. Even though your Linux system is set up automatically after installation to handle user `at` scheduling requests, you should know how to manage the `at` command facilities for at least one good reason.

By default, when a user uses the `at` command, the command is run with a default CPU priority. If too many users start running tasks with higher priorities, or CPU-intensive programs in the background, your system's performance could be affected. Read on to learn to manage your system's `at` command facilities to provide the best performance and control possible.

Your system's `at` command facilities are enabled by the `cron` daemon, which, after starting when you boot Linux, checks the `/etc/crontab` file, and sees the following entry:

```
...
# Run any at jobs every minute
* * * * * root [ -x /usr/sbin/atrun ] && /usr/sbin/atrun
...
```

As you can see, this is why the `at` command depends on the `cron` command; the `cron` command runs the `atrun` command, found under the `/usr/sbin` directory, each minute your system is up. The `atrun` command in turn, then searches the `/var/spool/at` directory to look for jobs to run. For example, if the root operator creates a job at 19:30 for that day, you'd see the following:

```
# at 19:30
echo Hello
Job 9 will be executed using /bin/sh
# ls -l /var/spool/at
-rwx------    1 root      root          3144 Nov 26 19:25 c0000900dff21e
-rwx------    1 bball     bball         3146 Nov 26 19:26 c0000a00dff21e
drwx------    2 daemon    daemon        1024 Nov 26 19:04 spool
```

As you can see, there is a job waiting for the root operator and the user bball. Each of the files beginning with a "c" contains a shell script to execute the job (in the case of the root `at` job, it is only to echo the word job, which will be emailed after the job executes).

JUST A MINUTE

> You can get more specific information with the `atq` command. If you're the root operator, you'll see all the jobs your users have scheduled, instead of just the ones you've scheduled.

Controlling the batch and at Commands

So now that you know how the at facilities run, how do you control how at works, and for whom, on your system? One way to control the performance, is to use the atrun command's -l (load average) option. This option will control any jobs submitted by users using the batch command (discussed in Hour 18 with the at command). You can limit when batch jobs are run by specifying a number lower than 1.5 (the default), which tells atrun to run batch jobs only when the system load average (determined by a value in the /proc/loadavg file while the system is running) is low.

You can see the current load average with

```
# cat /proc/loadavg
0.20 0.11 0.03 2/50 1228
```

This shows the load average for the last 5, 10, and 15 minutes. You can also get the load average by using the uptime command, for example:

```
# uptime
  7:40pm  up  2:44,  3 users,  load average: 0.13, 0.08, 0.02
```

To allow your users to use batch nearly any time, change the value of the -l option in the atrun command entry in your system's /etc/crontab file to a number higher than the default 1.5 value.

But how do you control whether or not users are allowed to use the at command on your system? By default, after you install Linux, anyone on your system can use the at command. There are four ways to control who can or cannot use the at command. If you look in your /etc directory, you'll see a file called at.deny. Because this file is empty, everyone can use the at command to schedule jobs. If you want to restrict a user from using the at command, put the user's username in the file. If you don't want anyone on your system to use the at command (of course, this doesn't apply to you, because you're the root operator!), then delete the at.deny file from your /etc directory. If you want to allow only certain users to use the at command, then create a file called at.allow in the /etc directory, and put the user's username in the file.

As a final, desperate measure, as the root operator, you can see all the at jobs scheduled on your system with the atq command, and if you see too many jobs scheduled, you can delete them with the atrm command, for example:

```
#  atq
Date                    Owner   Queue   Job#
20:00:00 11/26/97       bball   c       12
20:10:00 11/26/97       bball   c       13
20:15:00 11/26/97       bball   c       14
20:30:00 11/26/97       bball   c       15
...
# atrm 12 13 14 15 ...
```

Here I'm assuming you see a long, long list of job numbers, and have deleted them. This is an abrupt, rude way to handle enthusiastic users. A better method may be to email the user and find out if there are tasks being run that may be automated during off-hour or off-peak times.

As the system administrator, you have complete control of scheduling commands for the users of your Linux system. Think about tasks you should run hourly, daily, weekly, and monthly. With a little imagination, you'll soon automate any custom tools, command lines, and reports you've created to help you manage your system. You'll end up with more disk space, a better running system, and happier users.

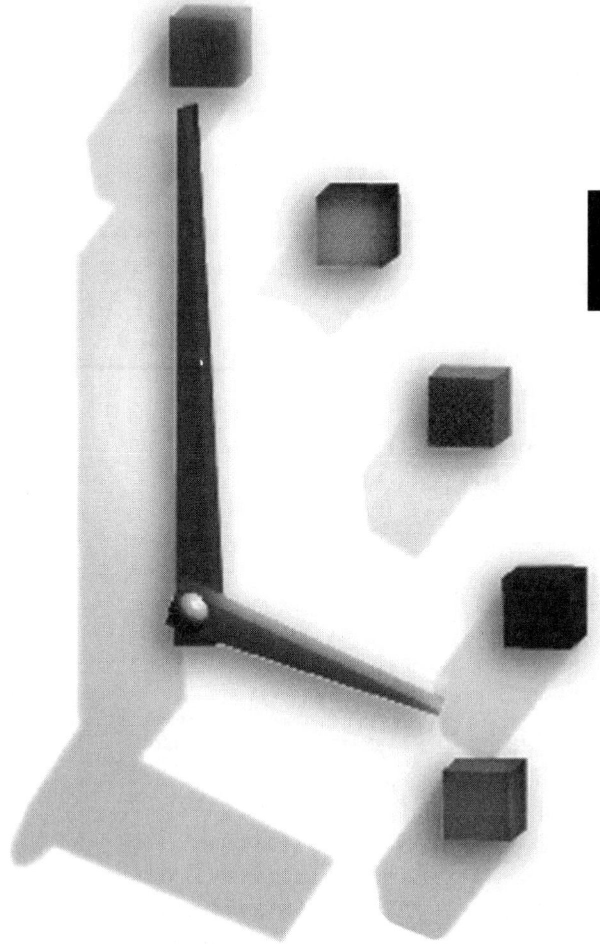

INDEX

Symbols

A

B

C

D

E

G

J-K

N

O

Q-R

S

W

X-Y

Z

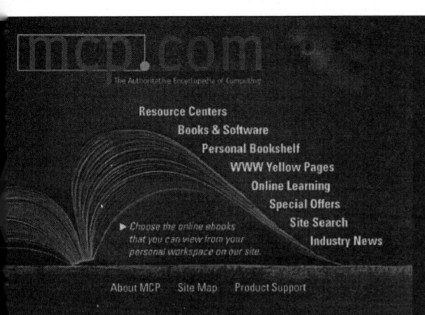

redhat
CDE
common desktop environment
LINUX

redhat
POWERTOOLS
LINUX
6 CD's Complete Easy-to-Use Red Hat
Linux with Compilers, Networking, Sources,
On-line Docs. and over 3 Gigabytes of Tools,
Utilities, Applications and Games.

Red Hat
Linux Library
Find immediate
answers from
the equivalent of
650,000
pages
of searchable
UNIX and
LINUX
reference material.